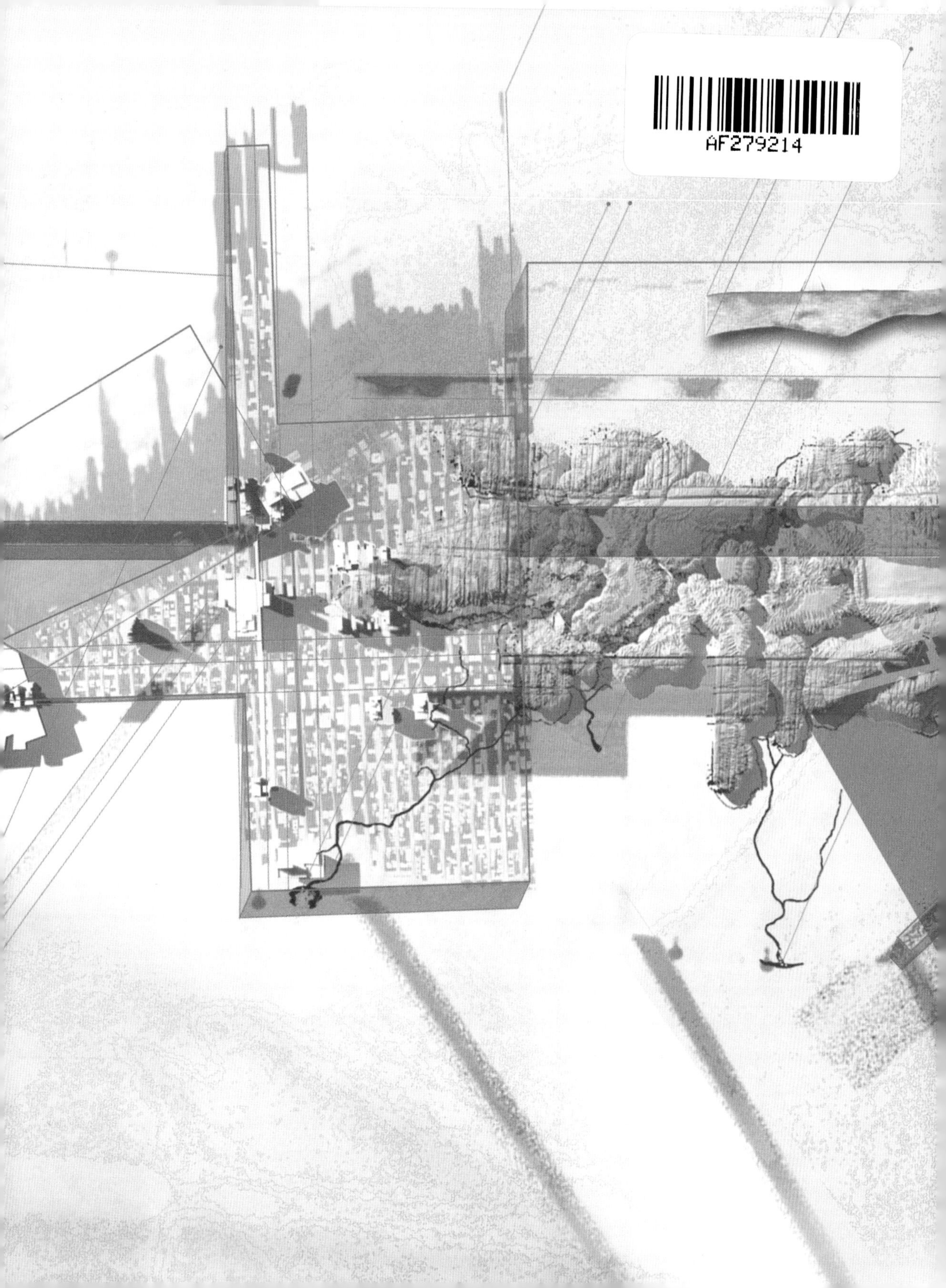
AF279214

New York Geologics

Representations of Manhattan from the Anthropocene

Tiago Torres-Campos

ORO Editions
Publishers of Architecture, Art, and Design
Gordon Goff: Publisher

www.oroeditions.com
info@oroeditions.com

Published by ORO Editions

Author: Tiago Torres-Campos
ORO Managing Editor: Kirby Anderson

10 9 8 7 6 5 4 3 2 1 First Edition

Library of Congress data available upon request. World Rights: Available

ISBN: 978-1-961856-39-4

Color Separations and Printing: ORO Editions, Inc.
Printed in China.

International Distribution: www.oroeditions.com/distribution

ORO Editions makes a continuous effort to minimize the overall carbon footprint of its publications. As part of this goal, ORO Editions, in association with Global ReLeaf, arranges to plant trees to replace those used in the manufacturing of the paper produced for its books. Global ReLeaf is an international campaign run by American Forests, one of the world's oldest nonprofit conservation organizations. Global ReLeaf is American Forests' education and action program that helps individuals, organizations, agencies, and corporations improve the local and global environment by planting and caring for trees.

Sometimes, from beyond the skyscrapers, the cry of a
tugboat finds you in your insomnia, and you remember
that this desert of iron and cement is an island.
– Albert Camus

New York is a diamond iceberg floating in river water.
– Truman Capote

'Well,' I said, 'Paris is old, is many centuries. You feel, in Paris,
all the time gone by. That isn't what you feel in New York.'
'What do you feel in New York?' he asked.
'Perhaps you feel,' I told him, 'all the time to come. There's
such power there, everything is in such movement. You can't
help wondering—I can't help wondering—what it will all be
like—many years from now.
– James Baldwin

New York had all the iridescence of the beginning of the world.
– F. Scott Fitzgerald

1   **Interact**   1
Indeterminant New York

2   **Imagine**   7
The Deep Section as a Tool for Thinking About Context

3   **Stratify**   33
Towards a Rhetoric of Ground

     3.1   Between Imagination and Myth: From *Lower Manhattan*   34
            (1999) to the *Viele Map* (1865)

     3.2   Stratigraphic Operations: Seismic-Architectural Devices,   48
            Heterotopic Fragments, and Geofollies

     3.3   SF and Other Metrical Strategies for the Underground   80

4   **Extrude**   87
Delirious Fields and Paranoid Critical Fragments

     4.1   Unfolding Urban Deliria: *The Commissioners' Plan* (1811)   88
            Through *Delirious New York* (1978)

     4.2   Paranoid Critical Extrusions   110

     4.3   From Gold to Light – Quarrying Manhattan's Cultic Dimensions   132

     4.4   Light Passes: Streams of Unconscious Consciousness   **156**

5   **De-Sediment**   **173**
Seismic Forces Through the Slightest Tremor

5.1 Weaving an Architecture of Anthropocenic Events   **174**

5.2 De-Sedimenting Manhattan: From *The Manhattan Transcripts*   **183**
(1981) to The Greensward Plan (1858)

5.3 Insular Events: Central Park, Seneca Village   **194**
and Other Stories of Erasure

5.4 Diffracted Archipelagos and the Fantasy of Erasure   **242**

6   **Intra-Act**   **269**
Architecture as a Geologic Condition

6.1 Contact Zones: Architecture as a Condition for the Fault   **269**

6.2 Towards an Ethics of Ground   **284**

Terminological Positions   290
Endnotes   302
List of Figures   338
Bibliography   340
Acknowledgements   353

In his 1925 novel *The Great Gatsby*, F. Scott Fitzgerald offers the reader what could be regarded as a quintessential literary depiction of Manhattan. He writes that '[t]he city seen from the Queensboro Bridge is always the city seen for the first time, in its first wild promise of all the mystery and the beauty in the world.' [1]

Conventional representations of Manhattan often offer an idea of the island as a dense city condition emblematic of twentieth-century neoliberal forms of capitalism. This urban condition reinforces readings of the city as a series of architectural extrusions along an orthogonal urban grid. Manhattan is also a laboratory of ideas that tells the 'social history of the world' but somehow has 'all the iridescence of the beginning of the world.' [2]

Yet, like many other coastal and insular conditions, twenty-first-century Manhattan faces adverse anthropogenic climate change. Stronger storm surges and sea level rise now demand that the island recalibrate its social and environmental positions. The city needs to consider once again its fluid archipelagic conditions at the mouth of a large watershed that engages in tidal fluctuation with the bay, and its old geologies inherited from glacial dynamics on which it has laid its foundations. Tangled in exponentially unstable planetary conditions, the city also needs to re-examine its ongoing indeterminacy influenced by unbalanced power and land dynamics.

The development of the island-city has responded, systemically yet with varying degrees of success, to logics that try to make capitalist progress compatible with the territory's geological, topographical and hydrological conditions. Even though these logics of land, water and ground – here called *geologics* – are perhaps less dominant than the dense urban culture and, therefore, less predominant in the city's representational cosmos, they are still important to explain why Manhattan has evolved to its current condition.

The examination of Manhattan's geologics requires a contextual

Standing on the northern tip of Manhattan, Inwood Hill Park can be read as an Anthropocenic-infused geology, where novel ecologies coexist in tension with scars of erasure through violence, theft and war. The apparent stability of the large rock on which the park stands is read against the fluidity of marshes draining to the Hudson and the Harlem rivers.

positioning of the city within historical processes of socio-political, cultural and environmental change. Chapter 2, 'Imagine,' explores how the deep section can become a tool to expand discussions on city datums and their delineations, and how they are conventionally represented (or not) in architectural discourse. It introduces a notion of context as being both informative and generative. Context allows for the study of the city as entanglements between nature and culture and how they are manifested across space and time. In establishing some of the terms for discussion, the chapter offers divergent entry points into the design explorations.

The book examines how some of the geologics that have supported the construction of Manhattan can be understood in relation to its urban characteristics and explores ways in which they have been brought – or can eventually be brought – into the realm of representation. To do so, it connects between impactful nineteenth century representations of a city in the making – *Commissioners' Plan* (1811), *Viele Map* (1865), or *Greensward Plan* (1858) – with three meaningful architectural manifestos of the late twentieth-century – *Delirious New York* (Rem Koolhaas, 1978), *The Manhattan Transcripts* (Bernard Tschumi, 1981), and *Lower Manhattan* (Lebbeus Woods, 1999). The wide recognition of the latter as manifestos comes not just from their construction as public declarations of intent for a new architectural practice, but also from their capacity to retrospectively synthesize and position significant architectural conditions of the twentieth-century city. In the book, their importance also comes from their critical focus on Manhattan's urban condition – described by Koolhaas as Manhattanism – as a lens to creatively address the indeterminacy felt at the turn of the century. Understood less as case studies, the pieces are conceptualized as probes to generate interrelated design explorations, which are, in turn, edited and curated as installations exhibited both physically and virtually.

The design experimentation that is described in the book is positioned in relation to these city representations. It aims to generate a critical and creative argument that seeks retrospectively to contextualize and reposition the manifestos and the plans, this time from the contemporary perspectives offered by the Anthropocene and the debates it has sparked over the first two decades of the twenty-first century.

Since it was coined in the early 2000s as a hypothesis in earth science for a new geological epoch in which humans have become the dominant geomorphic force altering the earth,[3] the term Anthropocene became ubiquitous in the sciences, arts and humanities, and is often used in colloquial conversations.[4] Its theoretical contours, both as framework and debate generator, are here explored less in relation to its initial disciplinary concerns and controversies in geology, and more specifically stratigraphy, and more in its slow but steady affirmation as a complex constellation of critical ideas that demand a repositioning of individual and collective ways of thinking and making. In other words, regardless of its acceptance as a scientifically accurate term to define the contemporary geological epoch – something the International Commission on Stratigraphy has yet to agree on [5] – the Anthropocene is studied in terms of the shifts it demands of theory and practice.

The recognition of earth's active agency in shaping the conditions of complex more-than-human assemblages has determined the consolidation of aesthetic and cultural attitudes and values where humans are regarded as an entangled subcomponent of an active *geo*. The Anthropocene carries with it the idea of an unstable earth in exponential, and potentially irreversible, change. In trying to detect, read and understand the logics involved in this human-geo entanglement, the book considers *geologic* as a central Anthropocenic term. Geologic reframes knowledge-making practices, which are personal and always already ethico-political.

Geologics advocate for architecture to become a productive mediation between city and geology. They propose a reconfiguration of urban territories as resilient hybrid possibilities that forge existence among dissonance, heterogeneity, and conflict. Geologics encourage architectural expansion towards more fluid practices for thinking with and feeling through the contemporary city as a forcefully unstable geologic becoming. And they propose alternatives for 'staying with the trouble.' [6]

It is perhaps relevant to recognize that the time frame separating the present moment of writing from the production date of *Delirious New York* – the earliest of the three pieces – is similar to the temporal distance between the latter and the golden age of Manhattanism (from the late 1920s until WWII). With this recognition, the manifestos become hinges in the exploration of a series of interactions in thought and practice that oscillate across the one-hundred-year period between the early twentieth and the early twenty-first centuries.

The period of conception of the three pieces coincides with a diffuse yet pivotal moment in architectural and landscape architectural theory and practice. Attuned to the registration of profound political, social and environmental change that reconsidered the role of human environments at the planetary scale, architects like Koolhaas, Tschumi or Woods invested in new forms of practice concerned with the role that cities should play as complex contemporary territories with global impact. While the manifestos mostly result from theoretical stances, they also shaped the architects' practices. For Koolhaas and Tschumi – both young practitioners at the time when their manifestos were published – the Manhattan studies served as the basis to experiment in their subsequent impactful proposals for Parc de la Villette in Paris (1982–1983), which in turn helped the disciplinary clarification but also expansion of landscape architecture in the following decades. Both finalists in the international competition to design the park – which Tschumi eventually won – the European architects saw in Manhattanism, and more specifically in the grid, the possibility to construct the twenty-first-century city with an operative frame that allows permeability, accepts contradiction and helps navigate through indeterminacy.

Of the three, Lebbeus Woods is the only American architect and a long-term resident of New York. His approach to Manhattan is concerned with the possibilities and limitations that the culture of congestion may have when connecting with the planet. Created twenty years after *Delirious New York*, *Lower Manhattan* already denotes a moment of particular vulnerability of city territories in the face of climate change. Its qualities as a transition in architectural discourse were helpful in grounding the beginning of the discussion and subsequently leading it into the other two manifestos.

Departing from the study of Woods' *Lower Manhattan* (1999), chapter 3, 'Stratify,' proposes a notion of ground as active earth media. Ground becomes a lens to question assumptions of Manhattan as a homogenized city grid and the island-territory as a coalescence of geological fragments that offer support to the city. Examined retrospectively from the Anthropocene, *Lower Manhattan* also generates an approach to study the *Viele Map* (1865). Together, the two representations support the production of several design experiments with which to construct a rhetoric of ground that frames architecture as a creative practice to deal with indeterminacy.

The fourth chapter, 'Extrude,' examines the *Commissioners' Plan* (1811) retroactively and through the lens of Rem Koolhaas's proposed theory of Manhattanism. Koolhaas' literary city in *Delirious New York* (1978) serves as the basis to discuss an iterative design experimentation that seeks to quarry, mine and extrude Manhattan's architectural icons from its Gilded Age entangled in their socio-political and environmental context. Using the Paranoid Critical Method (PCM) to steer several design operations, the work begins to suggest the creation of an imagined Manhattan within the space of the exhibition.

Chapter 5, 'De-sediment,' reflects on Bernard Tschumi's *The Manhattan Transcripts* (1981) and then looks retrospectively at Vaux and Olmsted's 1858 *Greensward Plan* to scrutinize Central Park as a curated construction of publicness that represents the American ideals of freedom and democracy at the expense of the histories of marginalized communities who were displaced or destroyed to build it. The *Transcripts* offer notational clues into a pseudo-archaeological design activity to uncover some of those stories and de-sediment the idea of park as a picturesque, gentil landscape. An experimental body of design work suggests a reading of the park as landscape fragments in constant tension with the city grid.

In making associations about Manhattan across the two centuries, the book explains the context that generated the design and writing experiments, the stories that motivated them, and what they may instigate.

The research and creative practice here presented spanned across a few years. It included the participation in international design competitions, the consolidation of theory through a PhD in Architecture by Design at the University of Edinburgh, the teaching of graduate design studios looking at Manhattan with both students from Edinburgh School of Architecture and Landscape Architecture and Rhode Island School of Design, as well as encounters, conversations and fieldwork in and about Manhattan.

The several arguments presented in the book are woven through writing in ways perhaps similar to the craft of iterative drawing or modelling. Writing is a craft attuned to two 'textual voices,' one related to theoretical and historical context and the other to design experimentation and the installations in the exhibition space. The latter also includes moments when distinct methodological approaches are foregrounded to propel the design forward.

The focus on representation as a form of synthesis and construction of knowledge encourages the expansion of key concepts in architecture, such as *ground*, *scale* or *frame*, so they become able to more strongly sustain readings that unsettle spatial and material conditions in the city and reposition them within temporal frames vaster than the more established temporalities used in the study of the urban. The design operations developed within this scope are experimented in different forms of representation to test how the foregrounding of alternative city conditions may question common epistemologies about them.

The sedimentation and critical reflection on the design experimentation seek to activate a second type of relationship in the book, in this case between image, text and installation. This close articulation is an open invitation to radically interconnected imagination, even when it activates tensions between all modalities. Sometimes text is treated as image, other times image can be read as text. The work benefitted from punctual moments of curation and edition in the form of installations in public exhibitions, which constituted not only opportunities for critical reflection through curatorial practice, but also moments that propelled the work forward. The installations progressively acquired more density, to the point where they began gesturing towards the formulation of a new Manhattan, an imagined city that emerges within the space of the exhibition. These relationships between text, image and installation ultimately become a form of (de)sedimentation, perhaps in the sense given by Jacques Derrida. [7] In other words, the construction of the book comes closer to some form of geological sedimentation, where text and image are slowly worked out and deposited throughout the book, but they are often questioned, unsettled and de-structured. The book as geology is counterbalanced by the idea that media also activates geology, both informing the study of the geologics. [8]

Riverside Park
Fort Washington
Fort Tryon
Inwood Hill
10th Avenue
Park Avenue
Morningside Heights
St. Nicholas
Jackie Robinson
Highbridge Park
East River Park
Marcus Garvey
Central Park
59th Street
Dyckman Street
125th Street Fault
125th Street Fault
Dyckman Street Fault
Geological constitution

2 Imagine
The Deep Section as a Tool for Thinking about Context

'Imagine yourself in Central Park one million years ago. You would be standing on a vast ice sheet, a 4,000-mile glacial wall, as much as 2,000 feet thick. Alone on the vast glacier, you would not sense its slow crushing, scraping, ripping movement as it advanced south, leaving great masses of rock debris in its wake. Under the frozen depths, where the carousel now stands, you would not notice the effect on the bedrock as the glacier dragged itself along.'[9]

Imagine Mannahatta one thousand years ago. You would be walking amongst broadleaf forests and tidal salt marshes terraformed by oyster reefs. Communities of the Lenni Lenape of the Delaware Nation would be travelling in their daily journey from their camping grounds on what came to be known as Collect Pond to the southern tip of the island along a crest that we now call Broadway.

Imagine yourself in Midtown one hundred years ago. You would be standing at the edge of the city extending south and watch myriad cranes constructing concrete behemoths. With each new floor a new sense of scraping the sky, a new paradigm of modern living away from the ground. You would not sense the slow crushing of the bedrock supporting the footings as it got pierced by the city's undercrofts.

Imagine Lower Manhattan ten years ago. Superstorm Sandy approaching the shore. You would sense its power transfigured in big waves crashing against the island and flooding the city plunged into darkness.

Imagine Manhattan a few years ago. Successive lockdowns in place to fight against a global viral pandemic. Looking out the window you would see, maybe for the first time in centuries, one of the most congested territories in the world almost completely empty, like a post-cataclysmic void produced in Hollywood.

Imagine yourself one billion years ago, or one billion years in the future. No island, no Manhattan. You would be standing on completely different geologic formations. You would still not sense them moving in tectonic planetary choreographies.

Manhattan read as a geo-constellation of dissonant territories coalesced by a homogenizing city grid. Architectural mediations between city and geology, between landscape conditions and passive geological faults crossing the island, and between diffuse and uncertain thresholds of landfilled territories and tidal waters.

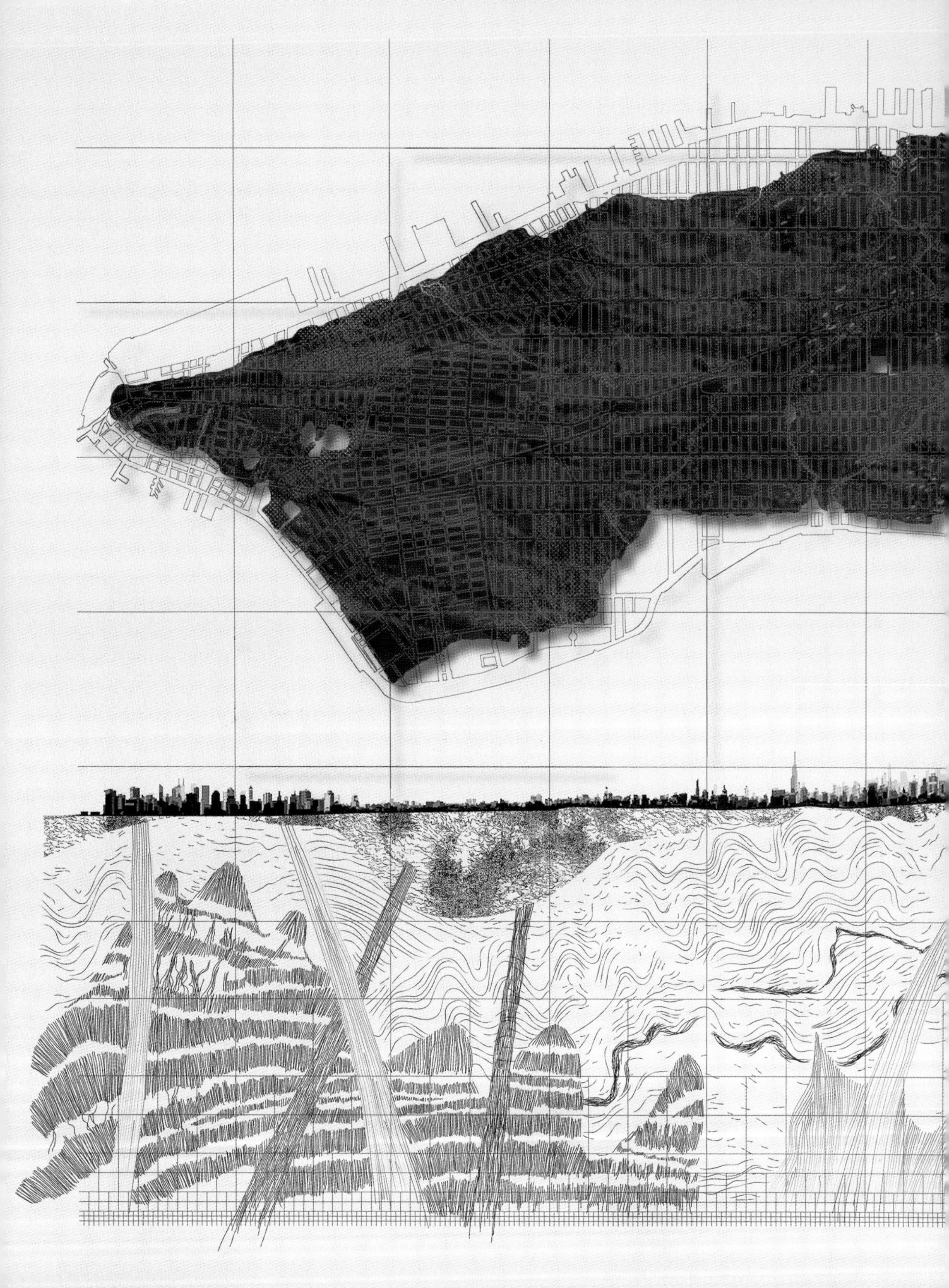

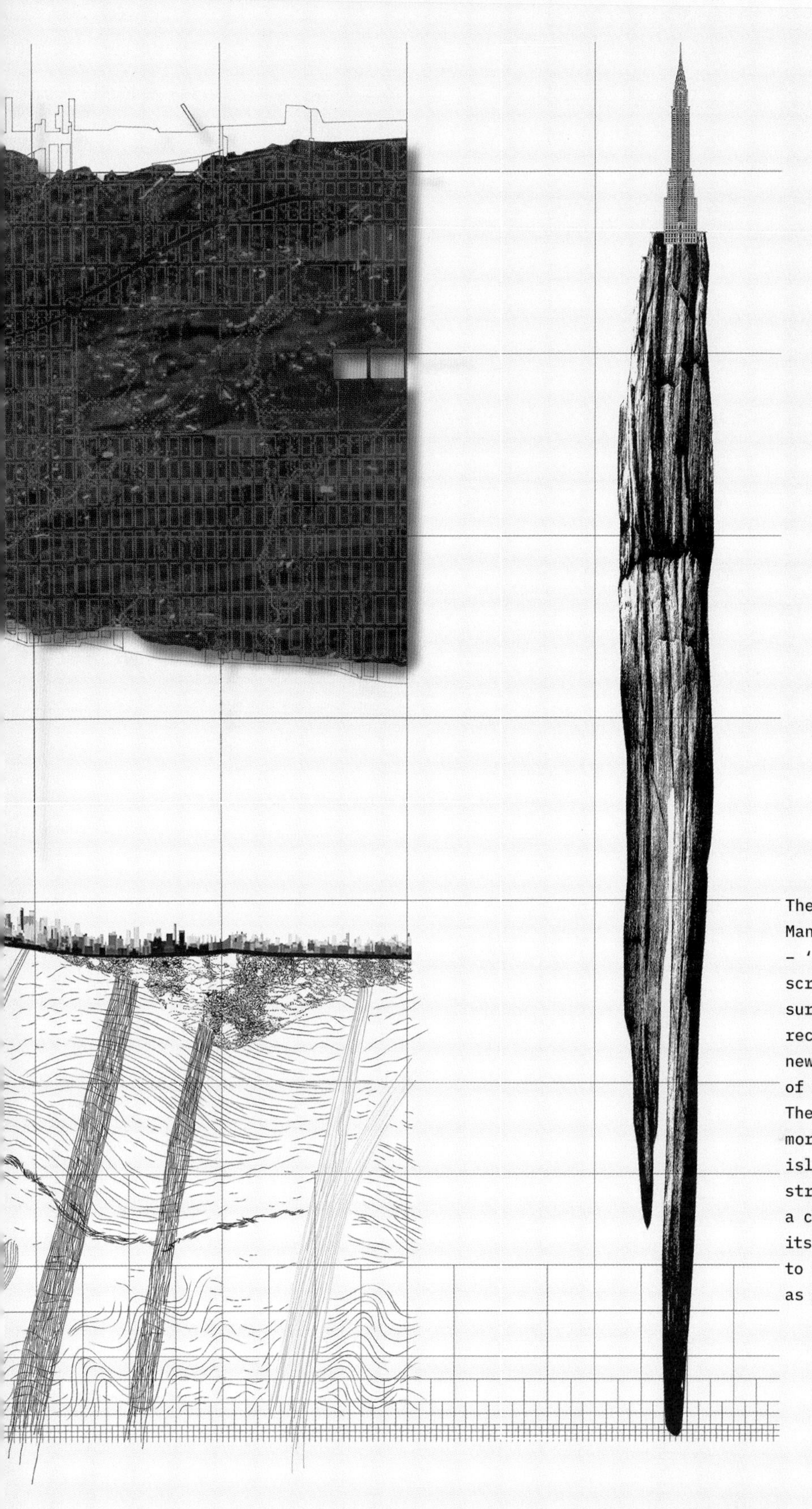

The old scale of
Manhattan's skyscrapers
– 'those small human
scratchings on the
surface of the Earth' –
recalibrated against a
new experimental scale
of deep space and time.
The city perceived as a
more recent layer in the
island's complex
stratigraphy also raises
a cognitive challenge to
its perceived limits and
to our own limitations
as humans.

This book requires an expansive type of imagination that triggers curiosity about an island-city, a dense territory mostly taken for granted due to how it is usually depicted. This is a type of imagination that allows for free movement across scale, space and time; across radically different sets of scales, spatial and temporal conditions; across material configurations that shift in temporalities radically different than human time – either atomically fast or glacially slow.

If architecture is conceived as a critical and creative practice that produces ways of thinking and crafting for noticing, bearing witness, and revealing alternative possibilities in the city, it can become a powerful tool to activate this type of imagination. How can architecture mediate between city, geology, atmosphere, and their radically different spacetime conditions? How can it speed up readings of geological formations in Central Park that

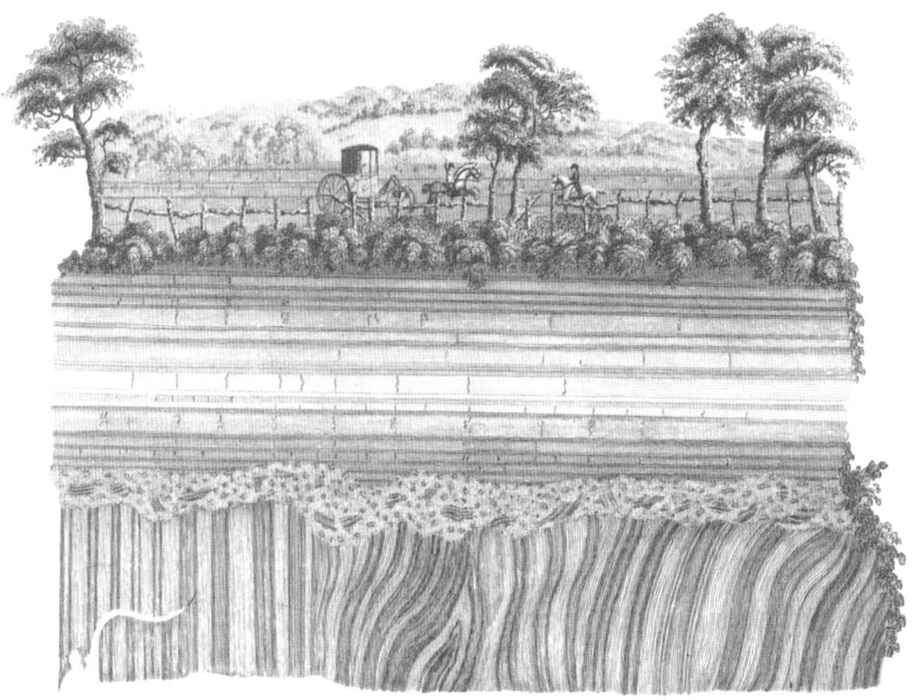

1 (above) *Hutton's unconformity at Jedburgh*, John Clerck of Eldin, 1787.

2 (right) *Géographie des plantes équinoxiales. Tableau physique des Andes et Pays voisins*, Alexander von Humboldt, 1803.

(next pages) The deep section as an experimental tool to trigger imagination about Manhattan's thicker context.

give an appearance of them slowly moving? How can it slow down readings of dust and light from billboards and giant screens so that they seem to quickly sediment on the gorges of Times Square?

Architectural representations are necessarily folded in their own cultural norms, and they usually depict the worldviews of their creators. They are always necessarily partial and partisan to those historical folds, even if sometimes they suggest the possibility of forging new worlds, or at least of de-sedimenting apparently established orders and value systems. If the representation is shown in section, for example, it requires a cut across an object, a building, a city, or a landscape to analyze and reveal spatial conditions in planimetric or sectional views. Architectural sections involve speculative thinking about assumed points of view that escape common perception and encourage representation across scale but also at specific scales where those perceptions can become meaningful.

When architecture commits to represent a city entangled with geology and atmosphere, it requires a deep section, one that is perhaps deeper, or thicker than most architectural sectional drawings. In relation to those more conventional sections in architecture, the deep section activates additional concerns about context. Deep section is a tool concerned with the representation of a wide range of thick site-specific conditions – architectural, geological, biochemical, hydrological, ecological, or infrastructural. In other words, the deep section activates concerns about context, which becomes both informative of those conditions and generative

of new types of associations between its different constituents, some of which escape more usual forms of representation. It often makes use of an expanded representational framing of the cut being performed to include the deeper layers of ground and atmosphere. The deep section has been used in the natural sciences to convey the complexity of the landscapes and territories analyzed, with the famous examples of John Clerk of Eldin's section to illustrate John Hutton's unconformity at Jedburgh or Alexander von Humboldt's annotated mountain and volcano *tableaux physiques*. More recently, it has become associated with urban and landscape design practices to represent the articulation of thick and unstable ground conditions. [10]

Imagine a cut across the city from the tip of the tallest skyscraper, descending
through every floor. It catches glimpses of human congestion, corporative
office life, familial domesticity, and entertainment culture. It
briefly captures the inner workings of an old machinic
technology: mountains of steel, wood, concrete, glass
and plaster; pipes, walls, slabs and windows;
elevators, shafts, wired networks and
escalators. It cuts through controlled
indoor atmospheres created with
complex systems of air and humidity,
disinfectant and air freshener.
The cut descends to the street
level.
It keeps cutting.
The cut breaks the
earth's surface. It cuts
across the building's
underground
foundations,
thick pillars
in reinforced
concrete and
steel, dark and
humid   basements pumping the water table out and into drainage pipes.
It cuts through layers of asphalt, coarse concrete, and soil
leftovers.
It keeps cutting.
It slices through a dense cloud of cables of electricity,
television, telephone, internet. It cuts through steel pipelines
of water, gas, oil, and sewage, as well as steam to control the
buildings. It briefly intersects with rhizomatic subway

systems leaking water and energy. It glances over brief
moments in the underworld of organized crime, amidst
rats, roaches and moles below.
It keeps cutting.
The cut grabs traces of the land's previous
uses in a temporal order expanding
backwards: first smaller skyscrapers,
then tenement buildings, old potter's
fields, remnants of fertile soil;
then farmhouses and wooden shacks,
pasturelands, and orchards; then
Native American hunting grounds,
rivers, creeks and marshland.
The cut hits the bedrock.
It keeps cutting.
The cut expands outwards to
the island's encapsulating   The
atmosphere. It cuts   atmosphere is
through the turbulent   made of compacted
lowest layers at the   pollution – carbon
human scale and close to   monoxide and dioxide,
street level.   nitrogen and sulphur –
congested human breath,
steam from subway ventilation
shafts, fumaroles and HVAC
systems. Weird ecologies of plants
from alien latitudes and small
resilient rodents thrive in the cracks

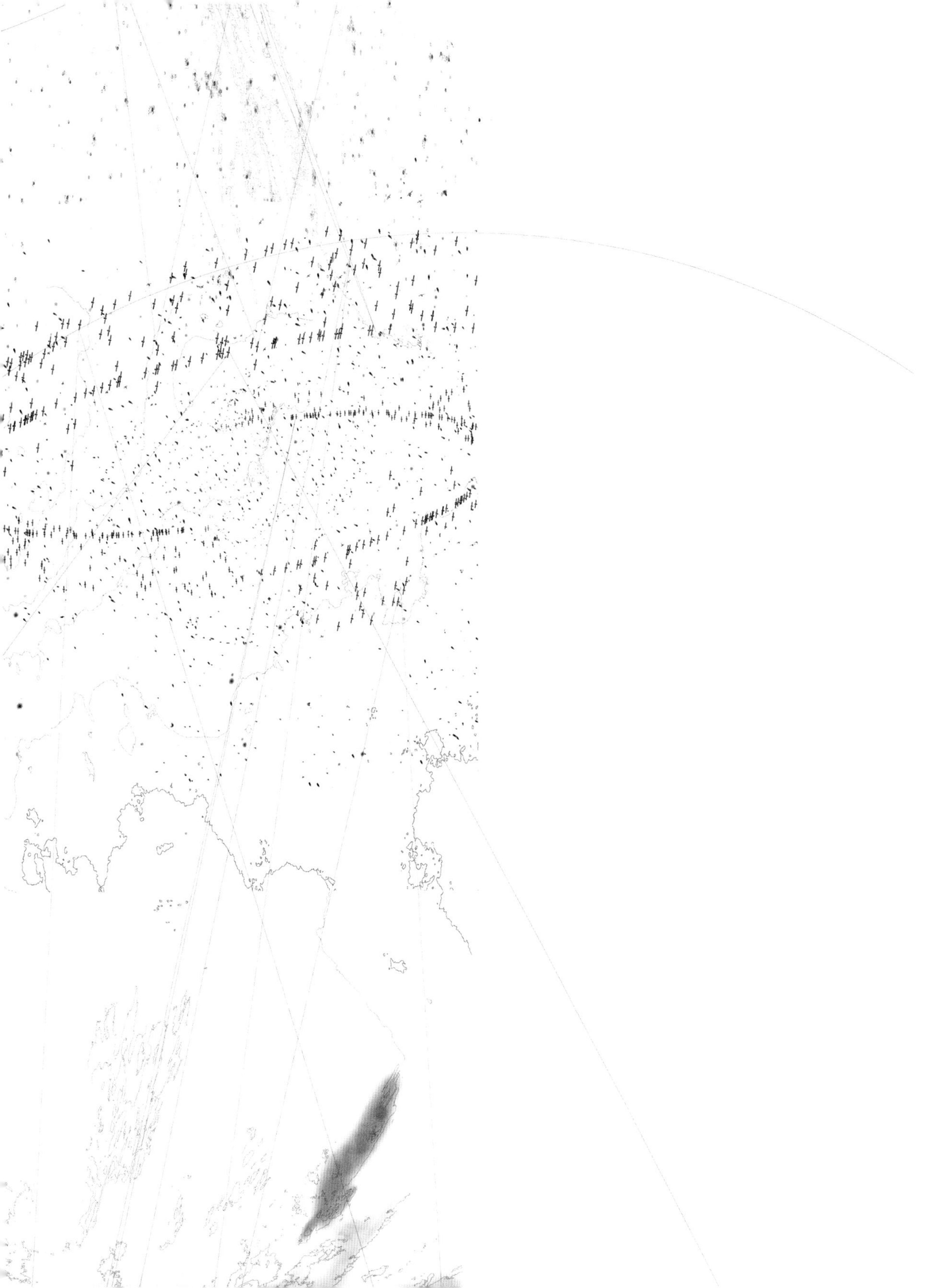

and in
plain sight.
It keeps cutting.
The cut expands upwards
through the wind tunnel
and the Venturi effects
caused by the skyscrapers. Wind
shifts direction perpendicularly
to flow along the grid. The deep canyon
gorges disorient birds and insects, the
perfect urban habitat for birds of prey.
It keeps cutting.
The cut grabs traces of the flight patterns around
the island; arches traced from the asphalt of
airport runways into the sky. It cuts through
the chemistry of polluted clouds made of
carbon molecules, nitrates and acidic water.
It grabs the direction of the dominant
winds blowing from the bay and the ocean
on the southwest.
It keeps cutting.
The cut expands further to capture
trajectories of satellites
scanning, triangulating, and
photographing from the earth's
low orbit.
It keeps cutting.
It cuts through brief
choreographies of planets,
meteorites, asteroids,
stars, gas and dust.
It keeps cutting.
The cut expands
inwards to the
deepest layers of
the lithosphere.
It cuts through
unstable
deposits of
alluvial
fans
and

outwash,
spoils
of glacial
retreat. It
catches the
flow of water
tables navigating
diagonally across the
island.
It keeps cutting.
The cut breaks with the
folded and deformed layers of
schist, marble and gneiss. It
cuts through the cracks and the
passive fault lines of much wider
geological systems the size of
the North American plate. It
catches glimpses of old ocean
floors, fossils, and fragments
from the unstable beginnings
of the planet.
It keeps cutting.
The cut expands further
into the inner, deepest
layers of the earth. The
viscous lava-flowing
mantle, magnetic infills
of iron, deposits of gold
and turbulent steam.
It grabs traces of
other temporal
organizations of
the universe,
when the earth
was still a
hot messy
fragment
of a star.
It keeps
cutting.

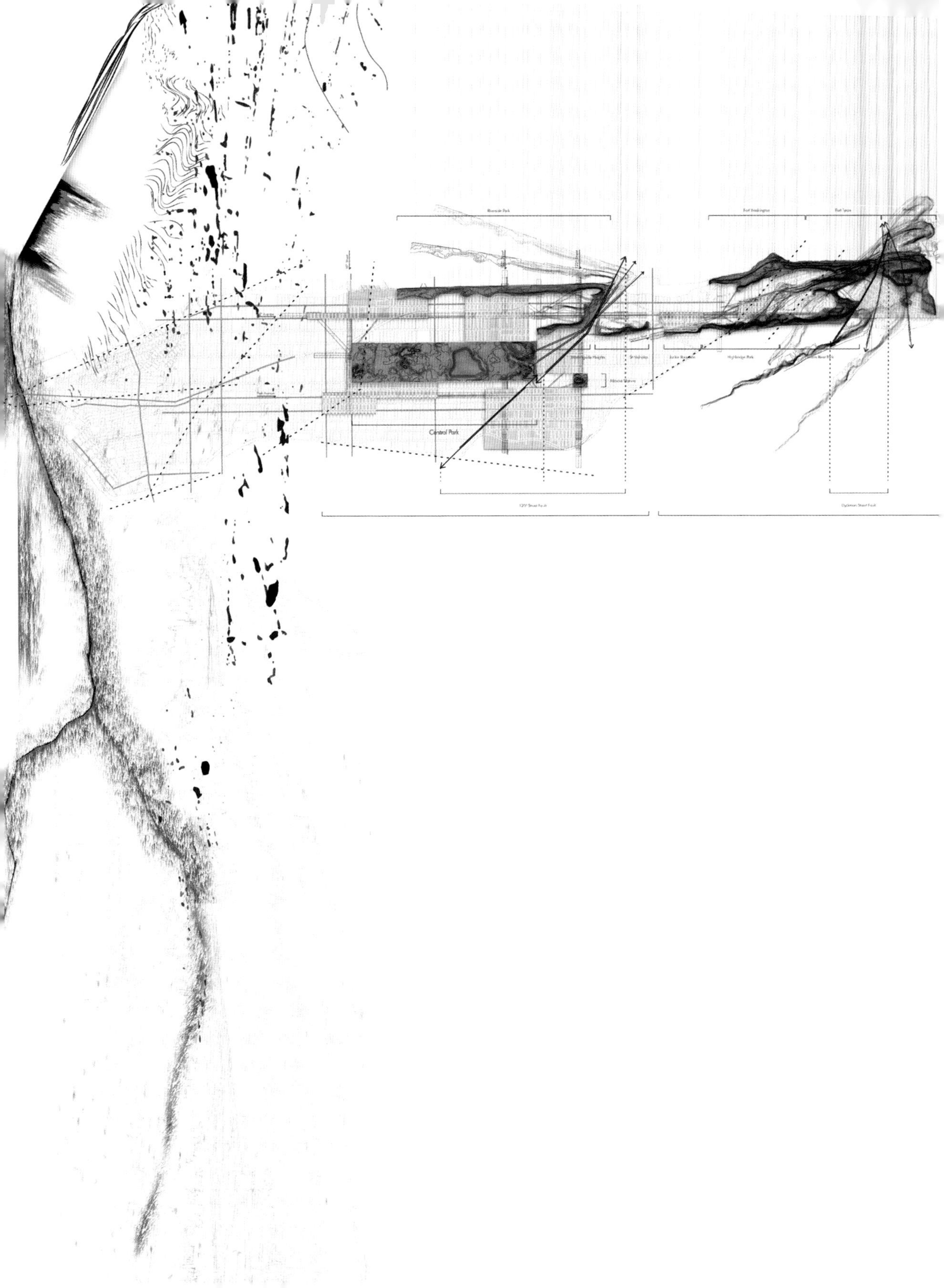

Riverside Park
Fort Washington
Fort Tryon
Morningside Heights
St Nicholas
Jackie Robinson
Highbridge Park
Harlem River Park
Mitchell Square
Central Park
125th Street Fault
Dyckman Street Fault

The deep section can be an interesting tool to begin an experiment of delineating Manhattan into a series of layers in an attempt to organize material assemblages. Rather than being isolated, these layers inevitably tangle with each other, and their characteristics eventually leak from one to another. Through this process, one may also gesture towards the imagination of some of the deepest, unfathomable, and unimaginable layers of the earth and highest, dizzying, ethereal layers of the atmosphere.

Any cut has the potential to become a representation of the world, in that the particular context being framed, or singled out, holds information about the vaster set of conditions around it, some of which may be well known – the thickness of a floorplate or a wall, for example – while others enter the more difficult domain of the unknown – the thickness of the rock beneath the building or the ephemeral densities of the atmospheric layers around it. The deeper the section, the larger the spectrum of precision involved, because the depiction must deal with the contingencies it cuts across and any eventual gaps in knowledge. A deep section does not always have the same level of precision throughout. Some parts of it may be extremely precise and supported by well-known facts, while other parts may be highly speculative, projective, or even hopeful.

The action of cutting through a particular reality – be it a slice of a

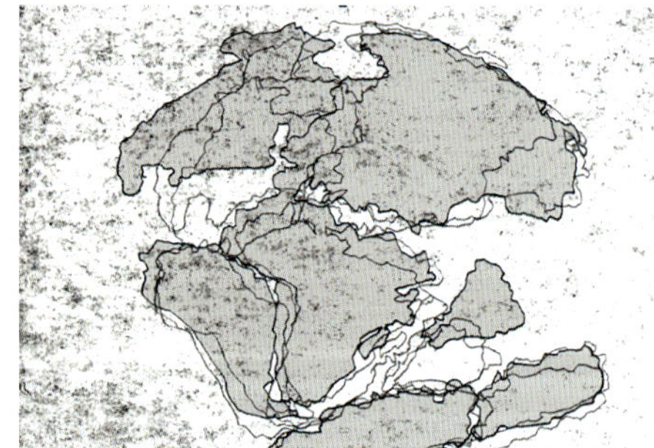

3 (above) Studies of exponential variation in Manhattan's geology.

4 (below) Earth's tectonic plates (series), in 'Lower Manhattan Revisited,' Lebbeus Woods (blog), March 8, 2012.

building, a planet, a galaxy or a nebula of knowledge production – has undergone an expansion as it nested more closely within the Anthropocene debate. When defining an ethics of matter, Karen Barad introduces the notion of *agential cut*, whose intention is not to separate the whole into parts or separate one thing from (an)other, but rather to cut with an ethics of 'responsibility and accountability for the lively relationalities of becoming, of which we are a part.' [11] The agential cut is performed as a subjectification, and it exists between the conditions observed with the cut and the possibilities inherent in the very process of becoming a subject. Similarly, Joanna Zylinska's minimal ethics propose the idea of *ethical injunction* as a series of incisions that are made in the world and allow for more accountability. [12]

It is possible to imagine a deep section of Manhattan cutting it vertically from the tip of its tallest skyscraper descending all the way down through the entrance at street level and its underground foundations. It could equally expand into the atmosphere's outer layers as well as into the bedrock's inner layers, which support the island and beyond.

Unlike more conventional architectural sections with a clear decision of where the drawing begins and ends, the approach here tries to work more deeply with the fundamental question of where and when to begin or finish a sectional cut. The exercise is not an attempt to capture the totality of the island-city in its wider context – one could argue, following Timothy Morton,

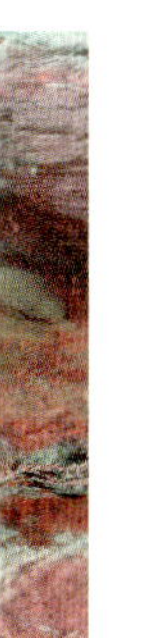

that any section is only a limited capture of a more complex spacetime condition [13] – but rather a preoccupation with what it may mean to stop and the spacetime moment that results from the choice. Lebbeus Woods reflects a perhaps similar preoccupation in his 1999 manifesto *Lower Manhattan*, and especially in the 2012 self-critique to that same manifesto 'Epilogue to Lower Manhattan,' when he writes that 'once we begin to consider what lies below Manhattan, it is hard to know where to stop'. [14]

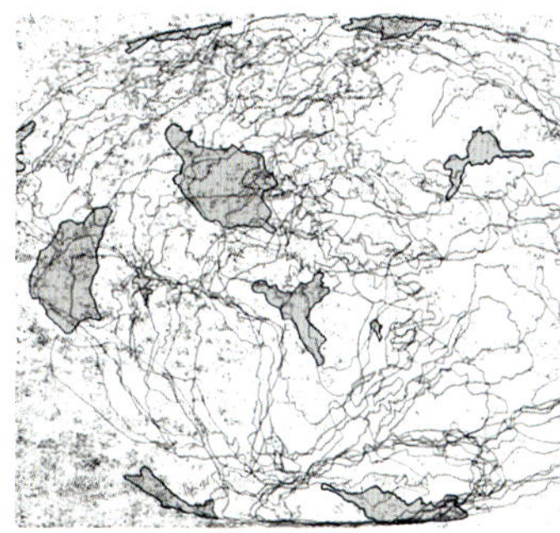

The deep section defines a methodological approach with which to recalibrate representations of Manhattan. By extending the limits of what is usually included in a section, the tool begins to reveal the city's different scalar relations with geo-bio-atmo-ecological conditions. This extension raises cognitive challenges both in representational and perceptual terms.

The experiment borrows from Humboldt not only thematic and aesthetic influences but also his ideas related with climatic and ecological organization. A significant difference from his drawings, however, lies in the conceptualization of scale. Despite their infographic character, Humboldt's mountain sections were constructed to a specific scale, at least up to a certain point. Manhattan's deep section as it is conceived here, however, does not necessarily rely on one scale but it unfolds exponentially across scale along its vertical axis.

The proposed multiscalar thinking used in the deep section shares some similarities with Charles and Ray Eames' *Powers of Ten*, namely on eventual meanings of the vertical expansion. Mark Dorrian suggests that the transcalar journey in the 1977 film might 'be read in terms of the domination and control of the realms that it pictures.' [15] Created during the Cold War and serving the American ideas and ideals of institutionalized capitalist corporativism – the piece was commissioned by IBM – *Powers of Ten* establishes a 'structural relation between the two [macro and microscopic] domains.' [16] Dorrian adds:

> … for only when we have first been in outer space, with all its connotations, are we then predisposed to understand the microscopic, or the interior of the body, as inner space. Likewise, through the sequential staging of "outer" and "inner" in the films, we develop the sense of a narrative unfolding, a plot-like effect that emerges from the structural relation that organizes them. [17]

The symmetric unfolding of scale 'endows the film with a strange circularity, almost as if the poles of the vertical line along which we have passed were bent to meet one another.' [18] The vertigo sensation of moving vertically across such a vast spacetime distance becomes, in fact, more of an unfolding that happens radially to earth in both the ascending and descending movements.

The investigative methodology necessary to experiment with an ever-expanding deep section shares similar geometric and geodesic implications. Despite its apparent verticality, the section becomes a two-dimensional radial plane cutting across an arc on the earth's sphere. Even when recognizing that any section eventually has always already the same implications – a cut of a sphere is always inevitably a radial slice – the extraordinary length of this proposed deep section foregrounds such preoccupations, which are here framed as a *spherographic* approach to Manhattan. [19]

There are, however, important differences between the Eameses' piece and the deep section here proposed. Unlike *Powers of Ten*, which gestures towards a totalizing contemplation of the universe, the deep section accepts that the views it allows of the conditions it cuts across are only partial. It is a fragmentary demonstration in space and time which reflects some form of representational organization of city-geology conditions and how they relate to a wider context. The ambition of the extent of its cut is also its inherent limitation in what it represents: a series of fragments that exist differently at distinct scales. This recognition brings the deep section closer to Derek Woods' notion of *scale variance*. Scale variance suggests that 'observation and the operation of systems are subject to different constraints at different scales due to real discontinuities.' [20] As a tool for a multiscalar way of thinking about the city, the deep section accepts that different systems exist within different constraints and at different scales. [21]

The crafting of the deep section encourages not only alternative ways of calibrating representations of Manhattan but also iterative experimentations over those alternatives. [22]

One such experiment comprises the translation of dimensions and conditions foregrounded by the deep section into a three-dimensional adjustable device. The speculative device aims to reveal fossilized accumulations of city and rock, together with land work related to cut and fill on the island. It further reinforces a reading of the city as a geologic force, and brings together, if only to an extent, the incommensurable scales of geological change in Manhattan taking place across deep space and time. [23]

With its extrusions of rock, soil, city and parks, the device models existing ecologies of scale with distinct spatial and temporal depths. But its construction gives it meaningful physical properties with which it then forges its own architectural relations defined by the materiality, weight and performance of the apparatus: white plaster carved with geo-technical information exposes long and interconnected rock profiles; 3D-printed translucent white fragments define layers of landfill where fertile soil was once removed to give place to the city grid; and 3D-printed opaque dark grey pieces reproduce the undulating fertile topographical ground of the main parks, especially north of Central Park.

Perhaps one of the device's most important formulations is implicit rather than explicit: the distinct layers extruded with the support of creative translations of geometric principles of dominance, size and scale, which are, in turn, determined by the distinct geological faults that run across the island and account for the fluidity, movement, entropy and erosion of the bedrock. The layers in the device are made visible by combined mechanisms

of fine-tuning that interpret these tectonic movements, operating in conceptual relation to levels of stress, pivotal and rotational axes and distances of displacement. Fine-tuning also has its own architectural properties: the device is supported by articulated pieces that operate as small cranes in the delineation of the movement, growth and reinvention of a congested urban condition.

Through proximity, distortion, rotation, fracture or partition, the device offers a recalibrated reading of the island. The faults are conceived physically as singularities or geometric distortions, but they are also proposed as possibilities for changing the current configuration of the island.

Two things are perhaps important to clarify at this point: the meaning and implications of creating such a device, and its potential implications for representations of the island.

In 'Epilogue to Lower Manhattan,' Lebbeus Woods shares a few of his preoccupations with the meaning of contextualizing Manhattan as something essentially geologic, namely by repositioning the island within deep time and according to the theoretical principles of *plate tectonics*. Although the movement of the tectonic plates operates across millions of years and has little to

Encounters with Manhattan's Geologic, Detailed views of the three-dimensional device used to experiment with Manhattan's deep section.

5 (right) *Geologic map and sections of Manhattan Island,* State of New York, 1898.

no expression in our human ways of living, the architect explains that the mere awareness of moving rock – and therefore of a moving city—may be enough to change forms of understanding and inhabiting the planet. Within the thirteen years that separate *Lower Manhattan* from its 2012 epilogue, Woods' architectural discourse evolved to include the planet's tectonic movements as something entangled in the city. *Plate tectonics* provokes the conceptualization of cities, especially when they are defined with relative insularity as Manhattan. The island may emerge as a sort of geological raft

adrift in an underground sea of semi-liquid rock, a city that in the vastness of deep time moves 'slowly but surely.' [24]

By accepting entanglements between city and geology, the Anthropocene makes any separation between the two difficult to reconcile. The focus of the design experiment was to allow for partial representations of some of the new scales of action that encourage for alternative configurations of the city-rock entanglement on this island. Some of these configurations were first enacted by the device and subsequently drawn out in a planar view. The drawing tests relations of size – e.g., the very large scale of the bedrock against the very thin

and almost imperceptible fault lines scattered throughout the island – and scale – e.g., the intricate relations established between different systems of city, rock, soil or water. The drawing synthesizes a series of geological operations which permit the recognition of important thresholds, discontinuities and singularities in Manhattan, some of which are presently covered by the homogenizing blanket of the city grid.

Both device and drawing offer distinct levels of precision when measuring Manhattan. They deliberately blur hierarchies of space and time in favor of successive actions of geological calibration. In a sense, they work in ways similar to a surveyor's chain. [25] Analogous to this distance-measuring device, which enables land to be more accurately surveyed for both legal and commercial purposes, so too do these design experiments instigate the creation of new arbitrary measurement units – of space and, in this case, also time – with their various assembled elements locked together like a chain.

One of the intriguing aspects of this consideration lies in the understanding of how the movement of one of the elements – a city fragment, a rock outcrop or a landfill slab – may have repercussions reverberating across the entire island's systems. This idea encouraged a posterior reappraisal, for example, of the park systems existing on the northern part of the island, where geology is harder, and therefore more visible and determining than in the island's lower parts. Most of these landscapes exist as fertile veils on top of rock outcrops and are limited by significant streets or avenues, which do not conform to the orthogonal grid but distort it instead. Some of these significant boundaries lie directly on top of geological faults spreading across the island, and they also divide the city into its different districts. [26] Even considering their apparent geological stability of these rocky organizations across the vastness of deep time, it is perhaps interesting to imagine them as geological constellations moving very slowly and according to choreographies constrained by some of the faults' geometric rules. [27] Some of these ideas are explored in the following chapter.

Encounters with Manhattan's Geologic, Detailed view of Central Park craned above the geo-technical profiles that supported its construction.

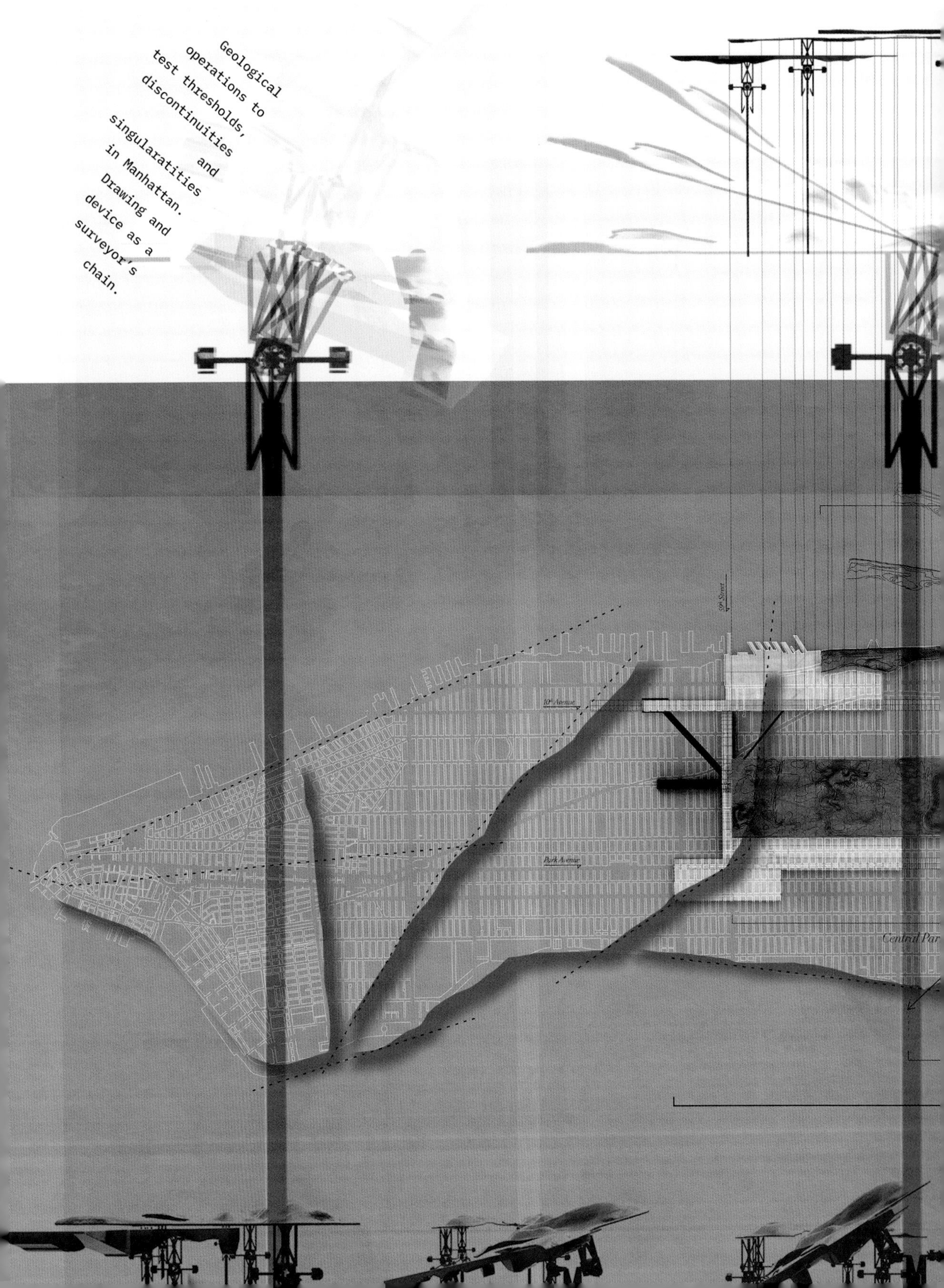

Geological operations to test thresholds, discontinuities, and singularatities in Manhattan. Drawing device as a surveyor's chain.
59th Street
10th Avenue
Park Avenue
Central Par

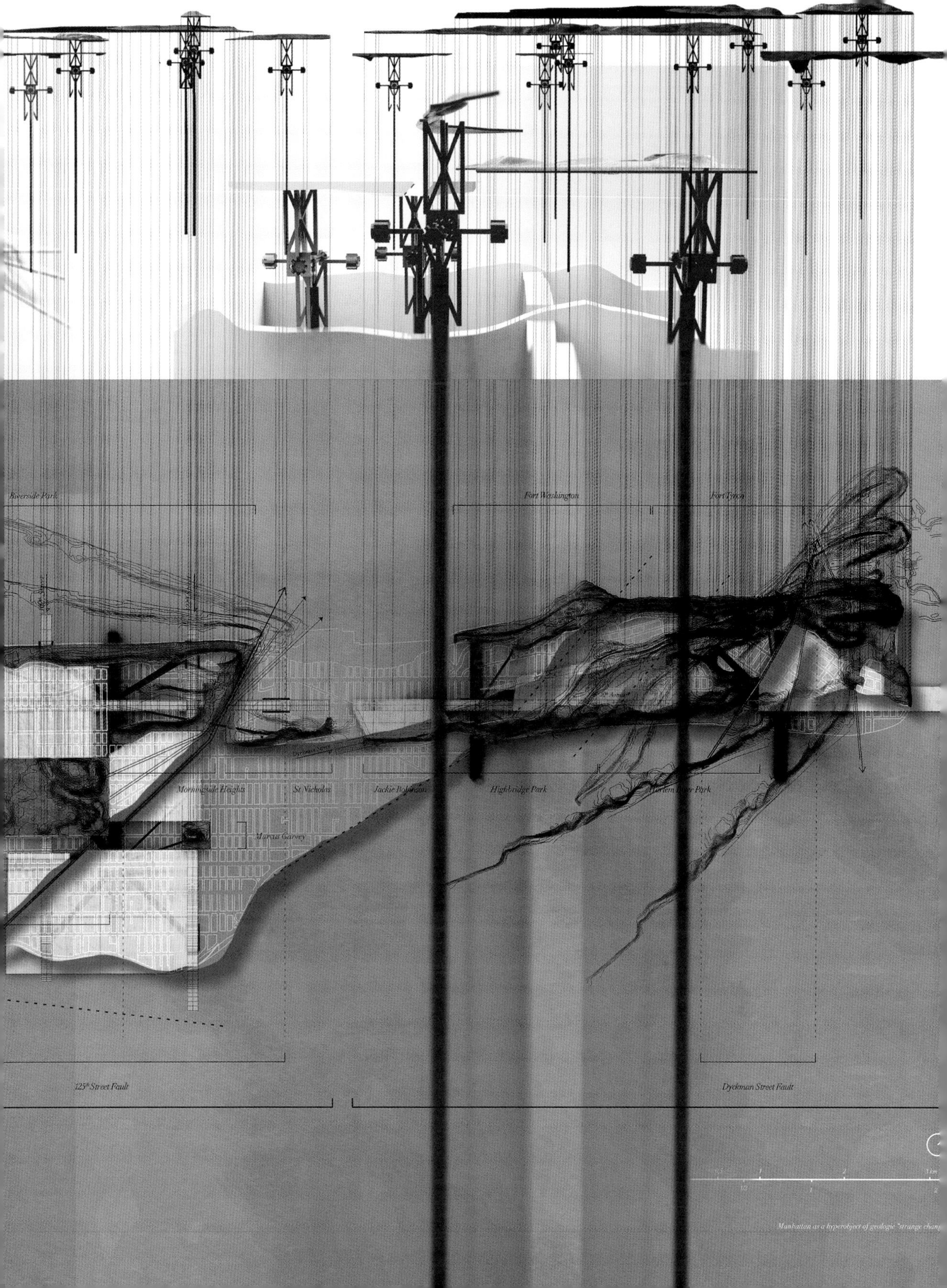
Riverside Park
Fort Washington
Fort Tryon
Morningside Heights
St Nicholas
Jackie Robinson
Highbridge Park
Harlem River Park
Marcus Garvey
125th Street Fault
Dyckman Street Fault
1 km
Manhattan as a hyperobject of geologic "strange change

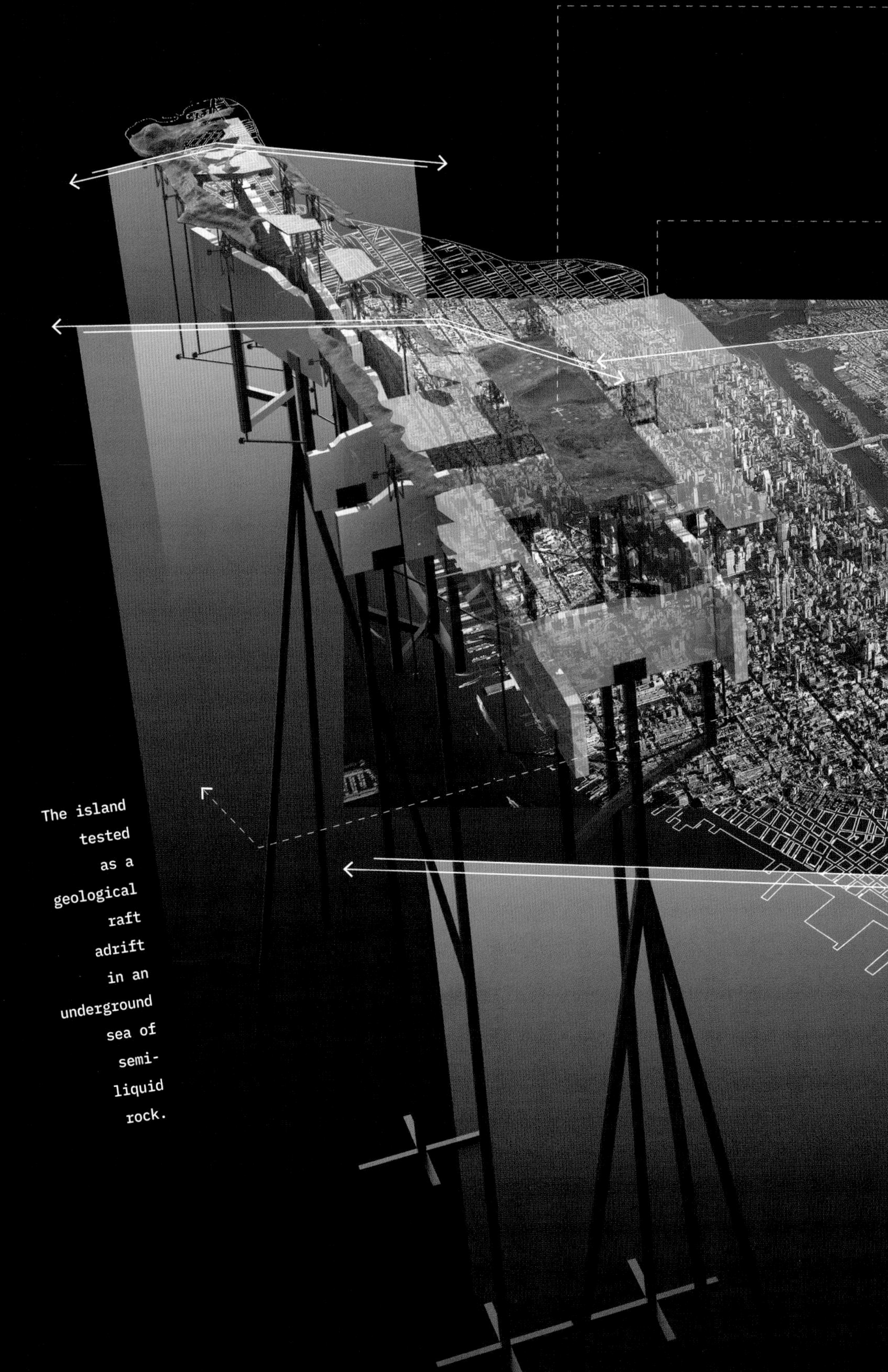
The island
tested
as a
geological
raft
adrift
in an
underground
sea of
semi-
liquid
rock.

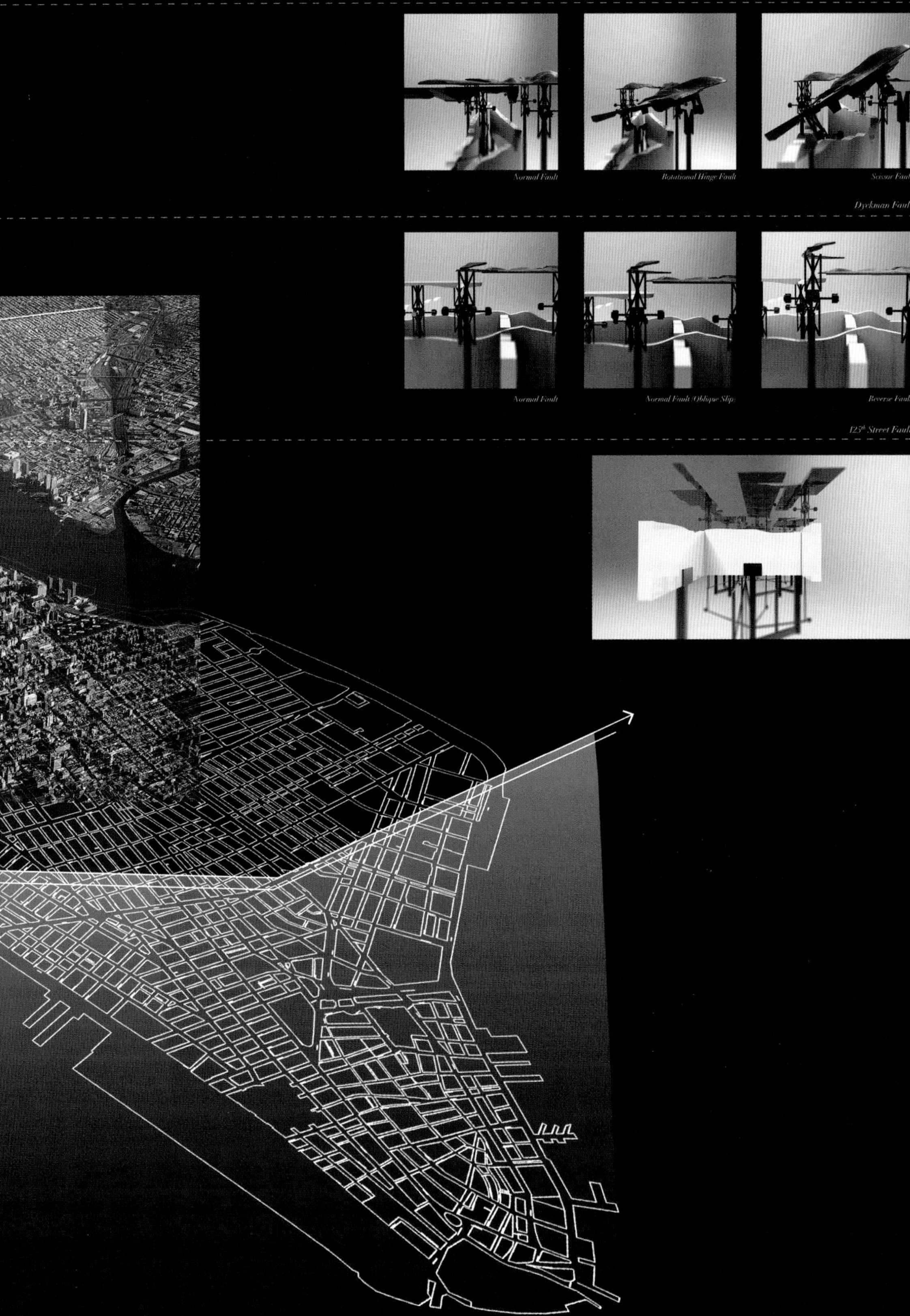
Normal Fault
Rotational Hinge Fault
Scissor Fault
Dyckman Fault
Normal Fault
Normal Fault (Oblique Slip)
Reverse Fault
125th Street Fault

3 Stratify
Towards a Rethoric of Ground

Through a close examination of Lebbeus Woods' 1999 manifesto *Lower Manhattan*, this chapter argues for a notion of ground as active earth media. Ground is used to question assumptions of Manhattan as a homogenized city grid, and instead to accept the island-territory as a coalescence of geological fragments that offer support to the city.

Examined retrospectively from the Anthropocene, *Lower Manhattan* is positioned along the line of pictorial tradition belonging to the American sublime and used as a critical lens to study the *Viele Map* (1865) as a transitional paper landscape that activates similar impressions. The research offers a retrospective contextualization of both pieces from contemporary perspectives and proposes that both interpretations of Manhattan be read as cyborgian urban conditions. This argument is supported by an understanding of *Lower Manhattan* as a techno-subliminal representation of the island deeply rooted in its own geologic condition.

The design work related to this study spanned a temporal arc of four years and culminated in an installation titled *Encounters with Manhattan's Geologic*, which was exhibited at the Tent Gallery, University of Edinburgh, in 2016. It briefly gathered a series of interrelated design experiments that reveal alternative ways of imagining and representing the island-territory.

The installation operated as a transitional moment along a longer period of experimentation and testing of possibilities inspired by *Lower Manhattan* (2015–2020). For the brief duration when they were exhibited as fragments of the island-city, the design explorations were mostly a demonstration of their fluid states of incompleteness and constant evolution.

In bringing together *Lower Manhattan*, the *Viele Map*, and the series of design experiments that critically appraise and reposition them, the chapter argues that Woods' rhetoric of ground, with which he formalizes his imagination, can be read more widely as an advocacy for architectural practice to engage with planetary instability manifested along expanded delineations and across vastly distinct scales.

Device for working with Manhattan's faults becomes a way of reading the city-rock entanglement stratigraphically. The iterative design process tests a rhetoric of ground that explores the urban condition as indeterminant possibility.

3.1 Between Imagination and Myth: From *Lower Manhattan* (1999) to the *Viele Map* (1865)

When Lebbeus Woods created *Lower Manhattan* there were a few major events he couldn't have predicted. First, the 9/11 terrorist attacks on the World Trade Center (WTC) in 2001, which devastated the city and violently brought the world into the unstable realities of the twenty-first century, amidst new geopolitical conditions of terrorism and war. Second, the extreme hurricane sisters, Irene (2011) and Sandy (2012), which left behind a trail of devastation and death, and temporarily repositioned environmental protection against climate change at the top of the American political, social and cultural agendas. Sandy, in particular, plunged New York into new conditions of flooding and darkness that would inspire many reactive projects to protect the island from sea level rise. [28]

Lower Manhattan is a manifesto comprising both a drawn aerial view of the island with the East and the Hudson rivers both dammed, and a short text reflecting on the eventual meaning of the image. Woods produced the manifesto to integrate a special issue on New York commissioned by the Italian architecture magazine *Abitare*. [29] It was created in 1999, a year of millennial transition and, therefore, a period prone to complex lines of flight between reflection and premonition. In a 2007 interview, Woods briefly reflects on *Lower Manhattan* and points out the tragic coincidence of his having depicted the WTC in an intriguingly diminished way, a weird anticipation that 'some kind of transformation was going to happen there.' [30] Also sadly intriguing is the coincidence between the timing of Sandy hitting the island and the moment when Woods passed away. The death of the architect of the unstable, the insecure and the inhospitable coincided with a moment when Manhattan's Lower East Side – Woods' long-time neighborhood – was momentarily swallowed by a raging Atlantic Ocean. Joseph Becker and Jennifer Dunlop Fletcher – the SFMoMA curators who had been preparing a solo exhibition called *Lebbeus Woods, Architect* (2013) – describe the bizarre coincidence between the death of the architect of chaos and climatic and geological events and Sandy as something that 'almost … had to be that way.' [31]

Though very succinct, the text in *Lower Manhattan* condenses significant lessons for architecture, the urban condition and the city, both implicitly and

6 *Lower Manhattan, Lebbeus Woods, 1999.*

explicitly. It reflects on the meaning of transformation between completion and uncertainty. It thinks about scale and its relational subtleties against size, utilizing the skyscraper as a vibrant instrument that can oscillate between the two. And it discusses the city's culture of congestion and the Koolhaasian post-modernist 'brilliant twist' in *Delirious New York*. [32] Manhattan's aerial illustration in the manifesto corroborates some of Woods' theoretical concerns in the text. At the same time, it synthesizes implicit preoccupations with planetary environmental conditions and, more specifically, the pursuit of meaning in architectural practice, both of which received Woods' attention throughout his life of experimentation. Nevertheless, for a discussion of *Lower Manhattan* as a critical idea contextualized retrospectively and from the perspectives offered by the Anthropocene theory, these implicit concerns acquire new meanings. Some of these concerns are analyzed here with the support of secondary sources in which the manifesto is referenced directly or by implication. [33]

Woods considered it one of his main professional purposes to devote architectural practice to the task of imagination, something he defined as

7 to 9 *Underground Berlin,* Lebbeus Woods, 1988.

stemming from his autobiography, a mixture of early experiences from the military-industrial complex and studies in engineering and architecture. [34] Aligning his practice with the Conceptual Architecture movement of the 1960s and 70s – led by influential studios such as Superstudio or Archigram – Woods was less interested 'in living in a fantasy world' than in raising questions and challenging conventions. [35] His friend and colleague at the Cooper Union in New York, Cristoph A. Kumpusch, believed that Woods '"wanted life and architecture to be a challenge" and "always wanted us to feel a little uncomfortable in order to make things change."' [36] But change, for Woods, did not forcefully include seeing his projects leave the conceptual plane of the paper into the three-dimensional world of the building, with an important exception to be made with the *Light Pavilion* in Chengdu, China, developed together with Kumpusch for a house complex by Steven Holl, another long-time friend. This late project, finished only a week before Woods' death, unites two foundational interests in his formation as an architect: light and geometry. The architect connects light with his personal aesthetic experience of the world's phenomena in ways that 'pierced [his] consciousness,' while geometry gave him a needed supporting order and precision to 'escape' the ordinary. [37]

Together with psychologist Olive Brown – who was his wife at the time – Woods created the *Research Institute for Experimental Architecture* (RIEA) in the late 1980s. His early involvement with the institute was relatively short-lived, but it gained traction in the American architectural milieu of that period. [38] The institute was one of Woods' contributions to the discussion on the meaning of experimentation in architecture, which could eventually lead – in his opinion, and whether institutionalized or not – to wider epistemological questions that could steer the foundations of architecture in new directions. [39]

Lower Manhattan congregates many of Woods' design preoccupations around tectonics, scale, ground, gravity and atmosphere. One can also derive from it other equally significant concerns that the architect explored throughout his conceptual practice: ethical dimensions implicit in architecture, the role of imagination in design experimentation, or epistemological understandings of knowledge production stemming from cybernetics and its eventual uses in architecture.

Lower Manhattan was conceived in line with a wider body of experimental work spanning across more than a decade – from the late 1980s until the late 90s – which includes some of the architect's most iconic projects, such as

Underground Berlin (1988), *Berlin Free Zone* (1990-91), *War and Architecture* (1993–95), *Havana* (1995), I*nhabiting the Quake* (San Francisco, 1995), or *Zagreb Free Zone* (1991). Rather than provide an exhaustive discussion around these projects, this chapter will attempt to trace the architect's compelling pursuit of meaning in and through architecture. More specifically, in relation to a study of *Lower Manhattan*, these conceptual proposals can be seen as tropes with which Woods reveals his reactions to and involvement with the orders of things, ideas of war and disaster, meanings of repair, cultural and political questioning of freedom. They can be conceived as his attempts to resolve what John Szot called the 'tension stemming from conflict, be it natural disaster, political turmoil, or otherwise', which eventually offers glimpses of a much wider Woodsian quest for a unified urban condition. [40]

Woods' conceptual involvement in global geopolitical conflicts gains visibility in the Sarajevo projects, but it had already been manifested earlier in his two Berlin projects: first, in the 1988 *Underground Berlin* – a subterranean city linking the eastern and western former divisions of the city [41] – and second, in *Berlin Free Zone* (1990-91) – a proposal for the reconstruction of the no man's land left by decades of separation. [42] Similar to his previous Berlin projects, as well as the ones that came after – *Zagreb Free Zone*, Sarajevo, Havana and San Francisco – Woods' imagined cities are only for 'those willing to explore new modes of thinking and living … They are neither public nor private in the prevailing use of the terms.' [43]

Both in the Havana and the San Francisco projects, Woods' concerns stem partly from a consideration of the possibility of environmental disaster. In the former, the architect proposes a cantilevered public terrace around Havana's waterfront – the Malécon – which becomes a storm-surge protection barrier-wall in emergency moments when hurricanes hit the island. In the latter, along the San Andreas active geological fault, he wonders about an architecture that accepts and benefits from the earthquake's seismic forces. [44] By becoming a part of the Californian lithology or the Cuban hydrology, Woods' architectures for the faults or the hurricanes inform an experimental approach to the creation of new meanings, 'grounded into a very specific "terrain," whether physical and/or conceptual, from which they stem.' [45] This set of projects, as well as the ones before rooted in geopolitical conflict, seem to respond to very specific and often extreme conditions, for which there is too 'little architectural history for [his] experimental projects to be alternatives to.' [46]

In thinking with ideas that he claims were being ignored by most architects at the time – 'earthquakes and other natural, if violent, transformations, political walls, and wars' – Woods pivoted his modes of practicing. He became progressively more interested in unstable social and environmental conditions, thus pointing out the need for architecture to be contextualized within a larger frame of reference, one that accepts buildings, for example, as 'part of a complex human fabric that is being constantly woven and rewoven by many people, events, ideas.' [47] An expanded framework that triggers imagination. Woods' later projects – including but not limited to *La Chute* (2002), *The Storm* (2002), or *The Wall Game* (2004) – are examples of how this framework embraces indeterminacy and change: instead of being conceived as objects or products, these projects are constructed as fields of interactions. The definition of architecture as *field* dilutes the conceptual boundaries between architecture and its context and encourages an exploration of alternative ways of dealing with the possible entanglements between the two. [48]

Woods' architecture aims for its deeper inclusion within a wider context, from which it then becomes impossible to disentangle. It is an architecture of probabilities, of synthetic technoculture, of cybernetic thinking about networks and systems, an architecture that perhaps comes close to Haraway's figure of the *cyborg*, which results from the congealment of the machinic and the organic, and from delineations less concerned about 'skin than about statistically defined densities of signal and noise.' [49] Woods' architectural ideas can be conceived as cyborgs in that they fluidly converge machinic responses and socio-cultural constructs to earth systems, thus enacting alternative organizations of life conditions. The argument must be nuanced, for even if Woods recognizes a strong influence of cybernetics in his personal and professional understandings of the world, he never explicitly aligned his practice with New Materialism or Haraway's thinking more specifically. [50] But the suggestion allows for the positioning of Woods' practice more at the center of the Anthropocene theory. In many ways, the architect's willingness to work with human crisis – both philosophical and existential – can be regarded as an Anthropocenic preoccupation. This is a crisis derived from the increasing awareness, on one side, of the 'human species as a major geomorphic force altering the planet' and, on the other, of 'a human existential crisis stemming from an individual sense of total lack of control.' [51] Interestingly, this is the context in which Woods defines architectural experimentation – a 'very personally philosophical, and strongly existential' practice that demands of 'every really good architect ... a coherent worldview.' [52]

Woods defines Manhattan as a condition that exists vertically 'between the earth and the stars.' [53] His experiments in scale reveal a vertical abyss 'related to the earth deep below and the sky high above' the island-city. [54] With *Lower Manhattan*, more specifically, Woods proposes to reconcile the city with the bedrock on which it laid its foundations. Departing from the idea that 'the old scale of Manhattan is that of the skyscraper,' the architect defines scale as a relationship between the city – those 'small human scratchings on the surface of the Earth' – and the earth. [55] Woods is less interested in the accuracy of geological representation than in providing a visual experience of the city's geologic context in deep space and time.

As an experimentation with scale, *Lower Manhattan* interestingly resembles nineteenth century photographic experiences with geological formations. When investigating an 1886 photographic series by William Jerome Harrison, Adam Bobbette focuses on the limits the photographs expose, both in geology and photography. [56] Unlike common photographs of rocks using reference objects – rulers, coins, umbrellas – some of Harrison's close-ups were already too close for human objects to be used as scale devices. Without a reference scale, the rocks suddenly become scaleless, that is, they could be read as much larger mountain systems, or much smaller pebbles. Harrison's photo-geological impressions reveal complex relationships between figure and ground: fossils are figure when the rock is ground, but fossils become ground when the figure of an everyday object leans on them. Backgrounds are broken to allow comparisons with the foreground, and even scale devices gain fossilized contours and seem to be embedded in the rock. [57] But even when present, Harrison's everyday objects do not necessarily resolve the scale of the rocks. Instead, they complicate 'relations among scales,' not by dissolving the constructions of time and space but by revealing an 'accumulation of fossilized impressions expanding in space and time.' [58]

If read as a geological formation – or better a *geosocial formation* [59] – *Lower Manhattan* shows a complicated relationship between city and bedrock beneath, where the two already seem fossilized. The image depicts a formation

10 *Pinnacle of Chalk*, William Jerome Harrison, W. of Sheringhamm, 1886.

where city, bedrock and planet intersect with one another and seem to coalesce. These impressions are mostly revealed through an unusual inversion in the representation of the relationship between Manhattan and the bedrock, where the city is tangled with the rock.[60] Woods' image operates as 'a lens through which we may no longer see a city supported by a rock but can perhaps imagine a rock with a fossilized city above.'[61]

With city and bedrock entangled, *Lower Manhattan* attunes us to interconnections between large-scale entities that are 'massively distributed in time and space relative to humans.'[62] At the same time, it also reminds us that the configuration of this entanglement is only a glimpse of a geosocial formation that expands across deep spacetime.[63]

With the damming of the rivers, *Lower Manhattan* could be regarded almost as a perspectival section.[64] Yet, the section here becomes less of a cutting across the city-rock entanglement and more of a connection between relational possibilities that the cut itself enacts. Following Karen Barad's notion of *agential cut* – a cut done ethically and with 'responsibility and accountability for the lively relationalities of becoming, of which we are a part'[65] – *Lower Manhattan* relates and makes tangible temporary spacetime conditions of city together with bedrock that would otherwise be difficult to comprehend and almost impossible to visualize. In doing so, it transforms our understanding of both city and rock.

Delineations in this context cannot be traced as sharp lines cutting across and circumscribing clear layers of figure against ground, or of architecture against its context. Manhattan's geologic delineations, more specifically, cannot be assembled in clear sectional configurations of city, soil, rock or atmosphere. Precisely because of their entanglement, these layers do not fully exist on their own or completely detached from their wider context, and their eventual delineation should be understood as a series of interrelated cuts across an ever-expanding and ever-shifting section. As discussed before, the deep section – with all its long tradition in architecture and landscape architecture – can be an interesting tool to begin an experiment of delineating Manhattan into a series of layers that attempt to organize material assemblages but which inevitably leak from one another.[66] Through this process, one may also gesture towards the imagination of some of the unfathomable layers of the earth and atmosphere.

One of *Lower Manhattan*'s most intriguing qualities is its power to invoke a sublime representation of the island-city. With both rivers dammed and the exposure of the bedrock that sustains the city, the image reveals a massive geological support that seems to extend indefinitely towards the earth's center. It triggers the imagination to think about a large object – the city-rock entanglement – as an invitation to a glimpse into an unfathomable spacetime abyss, and it raises a sudden desire to see what cannot be seen.

The qualification of *Lower Manhattan* as an aesthetic experience of the sublime – 'a pleasure mixed with pain, a pleasure that comes from pain' [67] – may carry interesting observations in the context of both early philosophical definitions of sublime and some of its more recent formulations. As an image, *Lower Manhattan* is somewhat limited in conveying strong qualities related to overwhelming vastness or power. But in belittling human scale and exposing human vulnerabilities to the earth's vastness and force, it conveys an 'emotional reaction of excitement and delight tinged with anxiety.' [68] The image also portrays an experience of 'artificial infinite' characteristic of the sublime, where 'the eye moves successively from one part to the next, with those parts having a quality of uniformity, and without anything interrupting the imagination's expansion. Repetition is used in a vertical way …' [69]

Even if different both in context and period of creation, *Lower Manhattan* echoes traces of landscape-related works from the Romantic period, both in painting and, later, early photography. One example is the eighteenth-century folio of drawings done by John Clerk of Eldin to illustrate the last volumes of James Hutton's influential publication *Theory of the Earth.* [70] Another example, already mentioned, is Humboldt's series of deep sections to explain how climatic variation in altitude organizes vegetation. Even without the geological or botanical accuracy of these pieces, *Lower Manhattan* still reveals important similarities, namely in its attempt to encourage a thinking about the vastness of the earth in the form of a thick geological agglomeration.

In gesturing towards the limits in imagination required to conceive of the vast and largely unknown geology beneath the city, *Lower Manhattan* suggests an 'ontological dislocation,' which Jean-François Lyotard describes as 'something that transcends the object … a kind of immanent transcendence … where the "elevated" mind takes center stage.' [71] The limits in imagination reveal limits in the knowledge to address such deficiencies. Woods' depiction can offer an experience of the sublime not just in terms of the artificial urban infinite it reveals, but also in relation to these limits required to conceive and understand the unknown that lies beneath.

Even if not necessarily affiliated with any art movement or period, Woods' depiction of Manhattan can also be related to a more specific lineage of North American representations of the sublime. [72] The carefully chosen angle of the bird's-eye view, for example, allows for the depiction of a large swath of space extending from the bay up into the Hudson valley. Following the tradition of landscape paintings associated with the sublime, it depicts a grand landscape by projecting a sense of vastness into the progressively darker and intentionally less defined background. The image also contains an additional vantage point pushing the image downwards towards the earth center. The glimpse of the old bedrock creates a feeling of a vast temporal abyss into the unknown. Rather than attempting to control the eye, the image's vantage points expand visual possibilities. At the same time, this expansion creates a distance between the eye of the beholder and the city so that the latter renders unusually calm in the sense of an absence of human congestion one is accustomed to seeing or experiencing in New York City.

If one reads it as depicting a city without human presence and devoid of water around it, it could be tempting to frame *Lower Manhattan* as an environmental dystopia – a 'landscape that might be under pressure.' [73] Emily Brady defines these as experiences of the environmental sublime, which promote an appreciation of nature that, immersive and multi-sensorial as it may be, is not necessarily one of comfortable intimacy. Rather, it involves a necessary degree of discomfort, anxiety and exposure to vulnerability. [74]

The Anthropocene debate suggests a perhaps more critical view of these experiences related to conceptualizations of nature as a vault from which humans and life itself might be excluded. It presents an almost Nietzschean 'challenge of looking at the entire archive of the earth' with a material mode of seeing that does not assume any teleological or spiritual meaning behind the materiality of its traces or inscriptions. [75] In other words, it denotes an empathetic imagination of the earth by invoking feelings and perceptions of life without an immediate leap into the meanings of those experiences.

Woods was certainly not alien to dystopian architectures in the face of catastrophic challenges. *Lower Manhattan* may be a representation that imagines an entanglement between city and its geology to eventually construct a deeper understanding of human scale and impact on earth, but it is also the depiction of a city built 'as if humans were not [or no longer] present.' [76] It is, in a way, an architectonic construction of a vaulted nature in a vast world of solitude, perhaps evocative of a type of remoteness portrayed in paintings of the Romantic period. It almost becomes an invitation to engage in what Claire Colebrook calls a *post-apocalyptic sublime,* that is, a fetishized construction of a post-urban version of the world, one where Manhattan has lost its human congestion. [77]

But the act of looking down and the distance of the beholder – which might also justify the apparent sense of human absence – is somewhat evocative of, for example, photographs of the Grand Canyon, taken from the ridges looking down into an abyss of space and time, that is, something with a distinct American flavor. At the same time, and because of the clearly engineered dams that curve around the island to hold back the water and reveal the geological section, there is an inevitable sense that the alternative condition that Woods proposes is a specifically – one could say architectonically –

constructed city, as opposed to being a depiction of the city in the aftermath of a catastrophic event. In this context, *Lower Manhattan* becomes less of an apocalyptic rendering of dystopian doom and more of a speculative realistic approach with contours of science-fiction that will be explored later in this chapter.[78]

The sense of isolation one gets from *Lower Manhattan* is not unusual in representations of the island city, which reinforce its meaning as a cultural icon of the urban condition. At the same time, Manhattan weirdly feels less isolated than other islands. It is in fact a territory whose radical interconnectedness is excursive. The nineteenth century was a period of fast urban growth in the United States and of significant technological revolution triggered by the implementation of infrastructures at the extremely vast scale of the American territory and at an unprecedented speed. It naturally corresponded to a rapidly diminishing sense of remoteness and profundity in the wilderness, one of the reasons why the sublime largely fell out of interest in philosophy.[79] Nevertheless, very large infrastructural work of this period led to the development of philosophical ideas combining a reverence for techno-scientific and military-industrial might. David Nye describes experiences of these territorial transformations as a specific form of American *technological sublime*.[80] Matthew Gandy uses a detailed historical description of New York's water system not only as an example of such an experience, but also one that has prevailed to present times. He adds that trekking in upstate New York may quickly become nothing short of a Thoreauvian experience in the wilderness, yet it is important to remember that 'you are standing inside New York City's water system.'[81]

At the same time as it evoked experiences pertaining to the sublime, the growth of New York City's water network was intersected by growing concerns with the poor sanitary conditions in the increasingly congested city. The conditions intensified in the aftermath of the American civil war, a period of intense polarization but also of great ambition for urban growth and social consolidation.

These two seemingly distant experiences generated from New York's water conditions – one awe-inspiring, the other verging on repulsive – were synthesized, even if unintentionally, by the American civil engineer and mapmaker Egbert L. Viele in 1865, when he authored the *Sanitary & Topographical Map of the City and Island of New York*.

The *Viele Map* – as it came to be known – resulted from a superimposition of the city grid onto what were then the assumed original conditions of Manhattan.[82] In the crafting of the map Viele undertook a significant

11 *Sanitary & Topographical Map of the City and Island of New York*, Egbert L. Viele, 1865.

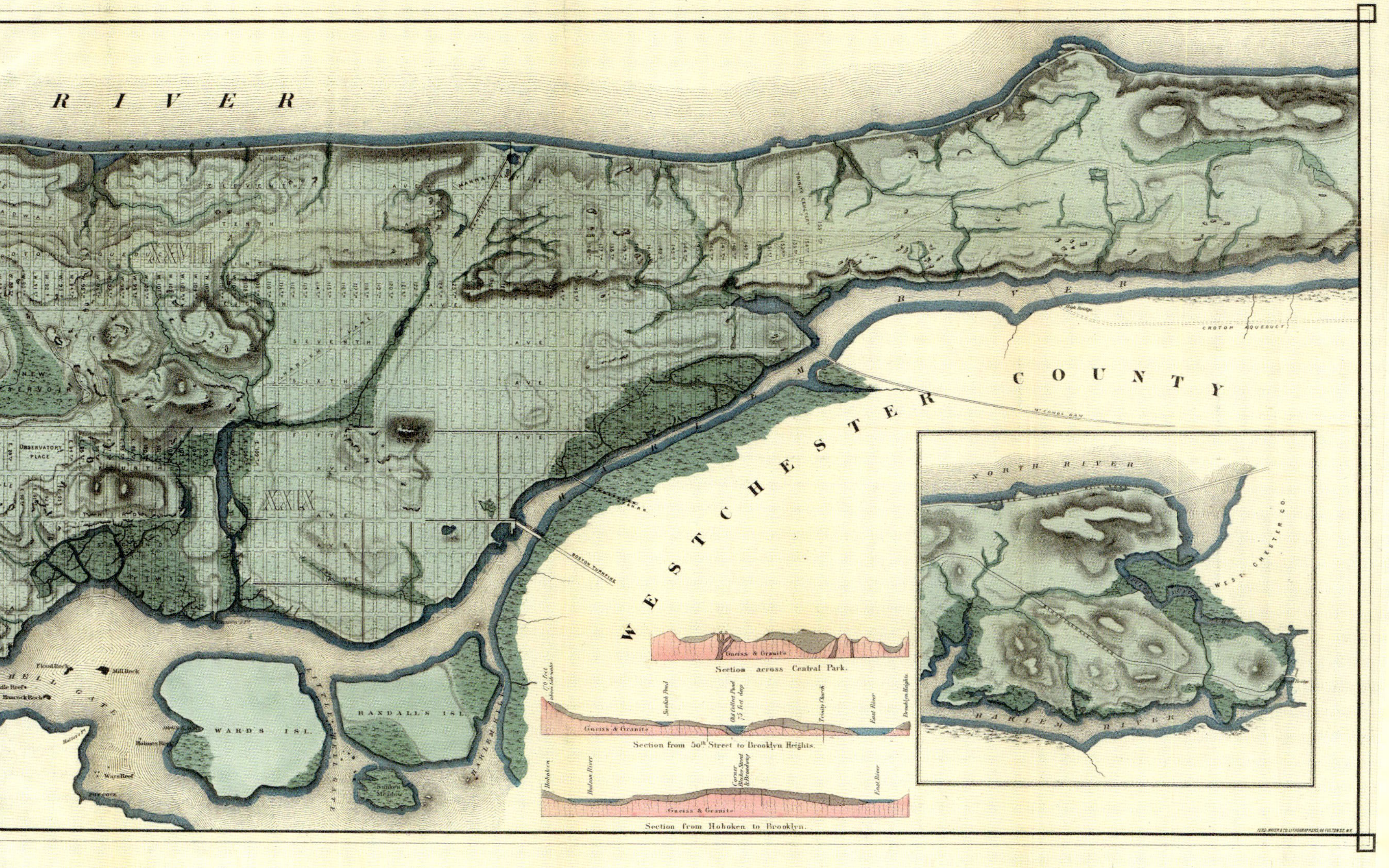

RIVER
HUDSON RIVER RAIL ROAD
WESTCHESTER COUNTY
HARLEM RIVER
CROTON AQUEDUCT
High Bridge
McComb's Dam
TRINITY CEMETERY
MANHATTANVILLE
BOSTON TURNPIKE
NEW RESERVOIR
OBSERVATORY PLACE
XXVII
XXVIII
XXIX
SEVENTH AVE
SIXTH AVE
FIFTH AVE
HELL GATE
Flood Rock
Mill Rock
Hancock Rock
Hallet's Pt.
Ways Reef
PO T COCK
WARD'S ISL.
RANDALL'S ISL.
LITTLE HELL GATE
HARLEM KILL
Sunken Meadow
Section across Central Park.
Gneiss & Granite
Section from 50th Street to Brooklyn Heights.
Gneiss & Granite
Scalish Pond
Old Croton Pond 75 feet deep
Trinity Church
East River
Brooklyn Heights
Section from Hoboken to Brooklyn.
Gneiss & Granite
Hoboken
Hudson River
Corner Hester Street & Broadway
East River
170 feet above tide water
NORTH RIVER
WEST CHESTER CO.
HARLEM RIVER
FERD. MAYER & CO. LITHOGRAPHERS, 96 FULTON ST. N.Y.

leap of creativity in the spatial narrative of the island's hydrological and topographical conditions, since most of the territory he depicted no longer existed, especially south of Central Park. [83] Thus, the map can be described as a speculative spatial fiction performing in at least two interesting ways: first, it enacts a temporal compression of the island by rendering some of its previous territorial conditions on top of the city in construction, thus, providing an impactful and immersive visual glimpse of the otherwise inaccessible foundational layers of bedrock.

Second, it stages a potent perceptual manipulation of territorial evolution by highlighting with yellow demarcations the edge portions of the island that were landfilled as additions to the original insular perimeter. [84] The map registers the material exchange involved in 'the consolidation of port commercial activities and their success for many years to come.' [85]

With a proposal to recalibrate the mediation between technology and nature, the Anthropocene theory advocates for the dissolution of boundaries between interior and exterior. The technological sublime is another way of referring to the resulting aesthetic engagement with and sensibility of nature associated with an increasing scale of human artifice. [86] The aesthetic experience of the sublime moves away from a feeling of being awestruck by the power of nature to an overwhelming sensation caused by the impossibility of escaping or even stepping outside of the technospheric milieu of which we are but a subcomponent. [87]

When studied from the perspectives offered by the Anthropocene, the *Viele Map* supports methodological approaches to conceiving of alternative recalibrations of city and bedrock, where both are conceptualized as transcalar *actants* that cut across an infinite range of connected scales. [88] Reconfigured as an artefact that contains the possibility of cutting through the island's spacetime conditions – in a way, a planar view that almost works as a section – the cartography informs a strategy with which to analyze and manipulate the city's present conditions and its future possibilities. The map activates readings of the city-rock entanglement across dispersed conditions of connectivity by gesturing towards what exceeds it and, in doing so, it indicates what can no longer be seen in the city. With an unusual depth in space and time, it evokes a perhaps unusual sublime experience of the island on a planimetric view; an aesthetic engagement that allows for the reading of what usually escapes comprehension and attention in more conventional depictions.

The map is, therefore, less of a cartographical survey and more of a speculative survey of conditions that no longer existed completely or existed in a not-completely solid way. It suspends time in this transitional paper space that translates the previous conditions that were no more on to a new city that was yet to come.

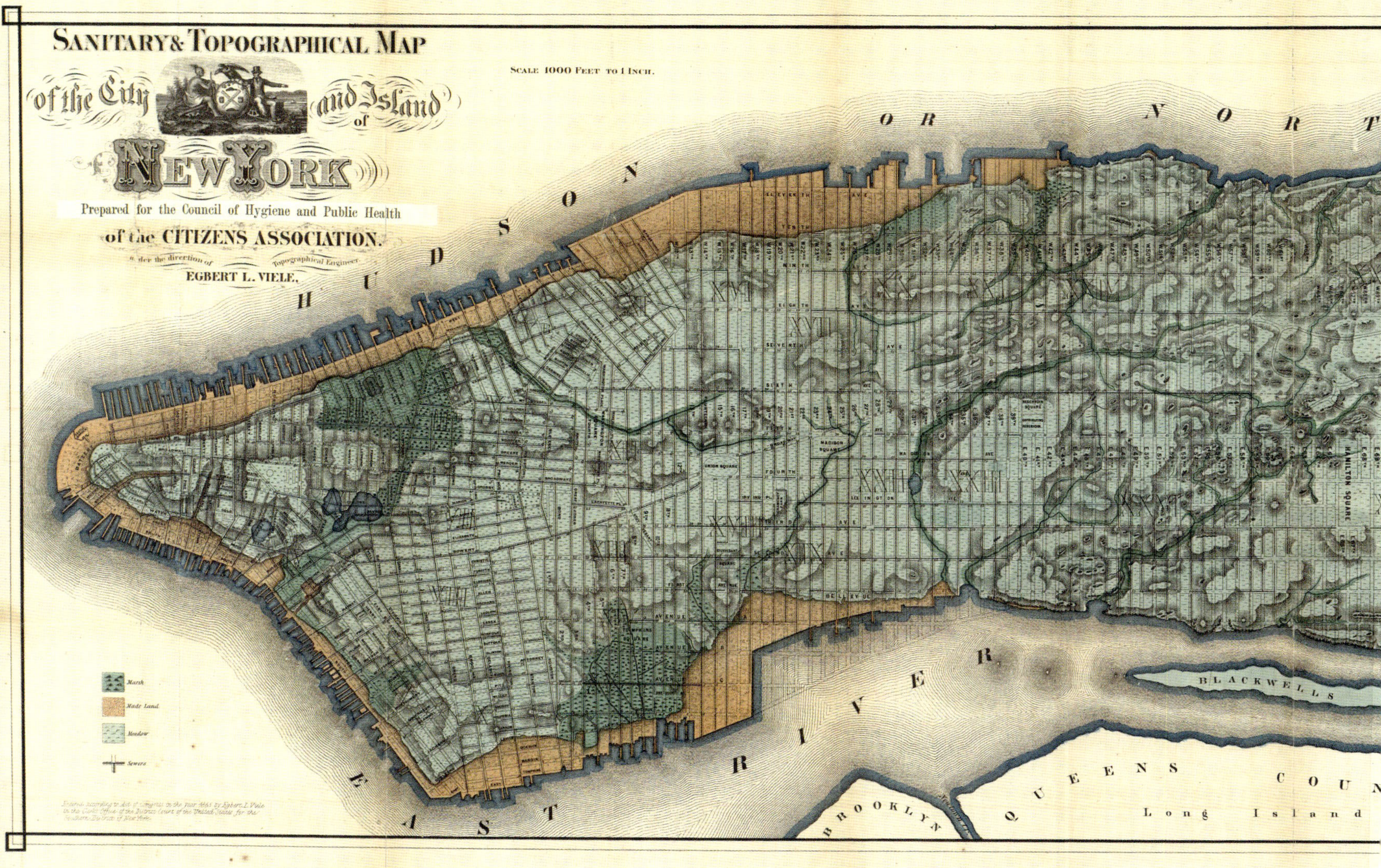

SANITARY & TOPOGRAPHICAL MAP
of the City and Island of
NEW YORK
Prepared for the Council of Hygiene and Public Health
of the CITIZENS ASSOCIATION.
Under the direction of Topographical Engineer
EGBERT L. VIELE,
SCALE 1000 FEET TO 1 INCH.
Marsh
Made Land.
Meadow
Sewers
HUDSON OR NORTH RIVER
EAST RIVER
BLACKWELLS
BROOKLYN
QUEENS COUN
Long Island
HAMILTON SQUARE
MADISON SQUARE
UNION SQUARE
TOMPKINS SQUARE
BELLEVUE

3.2 Stratigraphic Operations: Seismic-Architectural Devices, Heterotopic Fragments, and Geofollies

The retrospective study of *Lower Manhattan* as a lens to examine the *Viele Map* supported the construction of stratigraphic operations around ideas of *grounding, scaling* and *framing* to experiment with new delineations of Manhattan.

Most organizational principles that support Woods' architectural imagination are conceived as operations to investigate the extreme conditions of disaster from which the projects, then, emerge. These principles define a methodological approach, even if loose at times, for dealing with complex urban conditions. [89] In expanding the city's stratigraphic delineations, Woods' imagination gains contours of a new tectonic language made from abstracted conditions of ground; a language informed by conditions of fluidity and instability.

Ground sustains Woods' tectonic language and allows him to oscillate between the precision of his drawings and the contingencies involved in the complex realities in relation to which he thinks. It is a language that is simultaneously structural, geomorphologic and premonitory. Rather than providing the architect with stable delineations in which to root his projects, ground becomes something that shakes, breaks and moves; its structure is under perpetual conditions of change. Ground allows for the reading, understanding and imagining of the dynamics of change that support his ideas on war, disaster or instability. At the same time, ground means the possibility of imagining alternative value systems, of creating unconventional *lifeworlds*, of promoting different kinds of interactions, and of harnessing other types of energies.

Lower Manhattan can help enunciate some of the aforementioned preoccupations with ground. In the manifesto Woods focuses less on a grounded terrain on which to experiment with the spatiality of an idea than on ground itself. In other words, there is no expressed architectural proposal as such, other than the city itself as a sort of mineralogic agglomeration represented as a (necessarily temporary, crystalized and insular) whole, entangled in its geological support. Geology becomes a complex thickness of negotiation, where the usual datums of the city are embedded within vibrant rocky materials and their often-dissonant configurations of space and time. Through this negotiation, it could be argued, Woods finds and develops specific tools of persuasion. His practice could, then, be framed as a personal rhetoric of ground that instigates a dialectics between the city and interrelated operations with their meaningful stratigraphic qualities.

Scale in Woods' work is carefully distinguished from the notion of size. Scale allows the thinking of convergences between architecture and its context, as well as their eventual dissolution into one another. Woods uses a multiscalar way of thinking to identify city delineations that defy conventional architecture in relation to ground conditions, as well as conditions of interiority and exteriority. The architect focuses on 'a new kind of scale … of the city to the Earth, to the planet.' [90] Scale is an expanding notion necessary to establish conditions between subcomponents of complex assemblages. Interestingly, some of Woods' projects complicate scale, since they verge on *scaleless* architectural conditions, that is, configurations that don't have a clear scale established in relation to the world. Becker and Dunlop Fletcher point out that scalelessness was a point Woods often made in his invitation to the question of 'what if?' [91] This was a question, they argue, that was perhaps at the basis of his conceptual practice. 'No project is fully designed. ... This is intentional – Woods allows the viewer to complete the project in his or her mind.' [92] Embedded in this understanding of scale(lessness) Woods defines architecture – and its practice – in relation to experience. In this sense, his conception of *time* is 'ever of the present moment, the now, the precise but elusive moment of being.' [93] However, in articulating architecture as exercises of unfolding and enacting the future as a series of possibilities, time can also be understood as a constant becoming, where architectural futures (and pasts) are imagined and synthesized through experimentations in the present moment.

Frame supports the oscillation between precision and contingency, and it is used both in conceptual approaches and representational techniques. Architectural representations are a good demonstration of Woods' preoccupations with the framing of the city, and they help describe and question what is known. In the specific case of *Lower Manhattan*, for example, the geological extrusion revealed beneath the city through the damming of the rivers is less of an attempt at depicting geology 'correctly', or as it eventually is, and more of a vertical revealing of a vertiginous abyss where knowledge becomes progressively more diffuse.

Grounding, scaling, and *framing* are here proposed as some of Woods' stratigraphic operations to read the city and its spacetime conditions, but also as tools of persuasion with which to describe and imagine it.

Similar to Woods' approach, one of the main preoccupations in the crafting of these experiments is the navigation between precision and contingency in knowledge and how they affect representations of the city-geology entanglement. Different types of representational devices – drawings, models, photomontages – expose limits in knowledge of what lies beneath or above the city, and these limits have clear consequences in the design process itself. In other words, these representations of the city do not have the same level of precision all the way through, but they could be regarded instead as a constant process of negotiation between observation and imagination.

Departing from experimentation with Manhattan's deep section through the mechanics of a three-dimensional adjustable device – resembling a surveyor's chain, as mentioned before – the installation *Encounters with Manhattan's Geologic* (2016) occupied the exhibition space with fragments of the island-city. For the brief duration when they were exhibited, the design explorations were mostly a demonstration of their fluid states of incompleteness and constant evolution.

The experiments gesture towards the formulation of a new city that is imagined for and from within the gallery space, and which existed physically only for the moment of the exhibition. Each of the fragments expands stratigraphic delineations of both island and city. Each of them also becomes an island inside the gallery space, positioned inside a perpendicular grid aligned with the first fragment – oriented twenty-nine degrees east of true north. The walls of the exhibition space received a series of supporting drawings organized in clusters, some of which are the basis for subsequent explorations.

The design experiments inform different strategies for reading Manhattan's conditions of the geologic and, more specifically, for suggesting new ways to represent some of the city's underground conditions. The line of argument that they support through different formats – publications, presentations, competitions, informal conversations – aims to be less of a critique of Woods' practice and more of a critical and creative dialogue with the architect's interests in Manhattan and, more widely, with the rhetoric he uses to explore and push the boundaries of the conditions of relationality between city and ground. A dialectic that ungrounds and re-organizes the city stratigraphically.

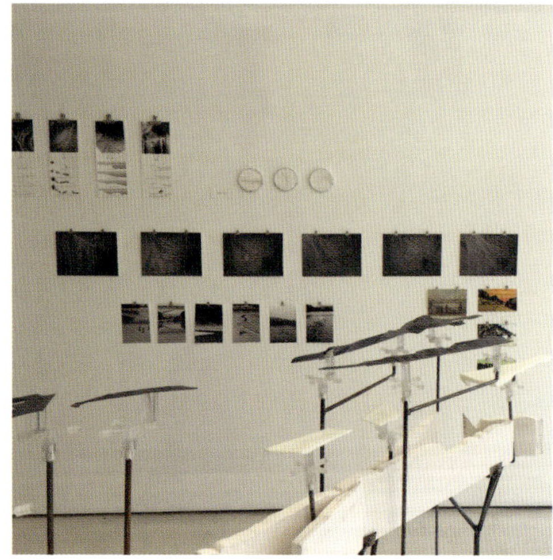

Encounters with Manhattan's Geologic, Detailed views of the installation.
(next pages) Plans and axonometric views of the installation.

51

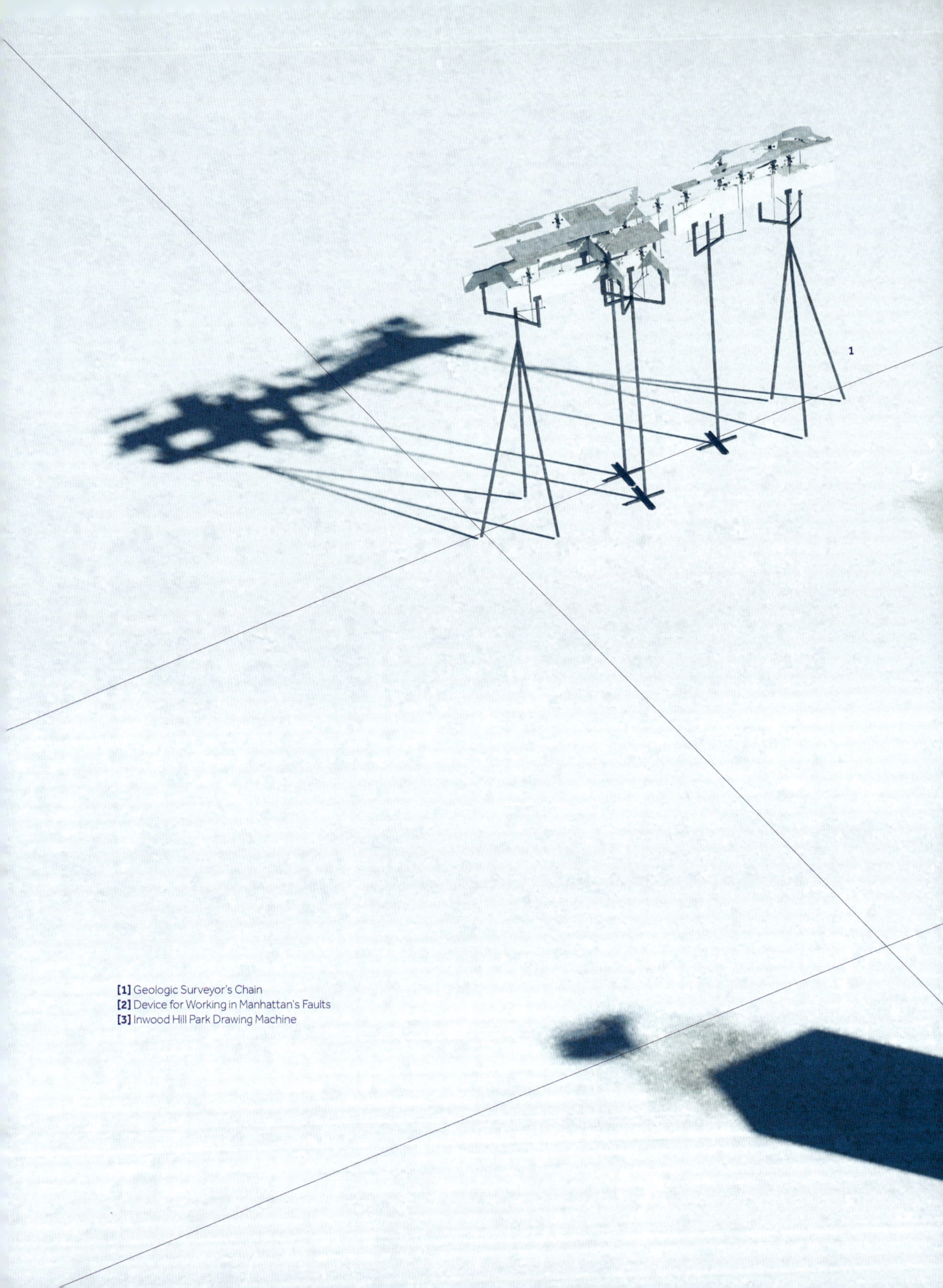

[1] Geologic Surveyor's Chain
[2] Device for Working in Manhattan's Faults
[3] Inwood Hill Park Drawing Machine

Orientation of Manhattan in relation to true north

3

2

[1] Geologic Surveyor's Chain
[2] Device for Working in Manhattan's Faults
[3] Inwood Hill Park Drawing Machine

A Device for Working with the Faults [94]

Despite its age, the *Viele Map* remains today as a fundamental cartographic document for many structural engineers facing the challenges of laying out foundations across the island, precisely because of the information it reveals about the inaccessible layers of the city, namely subterranean hydrological and topographical conditions. [95] In fact, infrastructural works of engineering scattered across the island offer a fruitful insight into some of Manhattan's geologic conditions.

In the quest to foreground how Manhattan's city grid might be affected and even distorted by the different passive fault lines that run across it, the trestle bridges become an interesting technology to investigate. They offer valuable insights to explore how architectural and geo-engineering inventions may challenge more conventional ways of reading the island. The trestle bridges that span 125th Street – where there is a geological fault line separating Manhattanville to the south from Harlem to the north and east – render these preoccupations with geological dynamics visible. Where they carry an elevated section of the Broadway Interborough Rapid Transit Subway System, for example, there are large hinges on the abutments, so that 'if vertical movement were to take place along the fault, the bridge would move on its hinges but remain intact, and the transportation system would be undisturbed.' [96]

The creation of a representational device able to reveal the role of the bridges within a thicker geologic exploration of the island implied a creative leap beyond the usual representational limits of Manhattan. The device becomes an architectural invention, whose main potential is to convey unexpected scales of space and time. Optimal distance and focal length become operative tools to generate multiple readings of architecture. Manipulation and abstraction are fine-tuned through successive acts of drawing and modelling to allow elements of the geological layers to interfere with the human-made layers that compose the city. The foregrounded conditions receive interferences coming from massively distributed spatial and temporal scales, such as the original conditions of the island – the once wet, hilly and densely forested *Mannahatta* – or the movement of the geological apparatus across deep time. [97] It is as though the lens of a microscope might have been deliberately used to blur city surfaces that are usually at the center of focus, and the samples being observed have been deliberately contaminated with unexpected dimensions of change. The change in focus becomes another way of registering a sectional understanding of the territory.

One of the consequences of this creative process is to encourage the conditions of some of Manhattan's faults to emerge from the background. Foregrounding the geologic through representation highlights an interesting *scalefulness* that verges on the *scaleless*. This is not unusual in the discipline of geology, for example, which moves diligently across exponential scales of both time and space in search of behavioral patterns, structure and material responses to environmental conditions. The strangeness of macroscopic depictions of vast territorial conditions, side by side with microscopic images of truncated mineral composition, leave us with an uncanny sense, not of mastering, but of losing control of scale.

Coalescence of Heterotopic Fragments Geo-Fragments

When focusing on a dialectics between the city and the unstable conditions where it exists, Woods' rhetoric accepts ground as dynamic, something that moves, shakes and breaks. Ground is in constant tension, reconfiguration and negotiation with the city. This understanding, it can be argued, is further reinforced through his preoccupations with planetary forces. Unsurprisingly, then, ideas concerning speculative displacement of the urban condition are deliberately tangled with scientific knowledge. As mentioned before, in 'Epilogue to Lower Manhattan' Woods claims that the island's geo-condition is what positions the city on the planet. The tectonic movement of the plates in the vastness of deep time forcefully conditions the city. [98] In forging stronger relationalities between planet and city, Woods encourages a provocative conceptualization of the city as a condition delicately balancing on top of an underground mantle of fluid rock.

The idea of Manhattan as a geofragment adrift in a fluid mantle evokes more classic examples of heterotopias – ships in the ocean or spaceships in outer space – all ideas with which Woods played in his projects, even if implicitly. Manhattan is, in many ways, a heterotopic condition, a world within the world, a place of a parallel reality that acts as a mirroring counter-site upsetting that which is both inside and outside; a displaced place of *otherness*, which accepts incompatibility, disruption or contradiction. [99]

Michel Foucault's notion of *heterotopia* has obvious implications for a reading of Manhattan as a condition of otherness, of overlaid contradiction and disruption enacted 'by [congested] relations of proximity between points or elements', which, he adds, one can formally describe as, for example, a grid. [100]

The characterization of Manhattan as a heterotopic island is not necessarily new, but in the context of this design experimentation the idea is to conceptualize the island less as unified heterotopia and more as a concatenation of several heterotopic islands within the island. To a certain extent, Manhattan's distinct boroughs have very unique, sometimes even isolated socio-cultural constructions manifested in architecture, urban life, public space or intangible heritage. But here, the idea becomes a methodological approach to facilitate a reading of geosocial formations as fragments of the geologic which eventually carry their own cultural and aesthetic meanings.

(next page) Device for working in Manhattan's faults.

(following pages) Studies of Manhattan's Geofragments.

CITY NEW YORK

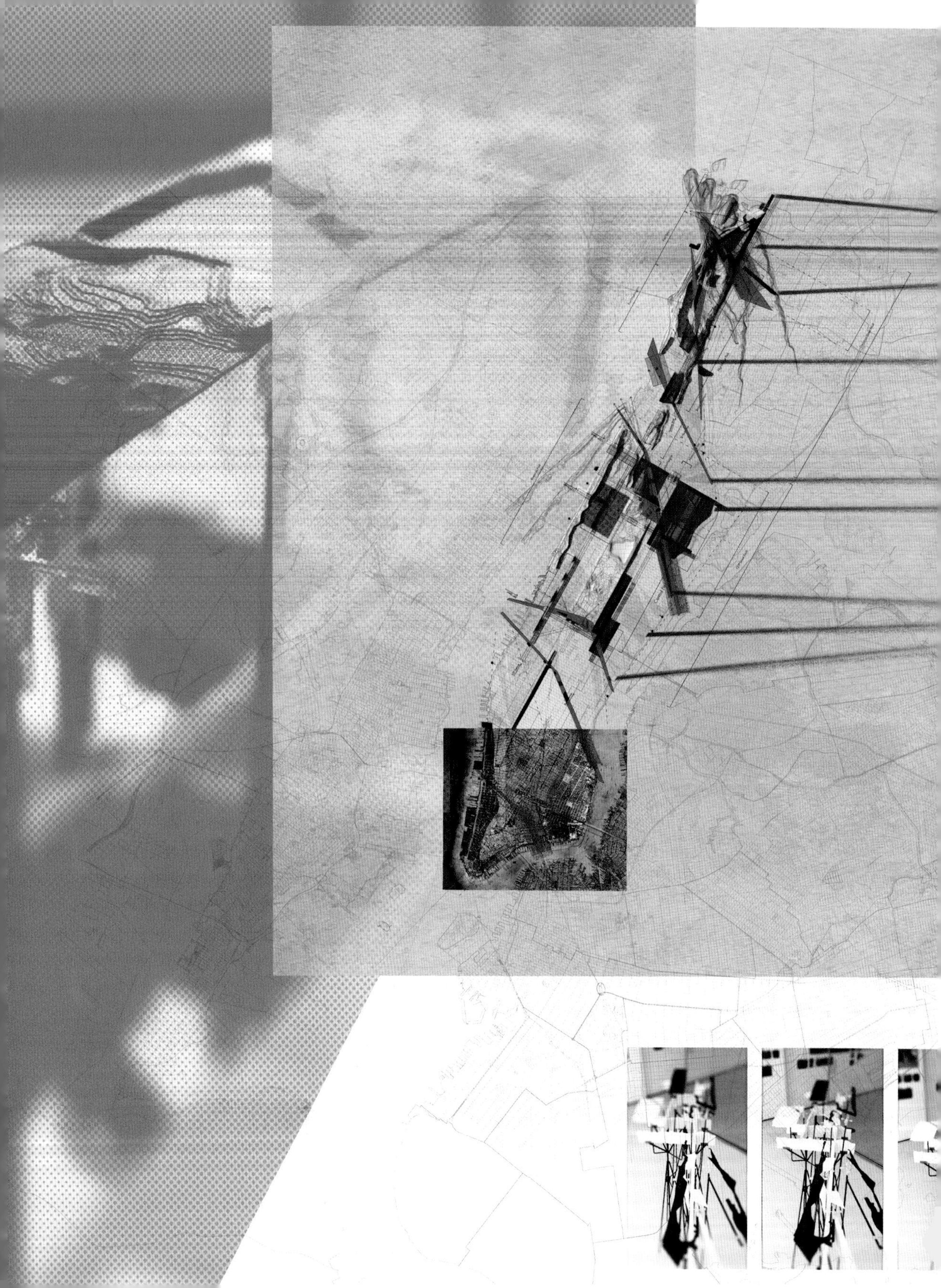

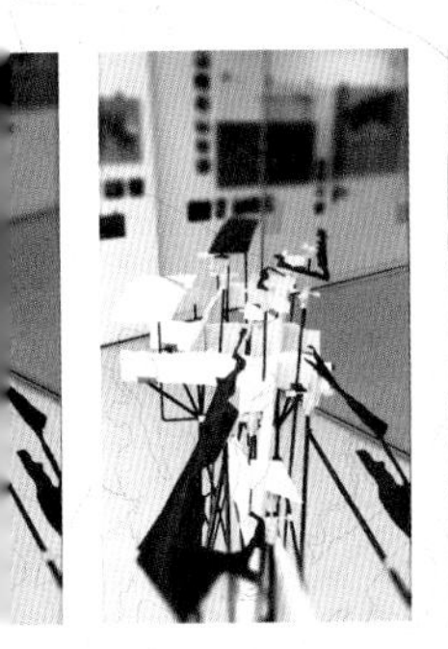
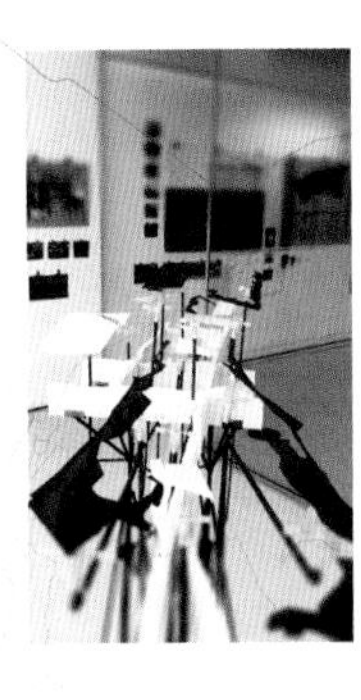
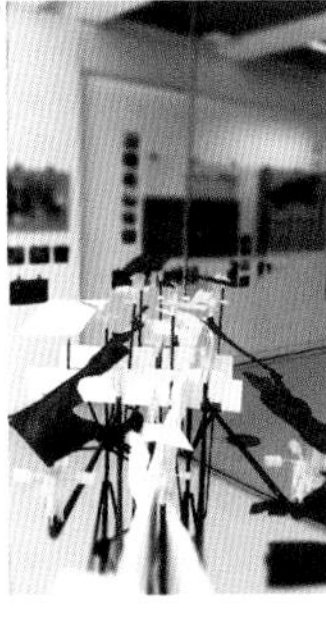

Geofollies and Other Witnesses of Dissonance [101]

Inwood Hill Park stands on the northern tip of Manhattan, spreading downhill from the top of a big rock that is in direct contact with the junction point between the Hudson and the Harlem rivers. The hilly landscape reveals steep slopes facing north and gentler slopes facing the city to the south. It is covered in a dense deciduous forest linked with a tidal salt marsh through a thick and dark valley. The rocky hill was forged by the glacial retreat of the Wisconsin Ice Sheet that once covered a big part of the North American plate. [102]

There is a common perception amongst contemporary Manhattanites that Inwood is the last piece of native forest and salt marsh on the island, a relic from another time. For today's local inhabitants, the urban eco-amateurs, the occasional tourists, and the groups of pupils and university students who visit it daily, the park is described as a natural haven. The bowl-shaped valley conceals the busy city and opens up to a glimpse of what once was a much longer tidal riverscape. This ecological vision of the park is, however, too simplistic and inaccurate.

If the Anthropocene can be conceived also as a 'politically infused geology' [103] – a contemporary situation where materials are vibrant witnesses and active generators of processes and aesthetic sensations [104] – then Inwood's landscape material inscriptions may testify to dissonant occupancies and register geological violence enacted by political, sociocultural and extractive actions. Disparate histories and stories of rock, salt and woodland gain preponderance throughout centuries of a city growing northwards through displacement, dispossession, demolition and cleansing. Rock, salt and woodland, therefore, inform a material palette inscribed in and erased from the landscape conditions of the park multiple times. [105]

Inwood's dissonant accounts across space and time demonstrate that ecology can erase narratives of violence through enforcement, theft or war. Yet, at the same time, this landscape's current state of maturity equally nurtures meaningful collective values of preservation and conservation. The landscape acquires heterotopic characteristics of an enclave inside Manhattan, a place where the condition of otherness emerges from its apparent resistance against the city and its own internal contradictions.

Inwood's Geofollies is a conceptual proposal which critically explores the tensions arising from these conflicting positions. It proposes the redesign of the existing salt marsh as well as a series of follies that accumulate around the marshland's tidal interfaces. Rock, salt and woodland are once again considered as a valuable material palette, this time for enacting contemporary landscape configurations and testing how they respond to, and eventually even trigger, new reactions in Inwood.

The redesign of the salt marsh focuses on the removal of the existing retaining wall to unleash the tides. The design process evolves with the creation of a drawing machine – where a mechanical device is attached to a physical model of the landscape – to test new topographical and hydrological conditions – in both plan and section – to explore new interfaces between

(right and next pages) Inwood's Geofollies.

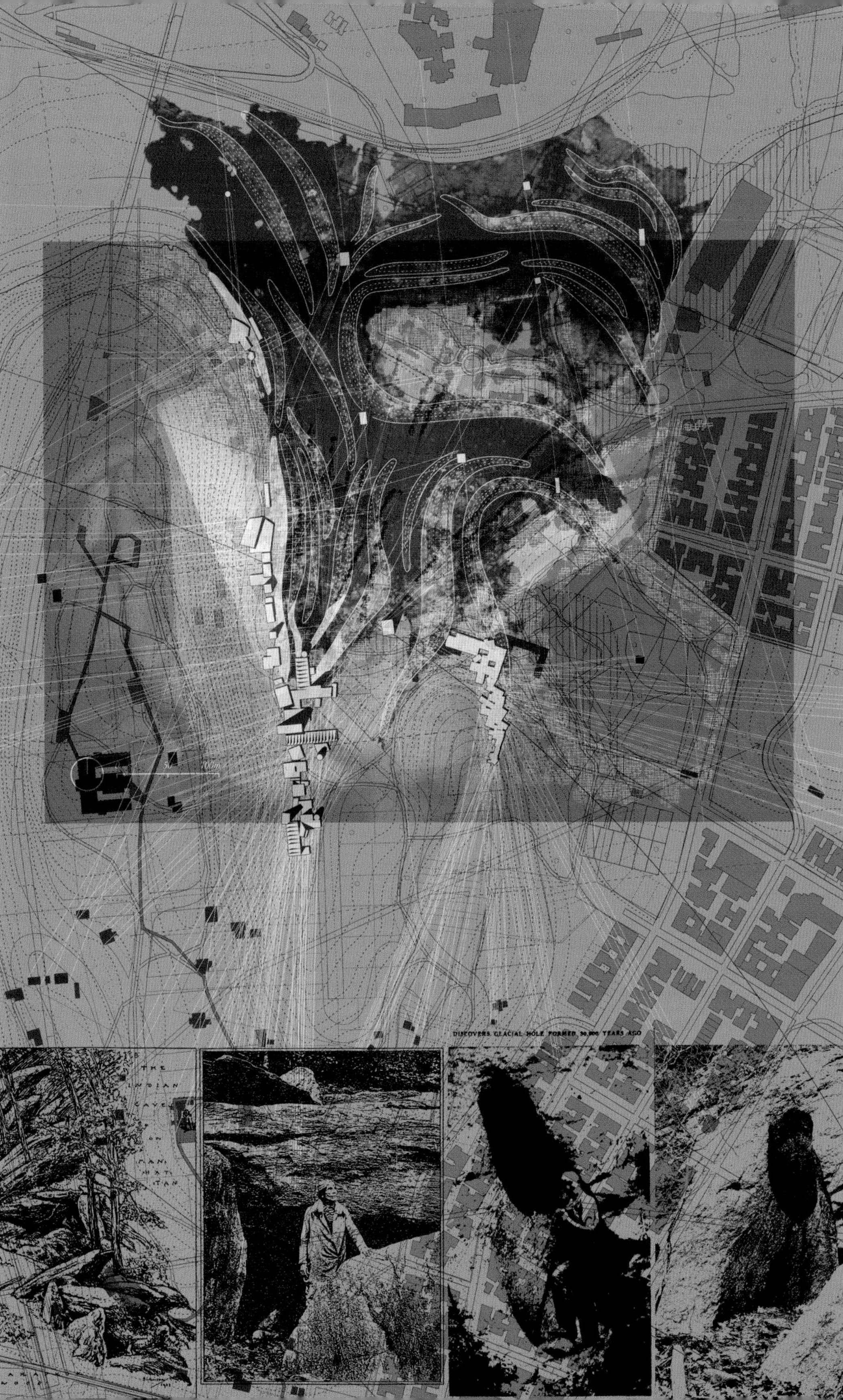
DISCOVERS GLACIAL HOLE FORMED 50,000 YEARS AGO
THE
INDIAN
CAVE
OF
MANHATTAN
100m

the sloped woodland and the tidal marsh. [106]

The project is supported by cartographic and in-situ mapping of the park's traces and scars left by previous dissonant occupancies, from building footprints to cave dwellings, and from glens to glacial potholes. The conceptual excavation – both architectural and geological – narrates stories of violence mostly by their evocative material absence. In the project, these voids are conceived as their reverse – extruded geological masses. The consideration of these conceptual volumes scattered along the hillsides suggests a potential gravitational dragging downhill, similar in many ways to the erratic boulders being dragged by glacial retreat and scattered across Manhattan, some of which can still be observed in their curated positions across Central Park. The final accumulation and recombination of the conceptual masses at the foot of the hill generate new architectural assemblages, conceived as contemporary landscape follies.

The idea of *folly* is meaningful here. Follies are forms distinguishable from the landscape context in which they exist and without explicit programmatic ambitions, sometimes without a program at all. In his reflection about the *Osaka Follies* – a series of follies developed by prominent architects for the Osaka Garden and Greenery Exposition (1990) – architect Arata Isozaki writes that a folly is 'a building that traditionally has no function'. [107] He adds:

> ... follies are small and fraught with difficulties. Designing a building normally entails responding to a specific use, or communicating a particular message. But with the folly there is no direct meaning to put across, no concrete function to fulfil. It isn't quite architecture. It isn't sculpture. [108]

In his reflections about Conceptual Art and Architecture, Mark Dorrian states that *utility* is less of a condition about the architectural *interior* and more the condition that has historically acted as the point of discrimination between architecture and art. [109] Historically speaking, architecture and art can be told apart because the former responds to a need, has a use, is determined and affected by the outside itself, and thus serves other ends. In other words, architecture cannot be free in the way art supposedly can. But when *utility* has taken 'the position of supplementary that had previously been occupied by art' – in a way still necessary but now disavowed – architectural pieces such as the folly draw attention 'insofar as they are understood as constructions of contingent, indeterminate or suspended use.' [110] *Use*, here distinguished from *function* – the 'culturally prescribed or ideologically determined use' – reappears in architectural discourses defunctionalized, 'in order to be posited as an open field of possibilities.' [111]

The proposed follies in Inwood remain as an attempt to forge possible relations with the existing context, geologically and topographically, as well as culturally and materially. The follies compress and distort space and time to offer alternative narratives which can influence new ways of reading, understanding and experiencing the landscape. Cedric Price discusses the folly's potential in promoting such a distortion:

> The true folly reaps the harvest of a silent eye, suspending truth itself in a delightful way.

... The folly distorts time, place and space and in so doing mixes magic with mystery, fun with fantasy, 'now' with 'then'. Humour is essential in its creator, and wit a bonus. [112]

Any sense of humor in landscapes like Inwood is not easy to find or accept. It is eventually coated with dissonance and the much-needed observation that some of these beautifully immersive landscapes carry with them violence of some sort. A humorous practice about Inwood is much closer to a sort of dark irony which nevertheless accepts 'serious playfulness' as a mode of thinking manifested through controversy or cynicism. [113] The Inwood follies question geological excavation and extraction, yet they are also born out of disruptive cut and fill. They question geological stability, yet they also require their own architectural solidity amongst the fluid tides. They question the manifestation of power in the smoothing erasure of dissonance, yet they further accentuate a series of architectural and landscape gestures driven by a personal design exploration. And, in the process of forging intimacy with the geologic, they become *geofollies*.

Together with the unleashed marsh, which invades them with the tides and cyclically sprays them with salt, the geofollies do not assume any educational or entertaining competencies. They quietly – but not silently – problematize some of the contemporary dynamics involved in landscape conservation as actions gesturing towards alienation through forcing the ever-changing landscape to be crystallized in tamed and known forms of acceptable outdoor museology. [114]

But they also question more widely historical assumptions that landscape is something that ought to perform in a certain way, usually optimizing ecological systems, or social functions, or cultural operations. Inwood follies serve purposes other than optimization. If anything, they complexify readings of the hill, blur distinctions between land and water, and interfere with existing and proposed ecosystems. In disrupting the current socio-ecological balances in the current park, while at the same time forcing coexistence with dissonant uses – present and past – the geofollies reveal the city-rock entanglement and reinforce the heterotopic character of the hill as one in a series of landscapes that organize, disrupt and affect the island.

Spring Tide
Mean High Tide
Salt water
Mean Low Tide
Existing retention wall
Spring Tide
Mean High Tide
Mean Low Tide
Spring Tide
Mean High Tide
Salt water
Mean Low Tide
Spring Tide
Mean High Tide
Salt water
Salt flat
—DRAPING—
—Cut&Fill—Microtopography—
STITCHING—SATURATING—CRYSTALLIZING—
Planting—Decompression—Flooding (tidal, permanent, seasonal)—Drainage—Consolidation—Permeability—Water quality

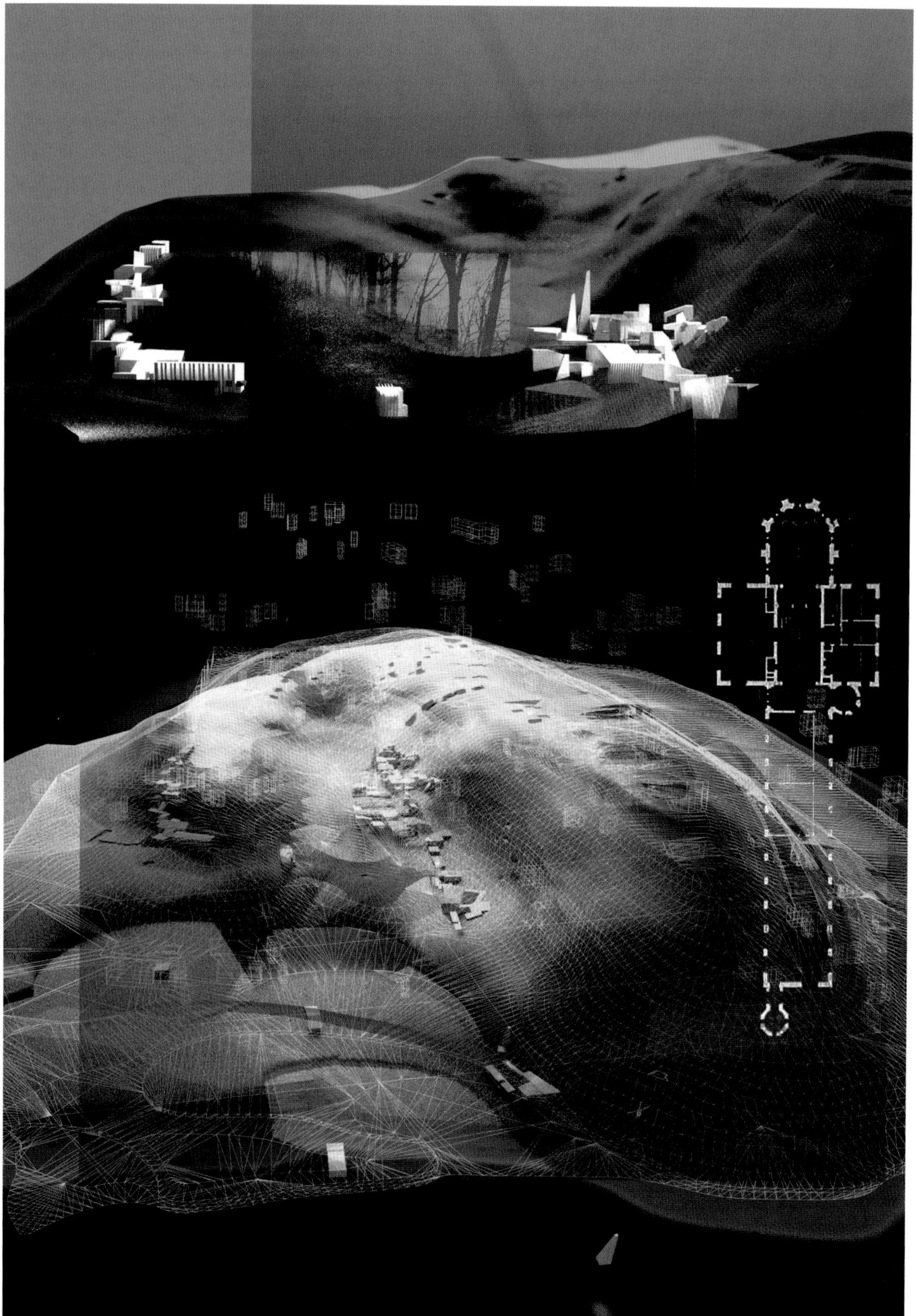

3.3 SF and Other Metrical Strategies for the Underground

In a 1988 lecture at Sci-Arc titled *Centricity: the unified urban field*, Woods described in detail his then-recent project *Underground Berlin* as a subterranean city powered by 'geomechanical forces', which he believed could promote an unauthorized reunion – political, social, cultural – between East and West Germanies. Moving away from the sun as a potential focus for renewable energy, the architect focused on the earth's electromagnetism and kinetics as alternative power sources. [115] When questioned about the reasons for proposing a new underground city below the surface's reference datum, Woods answered that:

> … there is something below even more compelling and powerful, something generating forces more powerful than all those from above, more powerful and immediate than history, than culture, than political conflict. The forces active within the planetary mass of the earth itself. … For what is happening in this city is much more than political unification. What is happening is acclimatation of people to new conditions of life. Beneath the surface, within the planetary mass of the earth, a new climate of forces exists, geo-mechanical forces that issue from deeper than the earth – gravitational, electromagnetic, and seismic forces that under shape the forms and relationships comprising life and the under city itself. And from a solemnly vibrating planetary mass of earth come seismic forces that move towards and bridges in equally subtle vibrations. The inhabitancy of the city feels them perhaps in a way we would call subliminal. [116]

Woods' proposed city no longer simply orbits around the sun; it is a city that also orbits around a spinning center of the earth and harnesses new forms of energy. The city is made of 'living laboratories,' which Woods describes as 'machines that play or are played to make a kind of quantum-mechanical music. For music too is number, geometry, metricality.' [117] Evolving from Woods' early interests in geometry, *metricality* is defined as 'measure in its pure form … the mathematics of the dynamic, the kinetic quality of both time and space unified in the idea of timespace, the continuous fabric of things kinetic and in some way living.' Arguing for a new myth in architecture based not on analysis or 'reinterpretation of history' but on imagination, Woods understands the notion as something

that results from a direct experience of a dynamic, ever-changing planet. Metricality, it could be argued, informs strategies for thinking across multiple scales where spacetime conditions operate fluidly and in configurations of infinite connectivity.

In drawing out the conditions of *Underground Berlin*, Woods explores the crafting of architecture as an iterative, explorative and speculative problem – a form of practice that is also contextualized in philosophy and cybernetics, as well as on ethical and aesthetic priorities. Through *Centricity* he conveys a much wider and somewhat synthetic reflection of his practice, both up until that point and throughout the rest of his life. Becker and Dunlop Fletcher talk about a practice concerned with disruption and confrontation of conventions by 'challenging the "omnipresence of the Cartesian grid."' [118]

In this context, *Lower Manhattan* can be used as an example where the grid is put into question through the city-rock entanglement. This is an idea of city that escapes the logics of the grid to reposition itself aligned with some of the island's geologics, and more specifically those which pertain to the domain of geology. In a different, even if related way of thinking, so too can the *Viele Map* be conceived as a challenge to a Cartesian understanding of the city. Awkward as this might sound at first – for the map is precisely an overlap of the grid on to the island's previous territory – when read through the lens of the geologic, it becomes possible to conceive of the cartography as a more vibrant set of temporal relationships; an aesthetics that results from a push and pull between city, water and rock, that is, a constantly renegotiated tension between a city being laid out and the water that was there, and continues to be, albeit in a different configuration. By suspending time, the map also suspends disbelief in space, allowing the possibility for a grid that no longer only subjugates water and rock but is also, and always, affected by them.

Centricity can be positioned along a series of projects where Woods opens the territory to new delineations. Some of the projects can be seen as a performative presentation aimed at unsettling conventional urban conditions and delineating new forms of city making. In other words, projects like *Centricity* organize Wood's architecture and his discourse about it stratigraphically. Metricality, then, becomes a meaningful concept with which to attribute scalar relations between architecture and city, city and ground, and finally, city and planet.

Similar to *Centricity*, *Lower Manhattan* reveals new delineations of

Manhattan, and confirms the importance of thinking about the island-city stratigraphically, in a gesture towards expansion rather than circumscription. Thinking about these expanded stratigraphic delineations allows us to problematize the idea of Manhattan as a unified whole – a cohesive insular unit – and to explore the notion of geological fragments – islands within the island – that have coalesced in these *geosocial formations* for a brief period within the vastness of deep time.

Woods' diffuse and conceptual practice has often been labeled attempted as deconstructivist. He rejected the inclusion of his work in the avant-garde architectural movement of *Deconstructivism*, even though he accepted certain affinities with what he considered to be the more serious Derridean cultural and literary theory of *Deconstruction*. [119] The categorization of Woods' work in this realm is complex and it will not be explored here directly.

Woods' work has also been qualified as *fantastic* and compared to science-fiction (SF). Once again, Woods rejected the establishment of a simple visual connection between his ideas and SF depictions. Throughout his career he persisted in the idea that what he did should be understood as architecture and not as storytelling or science fiction, as it was described innumerable times. On the other hand, in explicitly stating that his task was to imagine, he was also clear in his refusal to describe his practice as that of building, unlike some of his long-time colleagues. [120] And even if he didn't necessarily expect 'his designs to be built, he wished they would be — and believed they could be.' [121]

Reflecting on Woods' architecture in a SF context should not be mistaken by or interpreted through Woods' three direct experiences with Hollywood's SF film industry, all brief and unsuccessful. [122] Instead, they reinforce an argument that his practice can be regarded as a form of SF critical thinking and making. Woods' practice as a task of imagining alternative worlds is both speculative and fictional.

Architecture as speculative fiction (SF) is an exercise in storytelling which seeks to contextualize the world, both in space and time. Woods' conceptions of world as unstable and fluid – a world in the making – come close, in many ways, to Haraway's understanding of world as a 'verb, or at least a gerund; worlding is the dynamics of intra-action (Karen Barad's word from *Meeting the Universe Halfway*) and intra-patience, the giving and receiving of patterning, all the way down with consequences for who lives and who dies and how.' [123]

Haraway refers to the importance of understanding multispecies relations 'in the old art of terraforming; they [companion species] are the players in a mathematical SF equation that describes Terrapolis,' a terraformed world of infinite connection and relational and constantly adaptive *response-ability*. *Terrapolis* is 'rich in world, inoculated against post-humanism but rich in com-post, inoculated against human exceptionalism but rich in humus,

ripe for multispecies storytelling.' The companion species Haraway refers to – the 'SF critters' – are 'beings of the mud, not the sky.' [124] The idea of the *cyborg* is inevitably entangled here. Haraway reminds us that cyborgs are not simple tentacular conjugations of humans and machines, but rather the 'materialization of imploded (not hybridized) human beings-information machines-multispecies organisms.' [125]

Cyborgs are fabulated but they redo what counts as real. If one accepts a reading of Woods' architecture as cyborgs, one could regard them as SF architectures that remake the world and, in that *worlding*, they present themselves as alternative possibilities. In this context, architecture could, in fact, be described using Haraway's own words: as demonstrations of 'how to live and die in the adventure of worlding, the adventure of thinking, called SF.' [126]

As mentioned above, Woods' architectural understanding of the world does not necessarily coincide with Haraway's positioning, for the architect was not necessarily invested in a reformulation of architecture that would take it beyond the domain of the human and into a thinking with multispecies, at least not explicitly. However, Haraway's SF approach can be meaningful in a retrospective analysis and recontextualization of Woods' work. Similar to his interest in metricality as an ordering principle of speculative architectonic worlds, Haraway also describes Terrapolis as a formalism emerging from 'the mathematics of SF,' which, she adds:

> ... is that potent material-semiotic sign for the riches of speculative fabulation, speculative feminism, science fiction, speculative fiction, science fact, science fantasy — and, I suggest, string figures. In looping threads and relays of patterning, this SF practice is a model for worlding. Therefore, SF must also mean "so far," opening up what is yet-to-come in protean entangled times' pasts, presents, and futures. [127]

A rigorous analysis of Haraway's SF would go beyond the scope of this argument, but it matters to reiterate here that it ultimately corresponds to a thinking and making of and with the world as possibilities. In that sense, both Haraway and Woods are aligned in their relentless pursuit of 'what if' through speculative creative and critical thinking, a thinking that makes a rigorous use of operations – (un)grounding, (re)scaling, (re)framing – to navigate through lines of uncertainty that *are* the world. Terrapolis is made of these negotiations across scale: terrapolis, 'earth city', city *on* the earth, city *of* the earth, earth *in* the city, and so on.

Nigel Clark and Kathryn Yusoff mention that '[a] favorite trope of science fiction is to imagine other planets that are similar to earth in many respects but distinguishable by one or more significant variables.' [128] This, they add, allows for the construction of 'what if' scenarios while maintaining a degree of familiarity and identification on the part of terrestrial audiences.' [129] In a sense, Woods' favorite trope is to imagine the earth as other worlds through architecture. His work could be regarded as a *terraforming* of the planet to accommodate the urban condition, that is, less of an idea related to conventional science-fictional approaches to transform alien planets into earth-like *lifeworlds* and more of an idea of terraforming the earth itself 'if it is to remain a viable host for its own life.' [130] But at the same time, it is also a terraforming that accepts earth's inevitable dynamism, facing it less with a geo-techno-engineering approach, sometimes also called *techno-fixer*, and more with a conceptual navigation that cuts across many worlds as possibilities.

Geoff Manaugh describes this trope being folded in Woods' rhetoric of ground, or as he describes it, of an absence of a stable ground. Manaugh writes that for Woods architecture results from the recognition:

> … that nothing – genuinely and absolutely nothing – is here to welcome us or accept us or say yes to us. That there is no solid or lasting ground to build anything on, let alone anything out there other than ourselves expecting us to build it. [131]

Manaugh praises Woods' work as a 'delirious and amazing act;' a quasi-theological positioning that results from a 'lack of center elsewhere, [a] lack of world.' It is, thus, through architecture that humans spatialize – and one could also argue temporalize – experience in forms 'that would have been impossible under natural conditions.' Architecture is a becoming of possibilities 'offered, we could say, as a kind of post-terrestrial resistance against unstable ground, against the lack of a trustworthy planet. Against the lack of an inhabitable world.' [132]

Yet, from Manaugh's suggestion that architecture according to Woods is 'a counter-planet – or maybe it is the only planet, always and ever a terraforming of this alien location we call the Earth,' one could also think of Woods' poetry, mythology, premonition, lyricism as an Anthropocenic attitude of 'staying with the trouble of living and dying together.' [133] This is not a rejection of the world as is, but rather a speculation of what it could become once one accepts what it actually is. Woods' architectural practice may, therefore, be regarded as the power of architecture to tell or imagine stories about living unstably and fluidly with one (an)other. For Haraway these stories matter:

> It matters what ideas we use to think other ideas (with). … It matters what matters we use to think other matters with; it matters what stories we tell to tell other stories with; it matters what knots knot knots, what thoughts think thoughts, what ties tie ties. It matters what stories make worlds, what worlds make stories. [134]

The way in which Woods' rhetoric of ground has been framed in this argument can, in turn, become useful also in the study of city representations such as the *Viele Map*. Even though the map has been used by geo-engineers in the pursuit of stable ground to anchor infrastructure for the city, it is at the same time a story of an unstable ground and, perhaps even more importantly, of a ground that is indeterminant in relation to the urban possibilities it may activate.

Both *Lower Manhattan* and the *Viele Map* share what could be described as an American attitude of engaging with the world, at once both with a desire to control it and the awe-inspiring recognition of the limitations inherent in that control. Capitalist forces entangle in this approach by commodifying both control and its very opposite as possibilities for the city to happen.

If Woods' practice can be accepted as architectural stories that matter to conceive of the world as possibility, then retrospectively, it can be also proposed as an Anthropocenic form of critical thinking and making with the world that rejects 'both the *laissez-faire*, nihilist attitude that fundamentally nothing matters because the game is over, or in the techno-fixer belief that fundamentally nothing matters because we can make the rules as we go.' [135] Instead, the architect's ways of practicing, thinking, and making could be positioned in conceptual alignment with Haraway and the New Materialists' proposition to slow down, pay attention and bear witness.

Lower Manhattan depicts a city that should not forget its unstable conditions of congested existence on an island that resists the formidable forces of hydrological and atmospheric flow, a resistance supported by old geologies that inevitably shift, weather and erode. Like the story of Manhattan growing from the earth unfolding in the *Viele Map*, so too does *Lower Manhattan* depict a city that follows the logics of capitalism, but from time to time is forced to slow down and notice its own vulnerability. It invites an understanding of architecture as a practice of the geologic that is tangled with fluidity and instability, which in turn conceives of the city 'well beyond simplistic urban, architectural, or landscape architectural solutions enmeshed with capitalist logics of power, wealth, and forced stability.' [136]

The manifesto can be regarded as a synthesis of Woods' wider and richer practice and reveals his efforts in exploring an architecture of ground able to face the challenges posed to the urban condition and, eventually, to human existence. It is also, in a perhaps stranger way, a metaphor of his life as a conceptual practitioner and, more specifically, of his moment of death amidst the challenges of a chaotic moment on the island. In the aphoristic words of Manaugh, 'Lebbeus Woods would have had it no other way, and – as students, writers, poets, novelists, filmmakers, or mere thinkers – neither should we.' [137]

RECRYSTALLIZATION

4 Extrude
Delirious Fields and Paranoid Critical Fragments

'Extrude' examines the *Commissioners' Plan* (1811) as a probe to study Rem Koolhaas's *Delirious New York*, through which he proposes Manhattanism as a culture of urban congestion. The relation between manifesto and earlier cartography also serves as the basis for discussing a body of design experiments that quarry, mine and extrude Manhattan's architectural icons from its Gilded Age tangled in their socio-political and environmental contexts.

The design experimentation was formalized as a brief installation called *Manhattan's Geotaxonomies of the Fantastic* which was presented in the Tent Gallery, at the University of Edinburgh, in 2018. It proposes readings of the text as a city and focuses on plotting the book onto a newly reinvented territory, which in turn begins to suggest the creation of an imagined Manhattan within the space of the exhibition. With a focus on Koolhaas' use of the *Paranoid Critical Method* (PCM), the design experimentation invests in its own PC activity to identify, excavate and reposition city fragments described in the book within expanded temporal and material frames. Through this process, *Delirious New York* is retrospectively contextualized from the contemporary perspectives of the Anthropocene.

Throughout the investigation, *The City of the Captive Globe*, a 1972 piece created by Office for Metropolitan Architecture (OMA), is utilized as a methodological lens to calibrate readings of the book as city blocks. Koolhaas considers the architectural fragments depicted in the piece as shorter manifestos within the wider manifesto project and vehicles for a close examination of the use of the *Technology of the Fantastic*. The piece also anticipates OMA's approach to the urban condition that would characterize the practice – then still in its early stages – in subsequent years.

Using geology as a tool for critical and creative thinking, the experimentation proposes extrusion as a design operation to read the entanglement between architecture and its context. A posterior design exploration titled *Fault-Line City* aims to bring together Lebbeus Woods' ideas on ground with the Koolhaasian themes in *Delirious New York*.

Paranoid critical operations used to mine and quarry Manhattan in search of underground rhizomes of city infrastructures, dissonant occupations from the past, and phantom projects that only existed in the imagination. The activities unearth a newly reinvented city where the territory and its networks emerge entangled within wider planetary geo-social formations.

4.1 Unfolding Urban Deliria: *The Commissioners' Plan* (1811) Through *Delirious New York* (1978)

Rem Koolhaas wrote *Delirious New York: A Retroactive Manifesto for Manhattan* at the beginning of his architectural career. [138] He had recently graduated from the Architectural Association (AA) in London (1968–72) and was a visiting fellow at the New York Institute for Architecture and Urban Studies (IAUS) (1973). During his brief time at Cornell University, Koolhaas was influenced by Matthias Ungers and Michel Foucault and, even if indirectly, also by the writings of Roland Barthes. Coming into architecture with a previous background in journalism and scriptwriting, the young architect was invested in gathering evidence about the American city – and New York City in particular – and to synthesize it into what he considered to be a long-overdue architectural manifesto of the twentieth century. Nevertheless, Koolhaas notes, his interest 'was more literary than architectural. Maybe *Delirious New York* is about architecture, but it is more a literary creation – more writing than thinking.' [139]

Koolhaas regards *Delirious New York* as a strategy for carving out not just a malleable terrain – as in ground – from which to start analyzing the city, but also a malleable terrain – as in a milieu – where he could ground himself as an architect; 'a terrain where [he] could eventually work as an architect.' [140] Such a terrain could also, more widely, redefine architecture by deemphasizing artistic practice and reinforcing a focus on intellectual issues. Writing *in* architecture, and not simply *on* or *about* it, is a 'brute and primitive' need of the architect. [141]

In the book, Koolhaas constructs a narrative to support *Manhattanism,* the 'unformulated theory' behind the creation of Manhattan. [142] Manhattanism is a theory generated from articulated ideas of congestion, globality, power, capitalism, real estate and consumerism manifested in accumulations of vertical densities. [143] It has been described as a conceptual speculation so powerful to solve life in the city and to allow for the possibility of surreal wonder and ecstatic delirium that it gave Manhattan the strength to temporarily resist Modernism, if only to a certain extent. [144]

Koolhaas assumes the role of ghost writer and accepts that the dominant logics of the rigid two-dimensional grid have facilitated a specific kind of

12 *Delirious New York*, Original book cover, Rem Koolhaas, 1978.

Rem Koolhaas
Delirious New York

'undreamt three-dimensional anarchy' to speculate, congest, creatively and *cannibalistically* destroy a city, to reject the history of architecture and urbanism, even to forge 'a new system of formal values.' [145] Throughout the book the architect contextualizes, describes and interrelates some of the city's most iconic buildings – constructed during the first three decades of the twentieth century, a period considered by many as the city's Gilded Age – as applied examples of the use of the *Technology of the Fantastic.*

Ultimately, for Koolhaas, 'it's only when there is a text-like formulation of the problem that we can really start. The design is a demonstration of a thesis or a question or a literary idea.' [146] It is in writing, then, that *Delirious New York* may be considered a work of architecture. Koolhaas adds:

> The structure of the text is very architectural. I talk about blocks in analogy to New York itself; each block is subdivided in episodes that have a very architectural relationship to each other: i.e., they mostly coexist. Each component is extremely autonomous, nevertheless there are complementarities. Its written structure is analogous to the urbanism it describes. In terms of its layout, its fragmentation, it is also very architectural. Each minichapter has a title, and one of the main reasons is that otherwise you would have to spend inordinate amounts of words and time and whatever to create interesting "bridges," which correspond to the now, for me, completely impossible way of creating architectural "connections" in a building. It is a book without a single "however," and that to me is very architectural. It has the same logic as a city. Anyway, a crucial element of the work – whether writing or architecture – is montage. Ultimately, I'm still writing scripts, which is what I did when I was 22. [147]

If *Delirious New York*'s blocks of text are read as architecture, they help to conceptualize an urbanism that is at once fragmentary and interconnected. Like Manhattan, the blocks in the book foster a certain textual consciousness in relation to one another – what in literary terms would find a parallelism in intertextuality – as well as a level of autonomy. These two conditions – consciousness and autonomy – activate a non-sequential reading of the literary city through which blocks of text can be appraised as shorter manifestos within the wider manifesto project, as well as islands within the island.

Perhaps one of the most influential blocks of text in the book is also a city of blocks in and of itself. *The City of the Captive Globe*, which figures in the appendix of the book — 'the fifth block' – is a short project turned manifesto by OMA, and it comprises a drawing and a short text. The drawing was developed in 1972 by Madelon Vriesendorp – one of OMA's founding members – together with Koolhaas. In Koolhaas' own words, the project, which anticipates *Delirious New York*, is 'devoted to the artificial conception and accelerated birth of theories, interpretations, mental constructions, proposals and their Infliction on the World.' [148]

The City of the Captive Globe provokes in what it suggests, both implicitly and explicitly. Three provocations deserve special attention. The first, and perhaps most obvious, is the suggestion of how a city may capture a globe: in the depiction, the many disparate ideological laboratories, or iconic architectures, to which OMA pays homage, capture quite literally the globe. The globe — or in this case a captive globe – is circumscribed not only within a block in the grid, but also below the horizontal datum defined by the other architectural pieces. This is also not any globe, but earth itself. The city in this image is the captivator – as in capturer or incarcerator, but also influencer and dominator – of a whole planet. When applied to readings of *Delirious New York* it encourages a reflection on wider ideas of totality and their eventual implications for Manhattan as a field condition. The ideas explored later are, nevertheless, constrained, in that they are formulated from within Koolhaas' considerations about the foundational architectonic vocabulary of Manhattan – the needle and the globe – as well as hybrid constructions of the two.

The second conceptual provocation stems from the extrusion of the grid with plinths. Whilst the globe is kept captive inside a hole below ground, the architectural pieces extrude from it. It is not difficult to recognize the plinths' material properties as geology – soil, rock, mineral veins, sedimentary layers. In some versions of the image, the geology of the plinths is less crystallized, while in others is perhaps more organized into a

13 *The City of the Captive Globe*, Rem Koolhaas and Madelon Vriesendorp, 1972.

type of quarried rock – eventually marble. [149] A closer look also reveals intriguing excavations through the geological extrusions, such as holes, entrances, gates or tunnels. These elements, which are not completely part of the architectures above, are also clearly distinguishable from the geological materiality of the plinths. They encourage a way of seeing geology as holding the capacity for shelter, or a passage to something inside. Perhaps they give access to rhizomatic undercrofts beneath some of the ideological architectures, thus enacting geology as something with the possibility for architectural inhabitation. [150] *The City of the Captive Globe*, perhaps less an image than a design exploration, activates a specific vocabulary with which to operate in the city, even reinvent it altogether.

The third provocation emerges from OMA's proposition of the city as a laboratory of disparate architectural ideas. The drawing questions reality as something that perhaps doesn't have to forcefully exist in the world as a physical presence or material object. It provokes when it gives the imagined realities, architectural ideologies, theoretical discourses and iconic projects an existence between the conscious and the unconscious. [151] Navigating along this rather blurry boundary requires the activation of wider considerations involved in fragmentary ways of noticing which do not attempt to grasp totality, but instead contemplate the world through a multiplicity of disparate glimpses.

The City of the Captive Globe is interesting not just as an internal lens to read *Delirious New York* but also to read Manhattan outside the book. It attunes the attention to a series of speculative fictions composed of cultural phenomena, architectural theories and urban conditions, while facilitating a creative recalibration and repositioning of some of the city's *geosocial formations*, congested in space and time and manifested across scalar tensions between city, island and geology.

With an initial interest in a 'culture of congestion', initiated during his studies at the AA under the guidance of Elias Zenghelis – later also one of OMA's founding partners – Koolhaas wrote *Delirious New York* to assert that the city and its architectures not only have a program but are, in fact, a program. This curiosity about the programmatic conditions and eventual ambitions of architecture – which in his opinion came close to an agenda [152] – came to define his successful practice over the following five decades. [153] *Delirious New York* remained a reference for Koolhaas, 'a reference that we [the team at OMA] constantly suppress.' [154] The book influenced his subsequent writings, namely *S, M, L, XL, Generic City*, or *Junkspace*.

Delirious New York reinforces a reading of Manhattan as a city developed on an island allegedly acquired from the local native tribes of the Lenni Lenape. [155] It describes a city technologically tested in the dream-like urban laboratory of Coney Island and expanded northwards from the original colony through a series of extrusions on an orthogonal grid that rapidly occupied the whole territory. Through these linear readings, Manhattan is not only retroactively inscribed within a circumscribed historical period, but also defined, even if unconsciously, almost as an organism with pre-history, infancy period, maturity, decline and eventual death (with a few *post-mortem* dedications). These stages correspond, in fact, to the book's overarching chapters. By learning a story with a beginning, a middle and an end, one is left with the impression of a totalizing narrative that captures a whole city and inscribes it in a grid within which architectural deliria occur. [156] This is a city where 'each block is covered with several layers of phantom architecture in the form of past occupancies, aborted projects and popular fantasies that provide alternative images to the New York that exists.' [157] Koolhaas describes the grid as 'a matrix that captures, at the same time, all remaining territory and all future activity on the island,' and considers it 'the most courageous act of prediction in Western civilization: the land it divides, unoccupied; the population it describes, conjectural; the buildings it locates, phantoms; the activities it frames, nonexistent.' [158]

Delirious New York portrays Manhattan as a path to totality, both by registering the horizontal expansion and explaining the homogenization promoted by its orthogonality. In a sense, it could be argued that the book brings Manhattan close to an idea of *field condition*. [159]

Stan Allen supports this argument by suggesting Manhattan not only as an example of the American grid at the scale of the city, but also as an exception to any other American city, in that its grid expanded to its maximum capacity, that is, until it covered completely the insular territory. The grid as a field condition implies the path to totality of a synthetic carpet that covers the whole territory, as well as a sealing cap that has transformed the previous landscape in its entirety. [160]

Koolhaas's pursuit of Manhattan's culture of congestion situates the beginning of his narrative on cartographical instruments such as John Randel Jr.'s initial gridded plan for the street layout between Houston and 155th streets. Originally idealized as a tool for land sale and fast real estate development by the city, the State of New York eventually stepped in to solve local objections and appointed a commission with overruling powers to develop the plan and present it in 1811. In many ways, the *Commissioners' Plan*, as it came to be known, is a modernist project even before Modernism, in that it conceives the territory as a tabula rasa or blank canvas on which to then build the city. Koolhaas describes the plan as the generator of the urban condition as we know it in the city today.

In fact, the 1811 plan was the first of many versions of the grid throughout the nineteenth century (1832, 1836 and so on). This in turn allowed for a critical reappraisal of the magnitude of the gesture spreading across almost a century and documented in a series of subsequent plans that register not only the growth of the city but also the sequence of adjustments on the grid to existing landscape features and to changing social and economic needs and demands. Early twentieth-century Manhattan eventually allowed a few contaminations of the obsessively regular grid: from blocks, streets and avenues with different dimensions, to public parks and plazas, waterfronts and pedestrian walks. It was the confirmation that public city life needed far more complex urban patterns after all.

Departing from the *Commissioners' Plan*, Koolhaas' study implicitly activates two field conditions in the city: Downtown and Midtown. The former registers the transformational process from a European colony to a city of fertile architectural and urban experimentation, while the latter affirms and solidifies New York as the city born out of a capitalist culture of congestion. [161]

Allen argues that field conditions 'are inherently expandable; the possibility of incremental growth is anticipated in the mathematical relations of the parts.' [162] The idea is essentially multiscalar, moving from the city to the building and back to the territory. Readings of *Delirious New York* as text blocks allow for glimpses of vertical specificity (at the building scale) along the grid's horizontal expansion (at the territorial scale).

In a series of interconnected texts, Koolhaas identifies the skyscraper as the architecture of this verticality, which was only possible due to three mutations generated in the first decade of the twentieth century: '1. the reproduction of the World; 2. the annexation of the Tower; 3. The block alone.' [163] Manhattan succeeded precisely in integrating these three mutations into a '"glorious whole."' [164]

Koolhaas defines buildings such as the Woolworth – described in the book as '"Glorious Whole[s], quite beyond the control of human imagination"' – as automonuments, or buildings that are cities within the city. [165] These buildings have a scale that makes them another example of field conditions nested in the city.

Beyond the scales of the city and the building, the skyscraper as an idea of reproduction of the world through vertical multiplication triggers a third set of scales related to land ownership. It is possible to imagine, even if on a more conceptual plane, the implications of Manhattan's field conditions if the rights to build were to expand along a deep section towards both outer space and the earth's center. [166] As mentioned in the previous chapter, the city's horizontal expansion becomes an arc of the earth's curvature, and its vertical expansion becomes a radius cutting across the planet and expanding outwards, potentially infinitely. When expanding the temporal and spatial condition of the fields, they become infinite in their transscalar connectivity.

Koolhaas identifies needle and globe as two extremes in Manhattan's formal vocabulary, holding both symbolic and instrumental value:

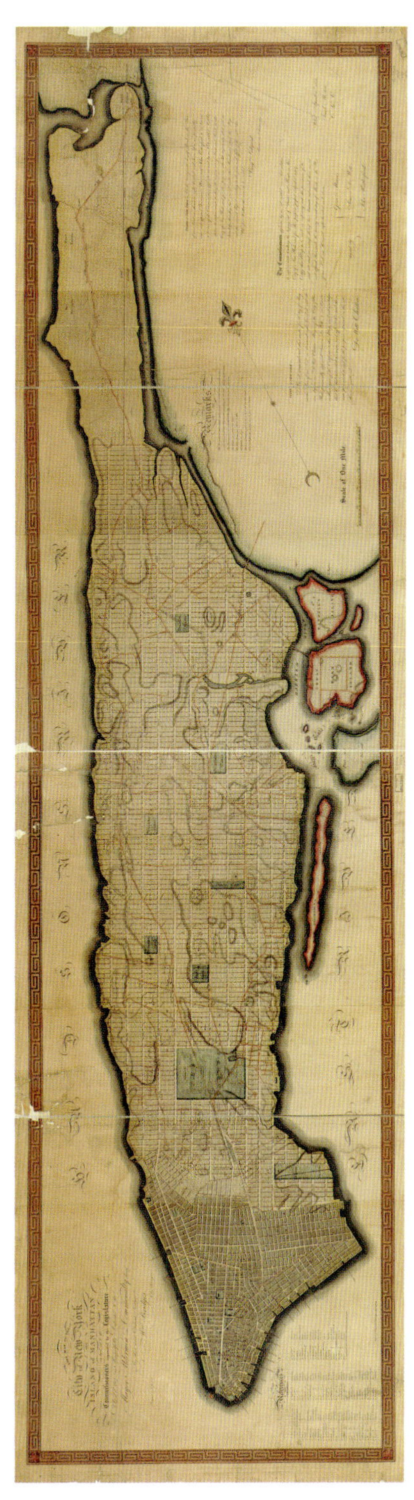

14 *Commissioners' Plan*, 1811. The definition of
Manhattan as a field condition.

The needle is the thinnest, least voluminous structure to mark a location within the Grid.
It combines maximum physical impact with a negligible consumption of ground. It is, essentially, a building without an interior.
The globe is, mathematically, the form that encloses the maximum interior volume with the least external skin. It has a promiscuous capacity to absorb objects, people, iconographies, symbolisms; it relates them through the mere fact of their coexistence in its interior. In many ways, the history of Manhattanism as a separate, identifiable architecture is a dialectic between these two forms, with the needle wanting to become a globe and the globe trying, from time to time, to turn into a needle – a cross-fertilization that results in a series of successful hybrids in which the needle's capacity for attracting attention and its territorial modesty are matched with the consummate receptivity of the sphere. [167]

The architect uses the two elements to frame 'the beginning and the end of Manhattanism,' a period between 1853 and 1939 – the dates of the first two New York International Fairs and also the only moments when needle and globe appear as clearly separate entities.' [168] He defines this period as an active reconfiguration of the city through hybridizations between the two elements. [169]

In Coney Island – Manhattanism's testing grounds – the 1876's 300-foot Centennial Tower arrives from Philadelphia, where it had pre-existed, and becomes the new needle-like observatory. It allows not only visitors to see the island as a cohesive whole, but also to cast a speculative eye onto its neighboring sister Manhattan. Soon after, forests of empty illuminated needles populate Coney Island's increasingly popular theme parks. The most spectacular of all the needles in this forest is perhaps the Beacon Tower, 'illuminated by over 100,000 electric lights' that 'can be seen for a distance of over 30 miles,' which eventually added a much-desired surrealist effect to the navigation routes across the bay. [170]

The globe too appears in different configurations, mostly as ever-expanding roofs encapsulating extreme forms of entertainment – from circuses and 'freak shows' to baby incubators, and from gardens of creation and domes representing the universe to synthetic sunbathing. By associating the globe with revolutionary moments in Western architecture – 'a simulacrum of the world' and 'a secular counterpart to the cathedral' – Koolhaas registers the conceptual Globe Tower as Coney Island's arguably most important sphere. [171] Over a series of interconnected text blocks, he describes the first attempt at creating an architectural hybrid of the needle and the globe – an impactful cross-fertilization for its innovation and size, which

15 (top) *Dreamland at Night*, Coney Island, New York, Unknown, Museum of City of New York, ca. 1905.
16 (bottom) 'From Fair to Fair', in *Delirious New York*, Rem Koolhaas, 1978. Koolhaas writes: 'Crystal Palace and Latting Obsentatory at first New York World's Fair, 1853. Double image appearing in background: Trylon and Perisphere, theme exhibit of 1939 World's Fair. At the beginning and the end of Manhattanism: needle and globe.'

resolved the apparent impossibility of a globe becoming a needle. '[T]he sphere is to be so colossal that simply by resting on the earth it can claim – through the height of its enormous diameter – also to be a tower ....' [172] Before becoming a fiasco-cum-financial fraud, the Globe Tower should 'be seen as the essence of the idea of Skyscraper; the most extreme and explicit manifestation of the skyscraper's potential to reproduce the earth and to create other worlds.' [173] The Globe Tower would nevertheless live on as a descriptive theorem for the ideal performance of the future skyscraper in Manhattan.

The annexation of the tower marks another important moment in the needle formulation. Iconic buildings in Manhattan, such as the Singer or the Metropolitan Life, evade their cubic outlines by receiving beacon-like towers, inspired by Venetian campaniles. Koolhaas calls them 'landlocked lighthouses,' [174] which anticipate the conception of 'Manhattan's paradoxical status' as a conceptual landlocked archipelago to which *The City of the Captive Globe* pays allegiance. [175]

Globes serving the entertainment industry carry on in Manhattan, progressively expanding their footprint on the grid until they eventually reach the size of a whole block. Madison Square Garden, in its different indoor and outdoor versions, is such an example. Equally, the city registers intriguing moments of inception where globes captivate other globes. Similar to an earlier space travel adventure to the moon in Coney Island's Luna Park, the Hippodrome – '"the largest dome in the world after the Pantheon,"' built between 1905 and 1906 – hosted the 'first Manhattan performance … called "a Yankee Circus on Mars,"' in an ambitious attempt to turn the surface of his [the developer's] entire block into a spacecraft.' [176]

Koolhaas refers abundantly to many symbolic representations of earth throughout the city and in the form of globes, some of which also become

significant architectural features. But with Raymond Hood, the iconographic value of the globe is refined as an interior architectural space. Radio City Music Hall (RCMH) – itself captive inside the Rockefeller Center – captures a globe as an entertainment dome. [177] RCMH, in many ways the initiator of John D. Rockefeller Jr.'s larger endeavor, became a machinic entertainment microcosm. On its stage, made as an 'uterine hemisphere' of plaster and gold paint, 'the 24-hour cycle of day and night is repeated several times during a single performance … Day and night are drastically reduced, time accelerated, experience intensified, life – potentially – doubled, tripled …' [178] The entertainment globe finally captivates and synthesizes multiple suns to become a sort of techno-utopian ideal of a dome interior. [179]

RCMH is successful for its spherical physical properties – a round space for congregation – while inside the Daily News Building – also one of Hood's creations – the globe is proposed as a conceptual sculptural piece. Protected by a dark, reflective and circular lobby, Hood designs a

ten-foot terrestrial globe, which slowly revolves on its axis while being
bathed by a carefully aimed stream of milky light. [180] Its reflections on the
surrounding darkness please Hugh Ferriss – Manhattan's prime renderer
at the time – who discovers resemblances between the lobby and his
conceptual proposal of 'an illuminated night inside a cosmic container.' [181]
Calling this proposal the 'murky Ferrissian Void,' Koolhaas describes it as 'a
pitch black architectural womb that gives birth to the consecutive stages of
the Skyscraper in a sequence of sometimes overlapping pregnancies.' [182]

17 and 18 (left) Interior of Radio City Music Hall
19 (above) Postcard 'Madison Square East, New York', 1909,
in *Delirious New York*, 1978.

Hood's Daily News globe is 'a three-dimensional realization of that murky
Ferrissian void – the pitch-black womb of Manhattanism, cosmos of
charcoal smudges – which has given birth already to the Skyscraper and
now, finally, to a Globe.' [183]

By capturing the globe and merging it with the needle, Manhattan further
congested its urban condition. When defining Central Park as a horizontal
skyscraper that subverts or even negates the orthogonality of the grid,
Koolhaas may be, in fact, reading the landscape as an 'architectural
mutation.' [184] Rather than reinstating an eventual virgin condition of the
island prior to the city, the park instead adds a new heterotopic layer of
artificiality. [185] Central Park's needle-like qualities of stratification – just
like a skyscraper, albeit horizontal – are brought together with its ambition
of becoming a globe that operates as a 'catalogue of natural elements …
taken from its original context, reconstituted and compressed into a *system
of nature* … Central Park is a synthetic Arcadian Carpet.' [186]

More than just successful hybridizations between needle and globe,

Manhattan accumulates density. Similar to Coney Island's forests of needles, Koolhaas identifies significant moments in the grid where the proximity between several blocks generates more complex urban forms. The proximity – and architectural affinity – between the Flatiron, the Metropolitan Life and Madison Square Garden captured in a 1909 multiple-vanishing-point postcard triggers a kaleidoscopic effect where the three architectural mutations – the reproduction of the World, the annexation of the Tower, and the block alone – at that point still existing in separate architectural fragments, may be imagined in future assembled hybrids.

When reading Manhattan's urban density through a geological lens, one could also imagine these urban form as crystals growing into progressively more complex mineralogic accumulations. The World Trade Center (WTC) – both in its initial formulation, built in 1973 and destroyed on 9/11, and in its current state – is another example of a mineralogic accumulation in Manhattan, where assemblages of needles and globes merge in complex hybridization. Conceived as the center of planetary capitalism, the Twin Towers became two iconic needles in New York's skyline. Occupying the complex's central plaza at the time, *The Sphere* – a cast bronze sculpted globe by artist Fritz Koenig [187] – was smashed during the terrorist attacks. In the current center, the skyscrapers occupy the edges of the void left by the twin buildings, while at the center lies the 9/11 Memorial, with a museum and surrounding gardens. [188] The memorial celebrates the void left by the destruction with two deep black pools occupying the same footprint as the Twin Towers did formerly. In a contemporary formulation of the pitch-black Ferrissian *void* as a city generator, the memorial captures the globe once again. This time, the conventional invitation to look up at the capitalist conquering of the Manhattan skies is counter-balanced with an equally meaningful invitation to reflect on the many human losses by looking down and inside into the earth. At the southern end of the memorial gardens, and looking back at the rebuilt complex, Koenig's now-smashed sphere returns to a central position.

Koolhaas' Field Conditions

The translation of Koolhaas' field conditions into drawing proves to be a challenging design exercise mainly because of how the architect writes about them, that is, in a deliberately congested form, both spatially and temporally. Therefore, the exercise is less that of mapping existing conditions and more of creatively drawing out the forces and lines of flight that Koolhaas uses to construct his argument.

Each architectural or city fragment described in the book is plotted onto its contextual conditions in the island. Yet, the establishment of the fields also begs for a deeper cartographical analysis to determine other, perhaps equally important, geophysical conditions affecting the urban territory. Thus, for example, a valley currently occupied by Canal Street – at a certain moment of New Amsterdam, a *de facto* canal – defines the northern boundary of Downtown; or a ridge currently defining Broadway determines the southwestern boundary of Midtown. Central Park, an urban landscape defined through a series of controversial political decisions, also seems to have had a significant impact on the northern delimitation of Midtown's expansion. [189]

The mapping of the two fields, as well as the fragments Koolhaas describes in the book, triggered curiosity about what he is not referring to, namely: the ground conditions on which these fragments and fields laid, past and present; the topographical work needed to construct them; or the hydrological conditions that had to be resolved in the city for them to exist. The mapping embarked on a pseudo-archaeological endeavor to analyze and subsequently excavate the architectures out of their context – a context suddenly made visible with the inclusion of the conditions not otherwise included in *Delirious New York*, but which nevertheless acquire meaning in the pursuit of the geologics that make Manhattan.

(above and next pages) Translations of Koolhaas' field conditions, 2019-20.

SANITARY & TOPOGRAPHICAL MAP

of the City and Island of

NEW YORK

Commissioners

Prepared for the Council of Hygiene and Public Health

of the CITIZENS ASSOCIATION

Topographical Engineer

EGBERT L. VIELE.

SCALE 1000 FEET TO 1 INCH.

References

Marsh

Made Land

Meadow

Sewers

Downtown Field loosely defined in Delirious New York

Canal St. becomes an important geological hinge in this field

Fragment of the Lower East Side added to the field [around Bowery and Sarah D Roosevelt Park]

The fie

Houston St stitches together the colony grid with the 1911 city

turally connected by Broaway [here considered as geo-logic on the island-city]
23rd St
34th St
42nd St
47th St
Extension of the Midtown Field to the south
to include Madison Square Park
Midtown Field loosely defined in Delirious New York
BROOKLYN
QUEENS
Long Island

DOWNTOWN ATHLE[TIC...]

TERRITORIES

'Of all the floors, the interior golf course [...] is the most extreme undertaking [...] The Skycraper has transformed Nature into Super-Nature.'

INCUBATOR

'The only price its locker-room graduates have to pay for their collective narcissism is that of sterility. Their self-induced mutations are not reproducible in future generations.'
'The bewitchement of the Metropolis stops at the genes, they remain the final stronghold of Nature.'

EQUITABLE BUILDING (1915) | ZONING LAW (1916)

TRIUMPH

'In 1915 the Equitable Building repeats its block 39 times, "straight up" [...] The higher the Skycraper goes, the harder it becomes to supress its latent revolutionary ambition...'
'[...] the Equitable is promoted as a "City in Itself", housing 16,000 souls.'
'From now on each new *building of the mutant kind* strives to be "a City within a City."'

SHADOW

'With the Equitable Building (1915) the process of reproduction loses its credibility through the grim deterioration – both financial and environmental – it inflicts on its surroundings [...] Its success is measured by the destruction of its context.'

LAW

'... the 1916 Zoning Law is a back-dated birth certificate that lends retroactive legitimacy to the Skyscraper.'

VILLAGE

'The Zoning Law is not only a legal document, it is also a design project [...] If Manhattan was in the beginning only a collection of 2,028 blocks, it is now an assembly of as many invisible envvelopes. [...] [it] defines Manhattan for all time as a collection of [...] phantom "houses" that together form a Mega-Village.'

4nd STREET (MCGRAW-HILL, BROADWAY, WORLD'S TOWER, AMERICAN RADIATOR, BRYANT PARK, NY PUBLIC LIBRARY, DAIL...)

domain. To have a sense of the island as a v
aware of its limitations [...]'

SPHERE

'As yet contained in the colossal cage of th
modes of mass transportation] will turn Ma
Galapagos Island of new technologies, whe
survival of the fittest, this time a battle amo
machines, is imminent.'

CONTRAST

'The Latting Observatory and the dome of
introduce an archetypal contrast that will ap
throughout Manhattan's history [...] The ne
represent the two extremes of Manhattan'[s]
[...]'
'[...] the history of Manhattanism as a separ
architecture is a dialectic between these tw
needle wanting to become a globe and the
time to time, to turn into a needle [...]'

THEORY

'In his vision the future Manhattan is a *City* o
modified version of what already exists; inst
extrusion of arbitrayry individual plots, large
will be assembled in new building operation
Towers will be a forested of freestanding, co
made accessible by the regular paths of the
Park.'

GOLD

'Hood [...] designs the first example of his C
'The top of the black building [American Rad
gilded. Hood's down-to-earth alibi for the to
connections between gold and any possible
Ecstasy.'

SINGER AND CITY INVESTING BUILDINGS | (NOW) ONE LIBERTY

WOOLWORTH BUILDING

CATHEDRAL

'The first *built* ammalgamation is the Woolworth Building [...] Its lower 27 floors are a straightforward extrusion [...] the g[raft] occupies an entire block.'
'If its interior is business only, its exterior is pure spirituali[ty]'
'The Woolworth does not actually contribute any radical modifications or breaks to the life of the city, but it is sup[posed] to work miracles through the emanation of its physical presence; a larger mass than constructed before, it is at [the] same time seen as disembodied, antigravitational. "Brut[e] material has been robbed of its density and flung into th[e sky to] challenge its loveliness [...]"'

BUILDINGS

'[...] in 1908 Ernest Flagg designs a Tower and places it on top of his existing Singer Building, a 14-story block built in 1899. This architectural afterthought alones makes it "from 1908 to 1913 America's most famous bulding"'
'"Thousands of travelers com to New York especially to see this Modern Tower of Babel, gladly paying fifty cents to ride to the 'observation balcony'". In akcnowledgment of the darker side of the Metropolis it is also the first "Suicide Pinacle"...'

TRIUMPH

'The builders of the Benenson (City Investing) Building multiply their lot 34 times.'
'Through volume alone, life inside the Skyscraper is involved in a

SQUARE PARK (FLATIRON, METROPOLITAN LIFE AND NORTH BUILDINGS, MADISON SQUARE GARDEN AND PARK TOWER)

FREEZE-FRAME

'A 1909 postcard pre
architectural evoluti
coexisting on Madiso
Flatiron, the *lighthou*
island of Madison Sq
At the time the post
vanishing points it is
Viewing Madison Sq
junction, the scene v
aspect..."'
'That the Square is a
urbanistic fertility in
apart from documer
postcard is also a pic
own, each of the thre
'But when the three
weaknesses become
meaning to the mult
for the metaphors o
conquest of the bloc
sole occupant of its
The true Skyscraper

The [Daily News] lobby is, after all, a three-dimensional
realization of the murky Ferissian void—the pitch-black womb
of Manhattanism, cosmos of charcoal smudges—which has
given birth already to the Skyscraper and now, finally, to a
Globe'
'The lobby is a chapel of Manhattanism'

ICEBERG
'With the McGraw-Hill Skyscraper [...] Hood becomes more
openly fanatic as he prepares a final dose of hedonism for his
City of Towers'
'Once again Hood has combined two incompatibles in a single
whole: its golden shades pulled down to reflect the sun, the
McGraw-Hill Building looks like a fire ranging inside an iceberg:
the fire of Manhattanism inside the iceberg of Modernism'

PREMONITION
'[...] all the movement that contributes to
congestion—horizontally across the surface of the earth—is
replaced by vertical movement inside buildings, where it
causes decongestion'
'The "City under a Single Roof" [...] "has been founded on the
principle that concentration in a metropolitan area [...] is a
desirable condition [...]"'

PERISPHERE
'The central feature of the [1939 World's] Fair is the theme
exhibit—Trylon and Perisphere [...] it is a stark reappearance of
the [...] Globe and Needle. Unconsciously, the exhibit marks
the end of Manhattanism [...]'
The Perisphere is nothing but the pure archetype of
Manhattanism's Skyscraper: a Globe tall enough to be a
Tower'

ROCKEFELLER

There is a series of strategies—the Great Lobotomy, the Vertical Schism,
real-estate calculations that have been geared, since the twenties, to
prove the impossible—and there is a construction industry specialized in
building it.
Finally, there is the doctrine of Manhattanism—the creation of congestion
on all possible levels'

TEST
'The Mountain must become architecture'

ARCHAEOLOGY
'Rockefeller Center is the most mature demonstration of Manhattanism's
unspoken theory of the simultanous existence of different programs on a
single site [...] Rockefeller Center should be read as five ideologically
separate projects that coexist at the same location. Ascent through its five
layers exposes an archaeology of architectural philosophies'

PROJECT #1
'The Grid assures every structure it accomodates exactly the same
treatment—the same amount of "dignity". In the city of the
Automonument, the isolation of symbolic objects from the main fabric is
meaningless; the fabric itself is already an accumulation of monuments.
In New York, the Beaux-Arts sensibility can only go where there is no Grid,
that is: undergound'
'In the Center's basement, Beaux-Arts planning establishes surreptitious
connections between blocks that are scrupulously avoided above ground:
a grand design that never makes it to the surface'

'By absorbing radio and TV, Rockefeller Center adds to its levels of
congestion electronics—the very medium that denies the need for
congestion as condition for desirable human interaction'

PROJECT #4
'Under any other doctrine of urbanism, Rockefeller Center's past
would be supressed and forgotten; under Manhattanism the past
can coexist with the architectural permutations it has given rise to.
The park extends over the three blocks'
'The garden is only a more advanced variation of the synthetic
Arcadian Carpet of Central Park, nature "reinforced" to deal with the
demands of the Culture of Congestion'

PROJECT #5
'Implanted in the synthetic vegetal past of their airborne site,
stsanding on the fabricated meadows of a New Babylon, amid the
pink flamingos of the Japanese Garden and imported ruins donated
by Mussolini, stand five towers, co-opted totems of the European
avant-garde coexisting for the first and the last time with all the
other "layers" their Modernism intends to destroy.
The roof of the Rockefeller Center is both a flashback and a
flash-forward: ghost of the Elgin Garden *and* Ville Radieuse,
masterstroke of architectural cannibalism'

FULFILLMENT
'Rockefeller Center is the fulfillment of the promise of Manhattan'
'From now on the Metropolis is perfect'

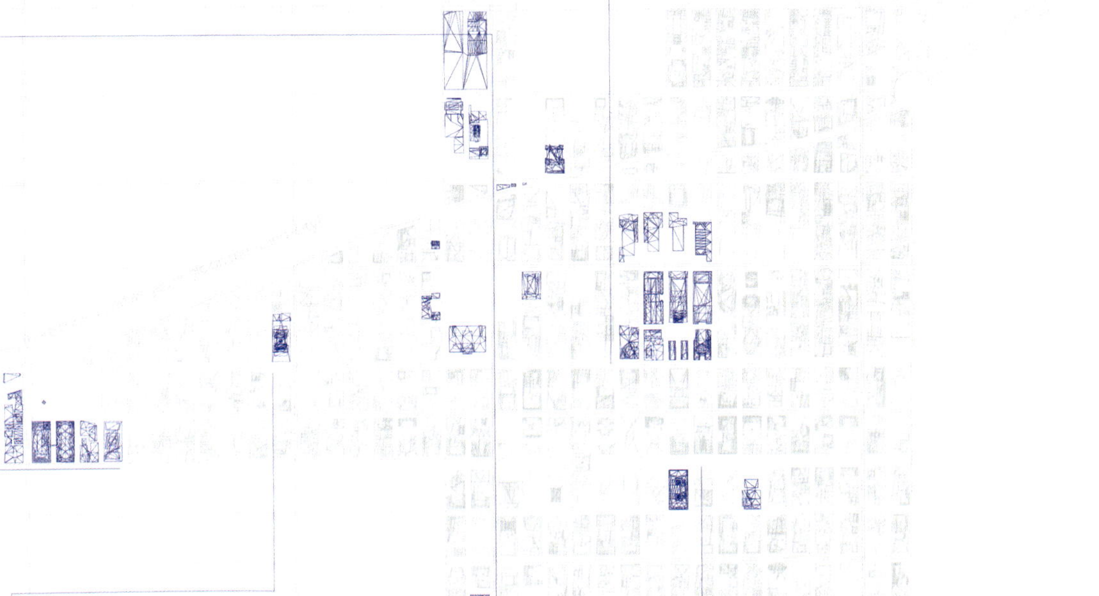

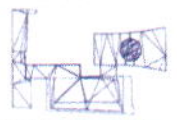

LIBERATION
'The *Empire State Building* is the last manifestation of
Manhattanism as pure and thoughtless process, the climax
of the subconscious Manhattan'

TRUCK
'The Empire State Building is a form of *automatic architecture*,
a sensuous surrender by its collective makers—from the
accountant to the plumber—to the *process of building*'
'The Empire State is a building with no other program than to
make a financial abstraction concrete—that is, to exist'
'"The end of the [old] Waldorf had come"'

SAW
'Five miles beyond Sandy Hook, the [old] Waldorf is dumped
in the sea'
'The dream's outrageousness activates dormant
nightmares: might the building's heaviness make it disappear
through the earth? No—"Empire State is not a new load
placed on bedrock. Instead, the inert load of earth and stones
put there by Nature has been dug away and a usefulload in
the form of a building has been placed there by man"'

DREAMPLANNING
'"Empire State seemed almost to float, like an enchanted
fairy tower, over New York. An edifice so lofty, so serene, so
marvelously simple, so luminously beautiful, had never
before been imagined. One could look back on a dream
well-planned"'
But exactly its character of dream, of automatic architecture,
prevents it from being also an example of the conquest of
the Automonument by higher forms of culture.
It was and is, literally, thoughtless'

AIRSHIP
'Only at the top is there symbolism'
'It is [...] an airship mooring mast and thus resolves

DENOUEMENT
'"New York will not after all crush the UN
in receiving it. On the contrary, the UN will
bring to a head New York's long expected
crisis, through which New York will find
the ways and means to resolve its
urbanistic deadlock, thus effecting upon
itself a startling metamorphosis, though
in this case it is a providential one. Life
has spoken [...]"'

INNOCENCE
'As Le Corbusier tried to drain Manhattan
of congestion, so Harrison now drains Le
Corbusier's Ville Radieuse of ideology.
In his sensitive and professional hands, its
abstract abrasiveness mellows to the
point where the entire complex becomes
merely one of Manhattan's enclaves, a
block like the others, one isolated island

TWIN
'The transplantations from the Astor mansions—literal or merely by
nomenclature—suggest that the Waldorf-Astoria is conceived by its
promoters as a haunted house, rife with the ghosts of its predecessors [...]
Manhattan the new and revolutionary is presented, always, in the false light
of familiarity'

LIBERATION
'The real problem of the [old] Waldorf-Astoria is that it is not a Skyscraper'
'The [new] Waldorf is the first full realization of the conscious Manhattan
[...] in the ideology of Manhattanism it constitutes a double liberation: when
the site is freed to meet its evolutionary destiny, the idea of the Waldorf is
released to be redesigned as the example of an explicit Culture of
Congestion'

TENTACLES
'Manhattan's first Skycraper House'
'A Hotel is a plot—a cybernetic universe with its own laws generating
random but fortuitous collisions between human beings who would never
have met elsewhere'

COW
'[Elsa] Maxwell's farm [party] completes the cycle: the super-refined
infrastructure of the hotel, its architectural ingenuity, all its accumulated
technologies together ensure that in Manhattan the last word is always the
same as the first. But it is only one of many last words'
'A haunted house such as the Waldorf is not simply the end product of a

DOWNTOWN ATH
EQUITABLE BUILDING (1915) | ZONING LAW (1916)
SINGER AND CITY AND CITY INVESTING BUILDINGS | (NOW) ONE LIBERTY
WOOLWORTH BUILDING
Canal St. becomes an important geological hinge in this field
Field loosely defined in Delirious New York
Fragment of the Lower Tower
[around Bowery and Sarah D Roosevelt Park]
4nd STREET (McGRAW-HILL BROADWAY, WEST TOWER, AMERICAN RADIATOR, BRYANT PARK, NY PUBLIC LIBRARY
MADISON SQUARE PARK (FLATIRON, METROPOLITAN LIFE AND NORTH BUILDINGS, MADISON SQUARE GARDEN AND PARK TOWER)

INCUBATOR
The only thing its locker-room graduates have to pay for their
collective narcissism is that of sterility. Their self-induced
mutations are non-reproductive, future generations
The bewilderment of the Metropolis stops at the genes: they
remain the final stronghold of Nature.

TRIUMPH
In 1915 the Equitable Building repeats its block 39 times, "straight
up" [...] The higher the Skyscraper goes, the harder it becomes to
suppress its latent revolutionary ambition.
[...] the Equitable is promoted as a "City in itself", housing 16,000
souls.
"[F]rom now on each new building of the mutant kind strives to be a
City within a City"

SHADOW
"With the Equitable Building (1915) the process of reproduction
loses its credibility through the grim deterioration - both social
and environmental - it inflicts on its surroundings [...] its success is
measured by the destruction of its context"

LAW
"... the 1916 Zoning Law is a back-dated birth certificate that lends
retroactive legitimacy to the Skyscraper"

VILLAGE
The Zoning Law is not only a legal document, it is also a design
project [...] If Manhattan was in the beginning only a collection of
2,028 blocks. It is now an assembly of as many invisible
envelopes [...] [it] defines Manhattan for all time as a collection of
[...] phantom "houses" that together form a Mega-Village.

SPHERE
As yet contained in the colossal cage of the
modes of mass transportation] will turn Ma
Galapagos Island of new technologies, whe
survival of the fittest, this time a battle anx
machines, is imminent

CONTRAST
The Latting Observatory and the dome of
introduce an archetypal contrast that will ap
throughout Manhattan's history [...] The ne
represent the two extremes of Manhattan's
[...]
[...] the history of Manhattanism as a separ
architecture is a dialectic between these two
needle wanting to become a globe and the
time to time, to turn into a needle [...]"

THEORY
In his vision the future Manhattan is a City o
modified version of what already exists; inst
extrusion of arbitrary individual plots, large
will be assembled in new building operation
Towers will be a forested of freestanding, co
made accessible by the regular paths of the
Park

GOLD
Hood [...] designs the first example of his
The top of the black building [American Rad
gilded. Hood's down-to-earth alibi for the to
correspondences between gold and any possible
to sky"
added to the field

CATHEDRAL
The first built amalgamation is the Woolworth Building. The
lower 27 floors are a straightforward extrusion [...] it
occupies an entire block.
"If its interior is business one, its exterior is pure spirituality.
The Woolworth does not actually contribute any radical
modifications or breaks to the life of the city, but is supposed
to work miracles through the emanation of its physical
presence, a larger mass than constructed before. It is at the
same time seen as 'disembodied', antigravitational: "Brute
material has been robbed of its density and flung into the sky to
challenge its lowliness [...]"

BUILDINGS
[...] In 1908 Ernest Flagg designs a Tower and places it on top of
his existing Singer Building, a 14-story block built in 1899. This
architectural afterthought alone makes it - from 1908 to 1913 -
America's most famous building
"Thousands of travelers come to New York especially to see this
'Modern Tower of Babel' gladly paying fifty cents a ride to the
'observation balcony' in acknowledgment of the darker side of
the Metropolis. It is also the first 'Suicide Pinnacle'

TRIUMPH
... building at the Bottom of fulfils the vertical Babylon, it simply
stacks 34 times
... through sheer rigor, it recasts the Skyscraper is involved in a

FREEZE-FRAME

POCKET PARK SQUARE PARK

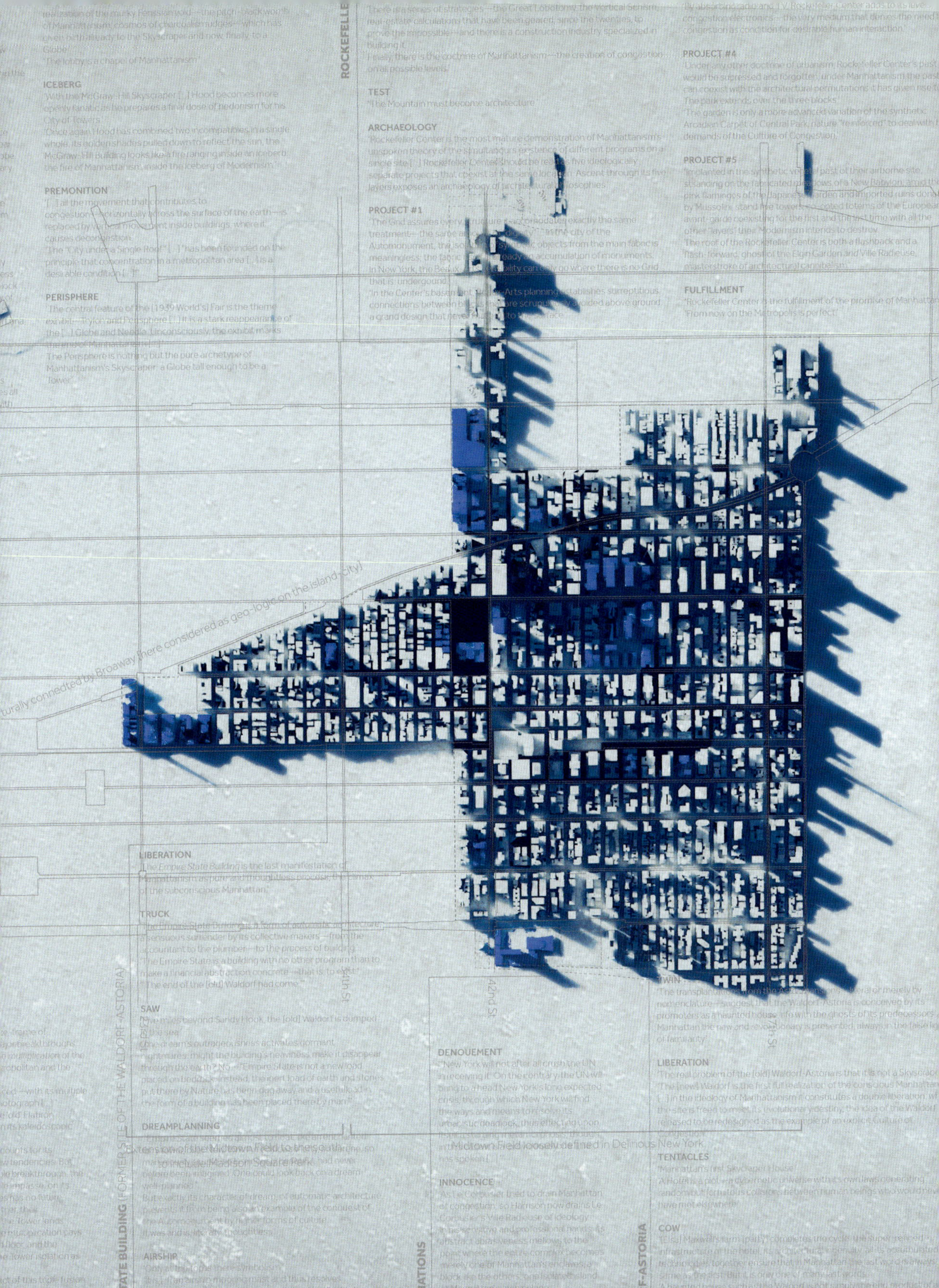

realization of the murky Piranesian void—the pitch-black womb of Manhattanism's cosmos of charcoal smudges—which has given birth already to the Skyscraper and now finally to a Globe.
"The lobby is a chapel of Manhattanism."

ICEBERG
"With the McGraw-Hill Skyscraper [...] Hood becomes more openly fanatic as he prepares a final dose of hedonism for his City of Towers."
"Once again Hood has combined two incompatibles in a single whole. Its golden shades pulled down to reflect the sun, the McGraw-Hill Building looks like a fire raging inside an iceberg: the fire of Manhattanism inside the iceberg of Modernism."

PREMONITION
"[...] all the movement that contributes to congestion—horizontally across the surface of the earth—is replaced by vertical movement inside buildings, where it causes decongestion."
"The 'City under a Single Roof' [...] 'has been founded on the principle that concentration in a metropolitan area [...] is a desirable condition [...]'"

PERISPHERE
"The central feature of the [1939 World's] Fair is the theme exhibit—Trylon and Perisphere [...] It is a stark reappearance of the [...] Globe and Needle. Unconsciously, the exhibit marks the end of Manhattanism [...]"
The Perisphere is nothing but the pure archetype of Manhattanism's Skyscraper: a Globe tall enough to be a Tower.

LIBERATION
The Empire State Building is the last manifestation of Manhattanism as pure and thoughtless process, the climax of the subconscious Manhattan.

TRUCK
The Empire State Building is a form of automatic architecture, a conscious surrender by its collective makers—from the accountant to the plumber—to the process of building it.
The Empire State is a building with no other program than to make a financial abstraction concrete—that is to exist.
"The end of the [old] Waldorf had come."

SAW
Now miles beyond Sandy Hook, the [old] Waldorf is dumped into the sea.
Only dreams outrageous shows activities dormant... nightmares might the building's newness make it disappear through its very thinness? No—"Empire State is not a load placed on bedrock; instead, the inert load of earth and stones [...] a there by Nature has been dug away, and a replica, in the form of a building, has been placed there [...]"

DREAMPLANNING

AIRSHIP

STATE BUILDING (FORMER SITE OF THE WALDORF-ASTORIA)
51st St
...naturally connected by Broadway there considered as geo-logic on the island city

There is a series of strategies—the "Great Lobotomy," the vertical Schism... real-estate calculations that have been geared, since the twenties, to prove the impossible—and there is a construction industry specialized in building it.
Finally, there is the doctrine of Manhattanism—the creation of congestion on all possible levels.

TEST
"The Mountain must become architecture."

ARCHAEOLOGY
Rockefeller Center is the most mature demonstration of Manhattanism's unspoken theory of the simultaneous existence of different programs on a single site [...] Rockefeller Center should be read as five ideologically separate projects that coexist at the same location. Ascent through its five layers exposes an archaeology of architectural philosophies.

PROJECT #1
The Grid assures every future skyscraper exactly the same treatment—the same as [...] the city of the Automonument, the isolation of symbolic objects from the main fabric is meaningless; the fabric is already accumulation of monuments. In New York, the Beaux-Arts sensibility can only go where there is no Grid: that is, underground.
In the Center's basement Beaux-Arts planning establishes surreptitious connections between buildings more scrupulously avoided above ground, a grand design that never dared to show its face.

By absorbing radio and TV, Rockefeller Center is the very medium that denies the need for congestion; electronics—the very medium that denies the need for congestion as a condition for desirable human interaction.

PROJECT #4
Under any other doctrine of urbanism, Rockefeller Center's past would be suppressed and forgotten; under Manhattanism it can coexist with the architectural permutations it has given rise to.
The park extends over the three blocks.
The garden is only a more advanced variation of the synthetic Arcadian Carpet of Central Park, nature "reinforced" to deal with the demands of the Culture of Congestion.

PROJECT #5
Implanted in the synthetic world-past of their airborne site, standing on the fabricated meadows of a New Babylon, amid the pink flamingos of the Japanese Garden and imported ruins donated by Mussolini, stand the towers—eroded totems of the European avant-garde coexisting for the first and final time with all the other "layers" Modernism intends to destroy.
The roof of the Rockefeller Center is both a flashback and a flash-forward, ghost of the Elgin Garden and Ville Radieuse use, masterstroke of architectural cannibalism.

FULFILLMENT
Rockefeller Center is the fulfilment of the promise of Manhattanism. "From now on the Metropolis is perfect."

DENOUEMENT
"New York will not after all crush the UN in receiving it. On the contrary, the UN will bring to a head New York's long expected crisis, through which New York will find the ways and means to resolve its urbanistic deadlock, thus reflecting upon itself its letting in at the end of it..."
...Midtown Field loosely defined in Delirious New York... has seeped in [...]

INNOCENCE
As Le Corbusier tried to drain Manhattan of congestion, so Harrison now drains Le Corbusier's Ville Radieuse of ideology. In his sensitive and professional hands, its abstract aggressiveness mellows to the point where the entire complex becomes merely one of Manhattan's enclaves, a block like the others, on Island-in-Island in Manhattan...

TWIN
The transplantations from the Astor dynasty—whether literal or merely by nomenclature—suggest that the Waldorf-Astoria is conceived by its promoters as a haunted house, rife with the ghosts of its predecessors. In Manhattan the new and revolutionary is presented, always, in the false light of familiarity.

LIBERATION
The real problem of the [old] Waldorf-Astoria is that it is not a Skyscraper.
The [new] Waldorf is the first full realization of the conscious Manhattan [...] In the ideology of Manhattanism it constitutes a double liberation: while the site is freed to meet its evolutionary destiny, the idea of the Waldorf is released to be redesigned as the example of an explicit Culture of Congestion.

TENTACLES
"Manhattan's first Skyscraper House."
A Hotel is a plot—a cybernetic universe with its own laws, generating random but fortuitous collisions between human beings who would never have met elsewhere.

COW
The Waldorf's turn [party] combines the cycle: the super-relaxed infrastructure of the hotel, its architectural density, all its accumulated technologies together ensure that in Manhattan the last word is always same, a protest but it is only one of many last words.

42nd St
7th St
UNITED NATIONS
WALDORF-ASTORIA
Delirious New York

tan is the 20th centur 's Rosetta Stone. [...] Manhattan as the product of an unformulated theory, *Manhattanism*, whose program – [...] to live inside fantasy – wa

tan is the 20th centur 's Rosetta Stone. [...] Manhattan as the product of an unformulated theory, *Manhattanism*, whose program – [...] to live inside fantasy – wa

*Philosophers and philologists should be concerned in the first place with
poetic metaphysics; that is, the science that looks for proof not in the external
world, but in the very modifications of the mind that meditates on it.
Since the world of nations is made by men, it is inside their minds that its
principles should be sought.*
—Giambattista Vico, *Principles of a New Science*, 1759

Why do we have a mind if not to get our way?
—Fyodor Dostoyevski

MANIFESTO

How to write a manifesto — on a form of urbanism for what remains of
the 20th century — in an age disgusted with them? The fatal weakness of
manifestos is their inherent lack of evidence.
Manhattan's problem is the opposite: it is a mountain range of evidence
without manifesto.
This book was conceived at the intersection of these two observations: it
is a retroactive manifesto for Manhattan.
Manhattan is the 20th century's Rosetta Stone.
Not only are large parts of its surface occupied by architectural mutations
(Central Park, the Skyscraper), utopian fragments (Rockefeller Center,
the UN Building) and irrational phenomena (Radio City Music Hall), but in
addition each block is covered with several layers of phantom architecture
in the form of past occupancies, aborted projects and popular fantasies
that provide alternative images to the New York that exists.
Especially between 1890 and 1940 a new culture (the Machine Age?)
selected Manhattan as laboratory: a mythical island where the invention

4.2 Paranoid Critical Extrusions

Koolhaas's description of the PCM in *Delirious New York* is woven into his narration of Salvador Dalí's first trip to New York. Paraphrasing the artist – and self-proclaimed inventor of the PCM – Koolhaas explains the method as '*"The Conquest of the Irrational"*' and '"the spontaneous method of irrational knowledge based on the critical and systematic objectifications of delirious associations and interpretations ...."' [190]

Initially associated with maniac types of persecution, the influence of the term paranoia expanded in the late 1920s, namely in art. Koolhaas describes this expansion as a 'delirium of interpretation':

> Each fact, event, force, observation is caught in one system of speculation and "understood" by the afflicted individual in such a way that it absolutely confirms and reinforces his thesis – that is, the initial delusion that is his point of departure. *The paranoiac always hits the nail on the head, no matter where the hammer blows fall.* [191]

Koolhaas presents an interesting analogy between the collective molecular pull in a magnetic field and the transformation that a paranoid makes of 'the whole into a magnetic field of facts, all pointing in the same direction; the one he is going in.' [192] To him, '[t]he essence of paranoia is this intense – if distorted – relationship with the real world: "The reality of the external world is used for illustration and proof ... to serve the reality of our mind ... ." Paranoia is a shock of recognition that never ends.' [193]

Dalí's PCM involves two sequential but discrete operations. First, the 'synthetic reproduction of the paranoid's way of seeing the world in a new light', and second, the critical 'compression of these gaseous speculations to a critical point where they achieve the density of fact.' Koolhaas extends the use of the PCM beyond the twentieth century, to a moment before Dalí allegedly invents it. [194] However, he also describes the importance of Dalí's injection of the method 'into the bloodstream of Surrealism':

> Instead of the passive and deliberately uncritical surrender to the subconscious of the early Surrealist automatisms in writing, painting, sculpture, Dalí proposes a second-phase Surrealism: the conscious exploitation of the unconscious through the PCM. [195]

It is with this conscious exploitation of the unconscious that Koolhaas feels more affinity. *Delirious New York*'s 'operation of retroaction' has been described as a PC activity that frames Koolhaas' theory in the 'unveiling of the city's unconscious.' [196] The architect's understanding of 'history as an invention' had already been tested in OMA's proposal *Exodus, or the Voluntary Prisoners of Architecture* before it was then used to construct the book 'from an amalgam of historical fragments set in new combinations.' [197] Koolhaas' retroaction works as a temporal compression that looks 'backwards and forwards, simultaneously,' presenting a four-fold approach 'containing a theory, a practice, a strategy, and an ethic based upon an "unconscious rhetoric."' [198]

Dalí's PC activity focuses on synthesizing paranoia to discredit the real, whereas Koolhaas oscillates between that and a retroactive construction of history that reveals a particular ambition to frame Manhattan as a path to totality. The architect organizes ideas, concepts and practices in New York that construct a narrative of paranoia

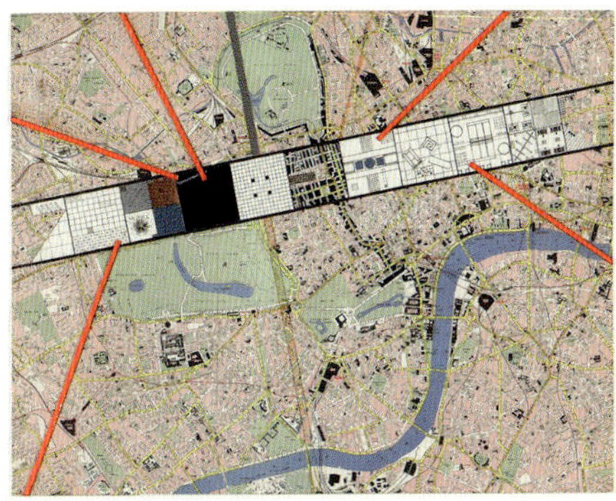

22 to 24 *Exodus, or the Voluntary Prisoners of Architecture: The Strip*, Rem Koolhaas, Madelon Vreisendorp, Elia Zenghelis, and Zoe Zenghelis, 1972.

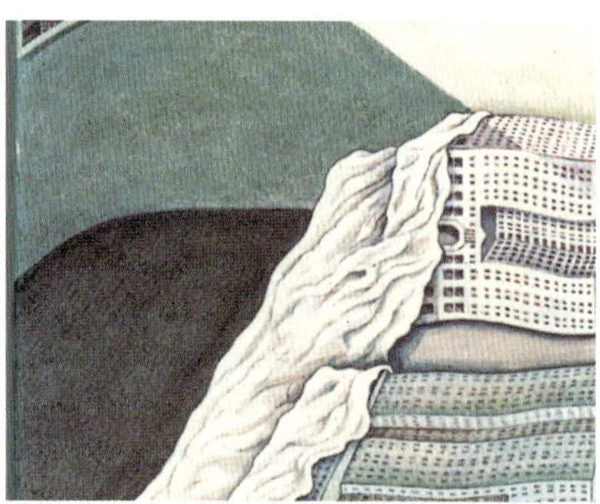

and fantastical artifice. He destabilizes the city with a constant temporal synthesis where phantom occupancies overlap with present and future uses. This synthesis also describes spatial and material exchanges involved in the creative destruction of architectural fragments. Koolhaas' retroaction can thus be described also as an invention of Manhattan as a fantasy of the Gilded Age. And, in theoretically quarrying the city for its history, he is also perhaps digging his invented golden treasure.

Koolhaas' city excavations assemble the city as a magnetic field constantly pulling the grid to the edges of the island. The Koolhaasian city is a tale of surreal technology that activates fantasy and delirium, something that might have even surprised Dalí upon his arrival. [199]

For the first book cover of *Delirious New York* Koolhaas used an adapted version of an earlier painting by Madelon Vriesendorp titled *Flagrant Délit*, originally from 1975. The painting depicts an affair between the iconic Chrysler and the Empire State buildings. [200] *Flagrant Délit* is not just one painting but slightly different adaptations of the famous scene, as well as a long-lost animated film that Vriesendorp created together with director Teri When-Damisch in 1976, narrating the events before and after the buildings' sexual intercourse. The painting is also part of a wider collection of sketches, drawings and paintings informing the series *Manhattan*. For the series, 'inhabited by anthropomorphic architectures and infused by oneiric imagination and surreal themes,' [201] Vriesendorp drew inspiration from

Dalí's 1933 *The Architectonic Angelus of Millet* to create a drawing titled *Manhattan Angelus* in 1975. Dalí's piece, in turn inspired by Jean-François Millet's 1859 *The Angelus*, results from the application of the PCM, through which he transforms the two original peasants into sculpture-like architectural fragments dominating a surrealist landscape. Vriesendorp also anthropomorphizes the two buildings, yet she goes further in inscribing the bowing buildings in a grid that simulates the proportions of Manhattan.

Dalí's influence on Vriesendorp's work has been studied before, but it is interesting to note that her use of the PCM precedes Koolhaas' use of the same method.'[202] Her series *Manhattan*, at least, precedes *Delirious New York* and, in the artist's own words, 'the paintings originally had nothing to do with Rem's book.'[203] Perhaps more importantly, Vriesendorp and Koolhaas mutually support their artistic and architectural explorations following Dalí's PCM, and even if 'using two different mediums, narration and illustration, to reinforce the credibility of the "retroactive manifesto," [they] were both heavily channeling the paranoid-critical method in their works.'[204] Koolhaas found in Vriesendrop's paintings the much-needed, though missing proofs to support his PCM in *Delirious New York*, thus creating a compelling, credible, fabricated and supportive visual narrative. In other words, to understand Koolhaas' PCM one must understand Vriesendorp's work.

Vriesendorp was fundamental in the creation of OMA's early representational microcosm. *The City of the Captive Globe*, from 1972, is an example. Just as with *Flagrant Délit*, the painting emerges from an iterative process of representation. As mentioned before, the geological plinths organized on a grid and supporting Koolhaas'

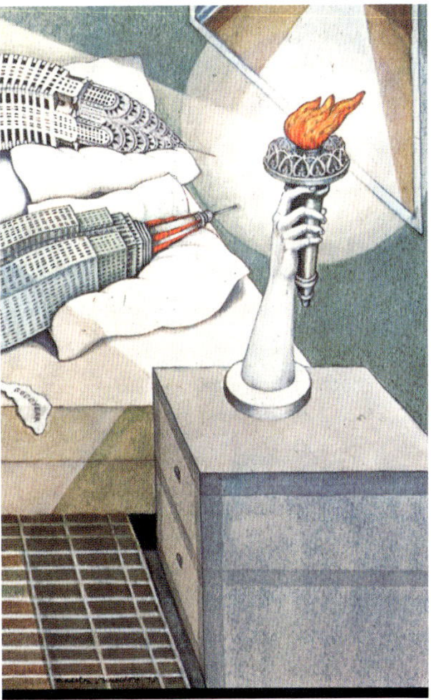

25–29 Fragments of *Delirious New York*, Original book cover, Rem Koolhaas, 1978. Image adapted from *Flagrant Délit*, Madelon Vriesendorp, 1975.

architectural laboratories are here explored as extruded geologies that may contain the possibility for architecture to exist both in and through it. Unlike *Delirious New York*, the image reveals an interest in structures that support the city and may be an early indication of Vriesendorp's curiosity about the representation of infrastructure. This interest is taken further in artworks such as *Freud Unlimited* and *A Casa*, both dating from 1975. In the first, the aqueous datum line of a round room – resembling the interior of a globe – is cut in section to reveal an infrastructural muddy ground supporting rhizomatic networks of transport, energy and communications. Similar rhizomatic infrastructures are depicted in *A Casa*, this time through a section cutting across a grid-like carpet covering the ground of what seems to be a museum room. The infrastructural plenum beneath her invented Manhattan and supporting its laboratorial culture of congestion is, for Vriesendop, a Freudian subconscious of the city itself, a series of inaccessible impulses and desires which create and nurture Koolhaas' *Technology of the Fantastic.* [205]

Vriesendrop's artworks create an implicit tension with some of Koolhaas' claims in *Delirious New York*. First, the idea of *extrusion* is mostly revealed through sections cutting across the city's ground datum lines and related with infrastructural architectures as rhizomatic possibilities. The extrusion in section expands the usual limits of representability of the city to reveal the architecture of its perhaps less known undercrofts. [206] This contrasts with Koolhaas' argument that infrastructure is repressed by architecture's idealizing impetus. For the architect, the city results from a synthetic carpet on top of which it then extrudes. Unlike Koolhaas, Vriesendorp explores extrusion in section via a 'conscious exploitation of the unconscious through the PCM.' [207]

The tension between architecture and its infrastructural support is enmeshed with descriptions of the former as geology. Hugh Ferriss' theoretical building envelopes developed to illustrate the 1916 Zoning Law, for example, are described as mountains, [208] and so are the '38 Mountains ... positioned on the intersections of alternate avenues and the wider streets of the Grid, roughly every tenth street', that architect Raymond Hood proposed in his *Manhattan 1950.* [209] Indeed, Hood's skyscrapers are often described as remarkable geographical features. 'The Mountain must become architecture,' Koolhaas writes when narrating the development of the Rockefeller Center, which he describes as a mountain range. [210]

It seems like Vriesendorp's representations go beyond *Delirious New York* also by enacting geology as more than just the geological material supporting architecture. In her depictions the extruded geologies sustaining the city, or the rocky foundations enmeshed with rhizomatic infrastructure in underground horizons, are positioned at the center of architectural debate and, in that sense, one could argue that they become architecture. The depictions unsettle more conventional understandings of architectural practice in that they tangle the ambition of indefinite growth in the city to serve its culture of congestion with the necessary limits of its geological, hydrological, even gravitational context.

Vriesendorp's paintings can be contextualized, even if only retrospectively, in the Anthropocene debate, since they enmesh architecture and geology as undetachable *geosocial formations* with important cultural meaning. They reveal the use of the PCM to extrude collisions between architectural conditions and geologic possibilities, thus representing Manhattan as something existing 'between still being a city and already being a geology.' [211]

Extending beyond Vriesendorp's work, the paranoid critical extrusion can be used to explain other coetaneous architectural projects, for example Superstudio's 1969-71 *Continuous Monument: An Architectural Model for Total Urbanization* or Lebbeus Woods' 1980 *Einstein Tomb*.

Continuous Monument results from an extrusion of heterogeneous, sometimes contradictory architectural elements onto a white superstructure that crosses, rather abstractly, cities and landscapes. [212] Working as an atlas of possibilities, each representation of the structure – usually in photomontages – reveals yet another particular condition of a fragment of the monument. [213] While placed in site-specific, and sometimes easily recognizable contexts – for example, when it crosses Manhattan – the depicted monument has an ambiguous scale against its many backgrounds. It unfolds in immeasurable scales that metamorphose from one representation to the next, an almost scaleless quality that emphasizes the authors' critique of architecture itself. [214]

Continuous Monument can be regarded as a utopian architecture being 'put into circulation' – or emitted – around the Earth. The relation between architecture and landscape is explained less in conventional chronological or spatial ways and more as spacetime taxonomies enveloping the earth. [215]

If *Continuous Monument* supported Koolhaas' 1972 provocative thesis at the AA titled *Exodus* (subsequently further developed by OMA), it may have also, even if indirectly, influenced the creation of *The City of the Captive Globe*. In the same year of the monument, Superstudio developed *istogrammi d'architettura*, a series of white plastic models organized in a grid which demonstrate the 'feeling of the need of control, even to categorize' architecture, and 'clearly offered as a series of typologies.' [216]

As proposed by various scholars, both projects by Superstudio critically revise the meaning of *monument*. [217] Defined as a 'moderate utopia,' the monument 'creates a territory with no history and no future, which does not belong to any particular place: a utopian design which imagines an alternative life where people can finally, and ironically, enjoy consumerism.' [218]

Lebeus Woods' *Einstein Tomb* is a conceptual memorial to Albert

Einstein. [219] Describing it as 'a symbolic structure in the same spirit as [Étienne-Louis] Boullée's *Cenotaph* to Isaac Newton,' Woods designed the memorial as an architecture 'to be launched into deep space, traveling on a beam of light, never to be seen in terrestrial space and time.' [220] The tomb is revealed in a pitch-black interstellar void and orbiting around a planetary body. [221] The proposal results from a deliberate 'synthesis between the tectonic and the cosmological, a relativistic and technical mystique of an effective engraver.' [222]

Though they are very different, comparisons can be made between these projects if they are analyzed as paranoid critical extrusions. Both proposals were conceived as orbital projects. Due to its sheer mass, vast distribution and enveloping around the earth, *Continuous Monument* becomes an orbital megastructure embracing the curvature of the earth and eventually enveloping the planet in the lower atmospheric layers. *Einstein Tomb* is an architectural satellite which also potentially explores the becoming of an orbital city through the continued extrusion of its own ends.

Both projects also explore notions of a captive globe and, in that sense, they encourage more layered understandings of T*he City of Captive Globe*. *Continuous Monument* captures the globe in a way that reverses OMA's proposition: instead of the shrinking of the globe into the city grid, it proposes the expansions of architecture to girdle the earth. *Einstein Tomb* captures the globe more metaphorically: as a satellite placed into orbit, it continuously delineates a quasi-spherical trajectory around the earth. Over time, the tracing of these potentially infinite orbits would result in an enveloping mesh capturing the planet.

Brought together as interferences within a more complex understanding of extrusion, these two projects may also trigger curiosity about potential emissions of the city fragments, and the placing of them into orbit, either of the earth or other space objects.

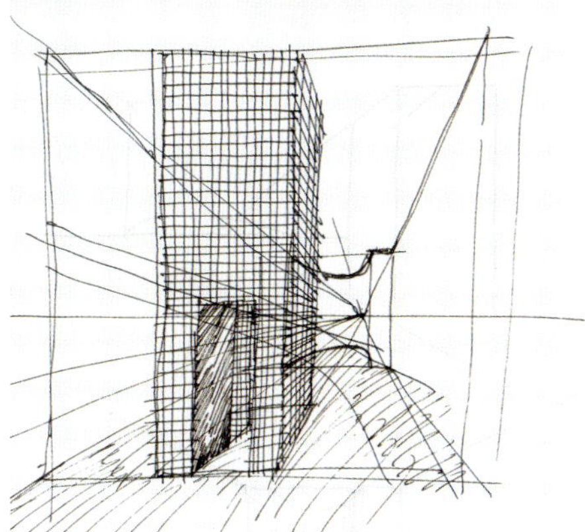

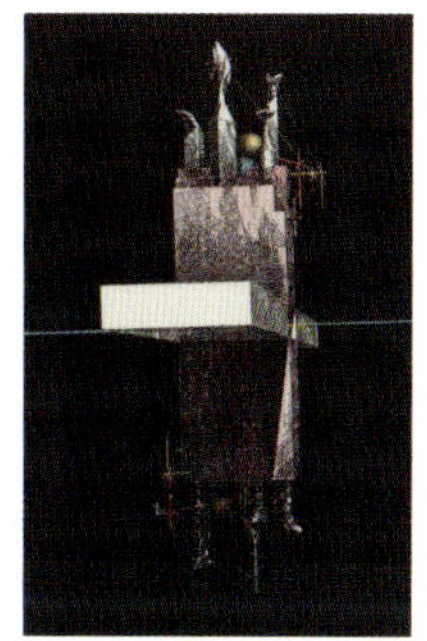

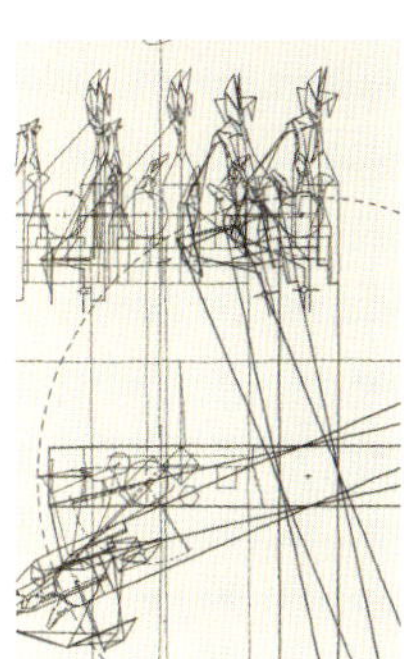

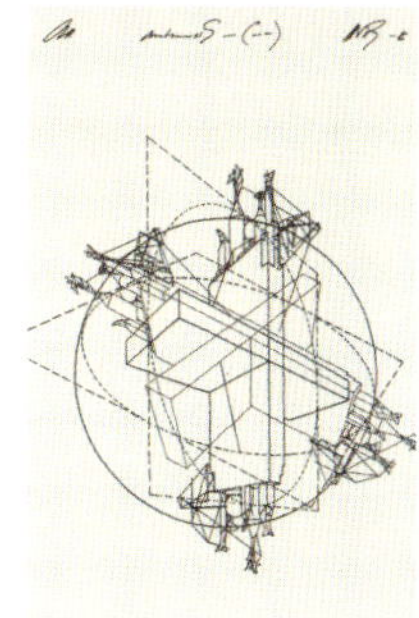

30 (top) *Continuous monument*, Superstudio, 1969.
The rendered collage first appeared in Domus
481, with the title 'Discosrso per immagini.'
31 (middle) *Modella della Zimmer in Graz,
Sketchbook 12,*, Superstudio, 1969. The installation
was produced for the 1969 Trigon Biennale, Graz.
The piece included mirrors above and below to trick
vision into becoming 'continuous.'
32 (bottom four) *Einstein Tomb*, Lebbeus Woods, 1980.

Manhattan's Geotaxonomies of the Fantastic

Delirious New York is less a book about Manhattan and more a literary construction of the island as 'an architectural delirium in which [Koolhaas] found his first prototype for the contemporary city.' [223] The book can be regarded as the result of Koolhaas' use of the PCM, something the architect refers to, even if only implicitly, in the chapter about Salvador Dalí's trip to New York.

Koolhaas accepts capitalism as a dominant logic leading to the conception of the city as a modern icon, a logic so dominant in how the city is conceptualized, constructed and represented that it generates a totalizing narrative of it, that is, a narrative that seems complete, or circular, or conclusive about the city and can only reinforce itself. This is, in a way, the result of the PCM. But if one is to understand the book as a grand narrative for the invention of the city, one should also equally question the ways in which that narrative corroborates its sustaining capitalist logics, namely by not offering counter narratives that could confront the dominant one – after all, and in Koolhaas' words, *Delirious New York* was written 'without a single "however."' [224]

The design enquiry here also follows a PC process, through which the actions involved in a critical and creative reading of *Delirious New York* and, more specifically, a plotting of the text blocks onto an invented territory, are reinforced through delirium. It was briefly consolidated as the installation *Manhattan's Geotaxonomies of the Fantastic*.

The exploration questions some of Koolhaas' assumptions about the city, namely by reading them retrospectively from the perspective of the Anthropocene. [225] In encouraging an expansion of the temporal and material frames to read the city, the Anthropocene theory facilitates a perhaps more distinct way of looking at Manhattan than the one Koolhaas proposes, one that expands the city beyond the limits conventionally attributed to architectural influence (even though conventions themselves should also perhaps be relativized when contextualized within much wider lineages of architectural discourse and debate). This becomes a way of reading the island-territory as a condition embedded in its own context. If in the previous chapter geology becomes a tool for critical and creative thinking about architecture, the city and the urban condition, here it sustains a series of design operations that extrude, quarry and mine the Koolhaasian synthetic carpet. Being also part of the PC process, the parallel narratives tangled with *Delirious New York* are used to reinforce assumptions that geologics – or logics related to earth, soil, land and landscape – offer alternative recalibrations of Manhattan that steer its urban condition away from the usual protagonism of the neoliberal forms of capitalism.

The proposed city in the exhibition space develops from a set of fragments and arguments in *Delirious New York,* which can be read in non-sequential ways in relation to the ideas they activate. They exist between Koolhaas' literary project and other complementary, yet sometimes conflicting, materials gathered from archival sources, fieldwork and design activities.

Koolhaas' fields of congestion are analyzed with the support of cartographies and drawings of past and phantom occupancies, ground conditions and patterns of land use, both pre- and post-grid. They consider the fields' magnetic forces to study, question and imagine power relations of proximity, affinity and kinship, tangled in conditions of contradiction and dissonance.

The installation consolidates a pseudo-archaeological process in which Koolhaas' congested fields of Downtown and Midtown are excavated. It quarries the architectures out of their context, which is made visible by rescuing to the realm of representation that which the architect did not describe. The extraction of these *geosocial formations* means the pulling out of the buildings enmeshed in their contextual conditions with which they are impossible to disentangle. The extracted and then exhibited city fragments do not hold the island-territory captive, nor do they gesture towards capturing it as a whole.

The architectural and city fragments that are slowly revealed result from iterative actions of negotiation between the city's present and past conditions as well as a juxtaposition with theoretical provocations and speculative futures, either narrated in *Delirious New York*, or dragged onto the new city by observation in related field activities. Thus, the fragments emerge from an investigative process where a paranoid critical extrusion is utilized to enmesh the Koolhaasian architectural PCM together with eventual contextual geo-conditions. The buildings on which Koolhaas focused his study are plotted together with some of the previous occupancies extracted from cartographies and textual descriptions. After being overlaid, each layer is then extruded and fused along a vertical section where distinct uses become organized in ways similar to geological stratification. Rather than a palimpsest of creative destruction, where each new use adapts, metamorphoses or destroys the previous ones, the actions of architectural extrusion here follow logics eventually closer to geological overlapping and entanglement.

(above and next pages) *Manhattan's Geotaxonomies of the Fantastic*, Views of the installation and critical operations of extrusion, 2018.

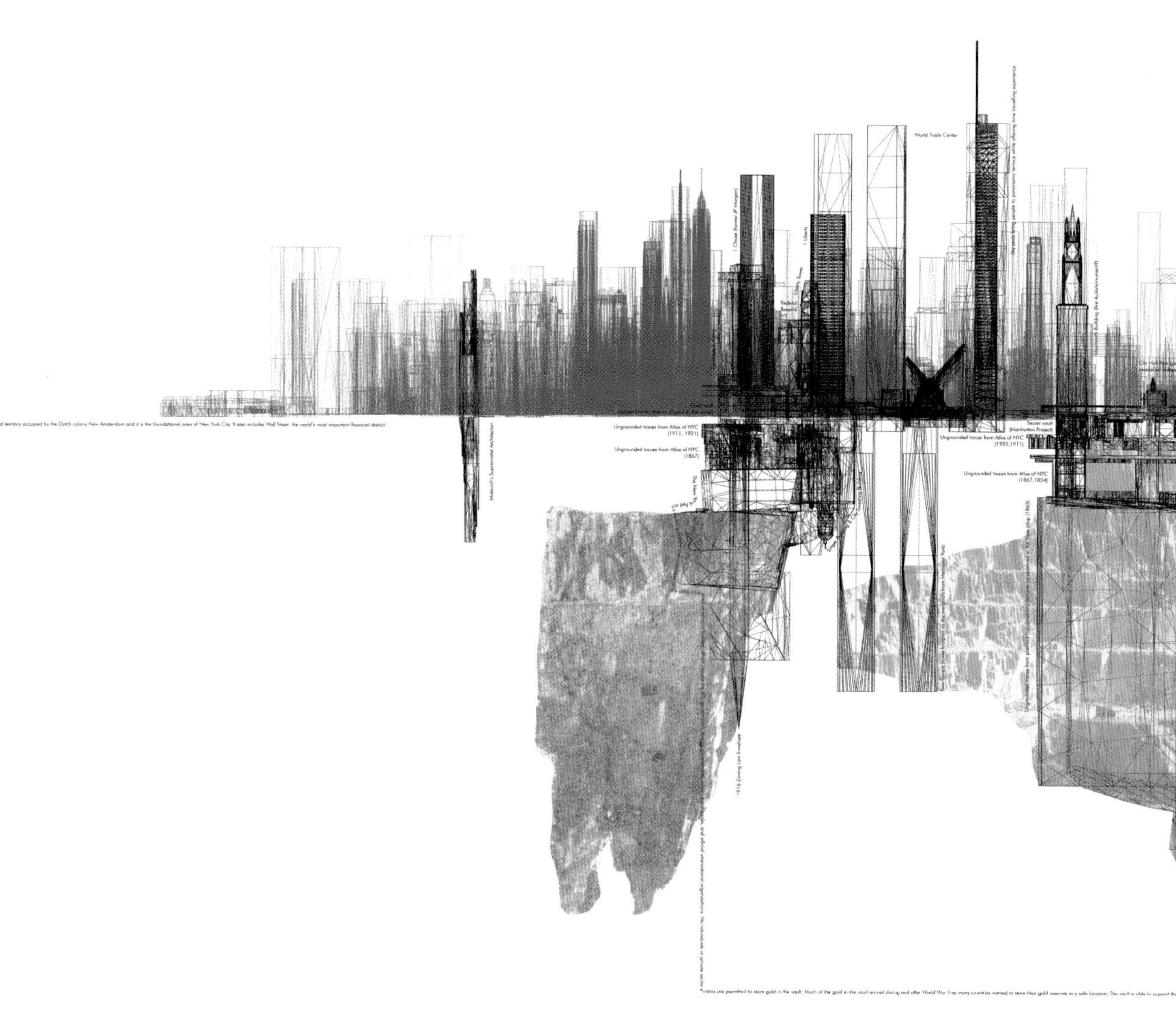
...ed territory occupied by the Dutch colony New Amsterdam and it is the foundational area of New York City. It also includes Wall Street, the world's most important financial district.
Malevich's Suprematist Architecton
Gold vault
World Trade Center
1 Chase (former JP Morgan)
1 Liberty
Liberty Tower
Federal Reserve NY
Woolworth Building (first Automonument?)
City Hall Park (few examples in depth)
Secret vault (Manhattan Project)
Ungrounded traces from Atlas of NYC (1911, 1921)
Ungrounded traces from Atlas of NYC (1867)
Ungrounded traces from Atlas of NYC (1955, 1911)
Ungrounded traces from Atlas of NYC (1867, 1854)
1916 Zoning Law Envelope
entities are permitted to store gold in the vault. Much of the gold in the vault arrived during and after World War II as many countries wanted to store their gold reserves in a safe location. The vault is able to support the...

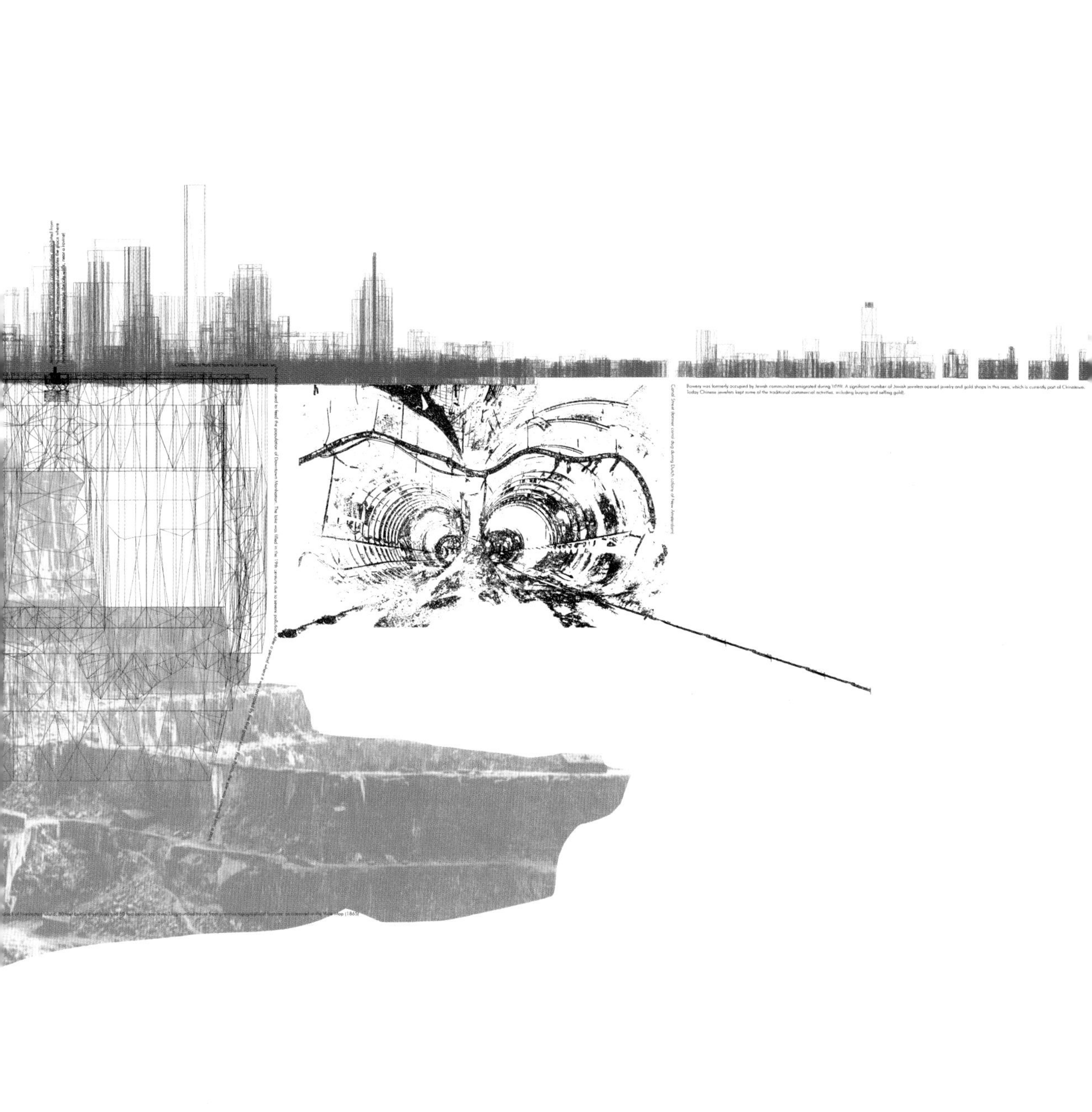

Bowery was formerly occupied by Jewish communities emigrated during WWII. A significant number of Jewish jewelers opened jewelry and gold shops in this area, which is currently part of Chinatown. Today Chinese jewelers kept some of the traditional commercial activities, including buying and selling gold).
Canal Street (former canal dug during Dutch colony of New Amsterdam)
dock of Manhattan Island, 80 feet below street level and 50 feet below sea level. Ungrounded traces from previous topographical features, as observed in the Viele Map (1865)

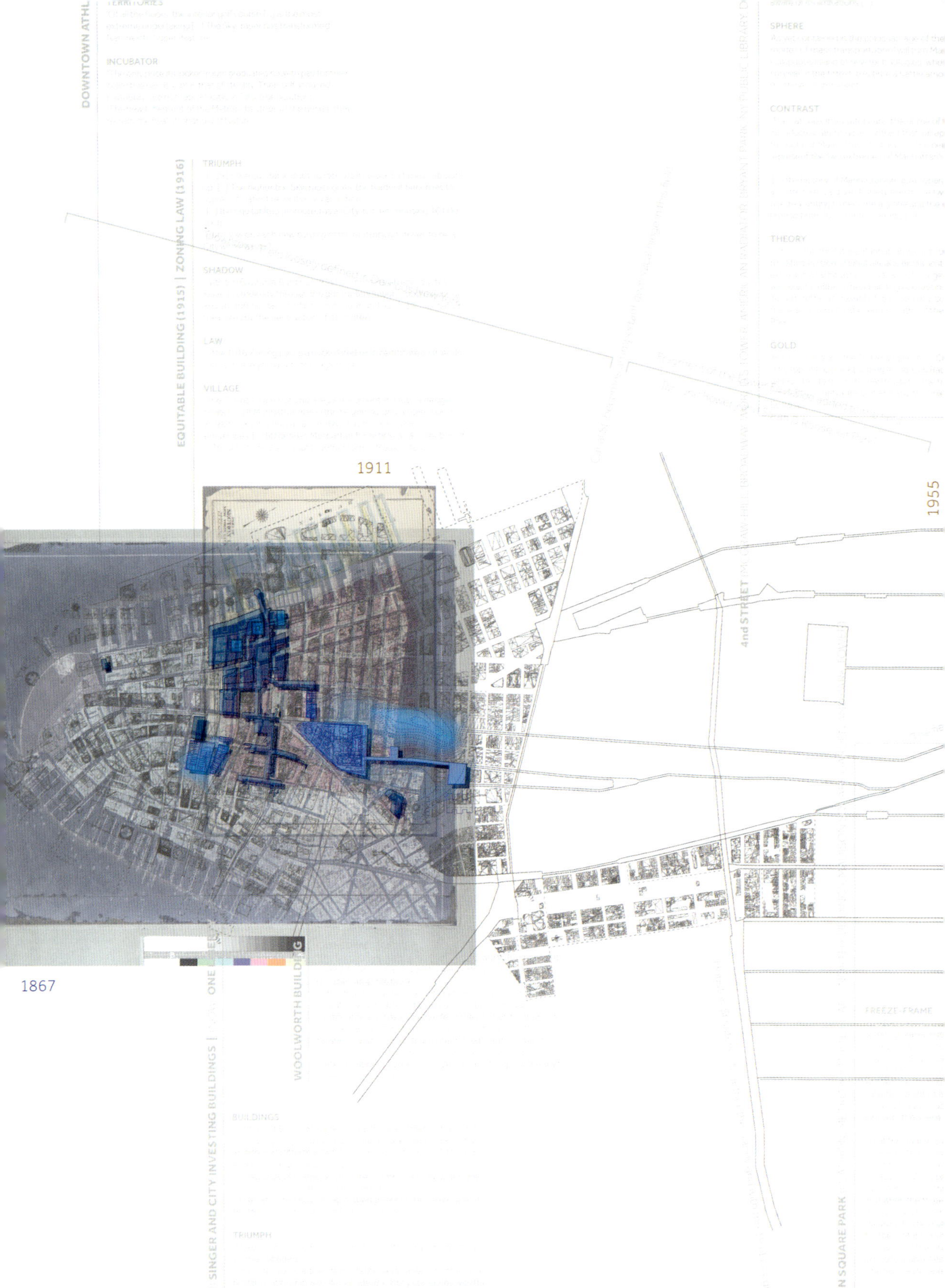

DOWNTOWN ATHL
TERRITORIES
INCUBATOR
TRIUMPH
SHADOW
LAW
VILLAGE
EQUITABLE BUILDING (1915) | ZONING LAW (1916)
1911
1955
4nd STREET
1867
SINGER AND CITY INVESTING BUILDINGS | ONE
WOOLWORTH BUILDING
BUILDINGS
TRIUMPH
SPHERE
CONTRAST
THEORY
GOLD
FREEZE-FRAME
MADISON SQUARE PARK

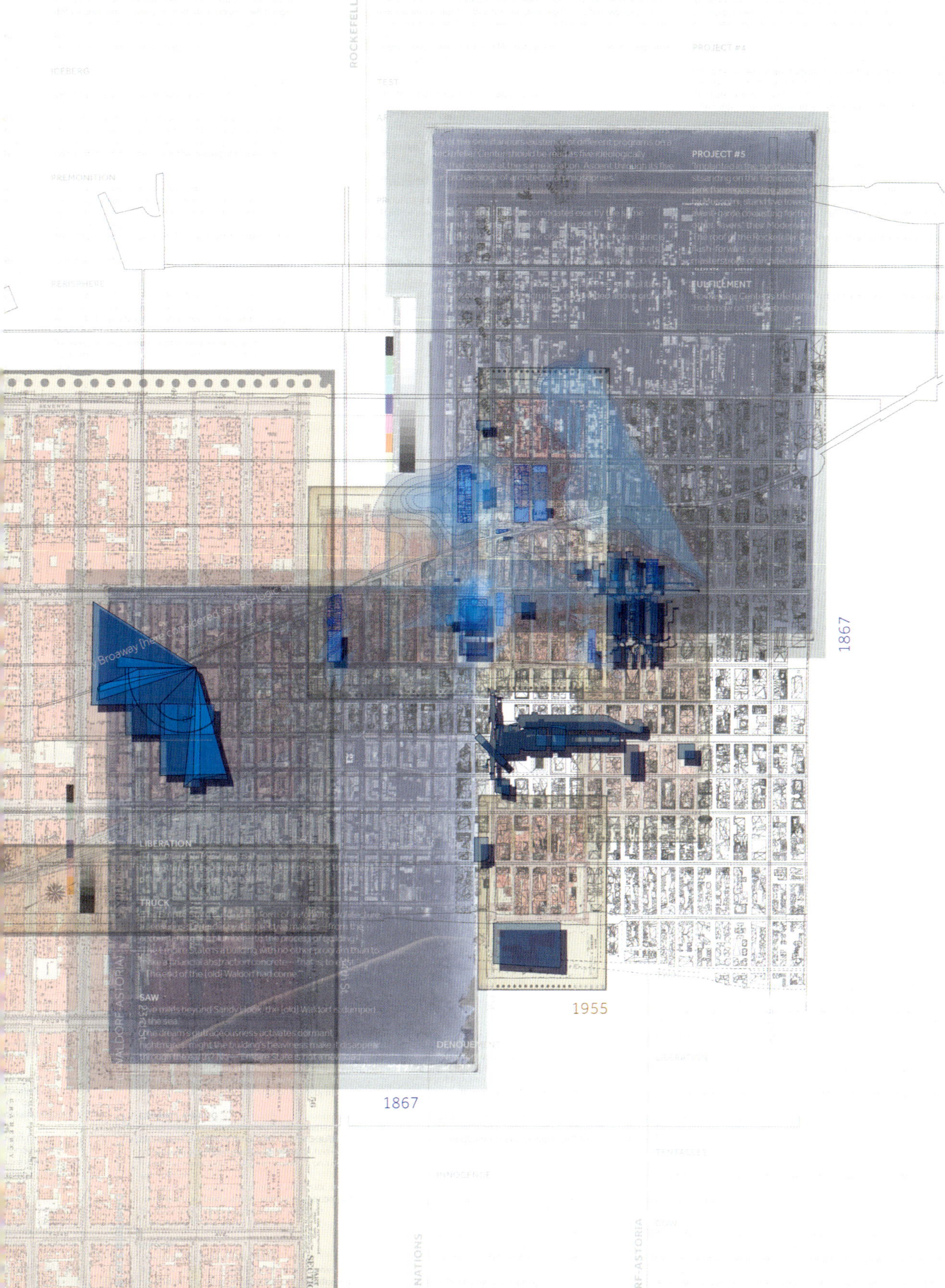
ICEBERG
PREMONITION
REHISPHERE
ROCKEFELL
TEST
PROJECT #4
PROJECT #5
FULFILLMENT
LIBERATION
TRUCK
SAW
WALDORF-ASTORIA
DENOUEMENT
1867
1955
1867

Collage of spectral Radio City in midtown

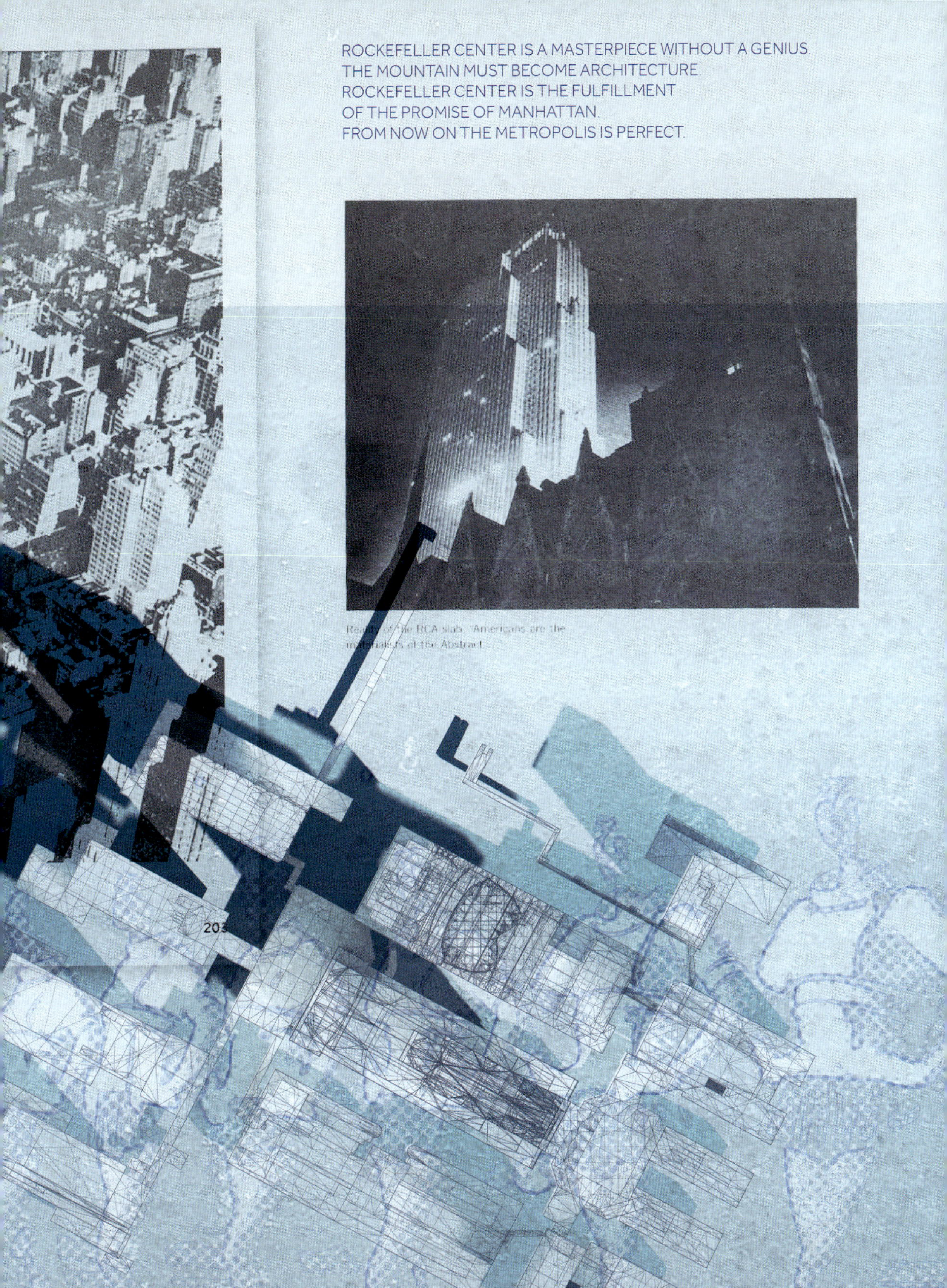

Reality of the RCA slab. "Americans are the materialists of the Abstract..."

THE EMPIRE STATE BUILDING IS THE
LAST MANIFESTATION OF
MANHATTANISM AS PURE AND
THOUGHTLESS PROCESS, THE
CLIMAX OF THE SUBCONSCIOUS
MANHATTAN. THE WALDORF IS THE
FIRST FULL REALIZATION OF THE
CONSCIOUS MANHATTAN.

luminously beautiful, had never before been imagined. One could look back on a dream well planned."*

But exactly its character of dream, of automatic architecture, prevents it from being also an example of the conquest of the Automonument by higher forms of culture.

It was and is, literally, *thoughtless.*

Its ground floor is all elevator; there is no place left between the shafts for metaphor.

The upper floors too are strictly business, for 80,000 people. Maybe a businessman finds himself puzzled by its grandiosity; secretaries gaze at vistas never before seen by man.

AIRSHIP

Only at the top is there symbolism.

"At the eighty-sixth floor level is the observation tower, a sixteen-story extension shaped like an inverted test tube, buttressed by great flanking corner piers…"

It is also an airship mooring mast and thus resolves Manhattan's paradoxical status as a city of landlocked lighthouses.

Only an airship could select its favorite harbor among all Manhattan's needles and actually dock to make the metaphorical literal once more.

DISPLACEMENT

Meanwhile, during its short period of displacement, the concept of the Waldorf continues to exist in the form of rights to its name, owned by Lucius Boomer, its last manager. It is left to him to reformulate the *tradition of the last word,* to plan and design the Waldorf's reappearance as the first Skyscraper fully conquered by social activity.

For over a century, Manhattan's lifestyle avant-garde has wandered from type to type in search of ideal accommodation. "In the beginning, private and detached houses were the only available residences for well-to-do New Yorkers. Then came the famous Brownstones, which were sometimes 'two-family' affairs; then the day of the flats arrived. Flats went up in the social scale and became 'apartments.' Next, because of their economic advantages, real or fancied, cooperative apartments had their day of favor. There then followed the vogue for Duplex apartments, with large rooms for entertaining purposes and many facilities of living that had previously been unknown…"

The stages of this quest correspond to ever greater accumulations of individual units that, however combined, do not surrender their independence,

writing unhindered by the author's critical apparatus.

The Empire State Building is a form of *automatic architecture,* a sensuous surrender by its collective makers — from the accountant to the plumber — to the process of building.

The Empire State is a building with no other program than to make a financial abstraction concrete — that is, *to exist.* All the episodes of its construction are governed by the unquestionable laws of automatism.

After the sale of the block there is a dreamlike ceremony of desecration, a performance for Truck and Hotel. "Promptly following the first announcement a motor-truck [was it driverless?] drove through the wide door which had received presidents and princes, rulers of states and uncrowned kings and queens of society. The truck, like a roaring invader, thrust its great bulk into the lobby, where surely such an invader had never been seen before. It churned across the floor, then turned and roared down 'Peacock Alley,' down that proud corridor lined with gold mirrors and velvet draperies.

"The end of the Waldorf had come."*

SAW

On October 1, 1929, demolition is formally begun. A second "act" is performed, this one for two gentlemen and a saw. With crowbars they dislodge the topmost stone of the cornice.

The destruction of the Waldorf is planned as part of the construction. Fragments that are useful remain, such as the elevator cores that now reach into the as yet immaterial floors of the Empire State: "We salvaged four passenger elevators from the old building and installed them in temporary positions in the new framework."*

Those parts that do not serve any purpose are carted off in trucks and loaded on barges. Five miles beyond Sandy Hook, the Waldorf is dumped in the sea.

The dream's outrageousness activates dormant nightmares: might the building's heaviness make it disappear through the earth? No — "Empire State is not a new load placed on bedrock. Instead, the inert load of earth and stones put there by Nature has been dug away and a useful load in the form of a building has been placed there by man."

DREAMPLANNING

According to the logic of automatism, workers on the site are described as passive, almost ornamental presences.

"… as Shreve the architect said, like an assembly line placing the

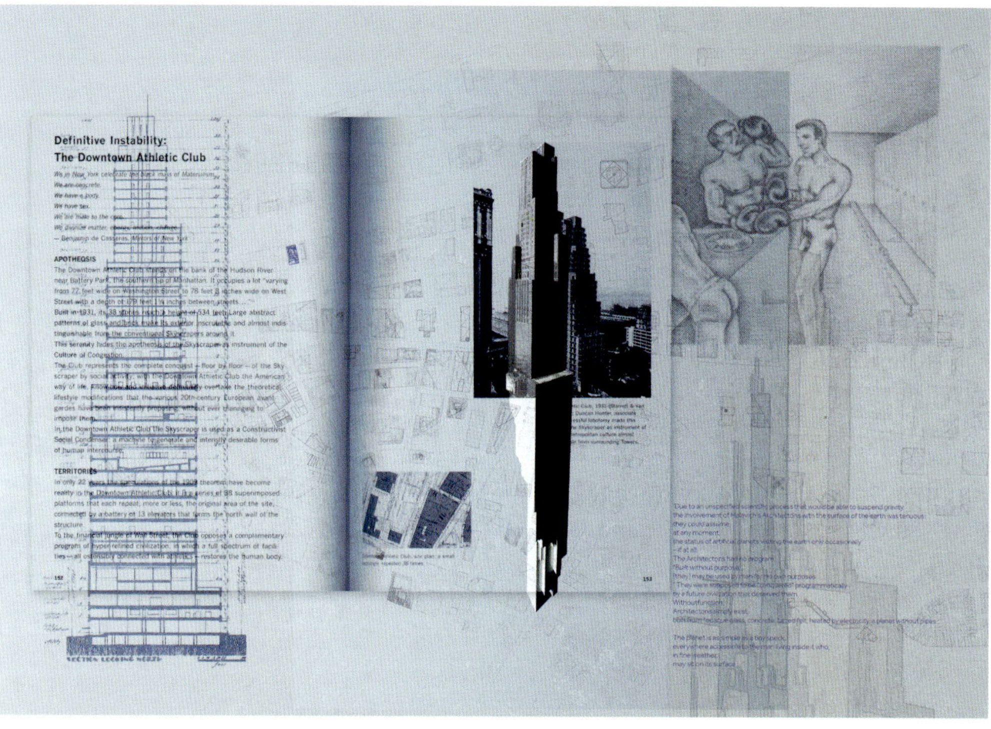

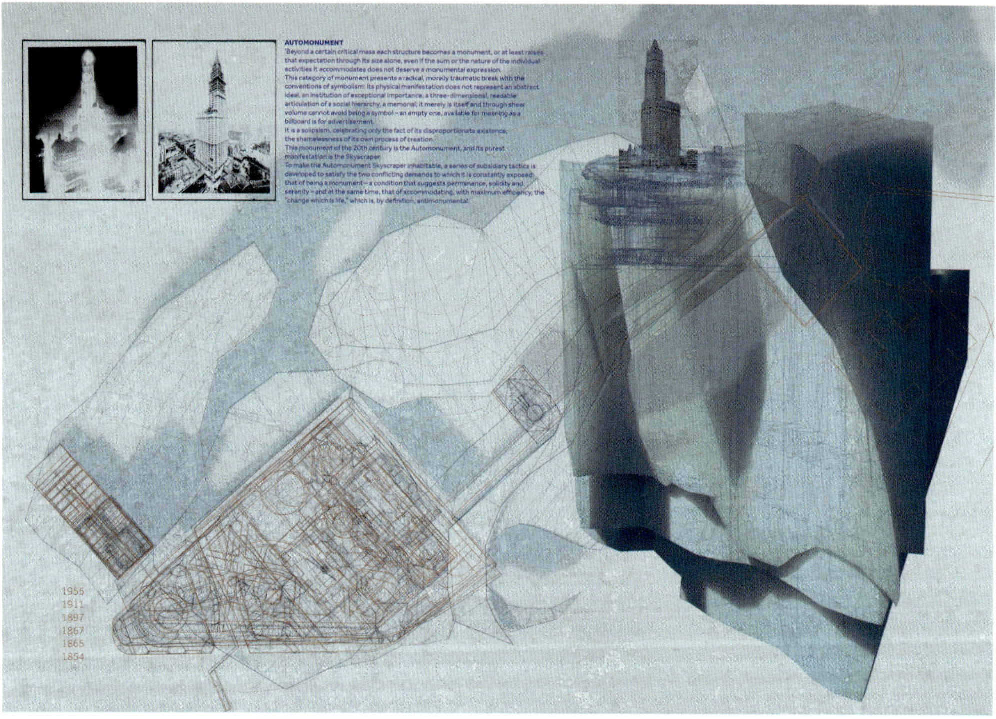

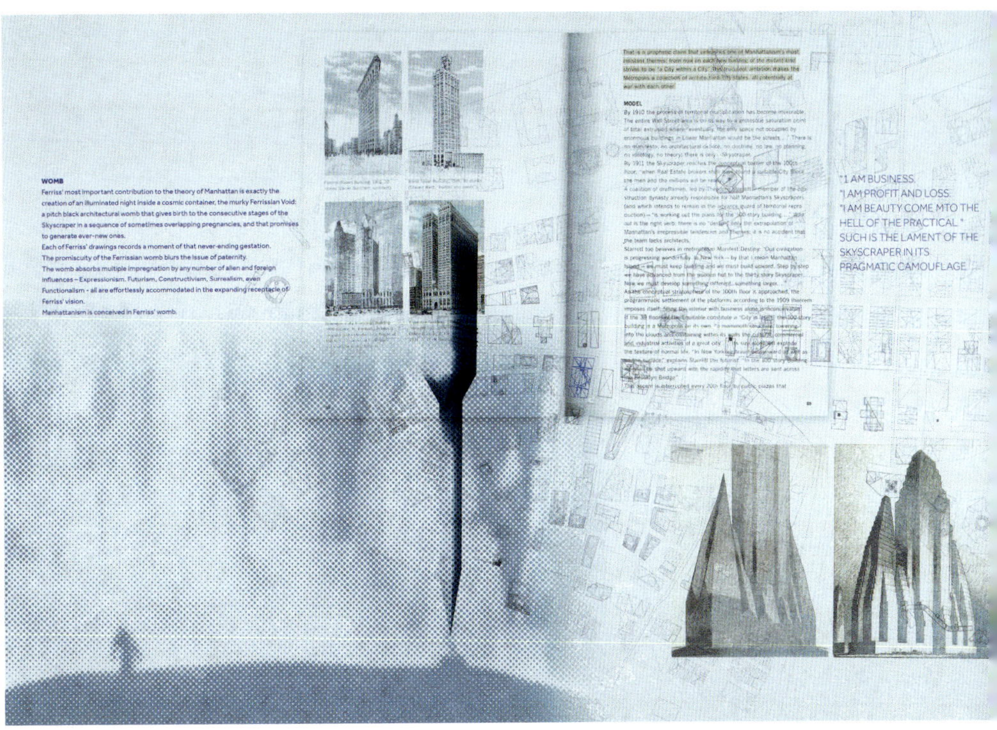

WOMB

Ferriss' most important contribution to the theory of Manhattan is exactly the creation of an illuminated night inside a cosmic container, the murky Ferrissian Void: a pitch black architectural womb that gives birth to the consecutive stages of the Skyscraper in a sequence of sometimes overlapping pregnancies, and that promises to generate ever-new ones.

Each of Ferriss' drawings records a moment of that never-ending gestation.

The promiscuity of the Ferrissian womb blurs the issue of paternity.

The womb absorbs multiple impregnation by any number of alien and foreign influences – Expressionism, Futurism, Constructivism, Surrealism, even Functionalism – all are effortlessly accommodated in the expanding receptacle of Ferriss' vision.

Manhattanism is conceived in Ferriss' womb.

"I AM BUSINESS.
"I AM PROFIT AND LOSS.
"I AM BEAUTY COME INTO THE HELL OF THE PRACTICAL."
SUCH IS THE LAMENT OF THE SKYSCRAPER IN ITS PRAGMATIC CAMOUFLAGE.

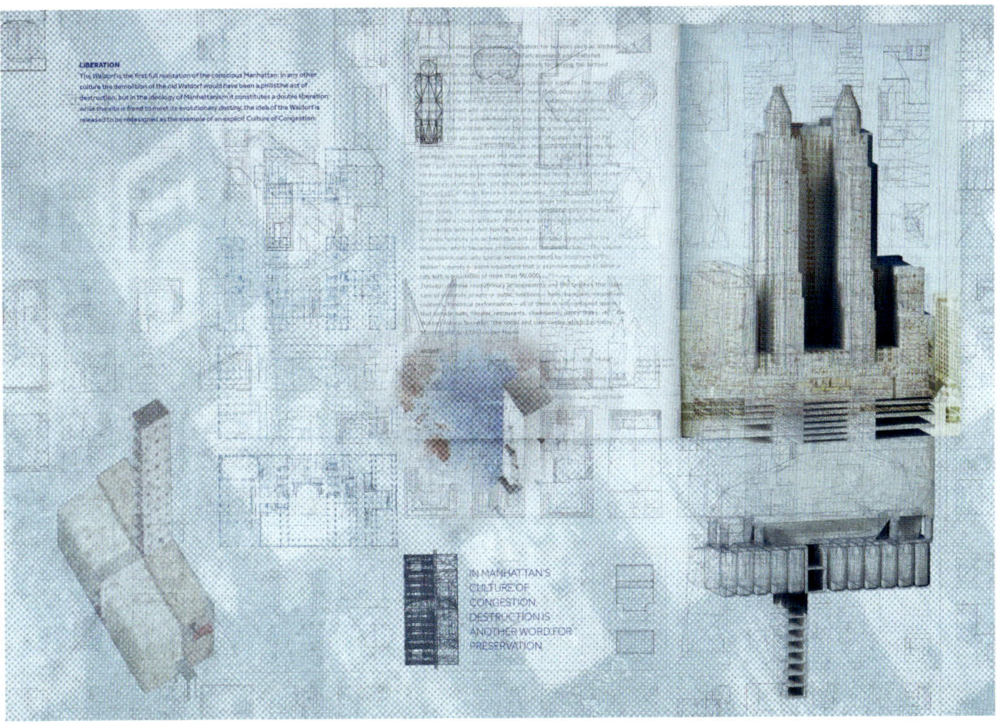

LIBERATION

The Waldorf is the first full realization of the conscious Manhattan. In any other culture the demolition of the old Waldorf would have been a philistine act of destruction, but in the ideology of Manhattanism it constitutes a double liberation: while the site is freed to meet its evolutionary destiny, the idea of the Waldorf is released to be redesigned as the example of an explicit Culture of Congestion.

Madison Square East, Ne

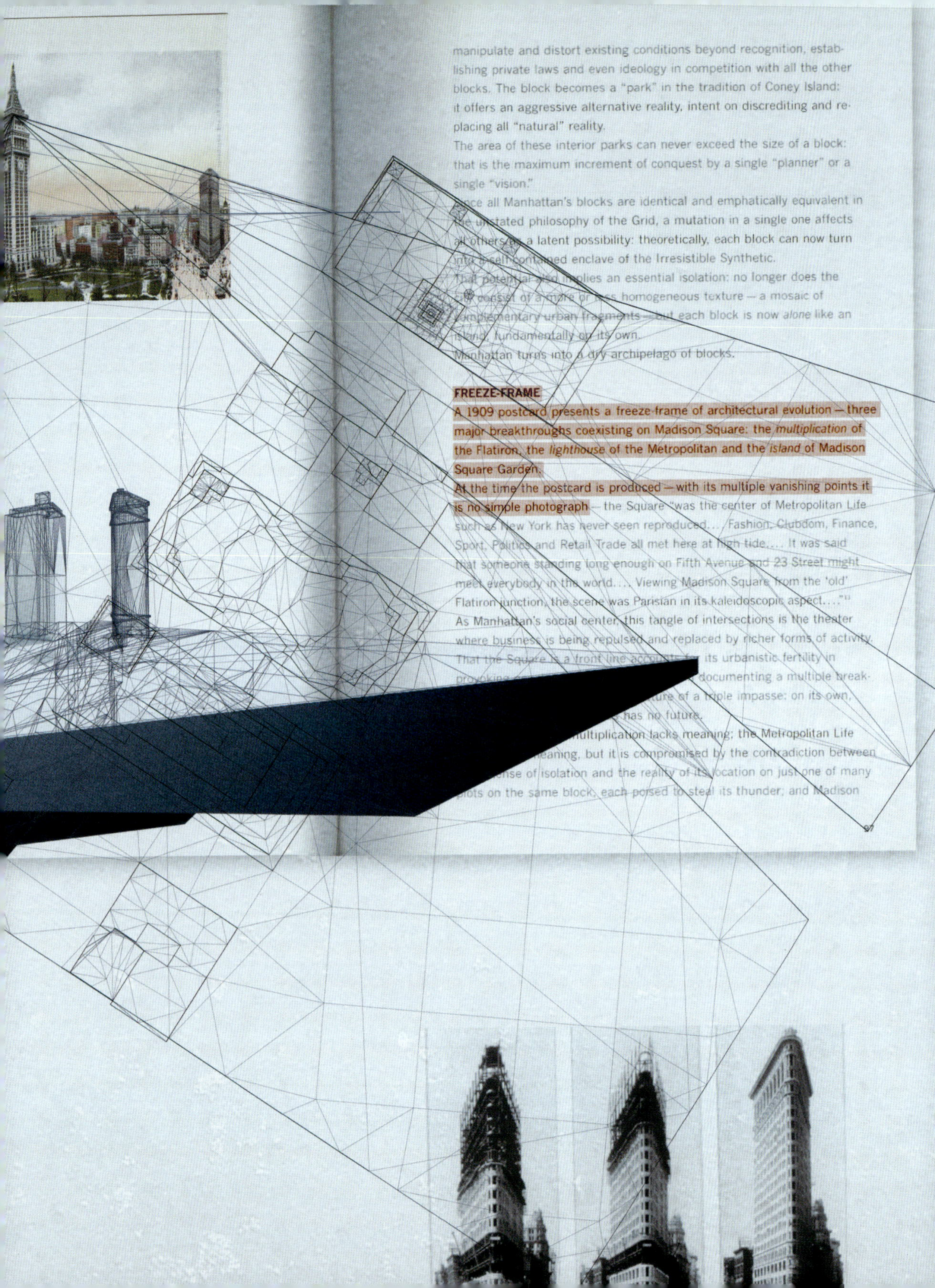

manipulate and distort existing conditions beyond recognition, establishing private laws and even ideology in competition with all the other blocks. The block becomes a "park" in the tradition of Coney Island: it offers an aggressive alternative reality, intent on discrediting and replacing all "natural" reality.

The area of these interior parks can never exceed the size of a block: that is the maximum increment of conquest by a single "planner" or a single "vision."

Since all Manhattan's blocks are identical and emphatically equivalent in the unstated philosophy of the Grid, a mutation in a single one affects all others as a latent possibility: theoretically, each block can now turn into a self-contained enclave of the Irresistible Synthetic.

That potential itself implies an essential isolation: no longer does the city consist of a more or less homogeneous texture — a mosaic of complementary urban fragments — but each block is now *alone* like an island, fundamentally on its own.

Manhattan turns into a dry archipelago of blocks.

FREEZE-FRAME

A 1909 postcard presents a freeze-frame of architectural evolution — three major breakthroughs coexisting on Madison Square: the *multiplication* of the Flatiron, the *lighthouse* of the Metropolitan and the *island* of Madison Square Garden.

At the time the postcard is produced — with its multiple vanishing points it is no simple photograph — the Square "was the center of Metropolitan Life such as New York has never seen reproduced.... Fashion, Clubdom, Finance, Sport, Politics and Retail Trade all met here at high tide.... It was said that someone standing long enough on Fifth Avenue and 23 Street might meet everybody in the world.... Viewing Madison Square from the 'old' Flatiron junction, the scene was Parisian in its kaleidoscopic aspect...."[11]

As Manhattan's social center, this tangle of intersections is the theater where business is being repulsed and replaced by richer forms of activity. That the Square is a front line accounts for its urbanistic fertility in provoking architectural breakthrough. But in documenting a multiple breakthrough, the postcard also suggests the nature of a triple impasse: on its own, each of the three structures has no future.

Without a context the Flatiron multiplication lacks meaning; the Metropolitan Life lighthouse has meaning, but it is compromised by the contradiction between its pretense of isolation and the reality of its location on just one of many lots on the same block, each poised to steal its thunder; and Madison

4.3 From Gold to Light: Quarrying Manhattan's Cultic Dimensions

Manhattanism illustrates a city that lives in a state of exuberance and exhilaration. Koolhaas' use of the PCM reinforces the suspended feeling of an alluring urban condition whose energy only increases with congestion. The architect refers to an emotional state of ecstasy, which:

> ... has generated a shameless architecture that has been loved in direct proportion to its defiant lack of self-hatred, respected exactly to the degree that it went too far.
> Manhattan has consistently inspired in its beholders ecstasy about architecture. [226]

Koolhaas's descriptions of buildings often reveal an emotional and mental state of delirium and ecstatic wonder that parallels the thrilling sense of adventure and conquering. The interior of RCMH, for example, is described as a delirious synthesis and condensation of multiple sunrises and sunsets during the duration of a single performance. The room is described as a 'vaguely uterine hemisphere whose only exit is the stage itself' and masked by a long curtain 'made of a specially developed synthetic fabric whose reflectivity makes it an acceptable substitute for the sun.' [227] The effect is intensified with the dispersion of rays from the stage curtain into the arches of the auditorium, which 'are covered in gold to better reflect the purple of the setting sun and the glow of the red velvet which Roxy insists on for the chairs.' [228] Roxy, the showbiz expert responsible for the room, resorted to gold with eloquence and sophistication to construct exuberance and augment the sensorial experiences of the exhilarated audiences. The room itself is designed to be as delirious as the shows it hosts.

The association between gold and delirium is not accidental here. Even if Koolhaas' direct references to gold in the book are circumstantial and disconnected, the alluring metal has an abundant presence in the city: in architectural details, both exterior and interior; in golden statues and paintings; and coating the crowns of skyscrapers. [229] The gilded tops of tall buildings, meaningfully inaccessible to passers-by on the street, also carry fraught spiritual connections as heavenly, perhaps galactic pointers.

Manhattan's Geotaxonomies of the Fantastic, Top view of the installation, 2018.

Gold's abundance yet inaccessibility in the city may contribute to a sense of adventurous delirium. Manhattan holds the largest known concentration of gold in the world, secured inside the subterranean vaults of the Federal Reserve Bank of New York, Downtown. Acting as the guardian and custodian of the gold belonging to nations, central banks and official international organizations, the vault represents a formidable accumulation of wealth embedded in the city's fabric and shielded in the bedrock, without which it would not be possible to hold so much weight. [230] Artists Elizabeth Ellsworth and Jamie Kruse identify the reserve bank as a place where the city's *geologic pulse* can be measured. [231] They describe the ascent from the vault as a time travel experience through cosmic and geologic time. The experience refers to the geological strata that visitors traverse, quite literally, on their way up from the inside of the vaults full of gold — a metal produced in supernovas billions of years ago, [232] even before the Earth coalesced into a terrestrial planet — through the 450-million year old Manhattan schist bedrock that supports the vault itself and the city at large, the building's exterior walls clad in Indiana limestone and Ohio sandstone, both around 350 million years old, and finally emerging on the street level where they can breathe, taste and partially see the Anthropocene. [233] The artists add:

> Here, humans instantly transform extracted and purified gold into an abstract mechanism of global exchange. The value of this rarefied geologic material has been driven by human needs and desires for thousands of years, bending cultures and civilizations around its lustrous core. [234]

The haunting presence and vast distribution of gold further contribute to what Deleuze refers to as an '"alienated, off-balance, embryonic, and hallucinatory" force which expresses a kind of deviant vitalism that is always in excess of the object and suggestive of its power to transmute living matter into forms of deadly life.' [235] In its hyperobjectonian conception, the abstraction of gold into entangled webs of capital and global markets is similar to Susan Schuppli's description of oil, whose 'smooth flows of finance capital were already pumping future dividends' for the major corporations involved in its extraction from the well. [236] Similar to oil, so too can gold be conceived across 'radically different time scales that cut across vast bio-technical and eco-social networks', and their 'image-making capacities' provide a defining 'future image … translated into a series of electronic ticker-tape digits flowing across the screens of market analysts and derivative exchanges.' [237]

Gold's power, beauty and allure have been studied and described but understanding its qualities and properties in the Anthropocene implies a more complex recognition of the metal's entanglement in networks of extraction, transformation, distribution and accumulation. [238] It also implies the acknowledgement of its massive dispersion as a chemical element, metal compound of important physical presence, civilizational and imperialist icon and instigator and destabilizer of power relations involved in socio-cultural hierarchies, including slavery, and globalized market mechanisms.

Human projects of glorifying gold and attributing to it divine-like qualities and status, of considering it the foundation, stabilizer and eventual destroyer of civilizational balances and world visions have emerged despite its un-reactivity and apparent lack of any qualities capable of operatively aiding survival. The drive for gold is not geographically, geologically, or temporally bound since it crosses different types of socio-economic collectivities across the globe and over time. Gold is a collective human fantasy, a fantasy of such a strong, rigorous and faithful pursuit as to '"discredit completely the world of reality."' [239]   Gold can be considered not only as the ultimate fantasy of a geological ground – that which will remain intact when everything else will be gone – but also the paranoid and fantastical stabilizer of capital, and therefore the ultimate logic of capitalism. In Manhattan, gold can also be a tool for understanding the gridded project of expansion, a sort of ultimate gilded paranoia.

In 'The Gold Bug' (1843), Edgar Allen Poe establishes an interesting connection between the pursuit of gold and the exhilaration of the treasure hunt – a sense of 'being bitten by a bug.' [240]   The connection supports the tracing of a long and rich literary arc where gold defines ever-expanding and more ambitious human projects of explorative endeavor. [241]

The publication of 'The Gold Bug' coincided with Poe's move to Manhattan, at a moment when the city was registering abrupt changes on the island as the grid extended northwards and around a rocky area that would become 84th Street. [242]   Even though the tale might not have been directly influenced by this territorial expansion – unlike ''The Raven', which most probably was written when Poe lived in Manhattan and during the writer's long daily walks in and around the island – Poe wrote 'The Gold Bug' after the Public Land Survey System was well underway across the United States. One might be tempted to say that, when observed retrospectively, the writings of Poe at this time incorporated, if only in a certain sense, a path to totality that aligns with an early American identity of expansion and conquering to the West. In 'The Gold Bug' the exhilarating sense of adventure with the treasure hunt can also be related to a conquering of the unknown that can lead to extreme wealth. [243]

As in most of his writing, Poe was interested in blurring reality with fiction in 'The Gold Bug.' His writing is less of a confrontation with the real and more of a realistic – as in rigorous – encounter with verisimilitude, with which he disarms the 'potential suspicions of his readers' and presents the events of the tale 'in an atmosphere of a kind of inevitability.' [244]   Such conditions of credibility are taken to an extreme in the description of the golden bug and its role in the story. The question of whether the beetle was made of gold is irrelevant to the story; the bug is not so much a valuable piece of jewelry or a rare insect but more a material trigger for an adventure leading to a treasure. An amateur entomologist and avid reader of scientific publications, Poe intentionally hybridized his bug with characteristics found in several scarab genotypes. [245] Poe's blended bug is part of a deliberate creation of a fantasy world so verisimilar as to open the possibility of '"discredit[ing] completely the world of reality."' [246] Poe's literary creations such as the bug tale may be regarded as a result of a literary PC activity.

When taken along more extreme lines of flight, exhilaration and delirium with gold can also help trace the constitution and development of a wider sense of adventure related to planetary and solar-systemic control. Gold has been an integral part of missions to outer space, either as an important element in micro-technological components, shielding surfaces coating astronaut suits and helmets, reflecting films coating telescope disks, or welcoming gifts to alien civilizations. [247]

The material conditions of gold have been often associated with solar being and becoming or cosmic renewal, as well as with an idea of life and death through a lens of energy expenditure. [248] When Georges Bataille frames the sun both as the origin of life and of its inevitable death from its unrestricted expelled energies in his 1927 essay 'The Solar Anus,' he provokes with a framing of solar propulsions as cosmic excrements. [249] In other words, the sun is conceptualized as a great cosmic anus that continuously expels matter, light and radiation, until its own stellar extinction. The sun's pure expenditure in Bataille's context is not calculated for return, an idea that can have a reasonance with the dung beetle's feces-sun movement along the Milky Way's arc. [250] Battaille's connection between gold and the sun as a support for human fantasy and delirium frames gold also as a kind of pure material expenditure.

An eventual Bataillean bug – a gilded mythological trickster as a god of the moving sun – could be conceived as the flow of energy and matter, the transformer of excremental solar energy into life, a parodic and mischievous creature whose 'selfish transgressions and their planetary consequences, like the Anthropocene itself, thoroughly undermine "any lingering notion that we can think of the environmental and social realms as separate or separable."' [251] As a trickster for alternative stories and histories of more-than-human entanglements, the gilded scarab may 'reinforce the need for humility and adaptive collaboration in the face of non-linear complexity, contingency and change in human-environmental systems', thus 'remain[ing] strikingly relevant in the Anthropocene.' [252]

Gold Haunters in the Continuous City

The new city imagined using the PCM conceptualizes gold and city as narratives of mineralogic accumulation organized stratigraphically, as well as horizons that delineate human existence towards inevitable entropy. The interchanges between the two, which can also be described as short literary exercises, are transformed into a visual narrative captured in and produced in the form of a video narrative that quietly interferes with the other fragments. The video piece can equally be thought of as an entrance into the installation.

Within the complex networks of gold's massively distributed presence across the globe, Manhattan emerges as a territory of extreme accumulation in space and time, with consequences both on a material level – with the necessary support offered by the bedrock to its accumulated weight – and on a symbolic level – with the iconographies of gold associated with the city's exuberance and exhilaration. From an Anthropocenic point of view, one that accepts the collision between earth and human temporalities, it becomes important to explore more-than-human interchanges that result from the collision between gold's extremely vast temporal and material frames and the city's also very vast, albeit more localized, ones. Yet, this collision does not mean that both material presences operate across similar scales. The idea of using gold as a delineator of the city exists in tension with its expansion on a grid. Even though both can be read in relation to logics of captivity, gold accumulates in specific deposits – either naturally or vaulted after extraction; it is located in specific geographic and geologic conditions of the earth. A grid, on the other hand, is formulated as a theoretically infinite mode of expansion. Both can be paths to totality, but gold is associated with accumulation while the grid is associated with expansion.

Rather than attempting to resolve this tension, the proposed methods of plotting the city accept their complex entanglement across intrinsically interconnected and multidimensional conditions. The design exploration seeks to work through the tension to conceive and develop the *Geotaxonomies*. Both gold and city grid become parallel conceptual probes towards the generation of the architectural fragments embedded in their contexts. Some fragments result from a site-specific quarrying and extrusion of present and past occupancies, while others expand beyond their initial architectural footprint, scoping for contextual conditions beyond them.

The exploration also attempts to notice, bear witness and make sense of Koolhaas's architectural descriptions. As mentioned before, it is then paralleled with a cartographic analysis of present and past occupancies, with which it then becomes possible to creatively extrude new contextual and stratified city fragments.

Given the character of this design methodology, sometimes necessarily loose or seemingly untidy, other times metonymic in the way it unfolds a constructed argument, the preference is to call it a methodological narrative. This is also related to the use of video as the media to narrate the eventual expansion and collision of scales between gold and the city.

The methodological narrative allows for the registration of two potentially meaningful intensities in the temporal and material frames of gold and the city. The first explores gold as a material of the geologic distributed across multiple stratigraphic horizons. The same stratigraphic idea is used to read the city, in which case the delineations resemble properties associated with mineralogic accumulation. [253]

The second intensity explores the idea of gold as a material trigger for a sense of delirious adventure that may power notions of urban progress. In Manhattan, progress has been associated with the idea of *creative destruction*. [254] Here it is studied also as a force of both expansion across the territory and of architectural extrusion.

Throughout the process it becomes possible to notice some of the typological conditions that frame the extracted fragments and how they repeat or diffract from each other. These new formations receive the name of *Geotaxonomies,* and they reveal an investment less in their own specificities than in the types of contexts they activate. They reveal typologies of context, which are then categorized pseudo-taxonomically.

Once quarried, analyzed and materialized, the *Geotaxonomies* are displaced a first time: they are rotated and realigned along a newly defined north-south axis centered on Madison Square Park and cutting across the city. Finally, they are captured inside a three-dimensional gridded megastructure extruded from the axis. The conception of the megastructure explores a specific formulation of *Continuous Monument*, albeit lighter and more translucent.

The dislocation of the city fragments from their initial position in the fields is explored through iterative drawing. The resulting process originates the *Continuous City*, which crosses Manhattan. Now freed from their original spatio-temporal contexts, the *Geotaxonomies* can find new relations of proximity, affinity and kinship with each other.

Continuous City is not a finished city. Rather, it aims to be yet a new city fragment that forges new scalar relations with the city and its geological and atmospheric conditions. It holds the potential either to be ejected into space, like *Einstein Tomb*, or to be chained to other continuous cities until it completes a lower orbit around the earth, like *Continuous Monument*. The delirious city was momentarily suspended in the exhibition through the material properties of light, paper and plastic. But it existed more fluidly before and after the exhibition.

The installation is a core part of the design exploration, and not the result of a subsequent set of editorial and curatorial decisions made necessary to exhibit the work. The creation and development of the city fragments ran in tandem with the creation and development of the architectural fragmentary constituents of the installation itself. Through this proposed and practiced imbrication, two observations are made: first, through this tight relationship, the installation constitutes architecture in its own right. Second, the use of the PCM is encouraged and explored to a point where it reinforces the idea of a new city being created.

While initially proposed for the front space of Tent Gallery, with a large window looking out onto the street, a desire to control light intensity and darkness motivated the relocation of the installation to a pitch-black space in the back of the gallery. This intentional move required a rearrangement of the exhibited fragments to enact some of the anticipated interferences between them. These interferences – as well as the initially assumed control of light – were determining factors in the construction and disposition of the installed constituents.

Though deeply connected, the exhibited fragments are organized under four main moments: a video piece; two concertina drawings; a thick field drawing of *Continuous City*; and two collections of framed images. The moments are explained below, yet these descriptions cannot substitute any in-person sensorial experience of the installation. The impossibility of offering such experience is also explored later.

The U-shaped table supporting the field drawing with *Continuous City* and the two concertina drawings was conceived to be walked around, potentially creating experiential moments of feeling outside and inside of it, or as least embraced by its extended arms. The central part of the table was designed to accommodate the field drawing and a model on top, while each of the arms received a concertina drawing. The U-shape also allows these drawings to be contemplated from nearly all sides, an important component of the experience, since none of these drawings prescribes a specific orientation.

The design of the supporting legs in a dark and gridded metal alloy is motivated by the design of the megastructure for *Continuous City*. The legs gesture towards the possibility of infinite extension, whilst also physically supporting the new city, and establish some form of connection to the ground, even if only metaphorical. This investment also motivates the distance between the legs as well as their alignment. The same system is devised for the two small stands holding the video projectors, with the idea of creating a horizontal datum in the room that could make a distinction between the illuminated conditions above the surfaces and the dark ones below them. Rather than advocating for any conceptual segregation between the city surface and its undercrofts – something defended by Koolhaas himself – the intent here is to explore and finally enact a distinction between the exhibited fragments and the technological machines and electrical equipment necessary to illuminate and project them. But by keeping the dark layer beneath the surface open, the creation also provides a glimpse of that infrastructural need, perhaps coming closer to Vriesendorp's representational approach.

The video piece explores relations between gold and the city as stratigraphic delineators. The narrative at two complementary tempos is projected onto two back-to-back screens, each focusing on a material condition.

The central field drawing activates Koolhaas' congested conditions in Downtown and Midtown. The drawing results from an iterative process of plotting the book onto a new city and through successive etchings that erode the paper conditions and create micro-topographies, as well as moments of light and darkness. The continuous subtraction of the architectures on the thick paper via a laser beam denotes moments of progressive collapse of the drawing itself, no longer able to support the pressure of the hot light on some of these carved absences. Standing directly on top of the field drawing and aligned with the north-south axis, *Continuous City* extrudes in an axial gridded megastructure built in translucent acrylic. *Continuous City* reveals the capturing of the *Geotaxonomies*, this time recrystallized in their new positions.

The two concertina drawings focus on two key moments of the design process. The first investigates how the city fragments were identified amongst the Koolhaasian fields and explores possibilities for their extrusion tangled with their context. Since the architectures are drawn out from their initial positions in the city, it becomes possible to understand any existing relations between them. The second drawing explores new configurations of the *Geotaxonomies* captured inside *Continuous City*. Both drawings are section-elevations cutting across computer-generated meshes, which solely depict the fragments without any other city context. The development of computerized meshes becomes important for their representational value in reinforcing the conceptualization of the city as a mineralogic agglomeration. As part of the process of assembling the sections, a series of textual annotations orbit around the depictions and explain both how they exist in the Koolhaasian imagined world, and also how they inform the pseudo-taxonomical organization of the equally fantastical *Geotaxonomies*. The concertina quality of the drawings is perhaps meaningful to open a conversation about the impossibility of grasping a city in its totality. This condition of a deliberately truncated sense of wholeness is exacerbated by the table's extended arms, too short in their length to eventually allow for the complete unfolding of the drawings. Without trying to force an anecdotal moment when standing before the drawings – one where the drawings are not totally unfolded only because the tables do not allow it – the interest in making the tables shorter than the drawings relates more to a suggestion that architectural fragments may exist in the same way as the city. One could equally say that the fragmented drawings representing city fragments contribute to an idea of the city in the same way as the city contributes to ideas of itself.

Standing on opposite walls in the room, each of the two collections of framed drawings further explore the potential of the megastructure to constitute a new fantastical city by either extending beyond Manhattan to eventually embrace the curvature of the Earth or by becoming a satellite orbiting around the terrestrial globe. [255]

The reduced material palette of the design production determines a horizontal datum made of paper representations and a vertical one made of projections and lights cast on acrylic. Both datums interfere with the extruded city, but in different ways. Giving particular attention to the flatness of both the horizontal paper drawings and the vertical acrylic screens, one becomes aware of how extrusion is not just enacted via the thickening of the architectural fragments through stratification, but also projected and necessarily distorted and compressed onto the two-dimensionality of the flat depictions. In other words, extrusion is an integral part not only of the thickness but also of the thinness of the installation. Here, once again, the meshes resulting from computer modelling prove to be effective in registering a great number of layers with enough transparency to let them affect the overall qualities of the representations. Equally important are the representational techniques

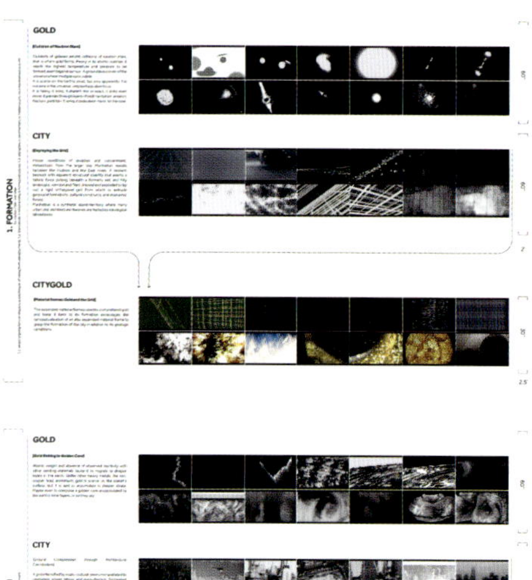

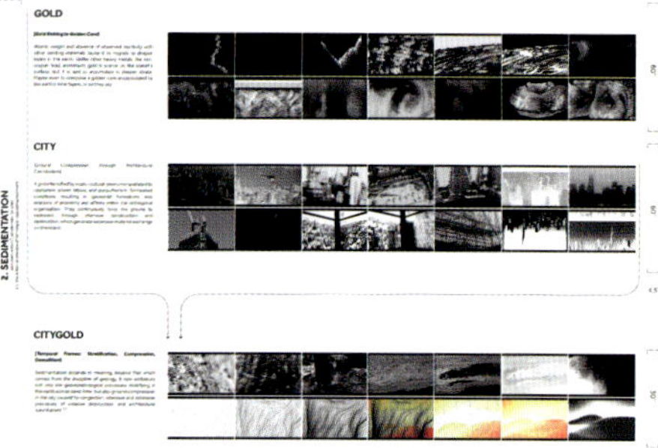

Horizons of Human Entropy, 2018.
The composite image includes still images from the video piece produced as a fragment in the installation.
(next pages) *Continuous City* and views of the installation.

explored through the process of drawing out the city fragments. Axonometric representations of the city are deliberately avoided to give the plan and the deep section not only more prominence in their interrelated architectonic relationship, but also the possibility for them to forge expected and unexpected contextual relationships.

Standing in a pitch-black room, where light cast onto the exhibition generates unexpected effects of distortion, reflection, refraction and spilling, the architectural fragments also distort common senses of scale. Each of the fragments is not only a representational device of Manhattan at a certain determined scale, but also a 1:1 conceptual architecture in its own right. Besides these two sets of scales, the relations forged by interferences between the installation's fragments – including via their projection onto one another and onto the black walls – generate other types of unexpected scales, either through sections enveloping the room, spills of light shards onto the ceiling, or even the field and zoom effects of the lenses in the camera apparatuses trying to capture them. These moments, living between deliberate creation and unexpected imbrication, distort scale itself, as well as the notions of space and time one progressively acquires in the installation. This third set of scales reinforces the possibility for discrediting the real; these scales reinforce a distorted sense of reality through which the imagination of the new city in the exhibition is reinforced.

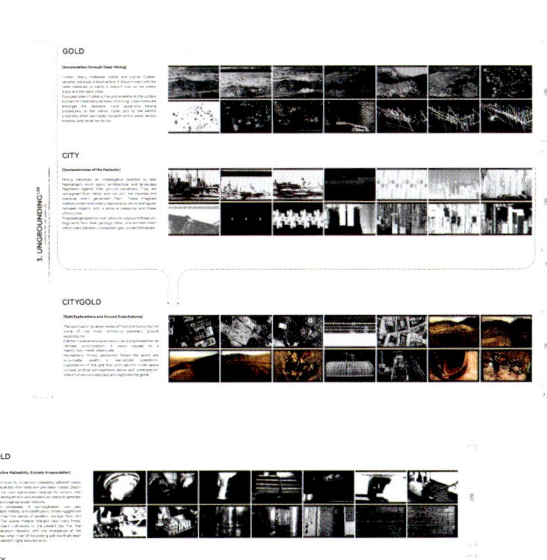

Of all the floors, the interior golf course[…] the extreme undertaking[…] The Skyscraper ha[…] Nature into Junior Nature.

INCUBATOR

THE NEW YORKER

[…] the new World Trade Center […] is pretty dazzling […] its long isosceles, mirrored faceting giving it the illusion of being torqued, twisted right, even as you stare at it—a look that, in the past, was called futuristic.

THE NEW YORK TIMES

[…] the 14-foot-diameter "sky portal" […] looks as if it is suspended over the streets below … The portal's glass floor is actually looking down on two dozen high-definition screens carrying a live feed from cameras mounted at the base of the building's spire. But the illusion is unnervingly convincing.

"You look out, and on a clear day, you can actually see the curvature of the Earth."

In truth, one has to be quite a bit higher than 1,268 feet to discern the curvature of the Earth. But One World Observatory is about showmanship, after all.

THE NEW YORKER

A celebration of liberty tightly policed; a cemetery that cowers in the shadow of commerce; an insistence that we are here to remember and an ambition to let us tell you what to recall; the boast that we have completely started over and the promise that we will never forget.

Although officially described as "reflecting pools," they are not pools, and they leave no room for reflection. Wildly out of scale with the rest of the site in their immensity, they are subterranean waterfalls—two huge sinks spilling chlorinated water from their edges, which then flows up and over a smaller platform at their center, and down the drain, only to rise and be recycled. Their constant roar interrupts any elegiac feeling that the lists of engraved names of the dead which enclose them might engender. In the pattern of falling, draining, and recycling, the sinks feel symbolically unsettled, too. Perpetuity is a favorite theme of memorial sites—that eternal flame on J.F.K.'s grave—but, emotively, these seem to suggest less the promise of eternal memory and more a cycle of endless loss and waste.

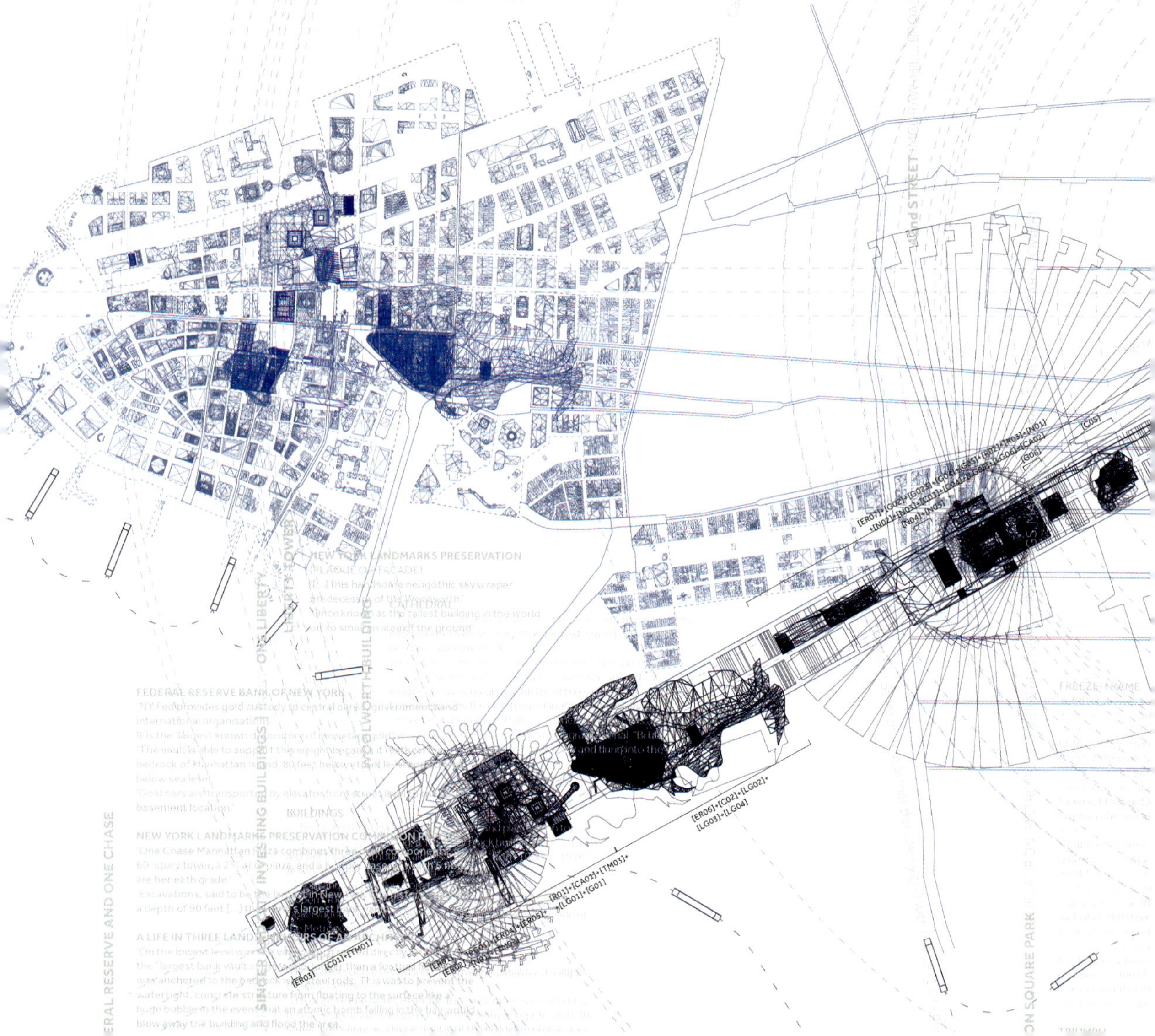

SPHERE

CONTRAST

THEORY

GØLD

TRIUMPH

SHADOW

LAW

VILLAGE

EQUITABLE BUILDING (1915) | ZONING LAW (1916)

WORLD TRADE CENTER, 9/11 MEMORIAL AND PATH INTERFACE

… TOWER, AMERICAN RADIATOR, BRYANT PARK, NY PUBLIC LIBRARY

ONE LIBERTY | LIBERTY TOWER | WOOLWORTH BUILDING | SINGER BUILDING | INVESTING BUILDINGS

NEW YORK LANDMARKS PRESERVATION (PLAQUE ON FACADE)

[…] this handsome neogothic skyscraper … predecessor of the Woolworth.

CATHEDRAL

once known as the tallest building in the world … on so small an area of the ground

FEDERAL RESERVE BANK OF NEW YORK

NY Fed provides gold custody to central banks, governments and international organisations.

It is the largest known depository of monetary gold.

The vault is able to support this weight because it rests on the bedrock of Manhattan Island, 80 feet below street level, below sea level.

Gold bars are transported by elevator from street level to the basement location.

NEW YORK LANDMARKS PRESERVATION COMMISSION

One Chase Manhattan Plaza combines three […] components […] 60-story tower, a 2½-acre plaza, and a 6-story base of which five are beneath grade.

Excavations, said to be the largest in New York […] a depth of 90 feet […]

A LIFE IN THREE LANDMARKS / COLOURS OF AN ARCHITECT

On the lowest level was the vault […] built directly […] the largest bank vault […] larger than a football field […] was anchored to the bedrock with steel rods. This was to prevent the watertight, concrete structure from floating to the surface like a huge bubble in the event that an atomic bomb falling in the bay would blow away the building and flood the area.

FEDERAL RESERVE AND ONE CHASE

[ER07]+[G06]+[G02]+[NG06]

[ER06]+[C02]+[LG02]+[LG03]+[LG04]

[R01]+[CA01]+[TM03]+[LG01]+[G01]

[ER03]   [C01]+[TM01]   [ER02]+[N01]+[TM02]+[ER05]

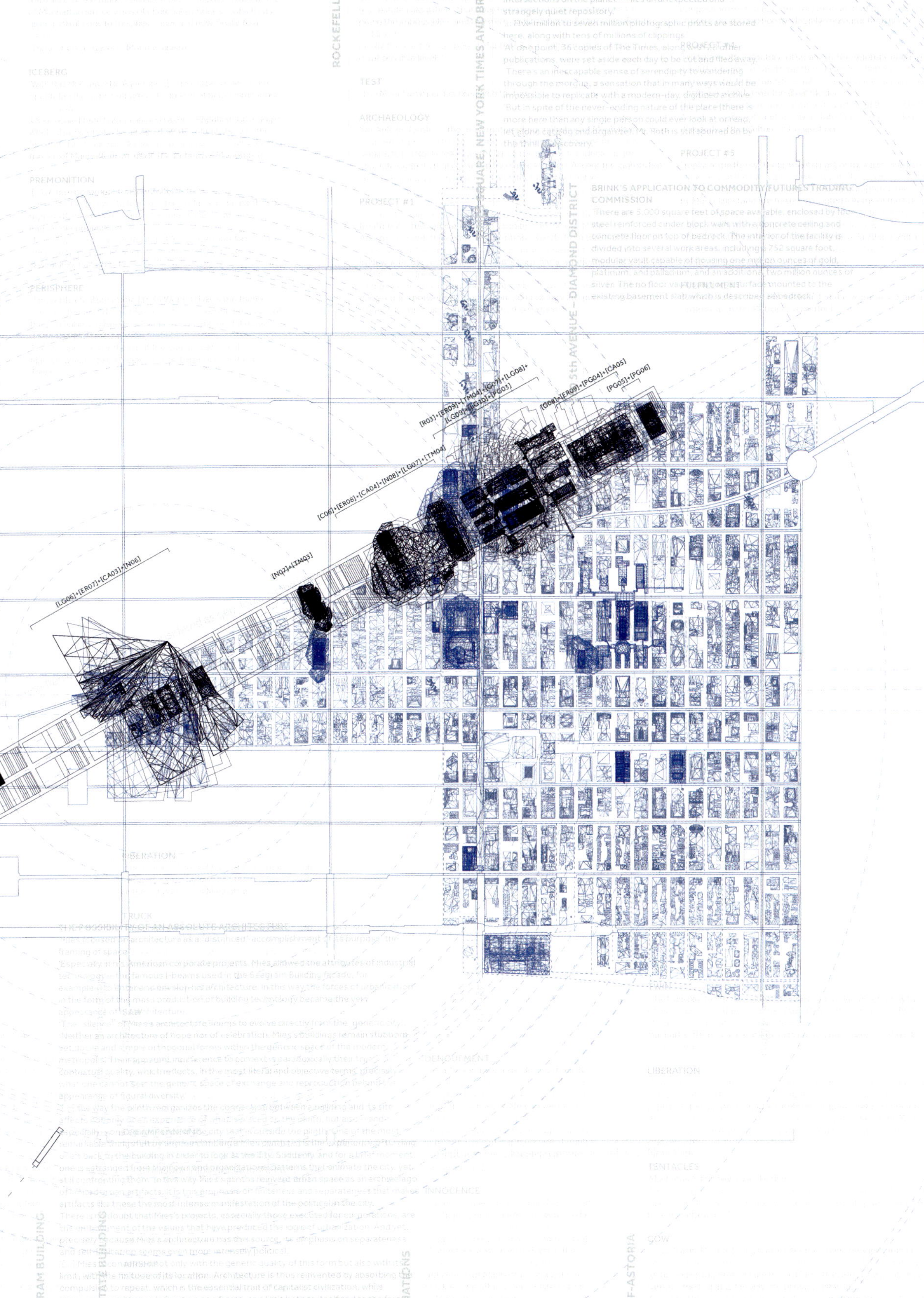

ROCKEFELL
TEST
ARCHAEOLOGY
PROJECT #1
PREMONITION
PERISPHERE
ICEBERG
5TH AVENUE – DIAMOND DISTRICT
SQUARE, NEW YORK TIMES AND BR
PROJECT #4
PROJECT #5

intersections on the planet... lies an unexpected and strangely quiet repository.
Five million to seven million photographic prints are stored here, along with tens of millions of clippings.
At one point, 36 copies of The Times, along... other publications, were set aside each day to be cut and filed away.
There's an inescapable sense of serendipity to wandering through the morgue, a sensation that in many ways would be impossible to replicate with a modern-day, digitized archive.
But in spite of the never-ending nature of the place (there is more here than any single person could ever look at or read, let alone catalog and organize), Mr. Roth is still spurred on by... the thrill of discovery.

BRINK'S APPLICATION TO COMMODITY FUTURES TRADING COMMISSION
There are 5,000 square feet of space available, enclosed by foot... steel reinforced cinder block walls, with a concrete ceiling and concrete floor on top of bedrock. The interior of the facility is divided into several work areas, including a 752 square foot, modular vault capable of housing one million ounces of gold, platinum, and palladium, and an additional two million ounces of silver. The no floor va... surface mounted to the existing basement slab, which is described as bedrock...

TRUCK
THE POSSIBILITY OF AN ABSOLUTE ARCHITECTURE
Mies focused on architecture as a "distanced" accomplishment of its purpose: the framing of space.
Especially in his American corporate projects, Mies allowed the attributes of industrial technology — the famous I-beams used in the Seagram Building facade, for example — to enter and envelop his architecture. In this way the forces of urbanization in the form of the mass production of building technology became the very appearance of his architecture.
The "shape" of Mies's architecture seems to evolve directly from the generic city. Neither an architecture of hope nor of celebration, Mies's buildings remain stubborn, yet supple and simple orthogonal forms within the generic space of the modern metropolis. Their apparent indifference to context is paradoxically their truest contextual quality, which reflects, in the most literal and objective terms precisely what one cannot see: the generic space of exchange and reproduction behind the appearance of figural diversity.
The way the plinth reorganizes the connection between building and its site affects not only the experience of what is placed on the plinth, but also — and especially — one's experience of the city that is outside the plinth. One of the most remarkable things felt by anyone climbing onto a Mies plinth is the experience of turning oneself back to the building in order to look at the city. Suddenly, and for a brief moment, one is estranged from the flows and organizational patterns that animate the city, yet still confronting them. In this way Mies's plinths reinvent urban space as an archipelago of individual artifacts. It is this emphasis on finiteness and separateness that makes artifacts like these the most intense manifestation of the political in the city.
There is no doubt that Mies's projects, especially those executed for corporations, are the embodiment of the values that have predicted the logic of urbanization. And yet, precisely because Mies's architecture has one source, its emphasis on separateness and self-limitation seems even more urgently political.
Mies... is concerned not only with the generic quality of this form but also with its limit, with the finitude of its location. Architecture is thus reinvented by absorbing the compulsion to repeat, which is the essential trait of capitalist civilization, while increasing architecture's function as a frame, as a limit both to itself and to the forces...

LIBERATION
DEMOLISHMENT
TENTACLES
INNOCENCE
COW
WALDORF-ASTORIA
STATE BUILDING
GRAM BUILDING
NATIONS

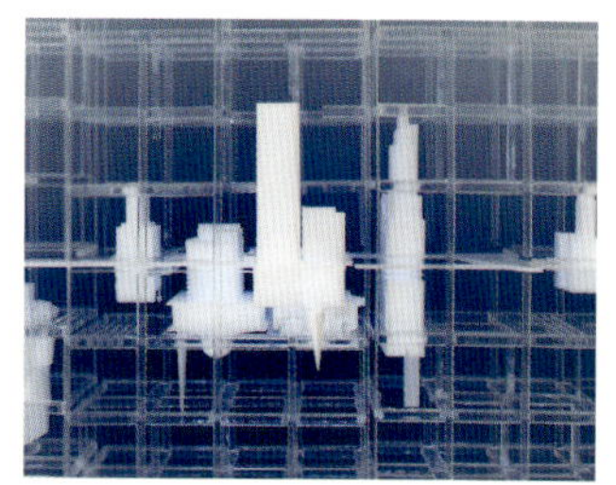

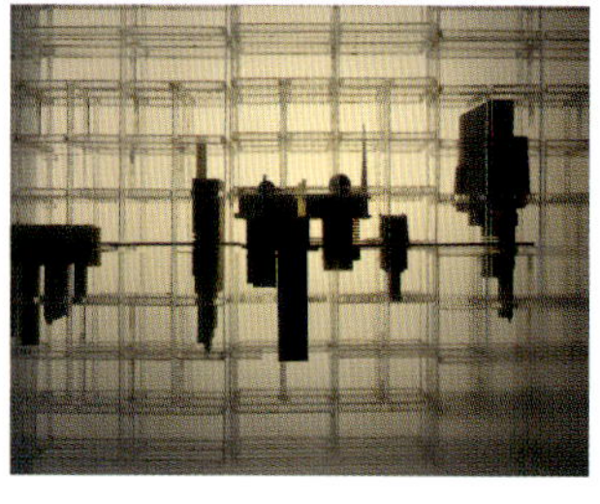

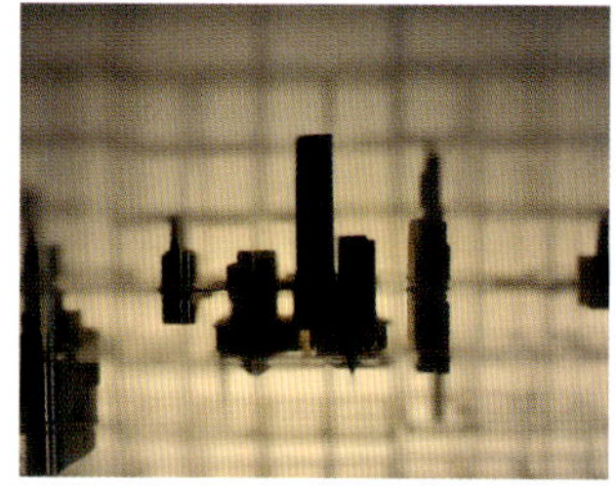

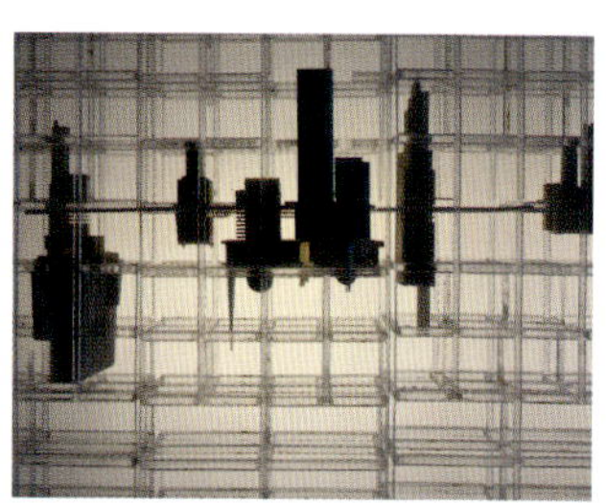

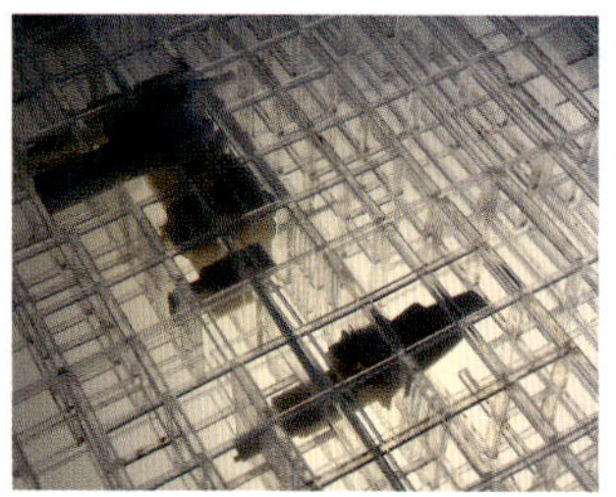

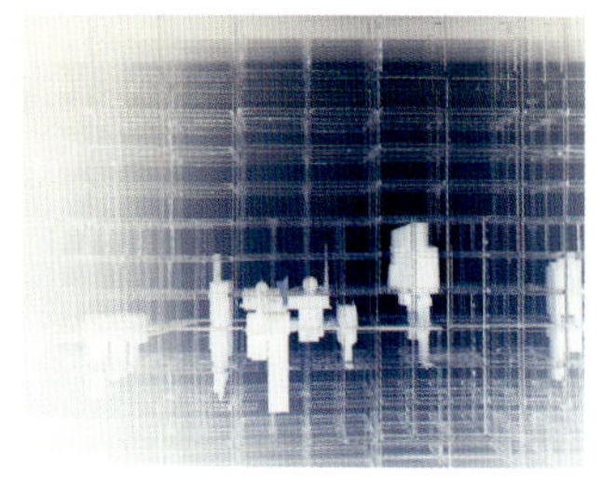

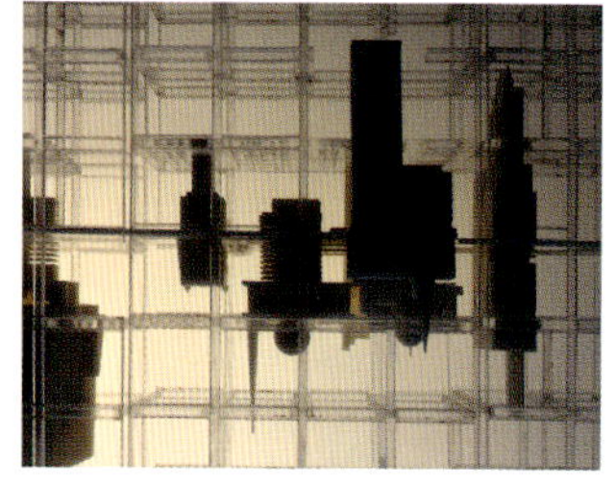

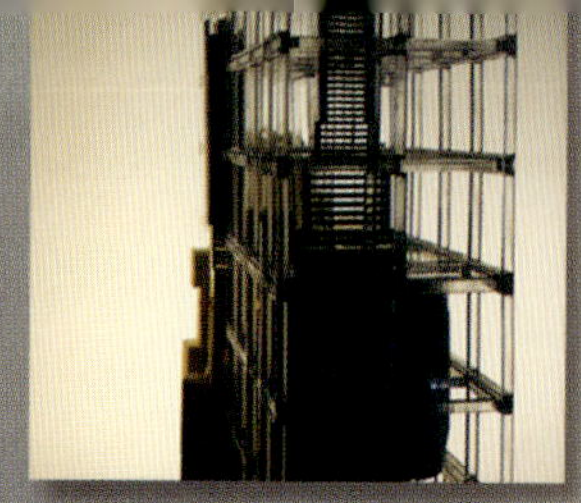

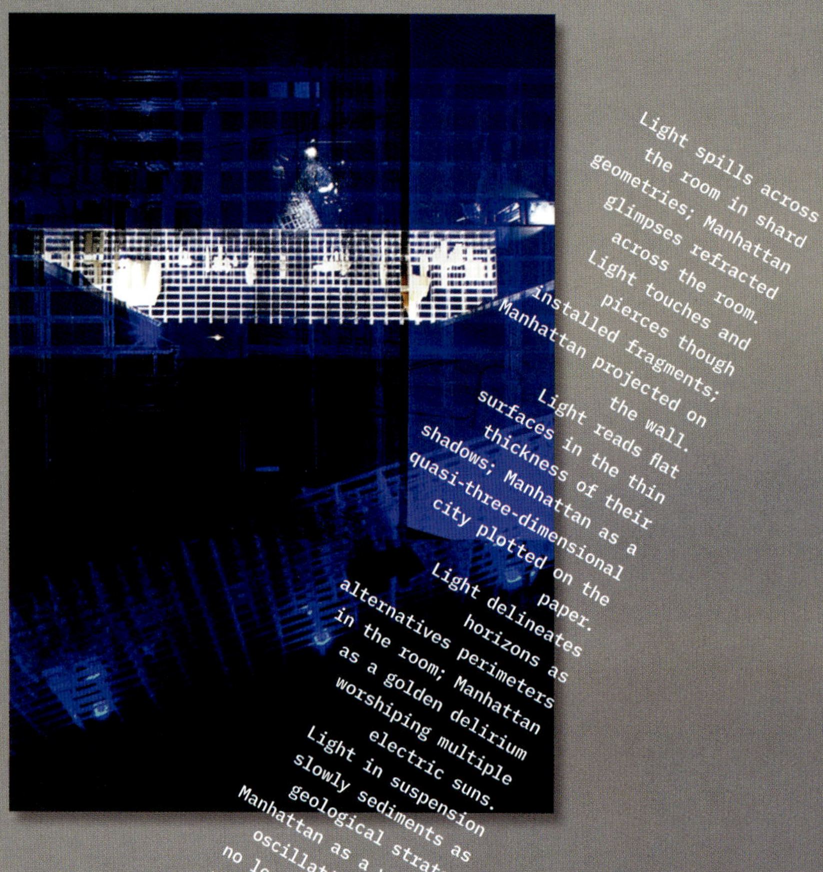

Light spills across the room in shard geometries; Manhattan glimpses refracted across the room. Light touches and pierces though installed fragments; Manhattan projected on the wall.

Light reads flat surfaces in the thin thickness of their shadows; Manhattan as a quasi-three-dimensional city plotted on the paper.

Light delineates horizons as alternatives perimeters in the room; Manhattan as a golden delirium worshiping multiple electric suns.

Light in suspension slowly sediments as geological strata; Manhattan as a vibrant oscillation between no longer being wave-particle city but not yet geological strata either.

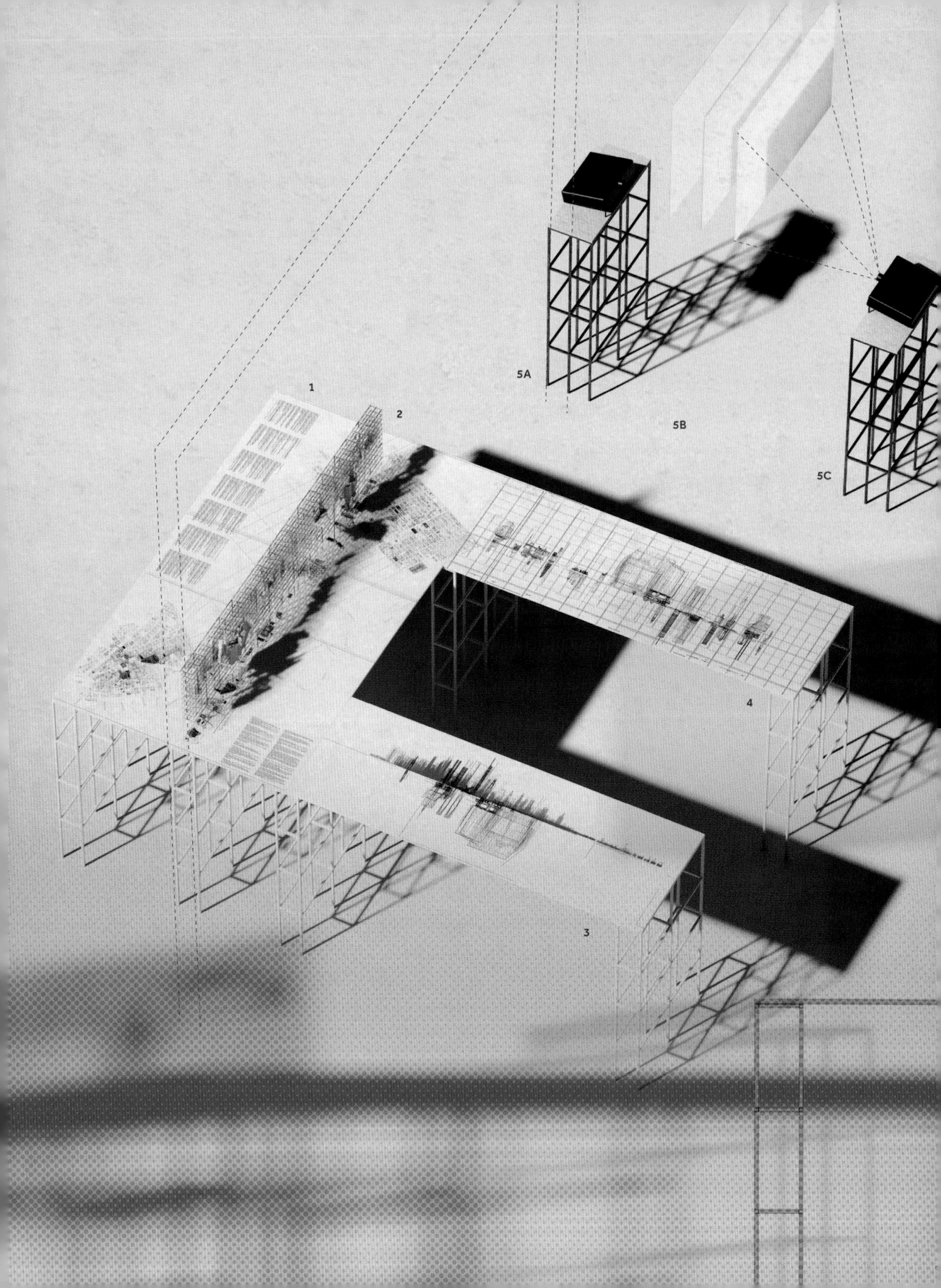

1
2
3
4
5A
5B
5C

[1] Field Drawing
[2] Megastructure with Continuous City
[3] Concertina Drawing exploring the Ungrounding of the Geotaxonomies
[4] Concertina Drawing exploring the Recrystallization of the Geotaxonomies
[5] Video Apparatus
[A] City | Projector 1
[B] Translucent Sreens
[C] Gold | Projector 2

[1] Field Drawing
[2] *Megastructure* with Continuous City
[3] Concertina Drawing exploring the *Ungrounding* of the Geotaxonomies
[4] Concertina Drawing exploring the *Recrystallization* of the Geotaxonomies
[5] *Recrystallization* | Framed Drawings
[6] *Emission* | Framed Drawings
[7] Video Apparatus
    [A] City | Projector 1
    [B] Translucent Sreens
    [C] Gold | Projector 2

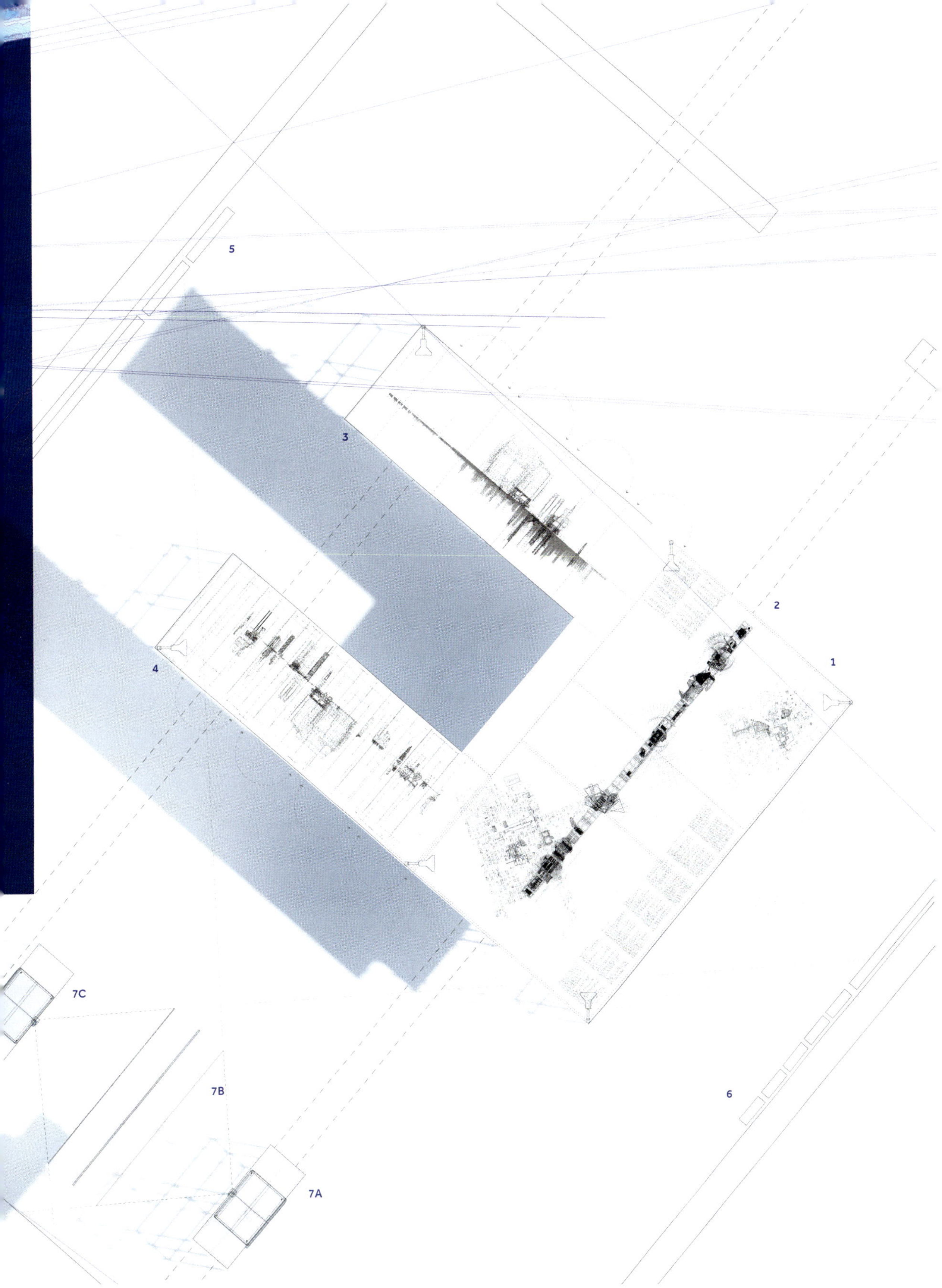

1
2
3
4
5
6
7A
7B
7C

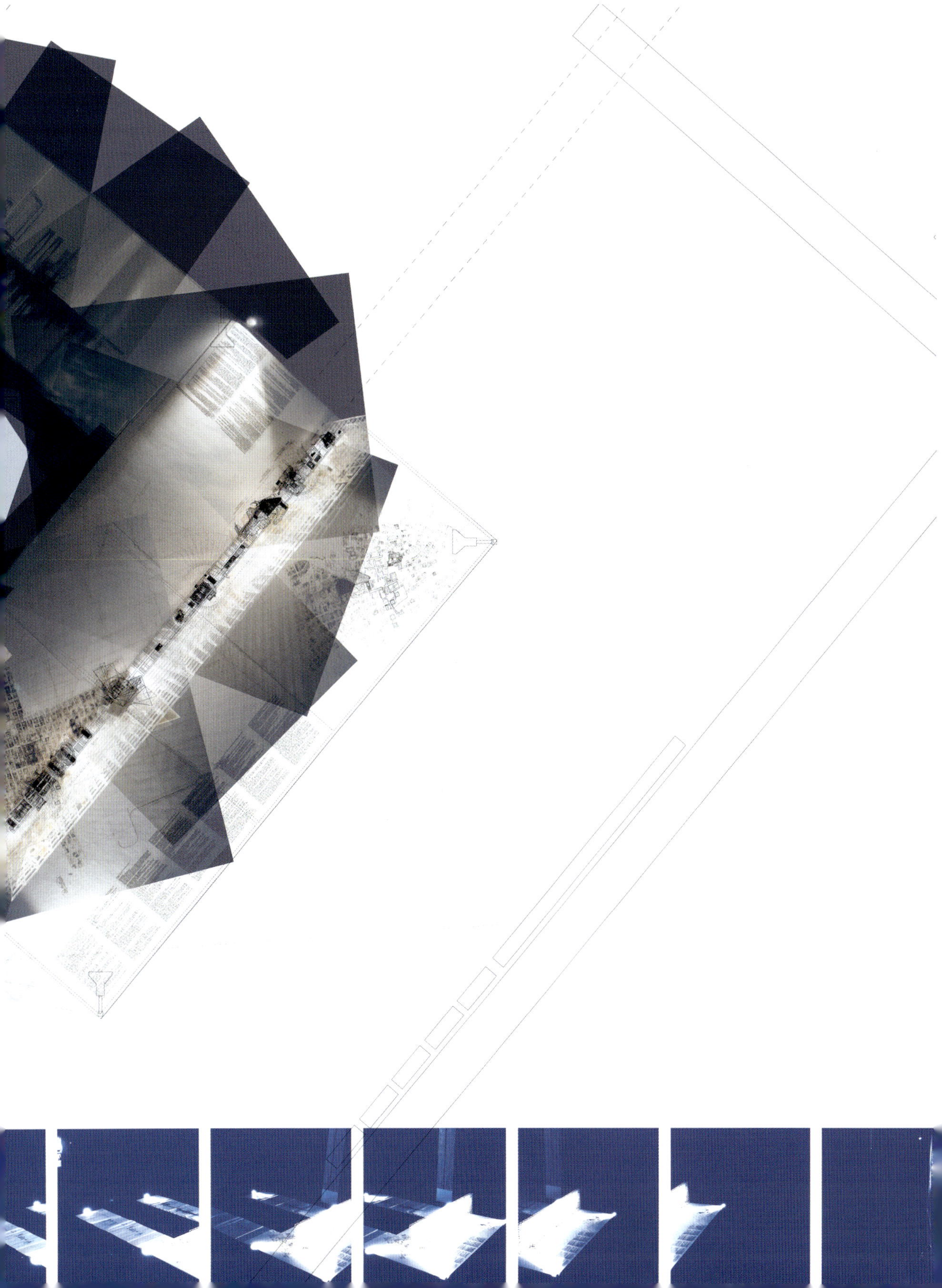

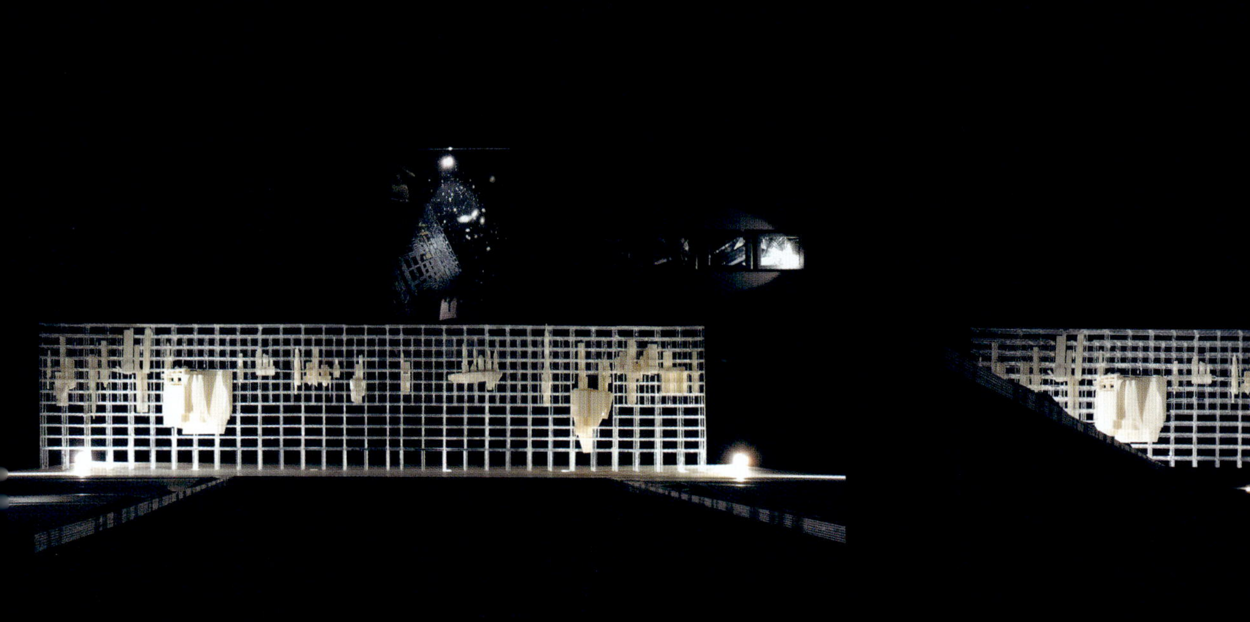

4.4 Light Passes: Streams of Unconscious Consciousness [256]

The city in the installation – and the argument unfolding throughout the text suggests there might be one – is an aggregation of a series of fragments which respond and can be understood in relation to the ideas, concepts and notions they activate.

The fragments exist between being something that forcefully needs to exist in the physical world as a built object and something without a palpable physical manifestation. Light in the exhibition emerges not just as a mechanism for reading the invented city but also for allowing the mind to move between ephemeral physical presence and imagination. Light encourages a discussion about the aesthetic qualities of the space, as well as the fluid conditions between the conscious and the unconscious, that is, between what is withdrawn and what is sensual about the fragments, or a correlation between their *essence* and their *appearance*. [257]

Light allows also for wider considerations about architecture as a thick and porous condition of boundary, or threshold, not unlike Virginia Woolf's description of a house in 'Time Passes,' the middle chapter of her 1927 novel *To the Lighthouse*. [258] In the short chapter with no people in it, Woolf weaves together two very different temporalities – ten turbulent years partially coinciding with WWI enmeshed in the stories of the Ramsay family – through the material properties of their crumbling house. Time both contracts to offer glimpses of war devastation and expands to the point where the reader becomes attuned to dust accumulating on the windowsill.

In 'Time Passes' the reader witnesses a world of entropy through the insentient 'eye' of the house and the help of a rhythmic lighthouse beam. Light testifies to entropy and it also diffuses boundaries across scale when it expands the threshold between the dusty interior and the much wider territory to which it is connected. Woolf describes the house as an architectural space-time that exists in between states of matter, in between still being solid and already disintegrating into particles. It is a space which narrates the passage of time, not as an internal and intuitive Bergsonian duration – as in other parts of the novel – but as an external and material poetic account of matter. It is a permeable membrane between an interior and an exterior, but not quite being any of those specifically, or in fact holding the possibility of becoming any of those at any given moment. It is a spatial and temporal threshold of light and particles. [259] It is something not quite architecture anymore but not yet geology either.

Light and dust become a geologic tuning in that enables a way of thinking about architecture geologically. One could argue that Woolf's stream of consciousness in the novel – which in 'Time Passes' becomes more of a stream of unconscious consciousness – comes close to an idea of architecture that verges on the geologic. [260]

Woolf's light is both cosmic and electric. The sun dictates the opposition between diurnal stillness and nocturnal chaos. It is cyclic also in relation to the passage of seasons and years, which augments entropy both inside the house and in the garden outside. On the other hand, the house is scrutinized by the blind rhythmic eye of the lighthouse — two short beams and a longer one. The properties and qualities of light help Woolf examine in detail the dust particles in suspension and observe their eventual deposition in layers that coat the house itself. In chemistry this tendency for particles in suspension to settle out of the fluid that keeps them in fluctuation and come to rest against a barrier is called sedimentation. [261] In geology, the definition of sedimentation differs; it often refers to the opposite of erosion and it involves actions of building up in layers or horizons. The description of the crumbling house in this chapter includes both. It is through light that Woolf eloquently describes sedimentation, both physically and materially. Just like dust sedimenting inside the house, light photons also accumulate on the surfaces inside it as they lose energy. Light sedimentation also occurs in materials weathering in the face of light, through bleaching or fading.

Light sedimentation adds yet another argument to the cultural study of gold and its many cultic dimensions. Cosmic light, first in photonic radiation hitting the earth's crust and then as de-energized photonic particles finally depositing on the geological layers, could be a conceptual trigger for gold deliria. One could argue the other way around as well: that gold is ultimately fantasized as materialized (sun)light. In this optic, the scarab's dung ball is a collection of Bataillean *solar excrements*. And if one were to push the fantasy a little further, by rolling the light dung under the Milky Way, the beetle would perhaps be guiding the sun in its cosmic path, thus aligning itself with the Ancient Egyptian conception of the insect as the god of the rising sun. Geology, then, may be regarded as a becoming of material possibilities inaugurated with every solar cycle.

The entanglement between gold and city that helps sustain the design experimentation requires layers of abstraction to ideate capture as a path to totality.

Unlike earlier modes of thought, which assumed a capacity for total abstraction that could lead to a complete conception of totality, modernity brought about a progressive awareness of the qualities and limits involved in the capacity to think abstractly about the totality of the capitalist system. [262] The difficulty in clarifying these qualities, as well as the limits of abstract thinking, may be a consequence of the enmeshed contextual definition of 'self-valorizing capital' as the social subject of modern history:

> ... capitalism can only be a polemical demonstration of the ultimate impossibility of *imaging* those forms of abstraction – harder to imagine than 'your own death' – which nonetheless become the common denominator of all values in the urban worlds ... [263]

As an iconic condition of the capitalist project of expansion and accumulation, Manhattan embodies this polemic both with its expansion on a totalizing grid, which started with the *Commissioners' Plan*, and its apparently unlimited extrusion both upwards and downwards.

Manhattan is a product of modernity in which the cultic dimensions of gold are as present as they are in our abstract ideas of Ancient Egyptian or Native American pre-Columbian cultures. Gold is the mythic substance that forms the (geological) ground of the abstract money economy on which it ultimately depends for some kind of material substantiation. Gold's allure and beauty happen through a self-reinforcing human desire to stabilize and eventually expand control, while at the same time delineating human entropy. In a way, gold is the ultimate PCM that prolongs, even if partially, what it is to be human.

Through his own PCM, Koolhaas' construction of a history for Manhattan activates the formulation of Manhattanism, which, besides being a retroactive theory traceable from the early 1811 cartography all the way through its many variations, becomes also a literary city that echoes the author's sense of delirium in at least two ways. First, Koolhaas denotes a paranoiac sense of searching for something in the city. One experiences a sense of adventure in searching for connections between different clues as in a treasure hunt. His research can be seen as a form of quarrying the city for phantom occupancies and the spoils of architectural cannibalism. It is not clear whether he eventually finds a treasure, but his text blocks reveal a crescendo to several climactic events with which the architect justifies the city, even at the expense of discrediting the real.

Second, the Koolhaasian PCM focuses on a path to totality that is imbricated in the expansion of the grid across the island. Koolhaas accepts the entangled logics of capitalism with little to no sustained critique, other than punctual and very localized observations. These logics reinforce the possibility of discrediting the real through a sense of totality that runs against the modern capacity for abstraction. Instead, it is complicit with the totalizing views of a paranoid who can only reinforce their beliefs in progress, congestion or accumulation in the making of the city.

When accepting geology as a tool for critical and creative thinking, the PCM gains new dimensions with a thinking activated by extrusion. The actions involved in quarrying architectural fragments and then extruding them tangled in their own contexts becomes yet another type of PC activity. Similar to Vriesendorp's representation of an infrastructural plenum supporting Manhattan, the design experimentation also extrudes and displaces the city, and finally explores options to nest it in a different configuration. With these actions, the project aims to push the limits of its representability, and to add possibility for architecture and its practice. In pushing the use of the PCM a new city is claimed. This new city results from the hybridization of present and past city fragments and future configurations, all of which exist across scale and amongst unresolved tension.

Woolf's glimpses of the house mentioned previously, and seemingly tangential to the novel's narrative, are unexpected appearances that materialize and immediately vanish. They resemble accidental interferences flickering on old cinema screens, which are marginal to the projected movie, but strong in triggering a way of thinking that is alien to the chronological order of the projection. [264] Instead, they dislocate the audience's attention and briefly detach them from the cinematic immersion. They augment the thick and porous threshold between the conscious and the unconscious.

As an immersive space, the installation affects in ways that, for example, a description of it could not. It seems to escape its own transformation into post-mortem descriptions, and instead exists as an impression of 'a close-up, where space expands; [and] with slow motion, movement is extended.' [265] These glimpses perhaps also relate to an internal lack of desire to organize them in a system that would linger on the conscious and gesture towards a forceful linearity of thought, or an implied chronological order of thought that never occurred in the assembling of the invented city. It did not happen in the processes of reading *Delirious New York*. It did not happen throughout the design exploration of plotting the text onto a newly conceptualized city territory. It did not happen in the attempts to provide the design exploration with a contextual background of some sort. It did not happen as the installation existed fluidly between ideation and physical configuration. The fragmentary nature of the exhibition, therefore, triggered an equally fragmentary critical reflection of it. Offering it as glimpses – the fleeting moments of something 'moving under the field of … vision' [266] – may perhaps be seen as the only way that does not constitute a deliberate spatial or temporal misrepresentation of the work itself.

The installation exists fluidly between a longer idea without a palpable physical manifestation and its brief existence as a physical presence. In its trajectory, the exhibition existed in many different formulations, all attempting to entangle the city fragments with the physical space. The installation progressively crept into darkness for the sake of concentrating the fields of the invented city, of fomenting interferences between its different fragments and of controlling light. Its final consolidated version was formalized inside a pitch-black box where the possibility of controlling light was initially assumed. Instead, and almost immediately, light acquired qualities and properties that thickened and warped the space.

Unlike Woolf's literary explorations, light in the exhibition is fully electric, permanent, and adjustable. It is cast onto the dispersed fragments; it beams across the room and spills over the metallic ceiling and onto the floor; once it touches materials, surfaces and dust particles, it reflects and refracts. What seems like a silent, rather dark and still installation when people occupy it, becomes a heavy, noisy, at times even chaotic spatial condition without people in it. Light is experienced as a perhaps unusually thick geologic media; it thickens as one withdraws from the space. The possibility of withdrawing is always limited, but it might be enough to notice how time passing could no longer be measured but light passing could.

The short duration of the exhibition wasn't enough to observe light particles sedimenting within the space, like dust on Woolf's windowsill. But it offered strong enough glimpses to imagine how that could affect the exhibition and, therefore, also the invented city. *Continuous City* is a project conceived as a fluid urban condition, which, after being quarried and materialized, also examines the spoils of these actions and accepts them as an integral part of its existence. This is a city fragment that accepts entropy as part of its own evolution, and ultimately embraces a larger timeframe for these conditions to evolve.

The city that briefly rests in the exhibition space offers glimpses of an invented Manhattan that discredits, or at least questions, the real in favor of possible alternative configurations.

(right) Glimpses offered by the concertina drawings in the installation.

(far right) *Continuous City* and views of the installation.

(next pages) Glimpses offered by the *Continuous City* in the installation.

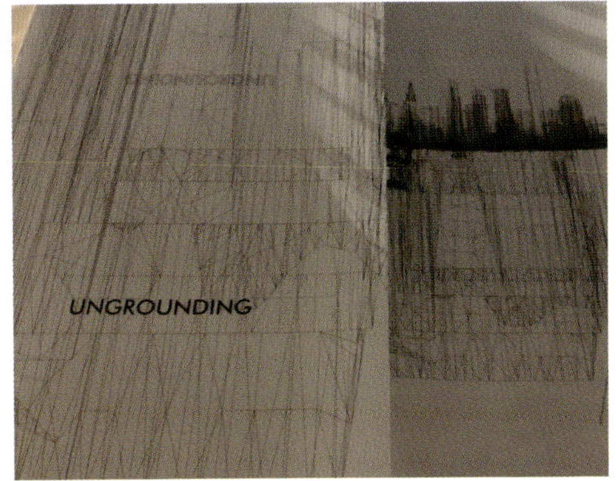

UNGROUNDING

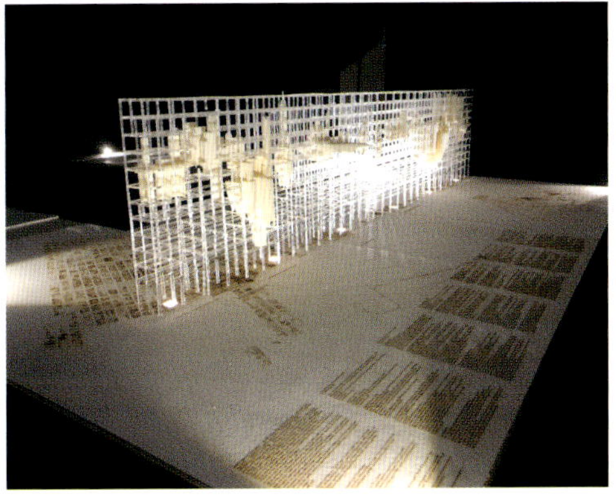

Fault-Line City

Once displaced from their original city contexts and re-materialized within the mega-structure, the *Geotaxonomies* can be utilized to test alternative urban conditions and city configurations. *Fault-Line City* is a strategy for a subterranean occupation of Manhattan along a major fault line, with the idea that the *Geotaxonomies* can become devices for scoping some of the geologics related to geomorphological dynamics. It combines the ideas resulting from the study of *Delirious New York* with Lebbeus Woods' rhetoric of ground.

In projects such as *Underground Berlin*, Woods probes the underground with disparate motivations, from political and cultural to environmental. [267] He explores the crafting of his architectural practice as an iterative, explorative and speculative problem – a form of practice that is also contextualized in philosophy and cybernetics, as well as on ethical and aesthetic priorities. The Berlin project reflects the architect's preoccupation with expanding the delineations and urban conditions of thr city. For him, a new myth in architecture is based not on analysis or 'reinterpretation of history' but on imagination. Architecture should be something that results from a direct experience of a dynamic and ever-changing planet.

Fault-Line City is yet another temporary fragment that results from a repositioning along the major passive fault line running beneath 125th Street, a previous site of experimentation. The *Geotaxonomies* here become tools to excavate, cut, mine and quarry the city's underground conditions. The experimentation is less a city than a project of excavation, that is, a subterranean thickness activated mostly by excavation that expands urban delineations. Instead of being understood as the opposite of extrusion – a conceptual relation explored earlier in the work – excavation assumes the speculative role of probing the unknown through acknowledged acts of architectural violence described by their material subtraction to geology. The resulting voids are celebrated as eventual underground possibilities for inhabiting a fault, here read as a spacetime moment of coexistence, a line of fluidity in deep time, an entity of potential instability.

(this and next pages) Studies of *Fault Line City.*

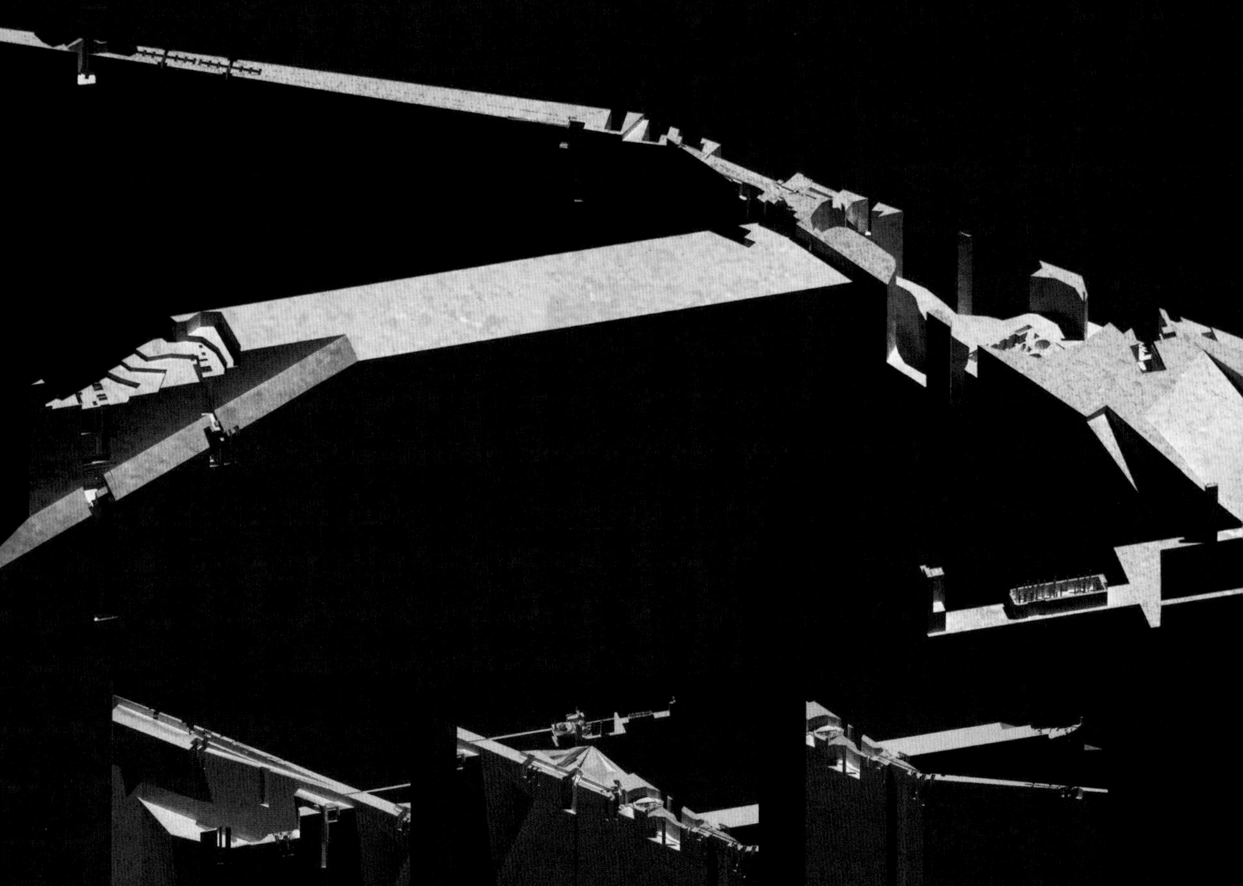

With an orientation southeast-northwest, *Fault Line City* extends along the fault line mostly underground. However, in key moments, it extends upwards to disrupt and affect the city above. It breaks with blocks and buildings. It connects them in unexpected assemblages which dilute what is above and below surface. It gives them a sense of directionality along the fault in key pivotal moments between boroughs.

It meets Central Park in its northeast corner, close to Harlem. Reclaiming a previous marsh draining to East River, this park corner is currently occupied by Harlem Meer. *Fault Line City* cuts across the lake and drains water into the underground. An extended arm aligns with the grid and permeates across the park to the west side. Just like the city, the arm does not have a program; it is deliberately ambiguous, even if the *Geotaxonomies* agglomerating along this axis result from architectural fragments of New York's International Fairs from 1853 and 1939.

Further northwest, it connects the topography of three parks: Morningside, St. Nicholas and the top of Riverside. The three landscapes hinge on the fault as part of a much older geological system on the island. Before the grid, the fault connected with a drainage system connected to the river. For now, *Fault Line City* finally projects itself on to the Hudson in two articulated points. But supported by the longer fault line, it could keep growing.

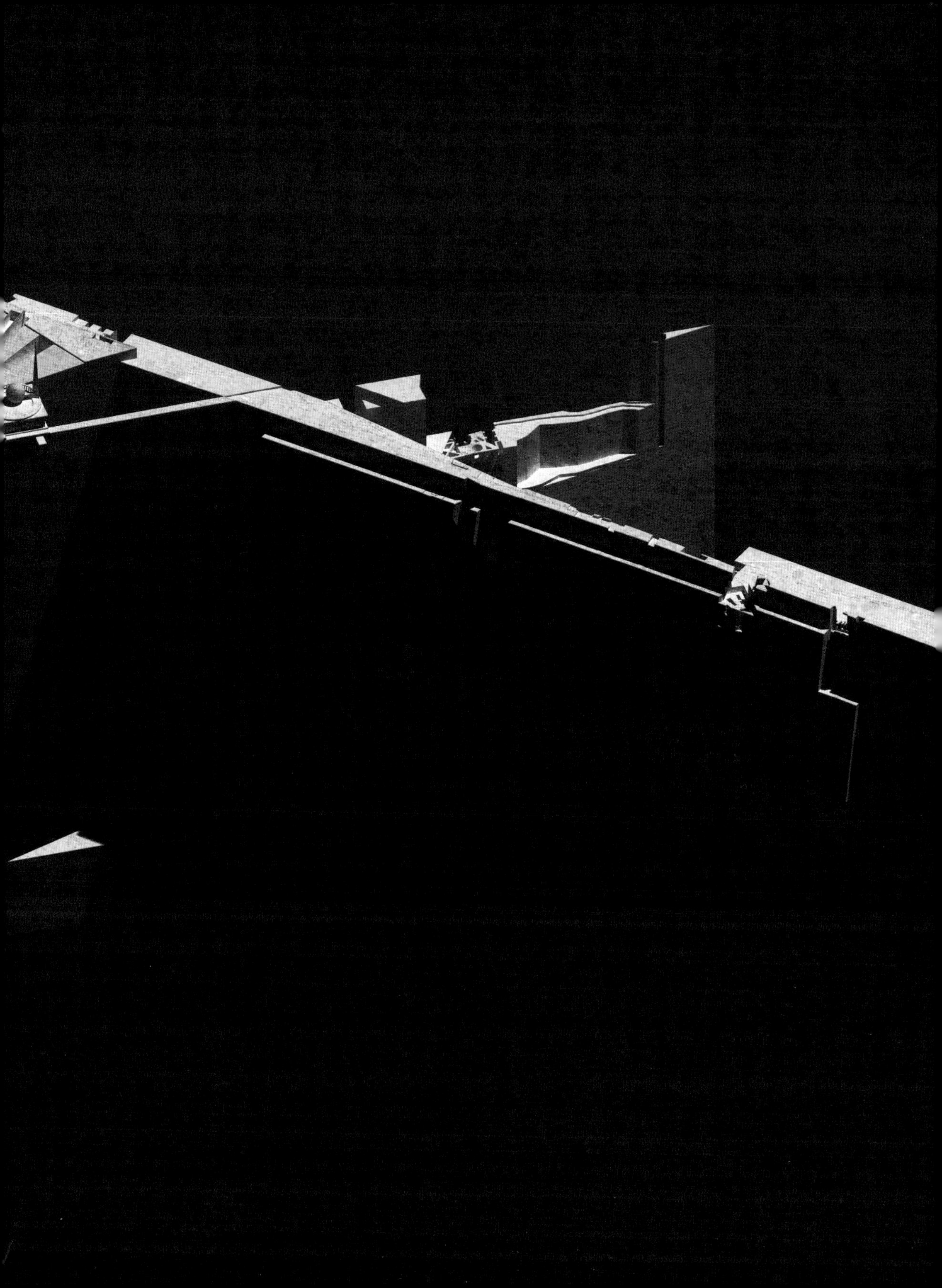

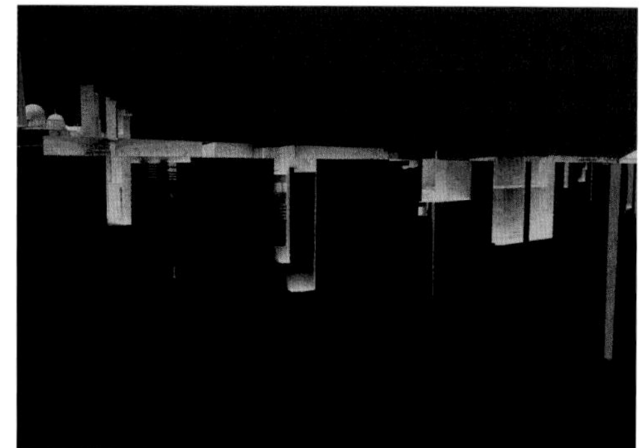

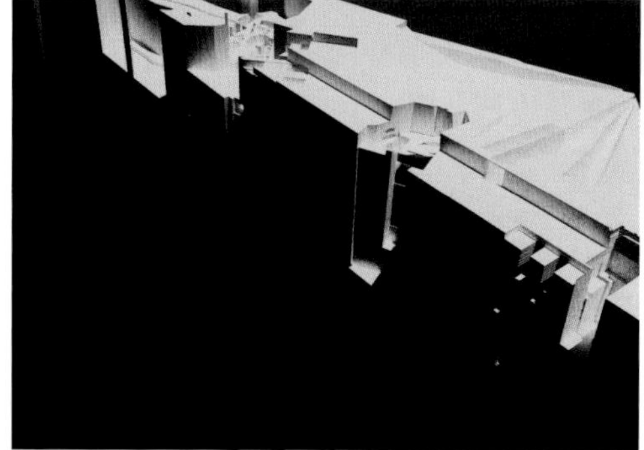
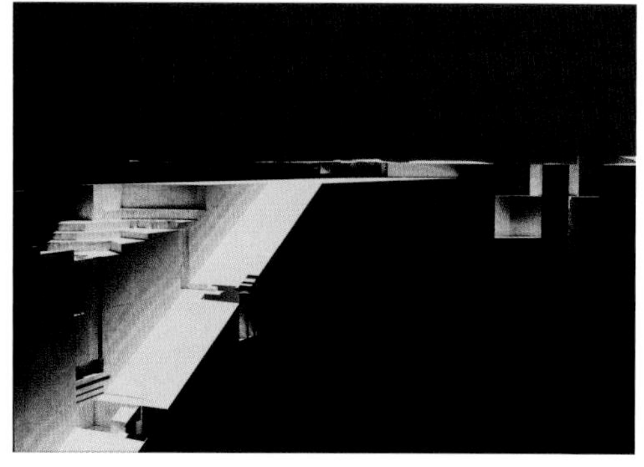
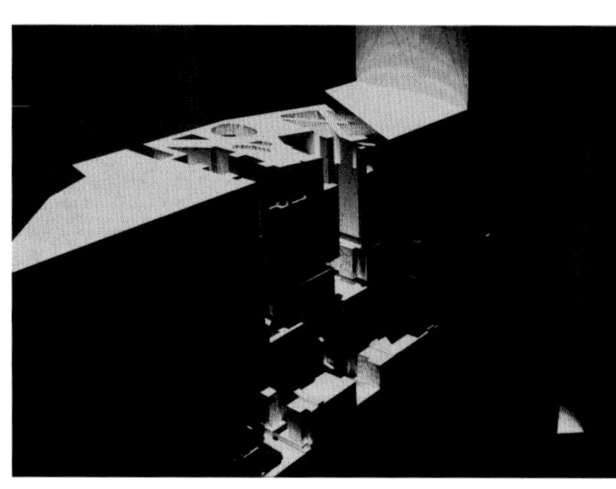

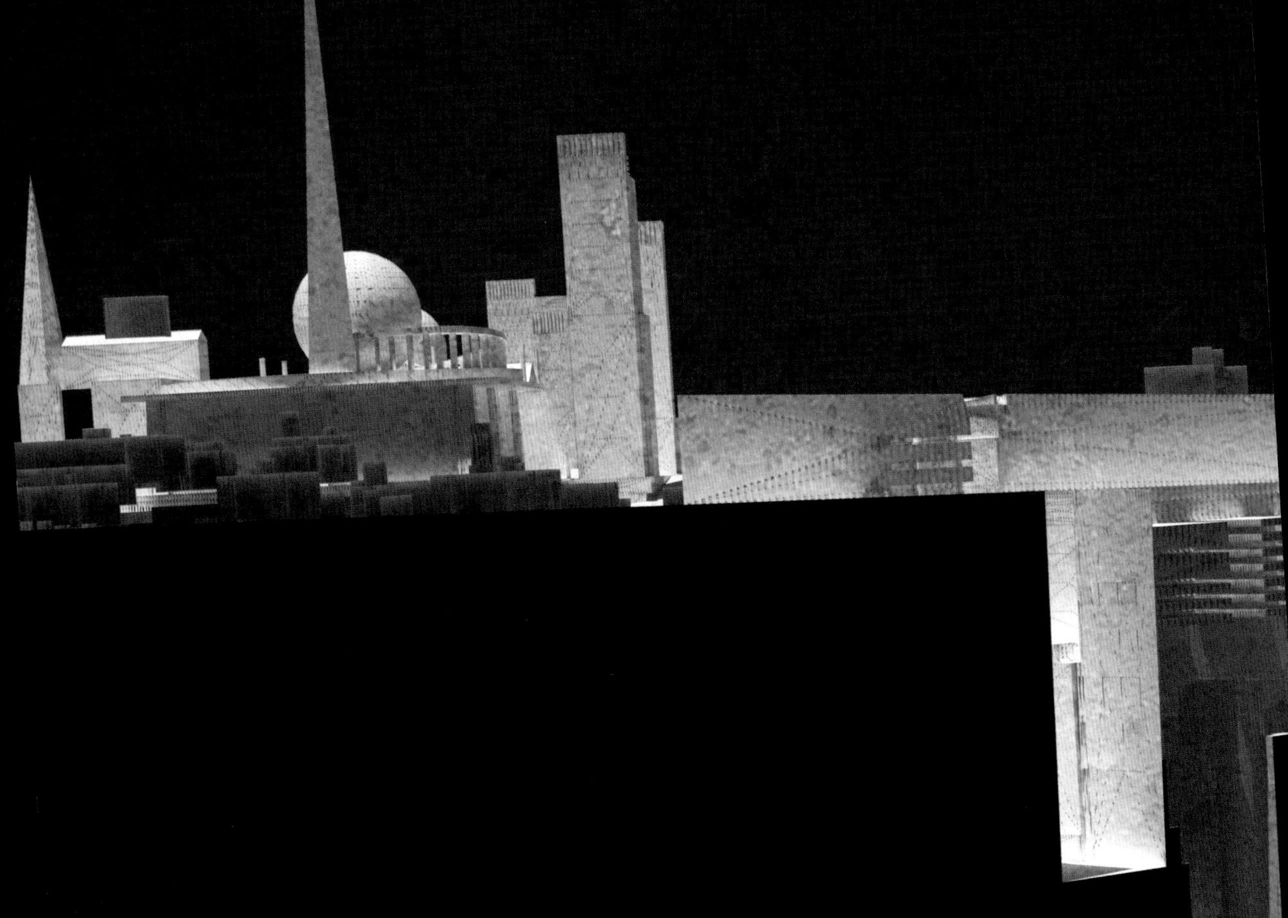

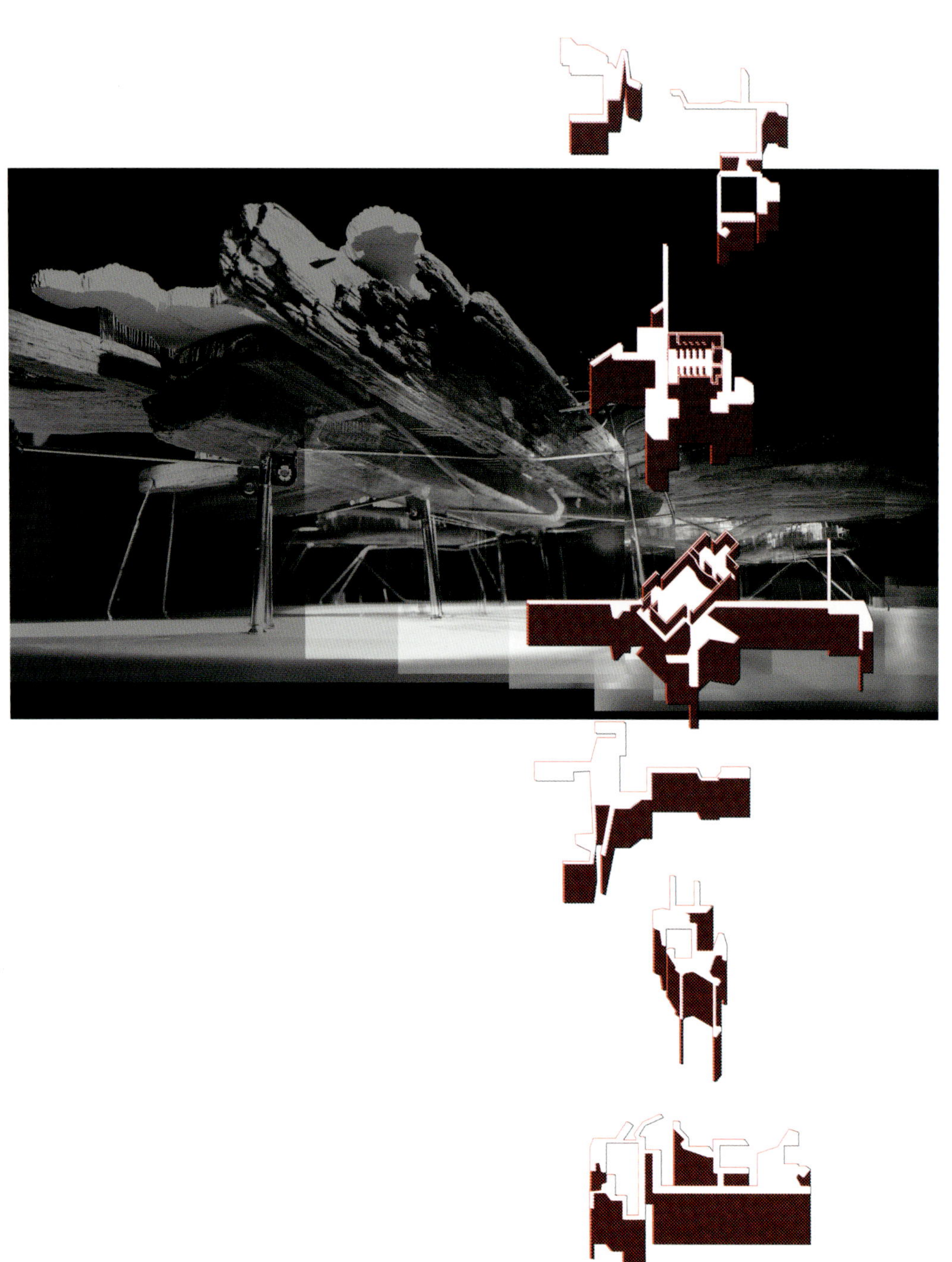

5 De-Sediment
Seismic Forces Through the Slightest Tremor

'De-sediment' studies Bernard Tschumi's *The Manhattan Transcripts* (1977–1981) by looking retrospectively at Vaux and Olmsted's 1858 *Greensward Plan*. The relational study scrutinizes Central Park as a curated construction of publicness that represents the American ideals of freedom and democracy, also at the expense of the histories of marginalized communities who were displaced or destroyed to build it. The *Transcripts* offer notational clues to a pseudo-archaeological design exploration that tries to uncover some of those stories and de-sediment the idea of park as a picturesque, genteel landscape. An experimental body of design work suggests a reading of the park as landscape fragments in constant tension with the city grid.

This chapter examines the *Transcripts* as a conceptual hinge in Tschumi's early practice. It also positions it retrospectively and from the contemporary perspectives offered by the Anthropocene, which encourage a reappraisal of some of the architect's defining concepts – event, space, movement or program – within expanded notions of *ground* and *sedimentation*.

The design experimentation was curated as a virtual installation titled *Insular Events* (2021) and structured in three related notational events, each focusing on specific transcripts in the book. *Part I – Under the Rug* studies the first transcript, *MT1—'The Park,'* as a conceptual probe to contextualize Central Park within wider geologic conditions and to question some of its main narratives. *Part II – Archaeologics of Domesticity* investigates the third transcript, *MT3—'The Tower' (The Fall)*, to excavate extracts of Seneca Village, an African American community that was demolished with the advent of Central Park. *Part III – Archipelago of Dependencies* moves more freely between transcripts to study cinematic sequences and how they are staged in Manhattan.

The design iteration throughout the chapter critically reflects on how a series of representational tools and techniques, such as montage or axonometric degree-zero, were utilized to explore ground as something that extrudes, fractures, and de-sediments the city.

Insular Events tells about a Park, a Village and other stories of erasure. Hovering over Manhattan, disparate events are continuously woven into the fabric of the park, until the landscape begins to be regarded as an island of islands in an island.

5.1 Weaving an Architecture of Anthropocenic Events

Rem Koolhaas once told an entertained audience that *The Manhattan Transcripts* (1977–1981; *Transcripts*) were the true manifesto about New York. [268] Public interactions between him and Tschumi are often abundant in entertaining controversy. On a separate conversation, this time in 2011, Tschumi said that, soon after finishing *Delirious New York*, Koolhaas realized it would have been easy to write the book about any other city. [269] The *Transcripts*, too, could have been about another city, Tschumi admitted, while raising the question of '[w]hy, then, New York?' [270]

The question was left unanswered at the time, but it seems to matter. The *Transcripts* are on New York, meaning that they are set in New York and register events in the city, but in a way, they are not about New York. They explore a murder in a park, clearly Central Park from its notated footprint, but that is never explicit. It doesn't even seem to matter that much, for the chasing is what Tschumi pursues, frame after frame. They also explore transgressions along a street, which is clearly 42nd Street in Midtown Manhattan, but that doesn't seem to be very relevant either, at least not from a geographical standpoint. They include a tower, which is a generic building from the top of which a body falls, and a city block, also generic and shaped by disparate yet converging programs. Still, the question of why New York seems to matter for both Koolhaas, who claimed to be interested in questioning the Avant-Garde, and for Tschumi, who was interested in practicing it. Tschumi was invested in the New York scene of the late 1970s. He wanted his practice to escape the realm of architecture and move into the space of the gallery. That curiosity eventually attracted him to New York, where he has lived ever since. Chronologically, however, that doesn't answer the question either, not fully at least, because Tschumi began his *Transcripts* while still teaching at the Architectural Association (AA) in London. But it might help explaining the angle the book eventually took and the main concepts it focused on, especially when positioned along a slightly longer trajectory of Tschumi's early practice.

When reflecting back on his early work of the late 1970s and early 1980s, Tschumi constructs a narrative about his practice that avoids more common chronological implications to, instead, forge 'pathways of thought by which

33 *The Manhattan Transcripts*, Original book cover, Bernard Tschumi, 1981.

BERNARD TSCHUMI
THEORETICAL PROJECTS
THE
MANHATTAN
TRANSCRIPTS
ACADEMY EDITIONS

we confront the implications that [architecture as a social and political practice] raises.' [271] Such a construct, often used as a literary device, could be described as a critical delamination of Tschumi's design attitude, which allows the architect to trace moving and movable lines of flight – or plot lines in a script – that speed up or slow down the narrative and build up anticipation towards what he considers to be climactic events in his work. Analyzing his own practice retrospectively, Tschumi constantly repositions himself, sometimes verging on manifesto-like affirmations where architectural discourse is externalized.

In the *Transcripts*, the script is activated with a triad composed of spaces, events and movement, which seem to be dragged laterally into the frame, almost like a long, uninterrupted shot scene. Tschumi uses this cinematic quality to 'transcribe things that are normally removed from conventional practice.' [272] In doing that, he also drags into his own architectural discourse several influences, questions and attitudes that unsettle representation and its conventions. Some of these lateral prompts are explored throughout the chapter and provide useful clues to further reviewing Tschumi's early work and its contemporary influence on theory and practice almost four decades later.

Tschumi's transcription of Manhattan seems to be, therefore, of a methodological nature. His '[n]otational sequences do not lie in the accurate transposition of the outside world, but in the internal logic [they] display.' [273] They focus on internal spatial relations in the city and offer them as a context in which architectural space emerges. The island-city is scrutinized as an internal set of conditions circumscribed inside the logics of the transcribed sequences, in ways akin to a Derridean deconstruction.

Jacques Derrida's literary and philosophical approach known as deconstruction was first developed in the late 1960s and continued to be redefined throughout his life. In its early stages it was mostly used to study relationships between text (and words) and meaning. [274] Strongly influenced by Nietzsche and Heidegger (from whom the German term *Destruktion* was first translated to the French *déconstruction*), *deconstruction* has no unique definition or description, it rather aims to correspond to a new way of thinking. The term eventually came to define a critical method of analysis of a structure and an operation to demonstrate that texts are equivocal and produce effects that problematize their apparent meaning. [275] But Derrida did not agree with its crystallization as an -ism. [276] In the English language, *deconstruction* seems to have been somehow monumentalized in ways that deviate from Derrida's more fluid original meaning. The philosopher often defined *deconstruction* as 'what happens' ('ce qui arrive'). [277] It is an event, but specifically one that comes from within, that is always already in the making. Derrida does not deconstruct text or words in search for meaning; he does perform an operation. *Deconstruction* is always already a part of those texts and something that is put into evidence – destabilized, decentered, described, transformed – in and through analysis. It is a way of writing that moves along lines and divisions and across the scale of the text, sometimes looking at the whole corpus, other times at one of its microscopic elements. [278]

Deconstruction is profoundly imbricated in the philosopher's notion of the present moment, or better, of the 'presence of present,' an event. [279] Derrida defines *event* as that which is happening in the *now* ('maintenant'), 'something singular and non-repeatable' associated to the singularity of organic life. [280] An event, therefore, cannot be planned or anticipated, nor even thought of, for it is impossibly incompatible with any form of repetition. Derrida defends that a thinking about the event is an impossible task, but also one that defines a project concerned with the possibility of forging relations between repeatability and singularity, neither as external nor homogenous, but instead as relations 'in which the elements are internal to one another and yet remain heterogeneous.' Derrida's writing – his project – is something that happens repeatedly but always differently, a *différance* able to describe a 'relation in which machine-like repeatability is internal to irreplaceable singularity and yet the two remain heterogeneous to one another.' [281]

Deconstruction is a kind of 'trembling, a "shaking" or "soliciting,"' that which dislocates in ways that, then, spread throughout the entire system. It is a 'force of irruption that "[disorganizes] the entire inherited order,"' something that de-structures, 'an earthquake' manifested through the slightest tremor, [282] a kind of 'seismic communication' attentive to the detail and along fissures and lines of friction, that *de-sediments* from within, until it makes writing itself uncanny.

When Tschumi first approached

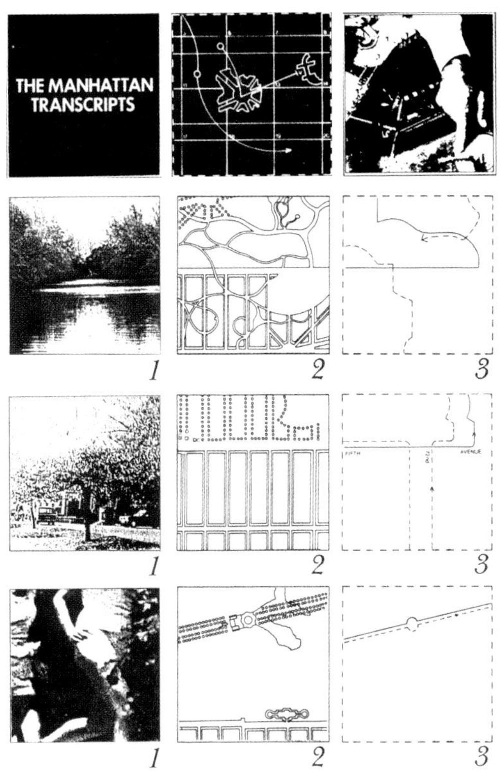

34 *The Manhattan Transcripts*, Introductory triptych and excerpt of *MT1–'The Park'*, Bernard Tschumi, 1981.

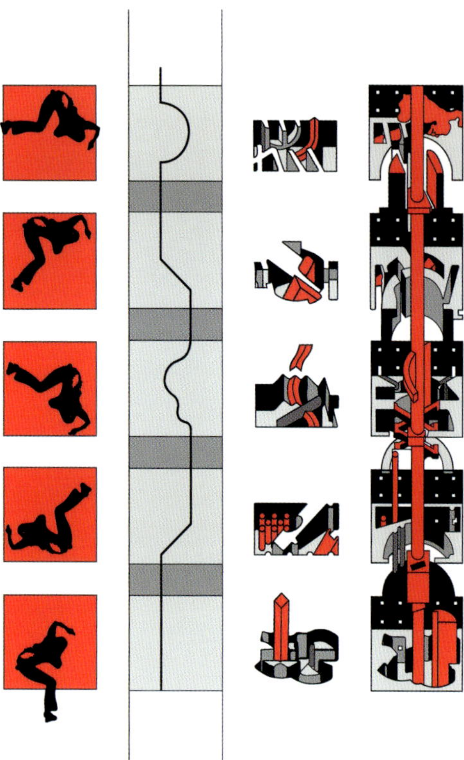

Derrida, the hypothesis that the architect's *architecture of the event* was an 'analogical transposition or even an architectural application' of the language of *deconstruction* was soon dismissed. [283] 'What could a deconstructive architecture be?', asks Derrida. '[I]s [deconstruction] not exactly the structural principle of architecture …?' [284] 'Is an architecture of events possible?' [285] This is not an architecture that 'constructs places in which something should happen or to make the construction itself be, as we say, an event,' but an architecture 'where the dimension of the event is subsumed in the very structure of the architectural apparatus: sequence, open series, narrative, the cinematic, dramaturgy, choreography,' [286] an architecture that 'not only programs a strategy of events … [but also] anticipates the architecture to come. It runs the risk and gives us the chance.' [287]

Event is a central concept for Tschumi. It is not a 'logical sequence of words or actions,' but rather a spatial expansion where the event may take place, which in turn may generate another spatial condition. [288] Together with *movement* and *space*, *event* defies 'hierarchical cause-and-effect relationship between form and function.' [289]

Tschumi's event is something generated by the coexistence, but not necessarily reconciliation, of 'multiple, heterogeneous, divergent, and even contradictory' dimensions. It results from the overlap of

differences synthesized across uninterrupted disjunctions. [290] Tschumi
adds:

> Events are everywhere and nowhere. How does one locate an event in
> architecture? An event is at once generic and specific; it can express
> itself in an infinite number of ways. In architecture, an event is an in-
> between: somewhere between an exception and the mold of things to
> come. ... There is no space without something that happens in it. There
> is no concept without an event that qualifies it. [291]

The definition of event that emerges from Tschumi's practice is perhaps
more diffuse than Derrida's conception, but they share similarities: they are
simultaneously generic and specific; they happen in-between, or from within;
and they happen uncontrollably, erupting in ways that cannot be anticipated.

Even though Tschumi never refers to Deleuze in this context, or at least
not explicitly, his considerations of the event as a qualifier of space align with
the philosopher's definition of event. For Deleuze, events are rhizomatic
multiplicities of processes of becoming and differentiation, only 'actualized
in space,' and it is 'through their spatiality [that] they also change and
reconfigure material reality.' [292] The event is always already a relation
between space and material. The relation, in turn, generates an interesting
question about the role of architectural design. How does spatial design
perform for the unimaginable? How can space be designed to accommodate
that which cannot be anticipated? The *architecture of the event* is an architecture
that happens, that is, it is carved by the event as it happens. It is an
architecture created by movement, an excavation of spaces in sequence.

Questions around materiality open the way for interesting considerations
of vibrancy and agency that have captured interest within the Anthropocene
debate. [293] For Tschumi, material is something that distorts, compresses,
and displaces. However, it may be useful to question the material conditions
the architect is, in fact, describing. The material seems to be architectural
– an architecture *on* the ground – where *ground* is taken for granted to the
point where it is almost always absent. The events happen on a seemingly
neutral ground. On the other hand, the Anthropocene theory blurs any easy
distinctions between figure and ground. It is interested in an architecture *of*
the ground as much as an architecture *on* the ground; it questions ground
conditions and studies their vibrancy and active agency. Operations on any
ground come with ethical implications, and they demand responsibility,
something that doesn't necessary occupy Tschumi's practice in the *Transcripts*,
but which nevertheless may have informed his interests, even if indirectly,
as discussed later.

If the *Transcripts* offer an 'architectural reading of the disjunctive, non-coincidental, interchangeable, and contradictory contemporary city,' [294] then it becomes important to consider what an *architecture of the event* can eventually mean from and for the Anthropocene. Here one returns to Tschumi's understanding of structure – of both city and book – for eventual clues. In the *Transcripts*, the architect accepts a tension between framing device and framed material, with the latter productively unsettling the former. In the contemporary city, the device is asked to capture much wider conditions of space and time and recognize in this expansion their infinite entanglements and conditions of connectivity across and at scale. If the human is synthesized with the earth – in multiple and irreducible ways – this also becomes an invitation to think about architecture as the 'juxtaposition and superimposition of differences' [295] across expanded temporal (and material) frames.

The device is reconceptualized as a more complex assemblage where observers and observed cannot escape each other. The frames do not limit the event in space; they mediate the entanglement between them and *us*, the observer. The allegedly polite framing of an event in the *Transcripts* needs to engage in a more vibrant dialogue with the material conditions it is intended to frame. The event cannot be isolated because it is enmeshed in a network. It becomes more of a network of related events – many of which occupy the margins of the frame or are left outside of it altogether – continuously colliding on and dissolving into its many components.

One is also reminded that 'the Anthropocene has reversed the temporal order of modernity: those at the margins are now the first to experience the future that awaits all of us.' [296] Tschumi's frame-by-frame sequence considers events happening at the margins of the screen or in the background. Marginal events are as important in his movie-like montages as the action taking place at the center. It is perhaps also at the margins of the montage that program is revealed. Tschumi's programmatic definition emerges as the event happens, before any procedural spatial formalization. [297] A discussion on program does not mean 'a return to notions of form versus function, to cause-and-effect relationships between program and type, or to some new version of utopian positivism.' Instead, it should focus on sequential motivation (in the sense of the Russian Formalists), whereby 'spaces are confronted with what happens in them.' [298] If the framing of the event is asked to expand, the sequential motivation also expands with it. It is within this continuous expansion that Tschumi navigates the edges of architecture, namely by dragging into the transcribed sequences events that are normally removed from it.

An Anthropocenic understanding of *event* is not radically distinct from the theoretical positionings offered up until this point, perhaps except for its focus. For Tschumi, event is something that essentially affects humans, or better, he is interested in how events particularly affect humans. Program is also a social, cultural, or political construct of the human. Tschumi's *architecture of the event* generates spaces through the interactions and overlaps between protagonists. It is a demonstration of a condition of latency, as opposed to the construction of something necessarily new. It doesn't always have to have meaning, which is perhaps why latency becomes so important. But the Anthropocene theory defends that human 'activities transform the earth at the global scale of geology.' [299] It proposes a dissolution between human and earth temporalities and spatialities. Architecture expands with programs that no longer privilege the human conditions in opposition to the non-human. With this expanded focus it can then contemplate more-than-human *geosocial formations* in the city, of which human is only a subcomponent. In doing so, architectural practice might be conceived also as a kind of seismic scoping moving along fissures and lines of friction, something that de-structures the familiar until it becomes unfamiliar, that de-sediments from within until it makes the city itself uncanny.

5.2 Transcriptions of Central Park: *The Manhattan Transcripts* (1981)
and *The Greensward Plan* (1858)

Derrida's interest in architecture extends beyond Tschumi's work. [300]
But at the time when the philosopher raised such questions, he was engaged
in a close reading of the follies in Tschumi's proposal for the Parc de La
Villette, a project that he reads in relation to the *Transcripts* (in some ways,
an anticipation of the park). [301] The follies forge a path of *affirmative
deconstruction*. (For '[d]econstructions would be feeble if they were negative,
if they did not construct, and above all if they did not first measure themselves
against the institutions in their solidity, at the place of their greatest
resistance ....'). [302] They are points of energy concentration, madness
accumulation and open-ended multiplicity. [303] Derrida calls them empty
boxes ('la case vide'); architectures that can't perhaps anticipate the event
(for that would be impossible) but which, nevertheless, can accommodate
the concretization of the architecture of the event in the *now*. As Mark Dorrian
defends, the folly can be read as a building with an 'indeterminate or
suspended use' but not necessarily a function, an architecture 'posited as
an open field of possibilities.' [304] The idea is useful for understanding the role
follies have had in Tschumi's practice and pedagogy, as moments of
architectural opportunity to his students in projects like *Finnegans Wake*,
but also to himself as a young professional.

The follies also reveal metonymic qualities in relation to the overall
structure of the. They activate a point-like grid that establishes an architecture
of multiplicity and heterogeneity, an architecture that does not depend on
any external forces – for there is no externality – but rather on the establishment
of inventive internal paths between the different points. An architecture
which decenters the park without the need of a pre-established coherence.
Derrida states that such a grid does not need to achieve totality, it rather
crosses through; it is an 'experience of permeability.' [305] It opens a 'field of
contradictory and conflictual events which deny the idea of a pre-established
coherence;' it is a strategy that weaves 'hostilities and negotiations;' Tschumi is
an architect-weaver. [306]

One could argue that Tschumi's follies – or Koolhaas' confetti in his
proposal for La Villette – are conceptually analogous to Central Park's erratic

36 *Proposal for Parc de la Villette*, General Plan, Bernard Tschumi Architects, 1982.

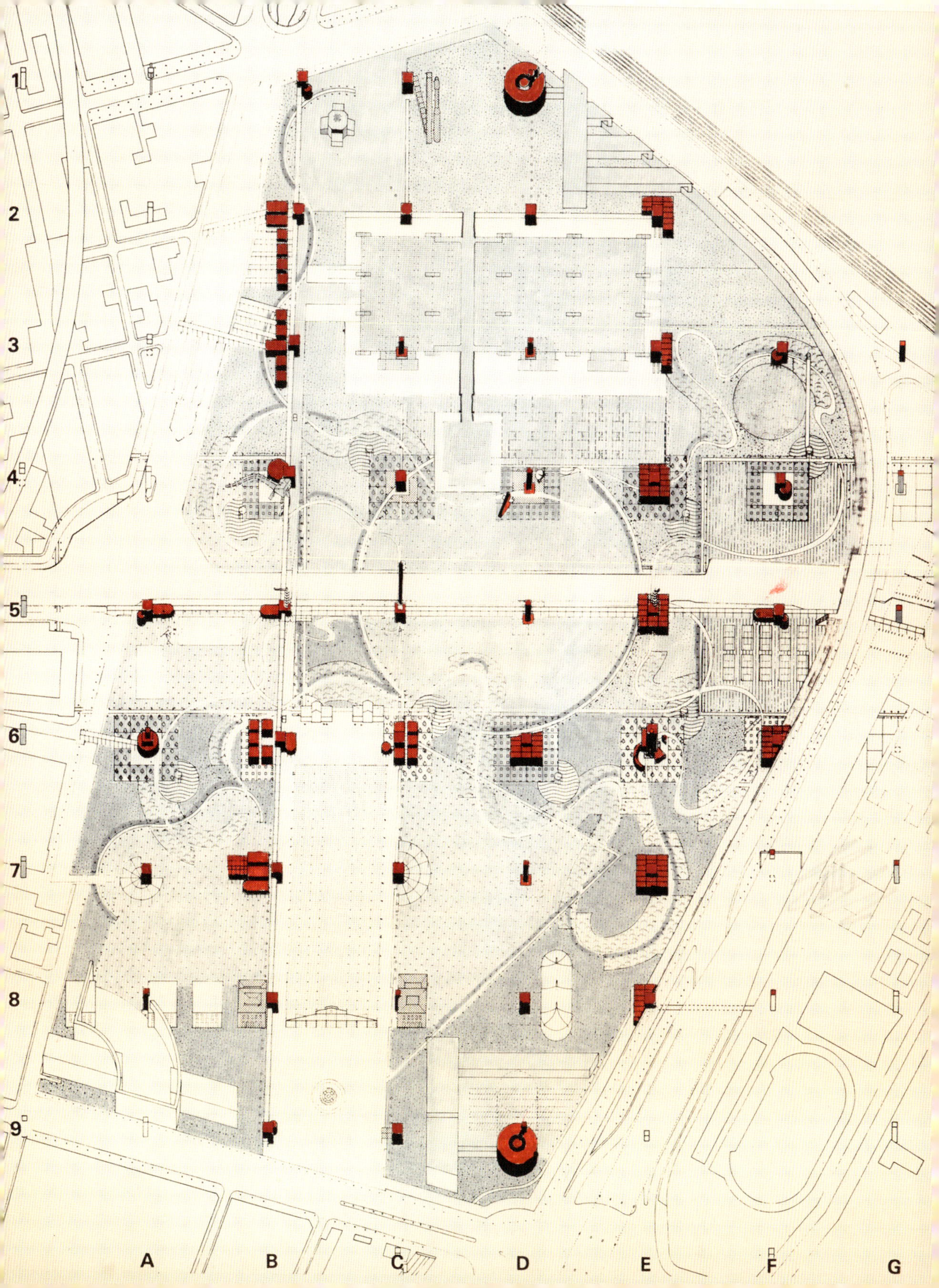

1
2
3
4
5
6
7
8
9
A B C D E F G

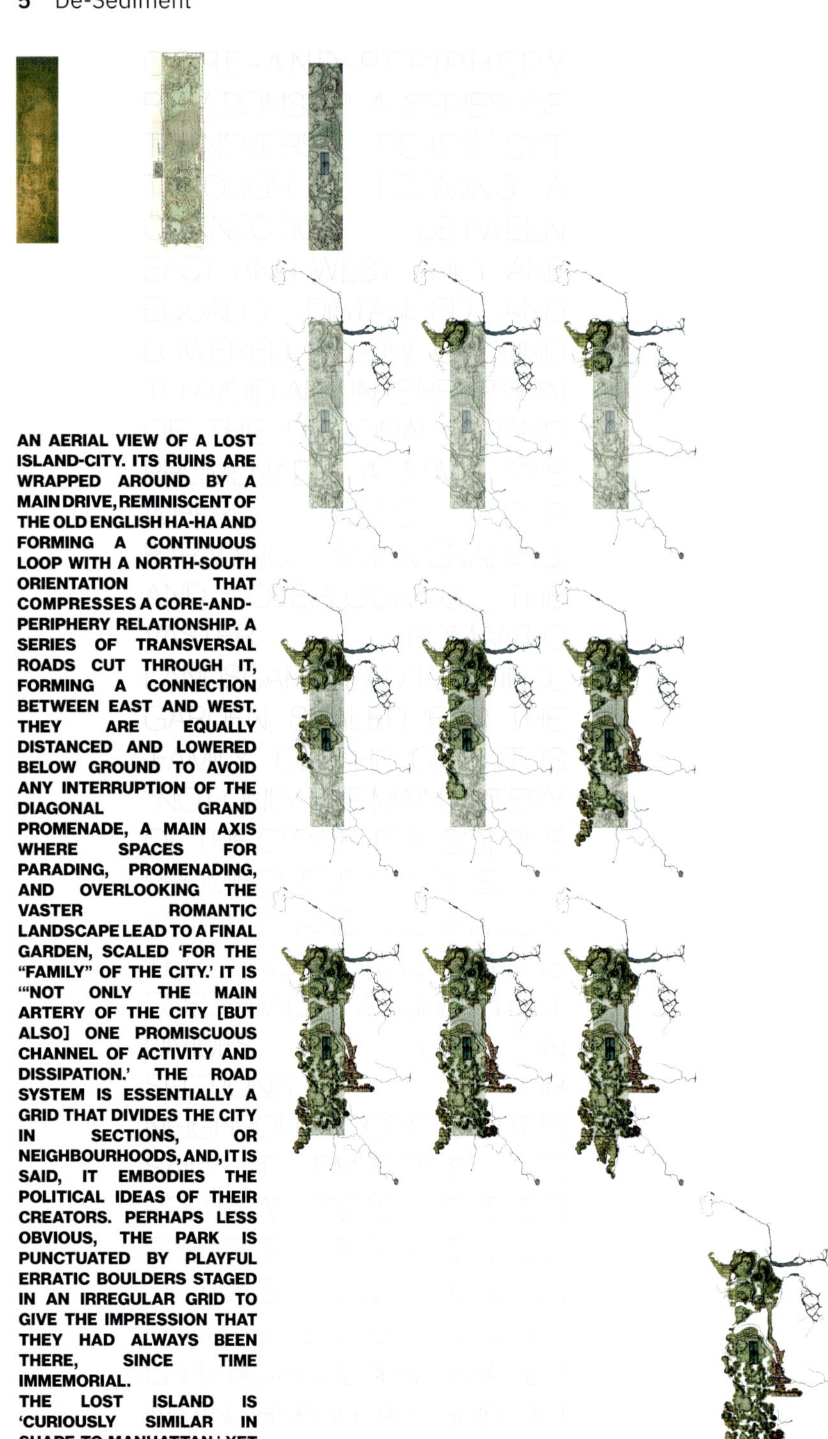

AN AERIAL VIEW OF A LOST ISLAND-CITY. ITS RUINS ARE WRAPPED AROUND BY A MAIN DRIVE, REMINISCENT OF THE OLD ENGLISH HA-HA AND FORMING A CONTINUOUS LOOP WITH A NORTH-SOUTH ORIENTATION THAT COMPRESSES A CORE-AND-PERIPHERY RELATIONSHIP. A SERIES OF TRANSVERSAL ROADS CUT THROUGH IT, FORMING A CONNECTION BETWEEN EAST AND WEST. THEY ARE EQUALLY DISTANCED AND LOWERED BELOW GROUND TO AVOID ANY INTERRUPTION OF THE DIAGONAL GRAND PROMENADE, A MAIN AXIS WHERE SPACES FOR PARADING, PROMENADING, AND OVERLOOKING THE VASTER ROMANTIC LANDSCAPE LEAD TO A FINAL GARDEN, SCALED 'FOR THE "FAMILY" OF THE CITY.' IT IS '"NOT ONLY THE MAIN ARTERY OF THE CITY [BUT ALSO] ONE PROMISCUOUS CHANNEL OF ACTIVITY AND DISSIPATION.' THE ROAD SYSTEM IS ESSENTIALLY A GRID THAT DIVIDES THE CITY IN SECTIONS, OR NEIGHBOURHOODS, AND, IT IS SAID, IT EMBODIES THE POLITICAL IDEAS OF THEIR CREATORS. PERHAPS LESS OBVIOUS, THE PARK IS PUNCTUATED BY PLAYFUL ERRATIC BOULDERS STAGED IN AN IRREGULAR GRID TO GIVE THE IMPRESSION THAT THEY HAD ALWAYS BEEN THERE, SINCE TIME IMMEMORIAL.
THE LOST ISLAND IS 'CURIOUSLY SIMILAR IN SHAPE TO MANHATTAN,' YET CLOTHED IN FOLIAGE.

boulders. [307] The Parisian park, then, becomes the displacement of the Manhattan ideal and the refusal of the park as a refuge. In that sense, Tschumi's concept for La Villette in Paris is the opposite of what Central Park allegedly stands for in New York: less of a picturesque void and more of a superimposition of programs through layering; the intensification of overlapping through design. La Villette's follies also differ from Central Park's boulders in that they steer the discourse even further away from the picturesque into deliberate cultural disruption. The follies result from the orchestration of a set of re-combinatory designed conditions.

The *Transcripts* anticipate La Villette in that they register a confrontation between Tschumi's ideas and a *real* city grid. Similar to the grid in Manhattan, La Villette aims to intensify urban congestion. Unlike New York, where the park is offered as an idea of release from that congestion, La Villette wants to fold the city into its internal structure. Even if Central Park has always arguably been as urban as the city, it still represents a landscape interruption of the grid that rejects the city. La Villette, on the other hand, explicitly epitomizes the triumph of the grid in the landscape – the landscape as an *architecture of the event*. [308] Tschumi admits that the ambition of this strategy also extends beyond the park, when he writes that 'the point-grid only gives the appearance of order, by simulating it. For material presence on a large metropolitan site is only one moment in a larger process which questions the very idea of structure.' [309]

Central Park in the twenty-first century remains remarkably similar to the *Greensward Plan*, the park's initial generator during the second half of the nineteenth century. Frederick Law Olmsted and Calvert Vaux's 1858 winning proposal for the first public park in Manhattan followed a naturalistic approach: a designed landscape with a 'natural feeling,' perhaps even a delirious state of mind of a pre-Manhattan landscape which has been a substantial part of its appeal over the last 150 years.

The concept of *public park* was new in the growing cities of the West at the time, and the initial plan privileged some of the European ideals as opposed to the vernacular landscape practices of the East Coast of the United States, but not without controversy and constant negotiation. The park's endurance and the appreciation it has continuously received from the city and its inhabitants over the years are also due in part to its slow adaptation 'through a vernacular process [from which] a natural landscape ... also became a social institution and city space.' [310]

The idea of a public park was neither neutral nor easy to define. As Central Park's first superintendent, Olmsted believed 'the public would have to be

Unleashing Central Park, Animated Sequence (text inspired by Lorna McNeur's 'Central Park City').

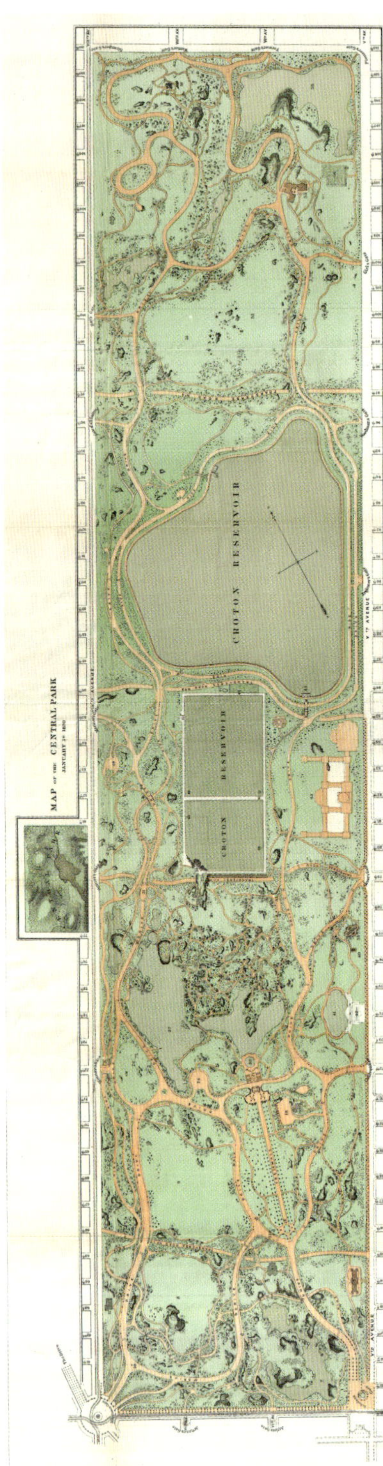

"trained" to use a park "properly so-called," by which he meant a picturesque landscape in the English tradition.'[311] In other words, the park was to be used by the wealthy and affluent who defended its construction for different reasons. Several rules on how to use the park were imposed on the city to, in effect, prevent lower-income workers and non-White people from using it. Questions about the meaning of *public*, as well as of *park*, raised equally complex questions about the meaning of democracy and the rhetoric involved in defining it in political, economic, and social terms.[312]

Besides requiring clarity on what a public park may mean to a largely polarized nineteenth-century society in New York, the construction of Central Park also demanded a shift in municipal management, and more specifically in the management of public resources. The creation of the park 'initiated a remarkable redefinition and expansion of city government's responsibilities to its citizens.'[313] Historians Roy Rosenzweig and Elizabeth Blackmar explain that the park not only meant a totally new attitude of public life in an increasingly congested city, but it also 'emerged out of a complex mix of motivations – to make money, to display the city's cultivation, to lift the poor, to refine the rich, to advance commercial interests, to retard commercial development, to improve public health, to curry political favor, to provide jobs.'[314] The idea of *public* was, maybe above all else, born out of necessity. The magnitude of the park's construction – more than ten million dollars, or 'three times the city's total

37 (left) *Map of Central Park*, Calvert Vaux and Frederick Law Olmsted, 1870.
38 (right) *Greensward Plan*, Proposal for Central Park, winning project, Calvert Vaux and Frederick Law Olmsted, 1858.

budget in 1850' – on more than three hundred hectares of prime real estate land meant that no single individual, or even isolated entity, could afford it on their own. [315]

The *Greensward Plan* has been explained by different scholars as Olmsted's strong reaction against the city grid. The landscape architect, who often referred to the park and the city seemingly interchangeably, advocated for a landscape that "'should present an aspect of spaciousness and tranquility with variety and intricacy of arrangement, thereby affording the most agreeable contrast to the confinement, bustle, and monotonous street-division of the city."' [316] For Olmsted, Central Park was not just the rejection of the city, it was an active *anti-city*, a 'Paradise Lost of New York,' an alternative vision for Manhattan, developed at scale – a living *colossal miniature of sorts* – based on the ideals of the European city. [317]

Few other landscapes have been as theorized, discussed and scrutinized as Central Park; none other holds as much symbolic power. The park is quintessential to the American rhetoric of democracy, and a powerful statement of the virgin land that resists the advances of the city or, even more appealing, that restores this virginity, once lost to the *city inferno*. It is widely known that this is not the case: that Central Park is as artificial a construct as the city on the island; that this is a highly curated and staged landscape that took more dynamite to get its smooth curves than the Battle of Gettysburg; that its species try to serve the ideal of a pre-Manhattan landscape but not all of them are endemic to the East Coast. Yet, the narrative is what persists, the way the park projects its image to media, and what people choose to believe in.

Central Park as an anti-Manhattan is intriguing also because it does not seem to be essentially true: the park has in it an implicit grid. Besides its obvious inscription in the city grid, with important alignments with streets and avenues both transversally and longitudinally, it includes a system

of follies across the park, sometimes in the form of elaborate architectural pavilions, other times with the meticulous curation of erratic boulders which activate a network similar to the ones found in picturesque English landscapes. Perhaps more innovatively, Olmsted and Vaux imprinted the park with a feeling of an old, rugged landscape which attempts to replicate assumed conditions on the island before the city. As mentioned above, the follies in Central Park are not that different from Tschumi's own expandable point grid for La Villette. Following a long tradition of designing parks as microcosmic city conditions – think of Stowe, and Versailles before it, and Villa Lante still earlier [318] – La Villette is to the twentieth century what Central Park is to the nineteenth century: an urban park that continuously tests the very city in which it exists and from which it cannot escape.

In 1856, two years before the design competition for Central Park, Engineer-in-Chief Egbert L. Viele began surveying the grounds that would soon be radically transformed. Roughly at the same time as he measured the topography and analyzed the hydrology *in-situ*, he began imagining what the park could look like. A summarized version of his report to the city and park commissioners was published in *The New York Times* in 1857, and included a plan for the improvement of the grounds for the future park, as well as a rough 'estimate required for active operations ... [that] a properly organized force may accomplish in favorable weather,' a total of 230,000 US dollars (roughly eight million US dollars in 2024). [319]

The thirty-three teams participating in the competition benefitted from the knowledge in the report, which was quite prescriptive in terms of any eventual topographical and hydrological decisions that should be made in favor of a satisfactorily functioning landscape operating in Manhattan's soil and climatic conditions. Yet, most proposals represented significant points of departure from the landscape's original conditions, as well as Viele's intentions to respect its intrinsic qualities. In a way, most of these projects can be conceived as suggestions of architectural violence towards an emancipation of pleasure in the city, albeit in perhaps a different context than what the concepts meant for Tschumi. The land was a ground of experimentation with extrusion, excavation, demolition and explosion. [320]

Throughout the second half of the nineteenth century, the park slowly opened itself to the city, a democratization process that began to attract larger crowds to the museums and local zoo, which eventually transformed it into a more 'eclectic and popular space.' The park's adaptation to the twentieth-century was not smooth; on the contrary, it demanded a continuous redefinition of its priorities and those of the city: a space for play and leisure or for conservation?; a space dedicated to the beautification of New York or of celebration of its urbanity and eclecticism? By the time Tschumi was studying New York to produce the *Transcripts*, the city

39 (left) *Map of the Lands Included in The Central Park from a Topographical Survey*, Egbert Viele, 1856.
40 (right) *Plan for the Improvement of The Central Park*, Adopted by the Commissioners, Egbert Viele, 1856.

was going through serious financial hardship, and eventually filed for bankruptcy. The park 'became less "public" as city officials turned to the private sector for money as well as administrative guidance.' [321] In this period, the allure with the juxtaposition of city and nature regained dark contours, namely with true or exaggerated accounts of murders in the park, occurring mostly at night, a recurrent trend since the creation of Central Park. Therefore, it should not come as a surprise to see Tschumi's exploration of the 'archetype of murder' in his notations. [322]

Tschumi defines works such as the *Transcripts* as 'books *of* architecture, as opposed to books *about* architecture,' that is, books that do not focus on buildings or cities *per se*, but rather on the search for architectural ideas. [323] Such books can explore the 'limits of architectural knowledge and ... [give] readers access to particular forms of research.' [324] The *Transcripts* were first conceived as 'successive paper spaces (on a wall) that defined a real space (in a room),' but their sequential organization was a natural fit for a subsequent book, with each drawing conceived as a frame of a longer and not definitive film of architectural inquiry.

Composed of four parts, or episodes – *'The Park,' 'The Street,' 'The Tower (The Fall),'* and *'The Block'* – the *Transcripts* emanate from programs of extreme nature that examine conflicts and tensions between pleasure and violence, their two driving theoretical forces. [325] Tschumi was interested in exploring an architecture of pleasure without a necessary moral or functional burden, even an architecture without responsibility. [326] His interest in pleasure, here defined as a dialectic between architecture as 'a thing of the mind' and 'the experience of space,' is positioned in the *Transcripts* as a sensation achieved when the two – concept and experience – coincide, that is, 'when architecture fulfils one's spatial expectations.' [327] The pleasure of space emerges in conflict with the pleasure of order, when limits are transgressed, a distortion or dislocation related not to destruction but eroticism (here defined as excess). Through his understanding of pleasure, Tschumi also clarifies his interest in books on architecture as media devices for the advertisement, production and reproduction of a fragmentary and desirable architecture.

Violence, on the other hand, is presented as not 'brutality that destroys physical or emotional integrity but a metaphor for the intensity of a relationship between individuals and their surrounding spaces.' [328] In the *Transcripts*, violence activates different readings of space at the 'intersection of logic and pain, rationality and anguish, concept and pleasure.' [329] Violence is a tool with which to construct action and activate movement through space; 'there is no architecture without violence.' [330] Describing them as sensations used *in extremis* to 'question past humanist programs that strictly cover only functional requirements necessary for survival and production,' the architect suggests that maybe architecture is all about 'love and death.' [331]

The distinction mentioned earlier is important in that the *Transcripts* notate events taking place in Manhattan, but they don't transcribe Manhattan-specific conditions. The *Transcripts* explore spatial, social and cultural confrontations in the city. [332] In that sense – one in which a city is confronted with what happens in it – they 'transcribe an architectural interpretation of reality.' [333] These drawings are a particular type of notation of what happens in a projected form. [334]

Notation is the first main method Tschumi uses for the transcriptions that interpret reality and probe the city. It works as a tripartite method used to represent spaces, events and movement to introduce the order of experience and time. It is also an investigative method with which the architect questions more conventional architectural representations: 'plans for "The Park" sections for "The Street," axonometrics for "The Tower," and perspectives for "The Block."' [335] The axonometric is of particular interest for this study. In the *Transcripts*, it is used mostly without rotation, that is, an extrusion that operates as a quasi-three-dimensional transition between a plan and section.

Sequence, the second representational method in Tschumi's drawings, depends on three types of relations: first, an internal relation connected to the 'method of work' – a transformational sequence described as a device or procedure, and second, two external relations, 'one dealing with the juxtaposition of actual spaces, the other with program (occurrences or events).' [336]

Architectural notational drawings 'already impl[y] a transformational sequence,' which tends to rely on 'rules of transformation, such as compression, rotation, insertion, and transference.' Borrowing from disparate influences such as Sergei Ejzenštejn's compositional montage (and later related to Luigi Moretti's theoretical writings on spatial sequences), Tschumi utilizes sequence to incorporate an architectural experience of time, or temporality, akin to film. [337] It denotes 'frame-by-frame techniques, the isolation of frozen bits of action.' [338] Sequencing implies a relationality between frames, so that each one is not understood in isolation, but carries the memories of all the preceding ones. It is used in articulation with framing, a relation that defines two conflicting fields in the *Transcripts*: 'the framing device – healthy, conformist, normal and predictable, regular and comforting, correct,' and 'the framed material, a place that only questions, distorts, compresses, displaces.' [339] Sequencing and framing are used in montaged combinations where the architectural space is continuously recombined and 'spatial relationships and physical dimensions of objects ... are like movie-shots from above ... intercut with those from below.' [340] Ultimately, Tschumi's transcription of the city into projected architecture is 'infinitely malleable, so that emotive, dramatic, or poetic attributes can change and unfold.' [341]

The design work showcased throughout this chapter explores the potential of conveying the *Transcripts* as a series of critical operations on Manhattan. The resulting methodology is concerned with both themes and issues of representation. First, it explores the representational tools and techniques that Tschumi innovatively developed in his notational drawings. Even though his drawings are regarded today as being more conventional than they certainly were at the time of their production in the early 1980s, they can still hold the potential to meaningfully engage with contemporary discourses and dynamics in the city, maybe precisely because the *Transcripts* are not about the city but on the city, as mentioned before. The focus, then, lies less on the external logics the architect utilized to anchor his translations of reality, and more on the rigor and critical creativity he applied to the internal logics of the sequences in the four episodes.

Questions of how thematic probes from the book can be transported (and transcribed) from the temporal context in which they were initially explored into more contemporary architectural and landscape-related discourses are perhaps more difficult to ascertain. On the one hand, there are themes that Tschumi identifies as being primordial to the project – space, event, movement, disjunction, notation, sequence or program, to name of few. These themes are explicitly formulated as preoccupations within the book, as well as outside of it, mostly in their relation to the architect's design practice. Like the *Transcripts*, the design work for *Insular Events* explores some of these themes, even if in expanded formulations brought about while using the Anthropocene debate as a framework of reference.

On the other hand, there are themes that Tschumi proposes as a secondary layer of support, and these are mostly of a contextual and geographical nature. The architect is explicit about some of them – for example, he explains that the park episode is set in Central Park, or that the street episode is set on 42nd Street. The reader is left with the impression that these references are used to sustain the argument that the book is about a *real* city and not a purely abstract geometric or formal exercise. But the context in which Tschumi operates is more concerned with the internal logics in the sequences and less with how they relate with Manhattan, whereas the logics developed in *Insular Events* place a lot of emphasis on the island's territorial context. The design exploration seems to be more heavily anchored at Manhattan's own contextual conditions.

Insular Events was developed in three interrelated narratives. The first exercise, called *Under the Rug*, examines *MT1–'The Park'* and reflects on Central Park's specific historical, geographical, geological and hydrological context. The internal logics used to produce a sequential series of drawings about the park – mostly in plan – are enmeshed in the park's own landscape and urban specificity. These logics are, to a certain extent, the events which propel the action in the storytelling act. The plan is also critically contextualized as a tool used politically to flatten the thickness of a city into its most dominant narratives.

The second exercise, called *Archaeologics of Domesticity*, takes *MT3—'The Tower' (The Fall)* to ponder how the contemporary geo-archaeologic entanglement postulated by the Anthropocene [342] can help design practice navigate some of the narratives that were forced to remain marginal to the city, or were erased by the city's own capitalist-driven evolution altogether. Tschumi's study of 'the movement of bodies in space through a simulated fall through the different floors that make up a skyscraper' [343] serves as the inspiration for the study of vertical movement of buried and forgotten objects vertically and along an unsettled, disturbed ground. The axonometric is used as the generator of the story that unearths and examines Seneca Village.

The final exercise, called *Archipelago of Dependencies* moves more freely between transcripts and their sequential motivations to deconstruct a dominant idea of Manhattan as a neatly framed territory of totality. It instead proposes a re-construction of the island-city as an archipelago of dependent internal and external islands, which superimpose and juxtapose different programs, in spatial or temporal coexistence or conflict.

Each of the three exercises is explained in more detail below, always with a complementary explanation of both the contexts in which they were formulated and any lateral or marginal events that further motivated them. The design exploration iteratively bridges more conventional methods of researching, drawing and modelling, and their sequential organization in the virtual installation. The structure of the latter was developed and used to create an experience of apparent control of the rhythm by which one sediments trains of thought about the work, and to coat storytelling with certain cinematic qualities.

5.3 Insular Events: Central Park, Seneca Village and Other Stories of Erasure

Insular Events was conceived as a virtual installation that weaves research with design as it narrates notational events mainly about and around Central Park. Divided into three instalments, the experience seeks to document a project that is both expository of certain island conditions and a critical retrospective analysis of Tschumi's work in the *Transcripts*.

Similar to Tschumi's *architecture of the event*, the work developed for *Insular Events* identifies and studies protagonists – a park, a village, a hydro-system, a topography – which then become representational devices; they trigger the production of space from their interactions, overlaps and superimpositions. Even if it is pointing at different conditions on the island, the project works out with the same tools as those used by Tschumi. Like the *Transcripts*, *Insular Events* also works on a notational style; both projects are discursive and not the things themselves. The change in focus proposed by the Anthropocene has correspondence in this work to a change in protagonists and the contexts in which they may be meaningful. The expansion to more-than-human assemblages suggests an effort in contextualizing them in their own historical, socio-cultural, political and environmental conditions. The resulting work seems more conservative than Tschumi's in what it tries to notice and protect. Its notations aim to offer meaning within a thickened context, and architecture's obligation seems to be, in a way, expanded.

Right in the first paragraph in the *Transcripts*, Tschumi explains the function and role of the modes of representation used to notate them. The architect compares the movements of the different protagonists in the stories to human actors on a stage set. [344] He adds that:

> The effect is not unlike an Eisenstein film script or some Moholy-Nagy stage directions. Even if the Transcripts become a self-contained set of drawings, with its own internal coherence, they are first a device. ...
> The temporality of the Transcripts inevitably suggests the analogy of film. Beyond a common twentieth-century sensibility, both share a frame-by-frame technique, the isolation of frozen bits of action. In both, spaces are not only composed, but also developed from shot to shot so that the final meaning of each shot depends on its context. [345]

In *Insular Events*, the plot lines appear on the screen through an action of consistent scrolling down. Sometimes they are dragged onto the screen frame, almost as if marginalia at the edges of a medieval manuscript were dragged into the main text. The scrolling down activates readings of the piece similar in many ways to Lázló Moholy-Nagy's graphic descriptions of scripts. More specifically, it borrows influence from Moholy-Nagy's sketch for the film *Dynamic of the*

A fixed camera hovers
over Manhattan in a
chronological flight
backwards.
Years, seasons.

Marianne Moore

Spring: masses of bloom, white
and pink cherry blossoms on
trees given us by Japan.

Local and continental
environmental
phenomena: fog, heat,
ice, rain, flood.

Pandemics.
Hurricane.
Terrorism.

Disparate events
continuously woven
into the fabric of
the park.

Marianne Moore

Winter: one catches sight of a
skater, arms folded, leaning to
the wind—the very symbol of
peaceful solitude, unimpaired
freedom. We talk of peace. This
is it.

An island
of islands
in an island.

Metropolis (1921–1922), an application of the artist's notion of *typophoto*, a form of 'modern synoptic communication' with the potential of being 'broadly pursued on another plane by means of the kinetic process, the film.' [346]

Moholy-Nagy's sketches offered a strong basis on which to then build a graphic strategy that helps organize the narration of the notational events throughout the virtual experience. This strategy relies on a form of *typophoto* combining text, image, photography and, in this case, also video. It is heavily noticed at times, while far looser at others.

Under the Rug

Under the Rug focuses on the exploration of two main questions. The first examines Central Park's rigid limits with the city and questions what the park could look like, were it able to escape the cartesian logic of the grid in which it was initially inscribed. The second ponders over the meaning of such an expansion if it were to follow more closely the landscape's topographical and hydrological conditions, instead of being forced to the political circumscription of land ownership and real-estate development.

The attempt to answer both questions triggered a cartographic analysis where several maps of Manhattan, and Central Park more specifically, were juxtaposed to confront territorial appearances and disappearances, political decisions about land registry, as well as processes of land valuation affecting the properties where the park was constructed and adjacent territories.

A close analysis of the geology and hydrology in Manhattan's central area also proved useful in the creative exploration of the park's limits. Scarred by glaciation, the old local geology of gneiss and schist guided the waterlines diagonally to the subsequent orthogonal grid. With a north-south crest roughly running to the west of Central Park, most waterlines in this part of the island drain from its core into the East River. The hydrology slowly eroded this landscape over time, creating a series of 'dry islets' in the area where the park is today and a series of marshes in the area currently occupied by the Upper East Side.

Through this initial exploration it became possible to identify conditions of wetness and dryness in and around the park. Several units were identified and conceptualized as possessing certain insular conditions. The resulting landscape is less like a unified rug, continuous in its surface extension, than a fractured archipelago, which breaks up the rectilinear limits of the park and expands into adjacent city territories, currently occupied by the grid. Fracturing becomes a ground operation that can mean different things: hydrological circulation; topographical erosion; geological entropy; as well as infrastructural support, mostly through the presence of reservoirs (still existing or not) as cuts in the rock for holding water.

Some of the park's paths and roads remain visible in the archipelagic fragments. Like the continental tectonic plates that preserved a geometric memory of each other suggestive of the unifying theory of *Pangea*, so do these islands with interrupted routes suggest a previously unified territory. Suddenly, the old cartographies from which these islands were initially constructed transport us to an eventual far remote future, where Central Park is no longer a landscape unit or surface at the center of Manhattan, but a series of territorial ruins that preserve some memorial traces of a long-lost past – a Paradise Lost of Central Park.

This design iteration relied on Tschumi's approach in the creation of *MT1*–*'The Park.'* Exploring the tension inherent in the squared frames of the triptych Tschumi used in his first transcribed iteration – Space, Event, Movement – the design work developed here argues for a disruption of the rectilinear boundaries of the park's own frame, something that acquires maximum expression when seen from above. The iterative work was rigorous in reading the park from top-down projections, using in effect maps and plans from different periods: pre-park and during its construction. The imagination of what Central Park could look like if it could escape to the city, as in some sort of revenge against the rigidity of the grid, took the form of a sequential notational event.

In *MT1*, the supporting narrative is linear and 'tend[s] to favor temporality.' [347] Furthermore, Tschumi explains that in this transcript 'each set of frames determined the following by acting as a starting point modified by a rule of transformation (such as compression), or by the addition of a new "existing" element (such as insertion).' [348] All three methodological principles – temporality, compression and insertion – became equally key in *Under the Rug*. First, the juxtaposition of maps or plans followed a close examination of the dates of their production and the period they depicted (which were not always coincident), to reconstruct the moments immediately before the construction of Central Park and the period of its initial establishment. Second, several map elements were either compressed or inserted into each other through collage, in an attempt to visualize temporal change in the territory. The making of temporality became a central preoccupation in the practice of an *architecture of the event*, where architecture is neither simply figure nor ground but an assemblage resulting from the dissolution of the two. Event in *Under the Rug* is something essentially more-than-human, which marks perhaps the biggest divergence from Tschumi's work, where the studied events are essentially human.

After the initial cartographic iteration, Central Park's conceptual archipelago was subsequently translated into a model. The clay pieces inherit some of the conditions of the juxtaposed maps from which they originated, and their extrusion results from both a negotiation with the topographical levels of the real city and the desire to exacerbate some of the insular conditions they suggest. Clay holds material qualities deemed relevant for the study – mineral plasticity, malleability and adaptability – and supports critical extrusion, thus challenging the idea of the park as a thin horizontal surface, or a landscape rug.

The diagonal orientation of the natural water systems inspired the creation of a support structure that sustains the clay pieces in place, in relation to their geographical position on the maps and plans. With the main pieces made from reclaimed wood – collected on East coast beaches, which conceptually activates the possibility of their having been 'drained out' of Manhattan through the very hydrological systems under analysis – the supporting structure also benefits from a series of metal insertions, a secondary scaffolding structure that holds the model's different components together.

Clay islets, reclaimed wood and metal scaffolding determine the model's three main datum lines. Together, they underscore the interest of this study in the thickness of Central Park, that is, a study of the park in section. The provocation here mostly relates to what conditions

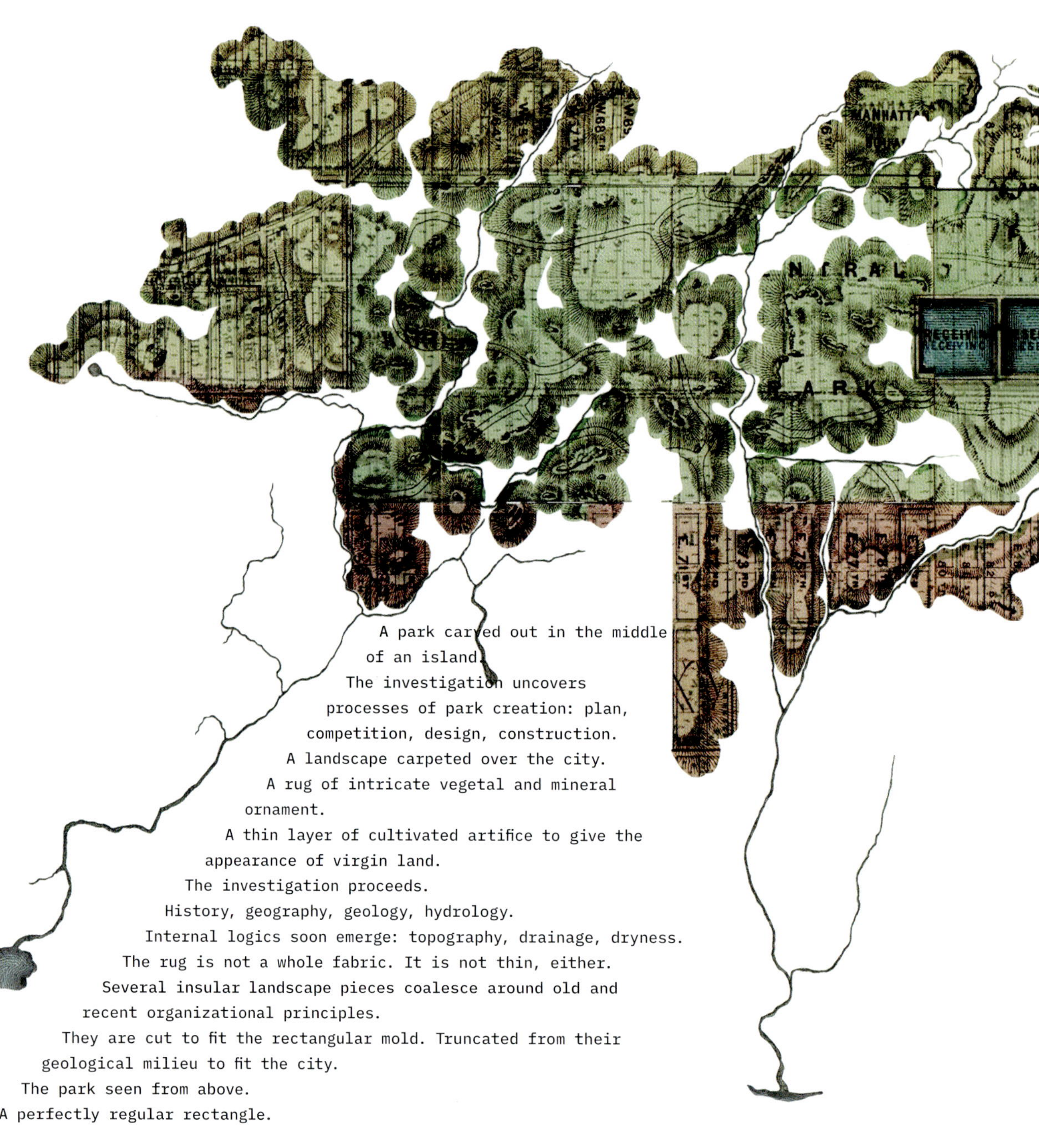

A park carved out in the middle
of an island.
The investigation uncovers
processes of park creation: plan,
competition, design, construction.
A landscape carpeted over the city.
A rug of intricate vegetal and mineral
ornament.
A thin layer of cultivated artifice to give the
appearance of virgin land.
The investigation proceeds.
History, geography, geology, hydrology.
Internal logics soon emerge: topography, drainage, dryness.
The rug is not a whole fabric. It is not thin, either.
Several insular landscape pieces coalesce around old and
recent organizational principles.
They are cut to fit the rectangular mold. Truncated from their
geological milieu to fit the city.
The park seen from above.
A perfectly regular rectangle.

What if
Central
Park
were
able to
escape
the
cartesian
logic of
the grid
in which
it was
inscribed?

What if it could expand following
the landscape's topographical and
hydrological geologics?

The investigation turns
into creative generation,
mostly in plan.
The landscape is laminated
in a series of sequential
drawings.
The sequence animates the
design.
Each new layer unleashes the
pieces from their rectangular
strangulation.
Each piece suddenly grabs the city
beyond the park limits.

the park might have erased as it was laid out. Acknowledging the political motivations behind the construction of such an ambitious endeavor brings out a curiosity of what might have been concealed along the way.

Seen from below, the model loses its initial definition around a recalibration of Central Park and begins to reveal other constructing principles related to gravitational support, material weight and balance. From this angle a new subterranean landscape emerges, with contours of a Waddingtonian *epigenetic landscape.* [349]

In the virtual installation the model is introduced as a flashback. Following a series of operations, some of which are illustrated, the three-dimensional piece was entirely produced as a physical artifact anchored at a scale and with very specific size constraints determined by space and material limitations. Each operation was defined in sequence and as a natural next step in the creation of the model's different layers.

Constructed as part of the design research process rather than because of it, the model was also a generator of new thinking, an artifact that steered the investigation into new possibilities. The folding of the model back into drawing and, subsequently, into the virtual world, included several operations applied systematically and in relation to each other: measuring, rotating, projecting, staging or lighting. Special attention should be given to the latter two in the production of a sequential photographic registration, which was then used as the basis for generating new drawings. In turn, these drawings raised new questions necessary to take the research further into the eventual meaning of contextualizing the park's thickness to reappraise its own insular conditions in Manhattan. What has this thickness created, what has it erased, and finally, how can it trigger the imagination of new ways for the park to relate back to the city?

The sequential drawings included top-down photographic assemblages of the model, inserted as background and middle ground layers of more complex cartographic impressions. Through the juxtaposition of these serial and successive laminations – based less on the landscape's current topographical conditions and more on the light contrasts modelled accordingly to its original (pre-park) features – it is possible to begin to conceive of the park as a field of material exchange. Laminated light conditions were considered both as waves and particles. *Light as fluid* drained like water from high topographical points to low, or, from the Upper West Side towards east, running through Central Park. *Light as particle* was swept like dust from dry areas (higher) into wet basins (lower), regions of light dispersion and regions of light accumulation. [350] The light studies become notational drawings with some interesting correspondences to material movements from the park out into the city and vice-versa. [351] Vegetal and mineral materials are continuously produced in the park and expelled out of it through the air, soil, and water systems. Conversely, the city is also a source of myriad materials that continuously contaminate the park's grounds.

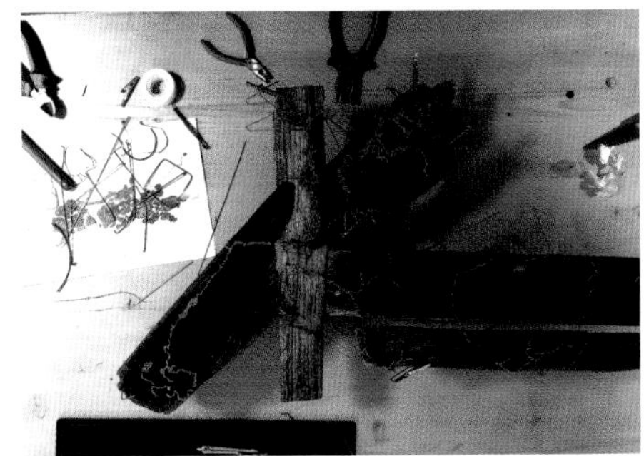

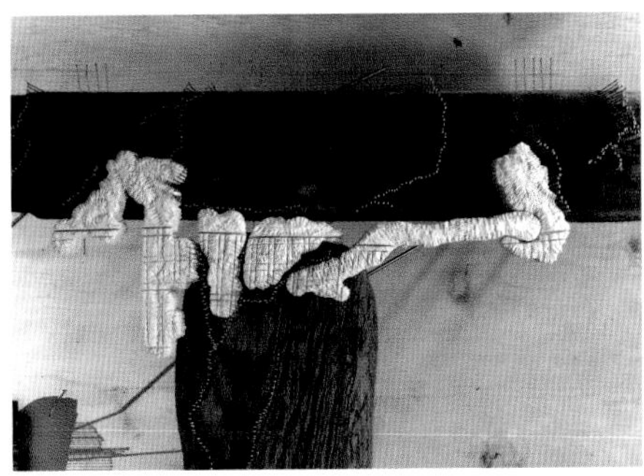

Under the Rug, Particular views of the model.
(next pages) *Under the Rug*, Clay pieces
catalogued and assembled, and additional
views of the model.

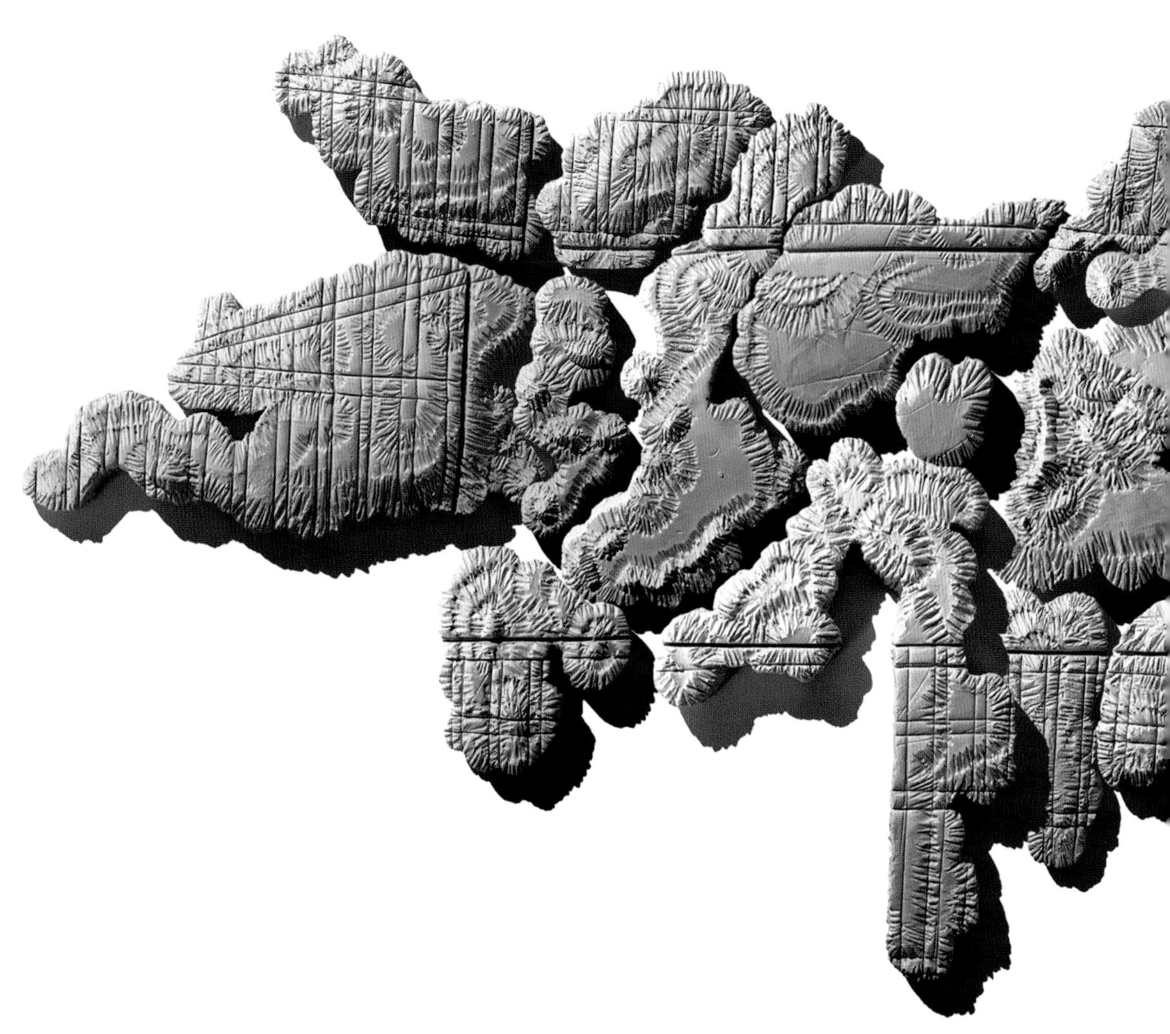

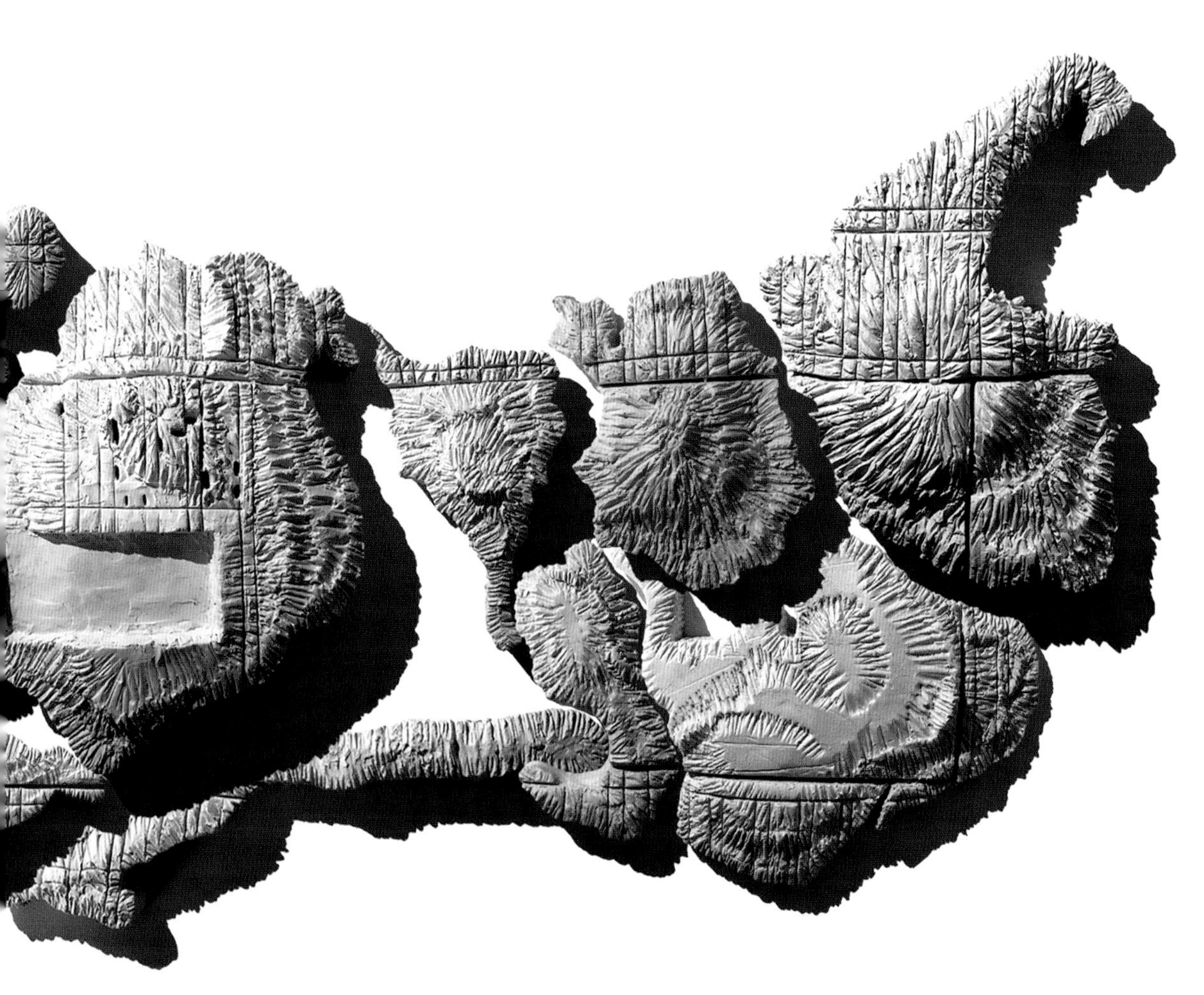

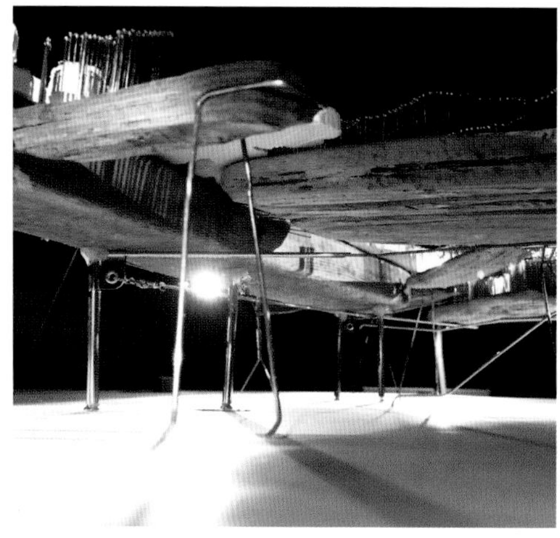

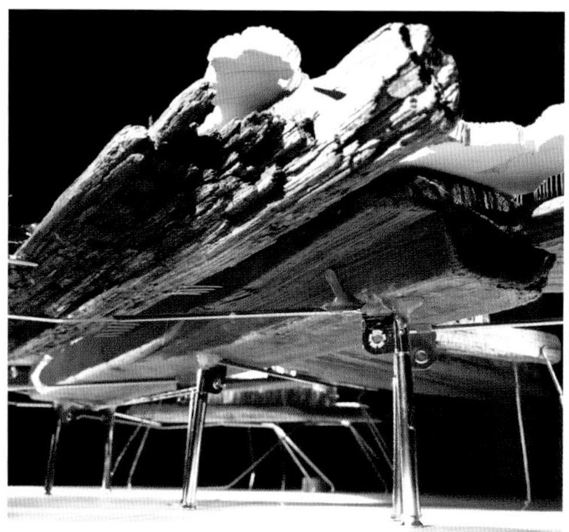

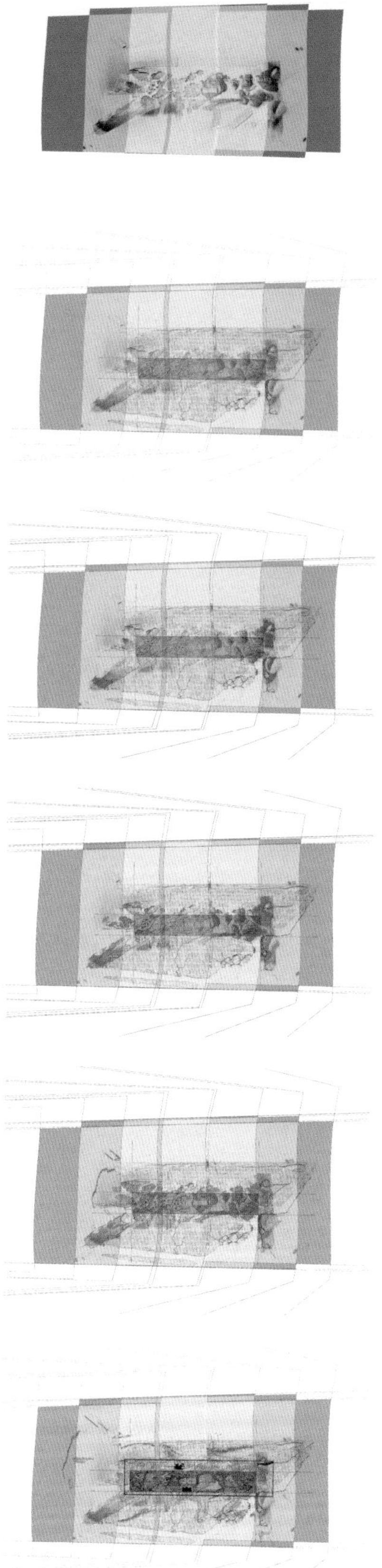

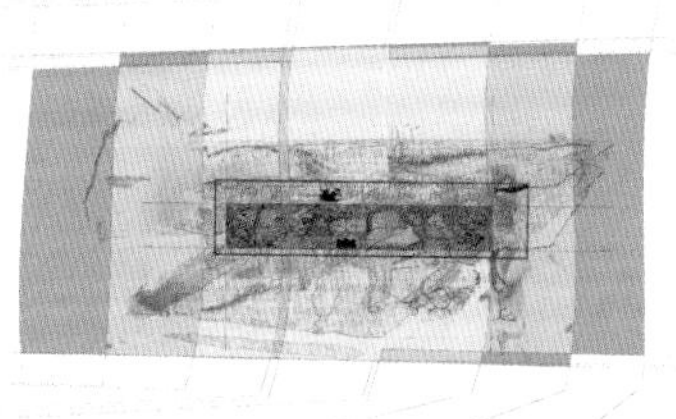

(this and next pages) *Under the Rug*,
Lamination of Material Movement,
serial studies.

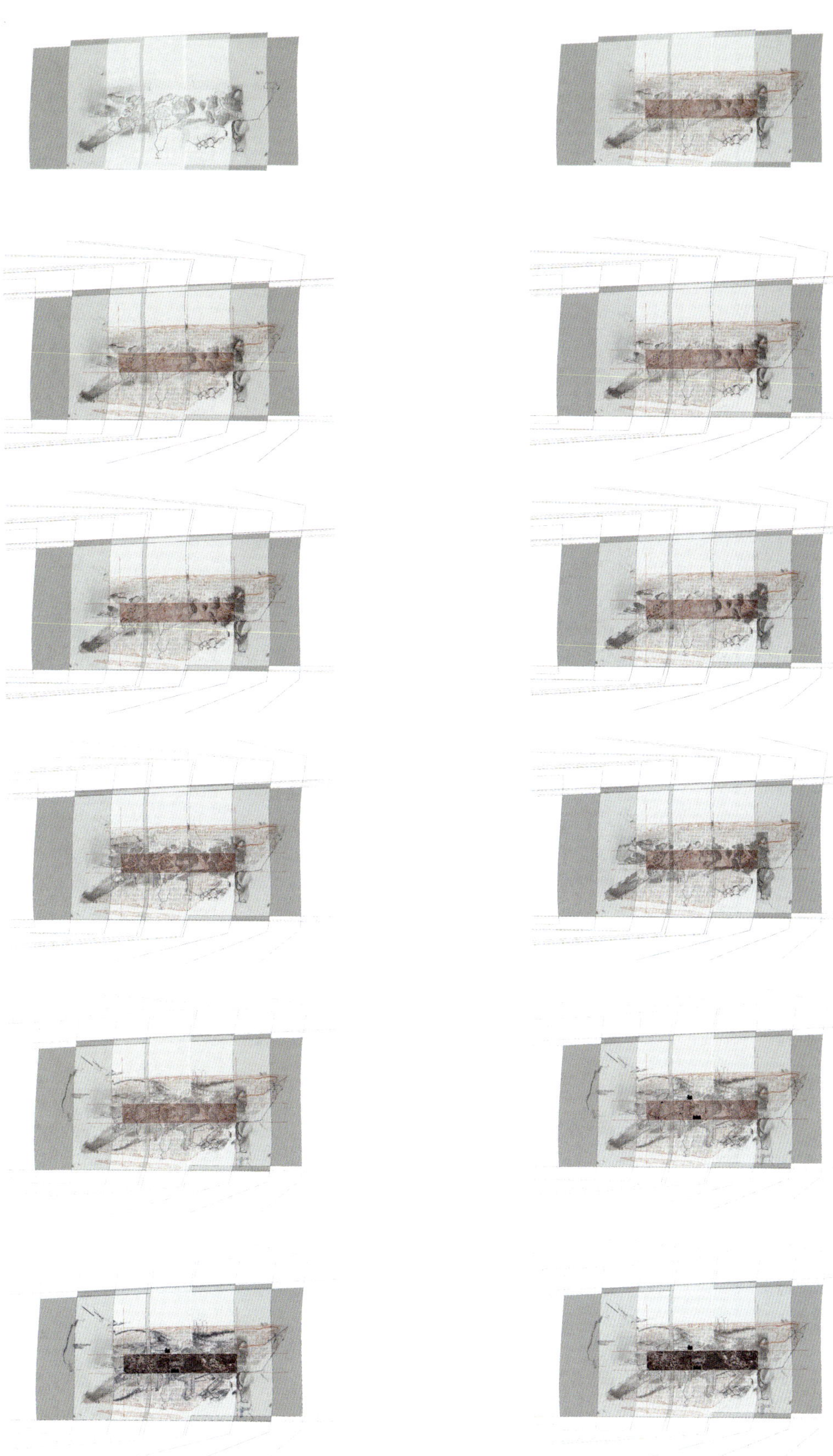

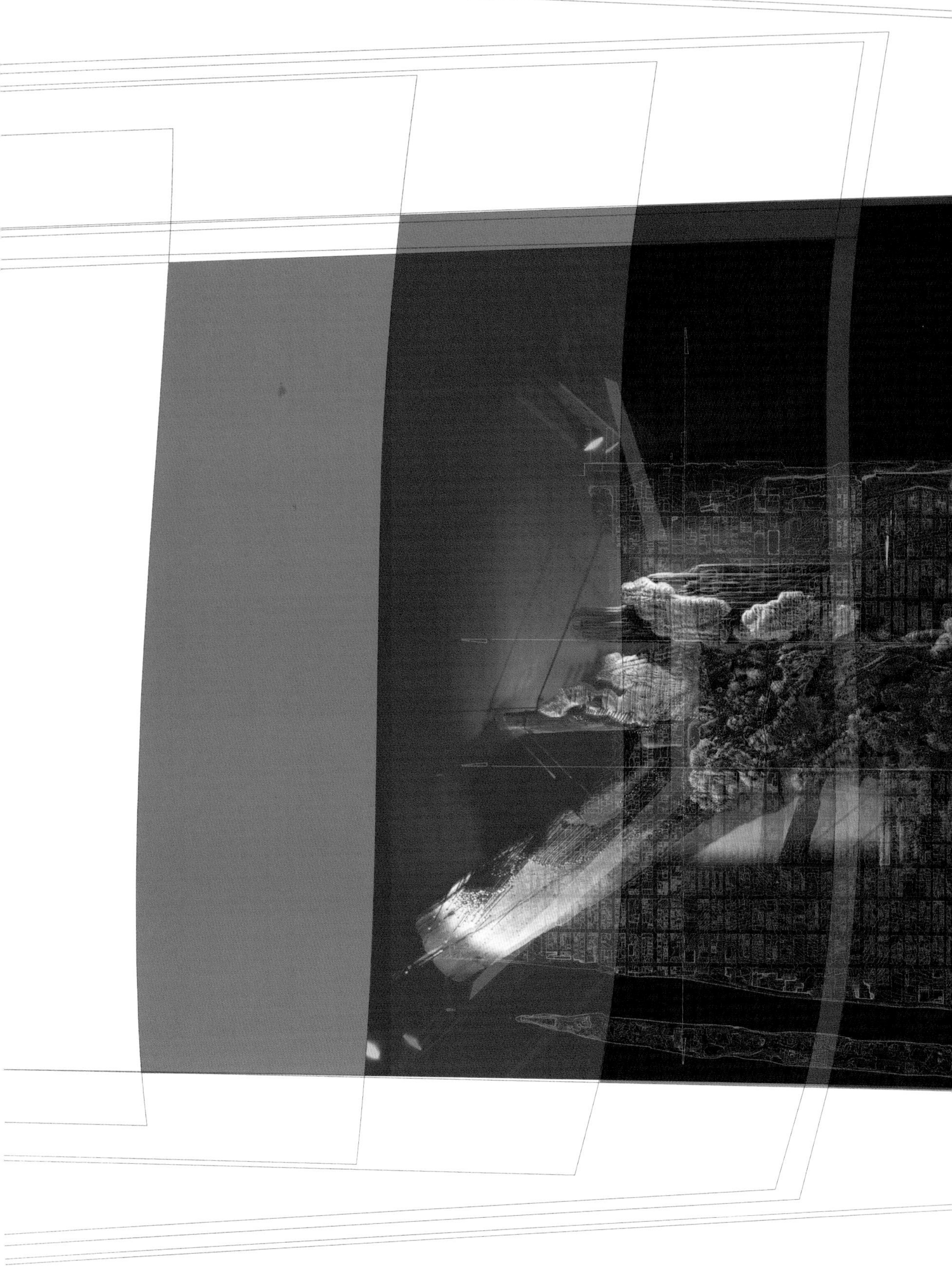

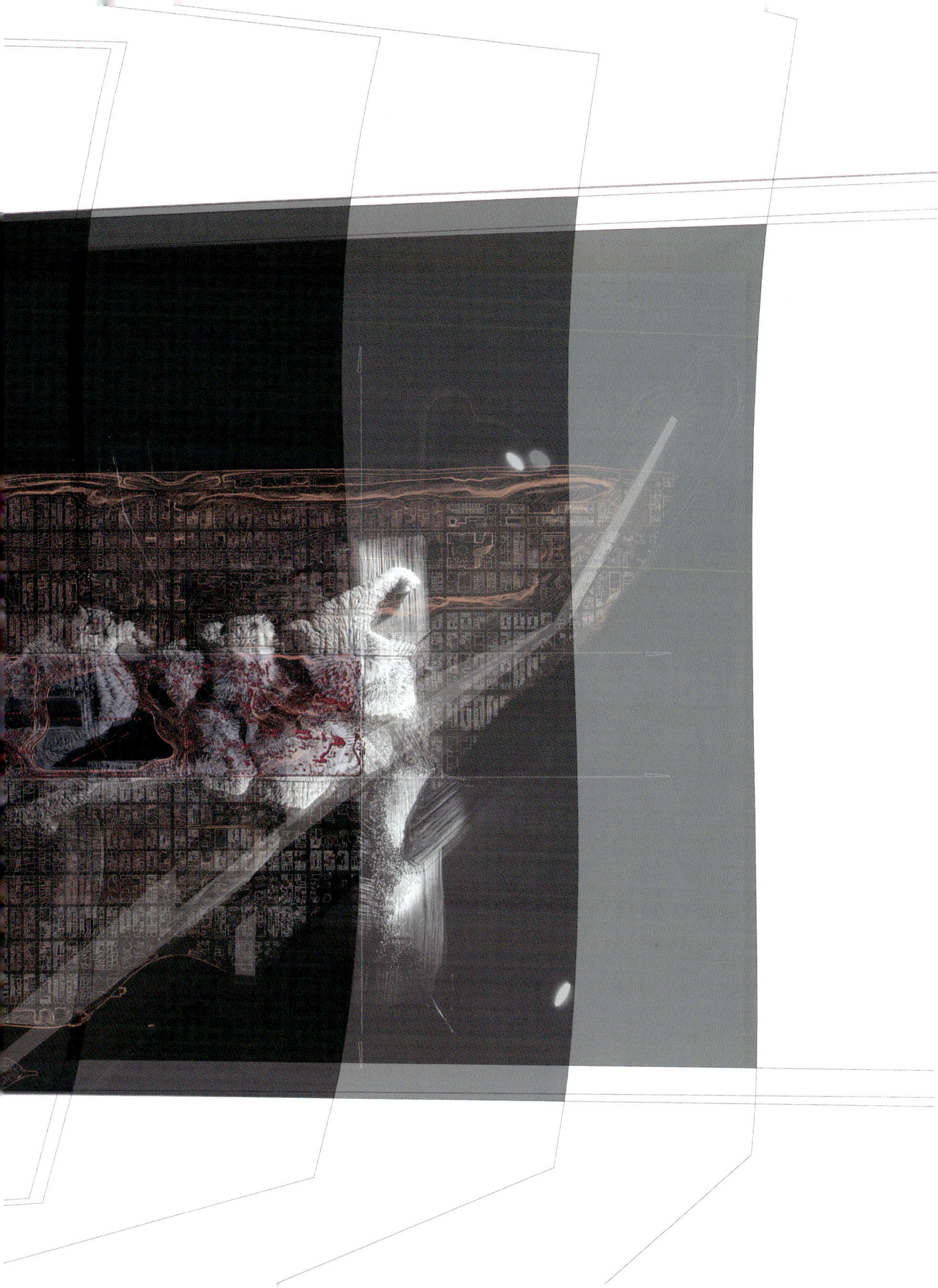

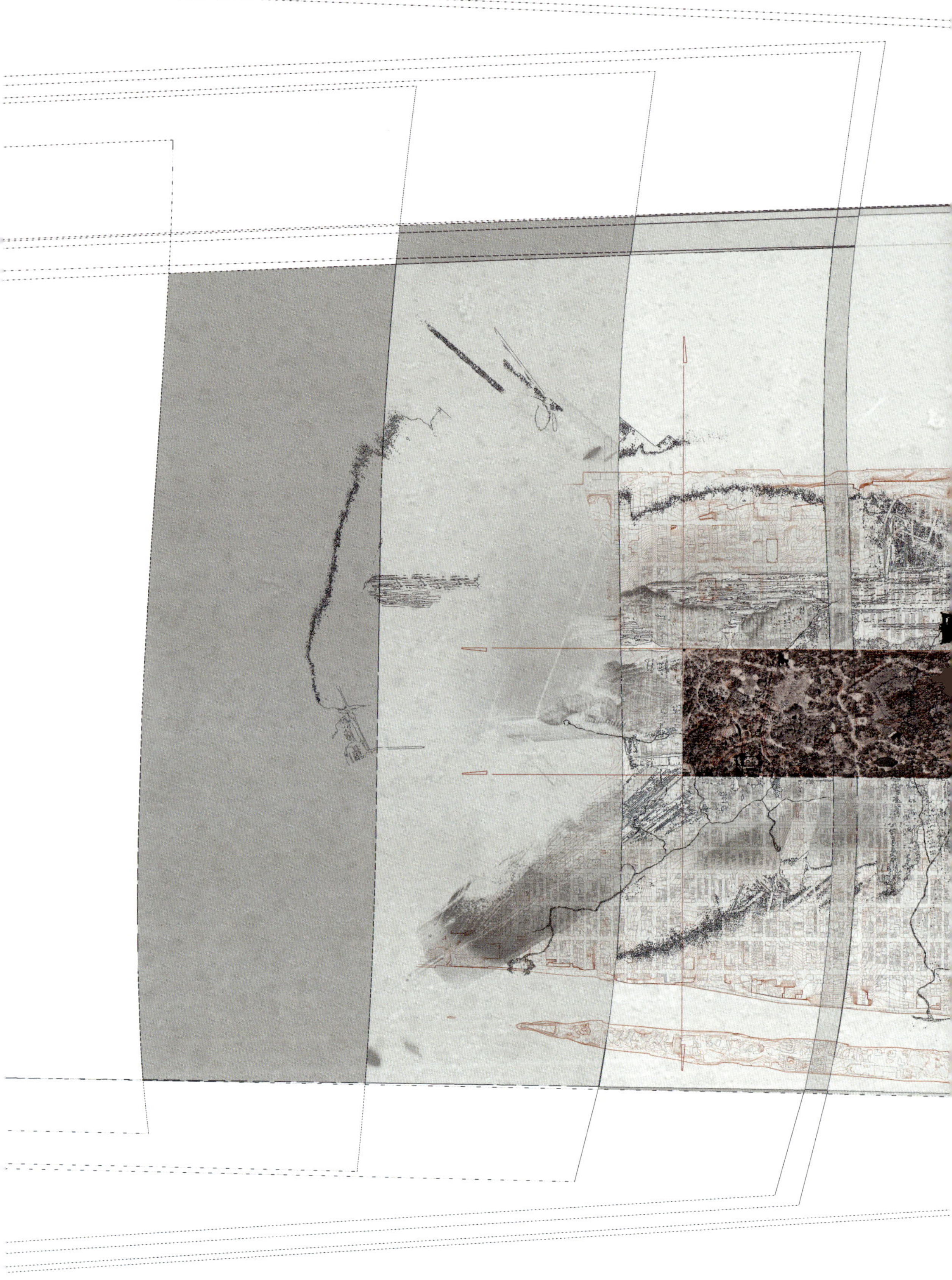

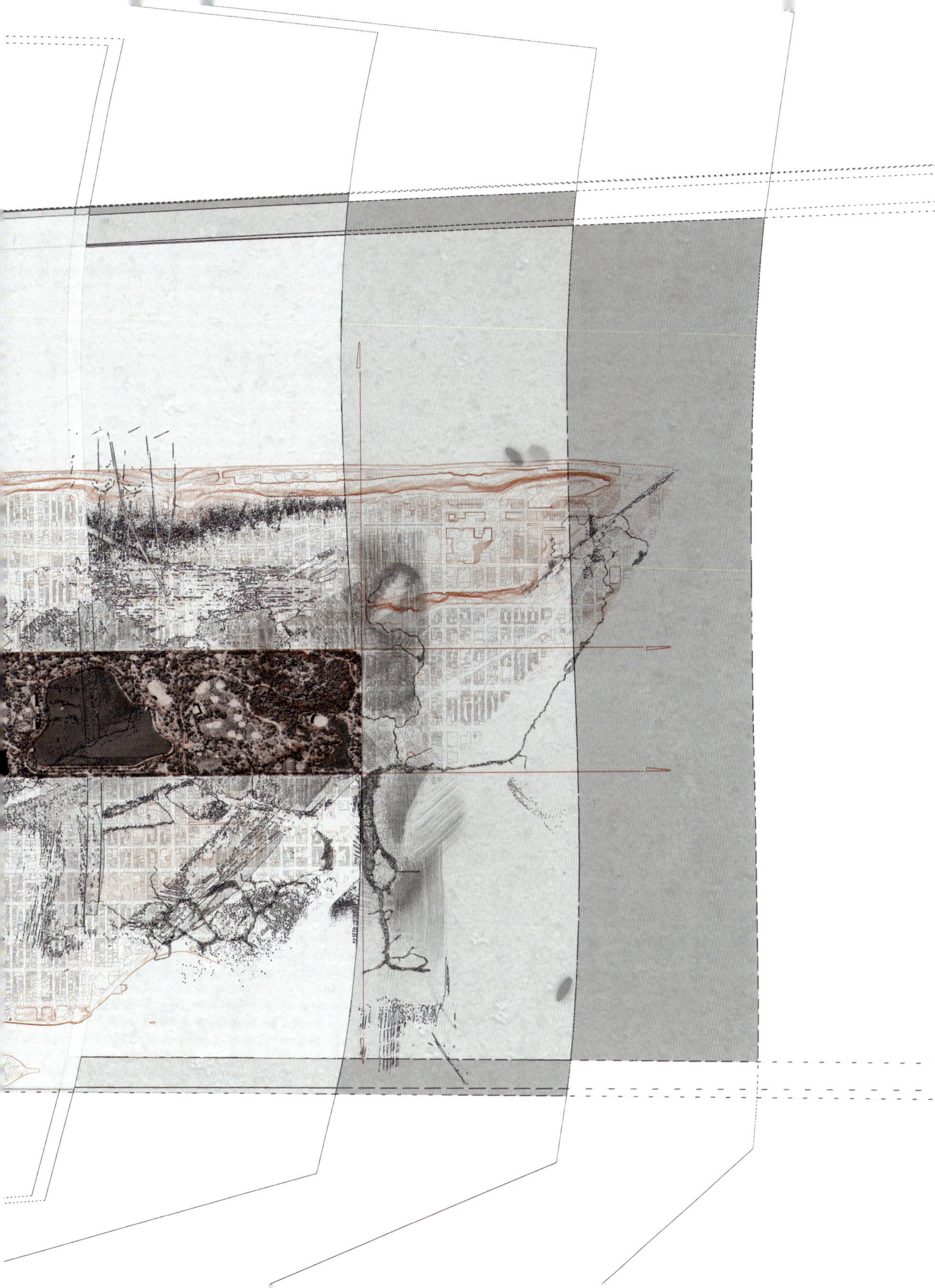

A Park and a Village.
Two main characters in a myriad of
mundane stories.
Domestic, even if *groundbreaking* stories.
The Village was there before the Park.
It was erased by its picturesque ambitions.
For more than a century the City forgot
the Village, the stories were reduced to
one character.
Some remained curious about the lost
Village. It was now the stuff of urban
myths.
The ground kept its promise: it preserved
the memory of the Village, shards of its
domesticity.
Slowly, it began to move inside, like food
along a digestive system.
Old artifacts emerged to the surface of
the Park. It was a new surface to them;
one they no longer recognized.
A long process led to an excavation.
Ruins were dug out, the footprint of the
villagers.
The artifacts were classified, attributed,
given retrospective meaning.
The pits were covered once again.
The Village remains as a character made
of fragmented memories.
The Park resumed its public life.

BROADWAY
ROAD OR PUBLIC DRIVE
72ND STREET
79TH
STREET
5TH AVENUE
6TH AVENUE
7TH AVENUE
8TH
Play Ground
The Green
DRIVE
THE LAKE
NATIVE
ORNAMENTAL WATER
CROTON

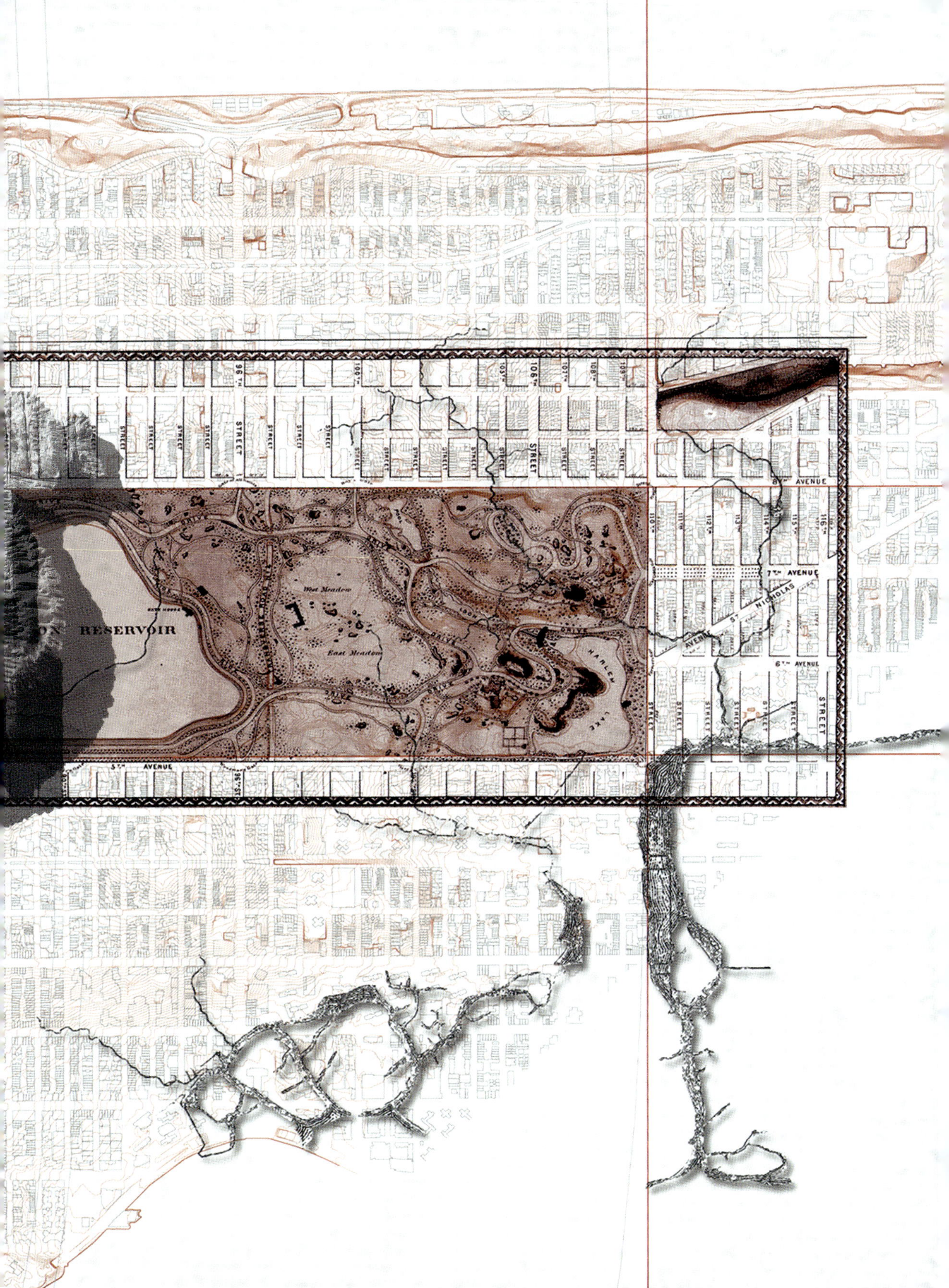
RESERVOIR
West Meadow
East Meadow
DRIVE
DRIVE
HARLEM LANE
96TH STREET
105TH STREET
106TH STREET
107TH STREET
108TH STREET
109TH STREET
110TH STREET
111TH STREET
112TH STREET
113TH STREET
114TH STREET
115TH STREET
116TH STREET
8TH AVENUE
7TH AVENUE
ST NICHOLAS AVENUE
6TH AVENUE
5TH AVENUE
96TH ST.

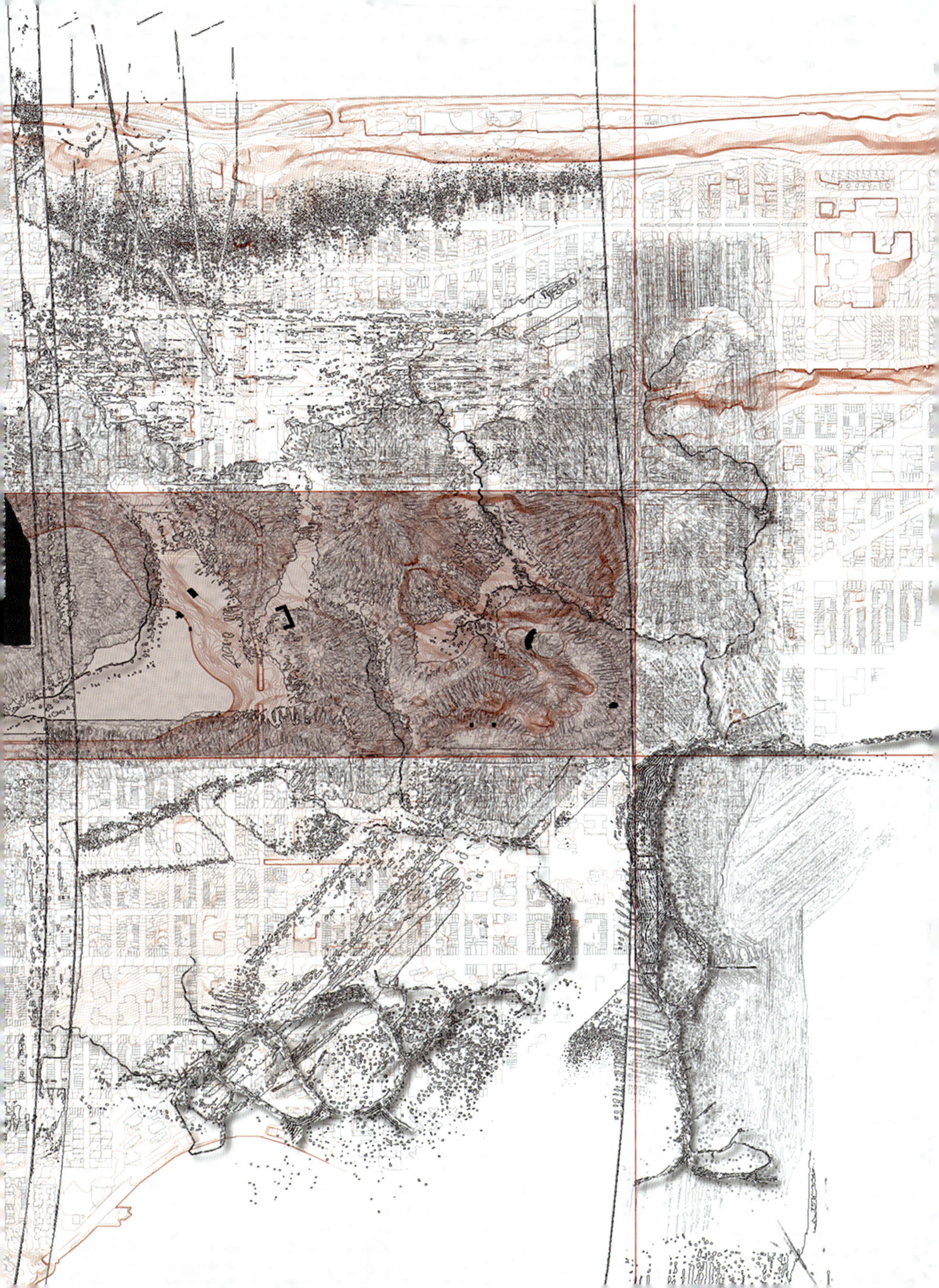

Archaeologics of Domesticity

Seneca Village was an antebellum middle-class Black community on the western edge of what is today Central Park, between 82nd and 89th streets and adjacent to the old Receiving Reservoir. Founded in the 1820s, the village thrived over the following two decades, mostly supported by free African Americans, who bought land and built their homes outside of the city edge, likely to escape from Lower Manhattan's dense and racist urban environment. [352] Seneca Village's grounds included rock outcroppings (Summit Rock) and damp lower lands, both of which made them unappealing for real estate development as the city grew northwards. But by the mid-1850s the village was included in the official surveys to build Central Park, giving the State justification to take the land by eminent domain and evict its roughly 1,600 residents. [353] The construction of the new park was circumscribed by a white-elitist narrative that depreciated Seneca's inhabitants as squatters living in shanties. [354] The park erased one of the first Black-led villages in the city to its near obscurity for over a century, making it the material of urban myths, until its brief but informative description in Blackmar and Rosenzweig's 1992 book *The Park and the People*. [355] What is currently known about Seneca Village is mostly thanks to the historical and archaeological investigations led by historian Cynthia Copeland, together with Nan Rothschild and Diana diZerega Wall, co-founders of the *Seneca Village Project* (1998). [356]

The stories and archaeological evidence about Seneca Village support the reappraisal of Central Park – a canonical landscape of the West – through the formulation of an expanded understanding of the park also as a landscape that erased pre-existing communities and their *lifeworlds*. [357] A more complete contextualization of the village informs a critique of the park that reformulates its iconic status also as a reinvented pristine nature [358] – or an Arcadian synthetic carpet, as Rem Koolhaas defined it [359] – towards its acceptance as an ever-evolving and fluid landscape that needs to be framed historically, politically and racially.

Such a recontextualization of the park benefits from a notion of *ground* where distinctions between natural and artificial are no longer possible. The Anthropocene theory accepts that ground is made of mineral and fossilized matter as much as synthetically produced materials that unsettle it and eventually sediment because of human activity. The entanglement emerges also from a reappraisal of geology, archaeology and the relation between the two. Questioning a disciplinary separation between the two fields – 'partly due to increasing academic specialization and division of labor, splitting respective subject matters along disciplinary lines' [360] – the Anthropocene proposes instead a convergence between divergent practices, with geology becoming increasingly more interested in the study of artificial ground and archaeology expanding the scope of its stratigraphic studies beyond human presence. [361]

If we accept that 'the Anthropocene is a politically infused geology,' as proposed by theorist Kathryn Yusoff, we have to acknowledge that it has also facilitated histories of erasure through racism inscribed in geologic violence. [362] Her remarks that the 'Anthropocene-in-the-making' is enabled by racial blindness should also be read as an opportunity to engage with often marginalized 'histories of [B]lack and [I]ndigenous' cultures. [363] The debate adds meaning to the study of the political motivations behind the construction of Central Park, and deserves close attention in the study of Seneca Village. The park's predominantly white elitist storyline systematically erased non-white, sometimes more specifically non-Anglophone or even non-British collectivities that existed in its territories previously. Seneca Village, similar to habitatoins of Irish pig keepers or German gardeners, just to name a few settlements in this area, was not only demolished by eminent domain to build the park and initiate one of the greatest real-estate operations ever seen up until that point. It was vilified and erased from the map, quite literally, as well as from the memories of the city. An Anthropocenic understanding of Central Park, one that conceives of the village through entangled geo-archaeological practices has, therefore, the ethico-political responsibility of forcefully dragging Seneca Village right back to the surface.

The production of the body of design work related to Seneca Village included the development of a methodology with two interrelated methods: first, a spatial interpretative mapping of Marilyn Nelson's poems from her 2015 book *My Seneca Village*, a literary 'portrait of a community, a collection of individual portraits that converge to form a communal portrait,'[364] and second, a series of extrusions that follow Tschumi's approach in the *Transcripts*.

Nelson's poetry, which comes supported by brief parallel descriptions offering insight into the scenes, summons other writings and portraits about other communities and individuals to create a parallel existence of invented characters and their world.[365] The poems, as well as the ways in which they are structured in the book, became the basis for imagining some of the spatial and temporal conditions of the everyday nineteenth-century landscapes of Seneca Village.

MT3—'The Tower', subtitled *The Fall*, focuses on the conditions of space that contain programs of containment: 'house, office, prison, hotel, asylum.'[366] The subtitle of this third transcript – the only document out of the four to receive one – is intriguing in how explicitly it conveys what the focus of this exercise seems to be: the free fall of a body descending vertically which activates an architectural excavation of the high building in elevation. In what is arguably the most cinematographic scene in the book, Tschumi notates 'someone's flight and subsequent fall through the full height of a Manhattan tower block, it's "cells" and its "yards."'[367] Descending produces a sensation of vertigo: the drawings invite our imagination of someone free falling alongside the building as well as an anticipation of the consequences. They drag the viewer into a vertical architectural world being carved out through the fall as the event unfolds. 'The drastic alteration of perceptions caused by the fall is used to explore various spatial transformations and their typological distortions.'[368]

Tschumi's short introduction to *MT3* in the book was first conceptualized as a script in the design iteration. The script was then adapted into a second edited version that suits the needs of the representational activities involved in unearthing Seneca Village. This led to a thought-

(next pages) *Archaeologics of Domesticity*, Unearthing Seneca Village and script for operations based on the *Transcript's MT3—The Park*

Seneca Village was there
before Central Park; it
was erased by picturesque
ambitions. For more than
a century there were only
stories about the Park.
The Village was the stuff
of urban myths. The ground
kept its promise; it
preserved the memory of
the antebellum middle-class
African American community
in shards of domesticity.

Slowly the remnants of
the Village moved up the
ground, like food along
a digestive system. Old
artifacts were spat to
the surface of the Park.
It was a new surface to
them, one they no longer
recognized. A long process
led to an excavation of the
villagers' footprint. Ruins
were dug out. Artifacts
were classified, attributed,

given retrospective
meaning. The pits were
covered once again. The
Village was reassembled
through glimpses of
fragmented memories. The
Park resumed its public
life.

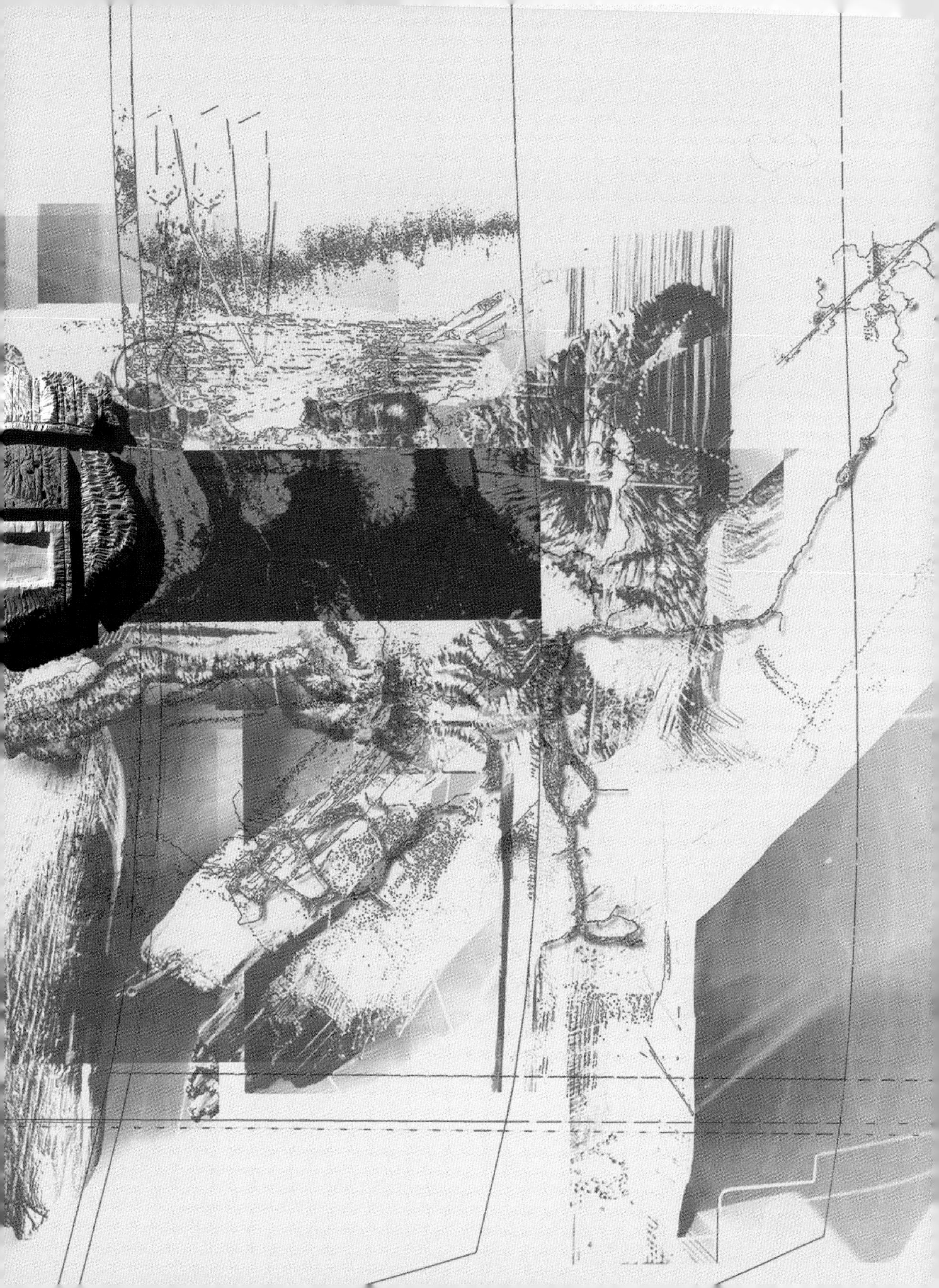

~~MT3~~ starts
with ~~five variations on an~~
~~archetypal sequence of~~
spaces (rooms along ~~a~~
~~corridor~~), then progressively modifies them
through the introduction (transgression of
movement patterns. On a second stage, it then
performs what might be called a 'zooming'
operation, as it suddenly focuses on one detail
of the final operation
and enlarges it to a new scale (the scale of ~~communal courtyards~~
as opposed to the earlier scale of single cells).
In turn, these ~~frames~~ (which here coincide
with the yards and their institutional
use: ~~prison, hotel, asylum, etc.~~) are transformed
(transgressed) by a further movement or event
(~~a falling body~~) and lead
to the final configuration of a continuous ~~and~~
~~vertical~~ sequence of spaces. ~~MT3~~ thus sees
event and movement coincide in formal
terms, even if the event's cultural implications
inevitably differ from the significance of the
movement pattern (which in this case
it taken to be neutral).

Archaeologics of Domesticity (AD) starts

with six regular perimeters prepared for

archaeological digs on three archetypal

spaces (landscape rooms along the park's

paths), then progressively modifies them

through the introduction (transgression) of

movement patterns. On a second stage, it then

performs what might be called a 'zooming'

operation, as it suddenly focuses on one detail

of the final operation on one of the perimeters

and enlarges it to a new scale (the scale of a pit

as opposed to the earlier scale of single cells).

In turn, these extrusions (which here coincide

with the yards and their archaeological

use: sites of excavation) are transformed

(transgressed) by a further movement or event

(fallen artifacts of a former village) and lead

to the final configuration of a continuous and

horizontal sequence of spaces. AD thus sees

event and movement partially coincide in formal

terms, even if the event's cultural implications

inevitably differ from the significance of the

movement pattern (which in this case

is taken to be neutral).

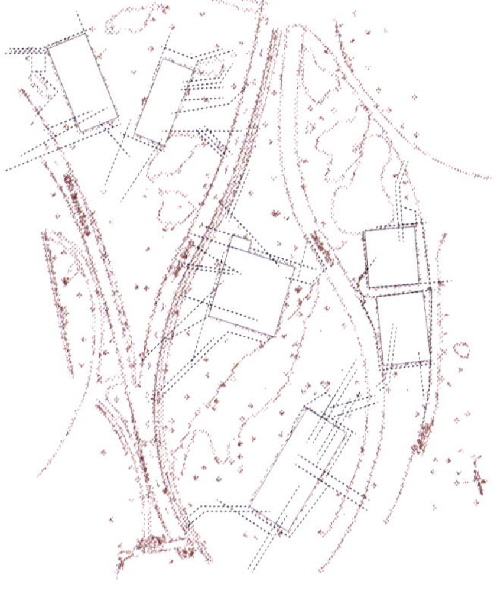

experiment where the second, adapted script emerges from Tschumi's original one. The script adaptation became a methodological tool used to structure the production of a sequential notational event that studies the village in its own geo-archaeological entanglements. It informed the iterative process involved in the extrusion and excavation of ground to study the spatial conditions that may have existed in the village.

Archaeologics of Domesticity departs from a plan prepared for an archeological excavation in Central Park in 2011. [371] The plan located the five pits initially delineated in the park. By studying the relation between the pits and the current paths in the park, a speculation was made on the main directions of movement around them, as well as the areas they determine. The areas were then extruded and analyzed in closer detail in relation to the new ground datums provided by the excavation. Three notational drawings were produced to speculate on the mundane landscapes that may have existed in the village. These drawings operate as animated sequences in the virtual exhibition. [370]

In *My Seneca Village*, several poems are dedicated to the land, beginning with 'Land Owner,' a poem about a bootblack with his own place, through which he can secure the right to vote. It includes 'Saplings,' about a working woman who plants an orchard, and two poems narrating actions set in gardens. And it also includes 'To Know,' about a woman packing her belongings as she is forced to leave her property behind. *Landscapes of Cultivation and Pollination*, the first of three drawings, explores the inner workings of a swampy and barren land that was transformed into a series of finely woven spaces of production, fertility,and diversity. The drawing examines different farmhouses and the properties around them devoted to agricultural production for subsistence. Besides the extrusion of the most heavily used areas around the houses, other types of circulation across the properties and between different properties were notated. The study of planted materials was supported by the landscape studies and botanical analysis included in the 2011 excavations report.

My Seneca Village also narrates the domestic life of an imagined community. Several poems describe female-led scenes in kitchens, central spaces of communitarian care, tradition and learning. [371] From inside these kitchens, in 'Sky Land' or 'The Park Theatre,' we learn about cultural events in the city, riots, revolts and weddings. Kitchens were sometimes hiding refuges of the *Underground Railroad*, a large network of exaping slace from the American South to Canada ('Conductor'). On a closer scale, the second drawing, titled *Landscapes of Pampering and Gossip*, experiments with intimate movements inside tight rooms related to braiding, grooming, cooking and gossiping. The drawing takes one of the houses from the first exploration and imagines its floorplan following the construction principles of the *dogtrot house*. [372]

Nelson's book also explores the socio-political tensions of a turning point in the United States, in the period immediately before the Civil War. New York, among other cities, was reluctantly accepting recently freed African American slaves to purchase land, become citizens and eventually take active part in the democratic processes, but that was not the case in the majority of Central and Southern States. Poems such as 'African Mutual Relief Society,' 'Address' or 'Babylon' describe the important role local churches played in social and anti-racist activism. Churches were also schools for African American infants ('Too Light for Gravity'), architectures of refuge ('Wild Night') and places of celebration ('Rejoice with Me') and mourning ('Council of Brothers'). Expanding in scale once again, the third drawing, titled *Landscapes of Activism and Mourning,* initiates a dialogue between the villagers and their other territories of departure, arrival or punctual adventure. Two local churches play a pivotal role in anchoring the notations in the drawing as well as the movement along the virtual piece.

(next pages) *Archaeologics of Domesticity,* Based on the Excavation Site Map of Seneca Village, extrusion became a tool to unearth the site. The study continued with a sequence of animated drawings divided into three chapters: *Landscapes of Cultivation and Pollination, Landscapes of Pampering and Gossip,* and *Landscapes of Activism and Mourning.*

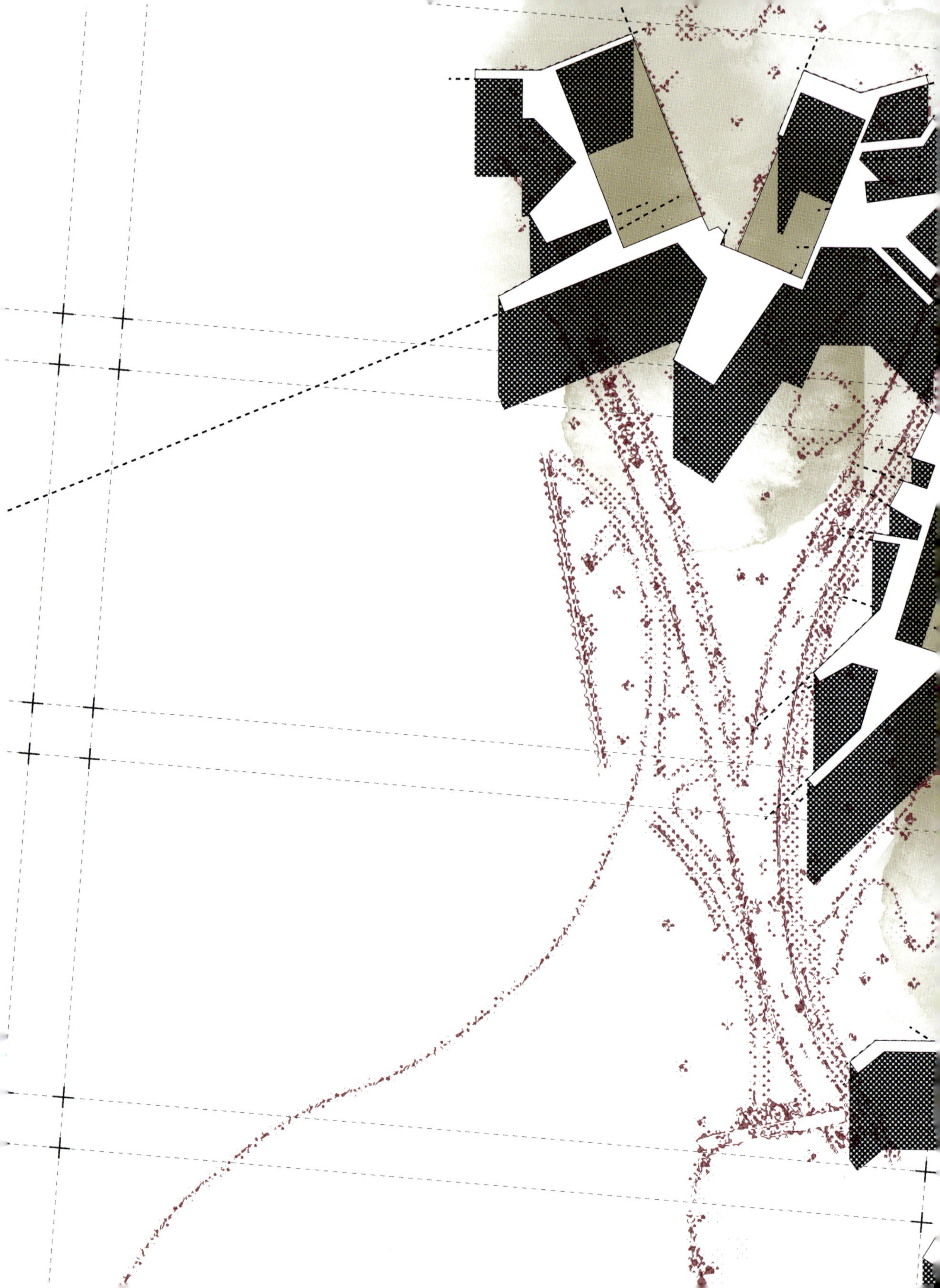

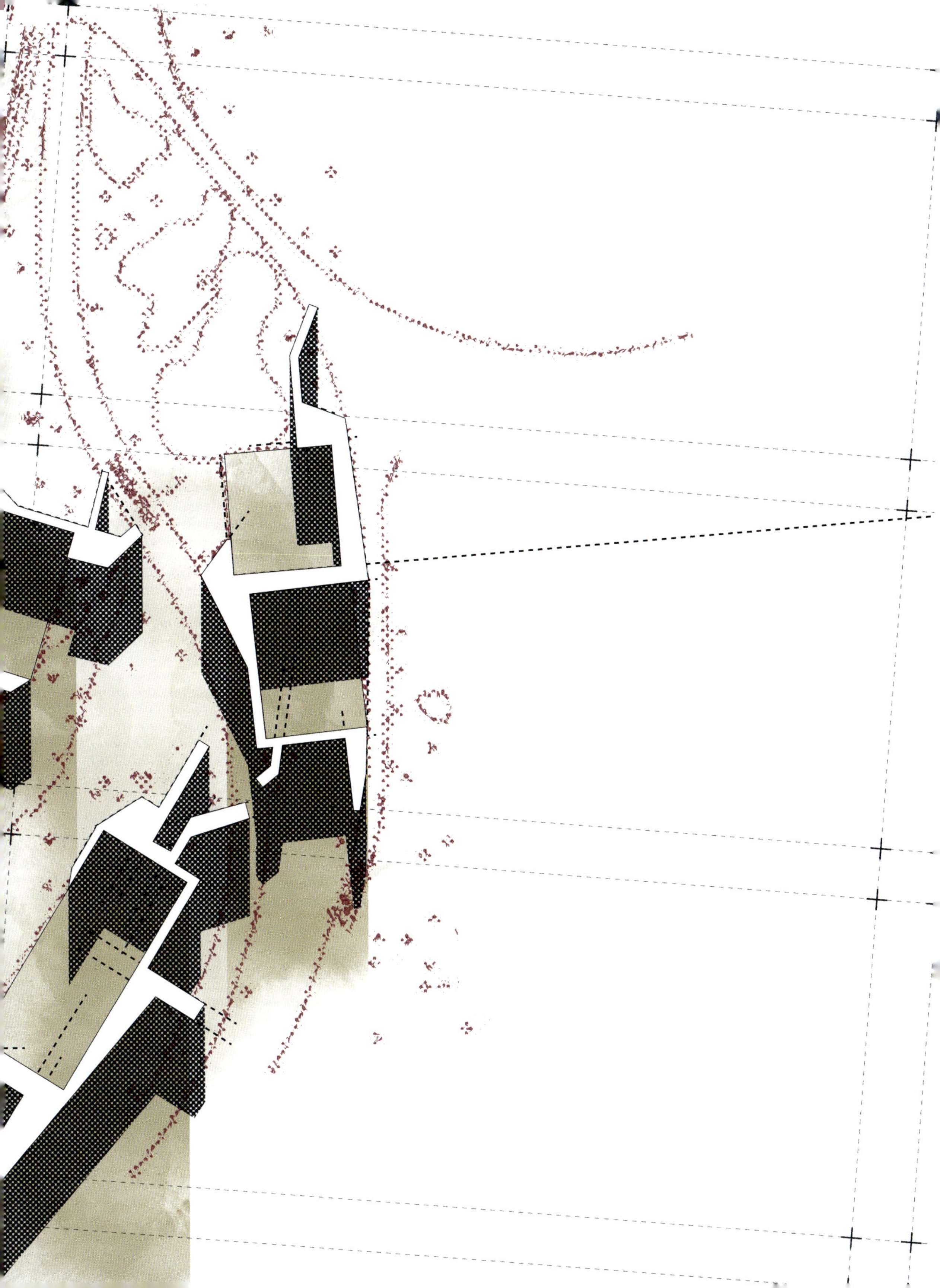

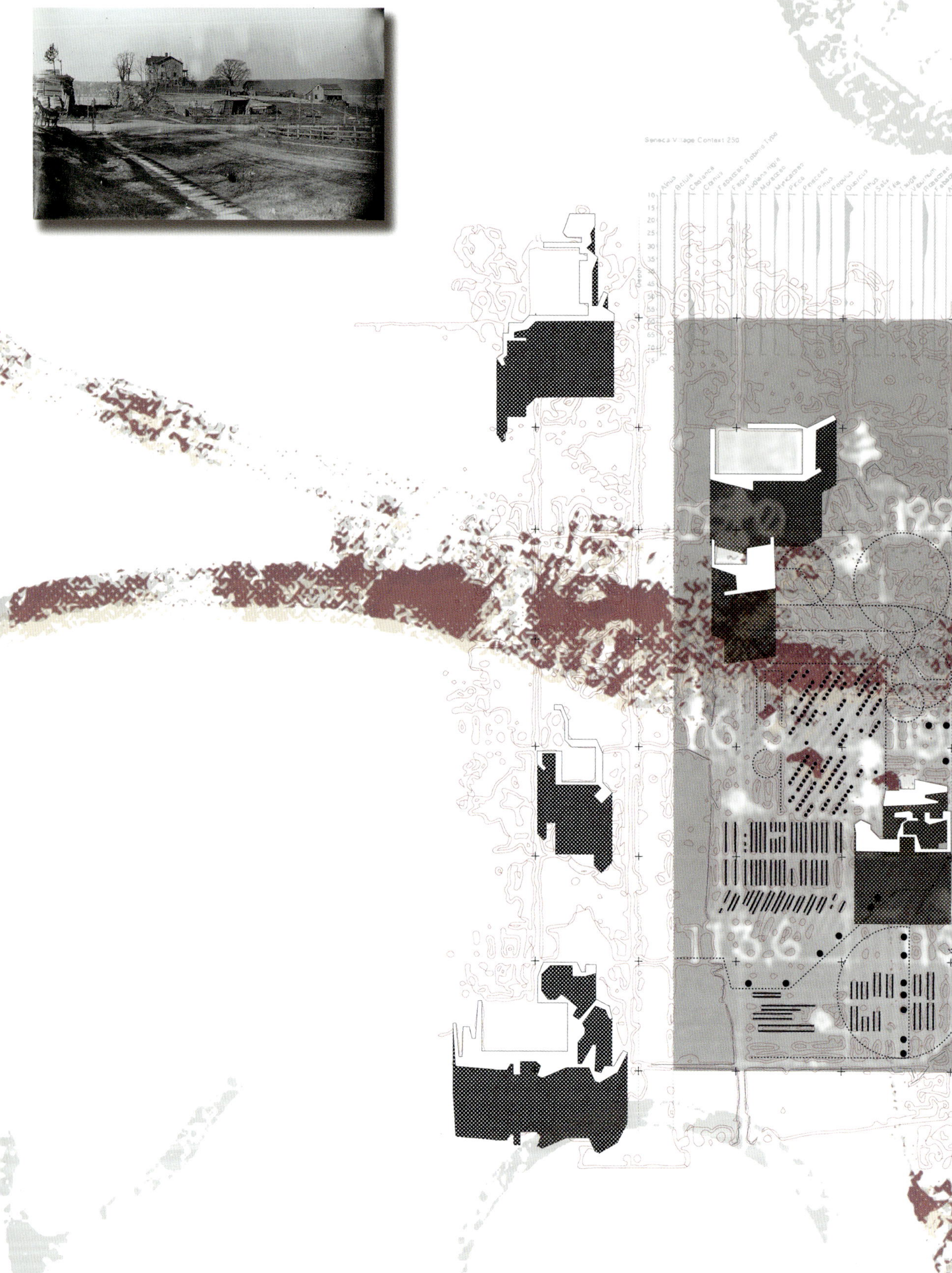

Seneca Village Context 250

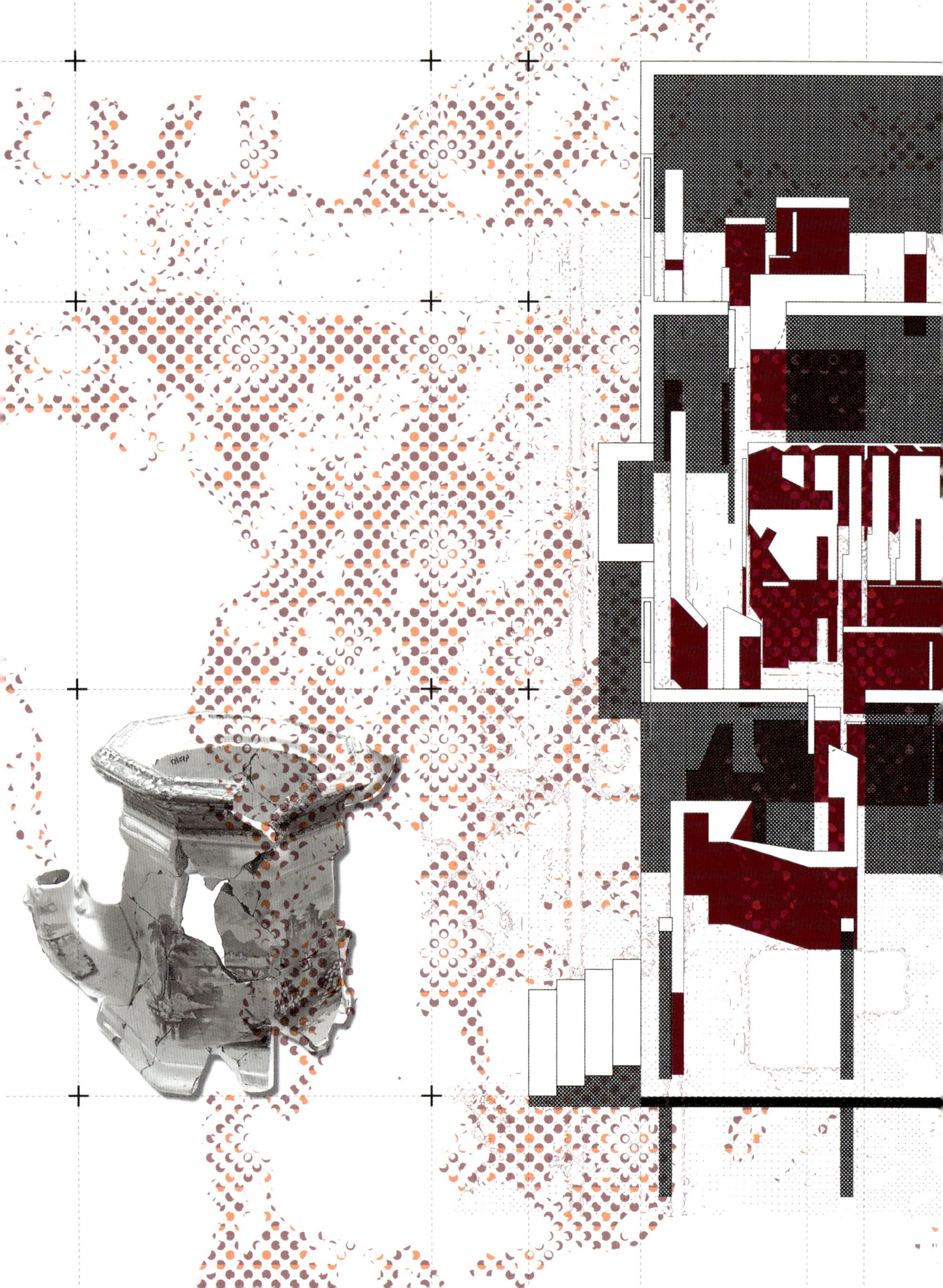

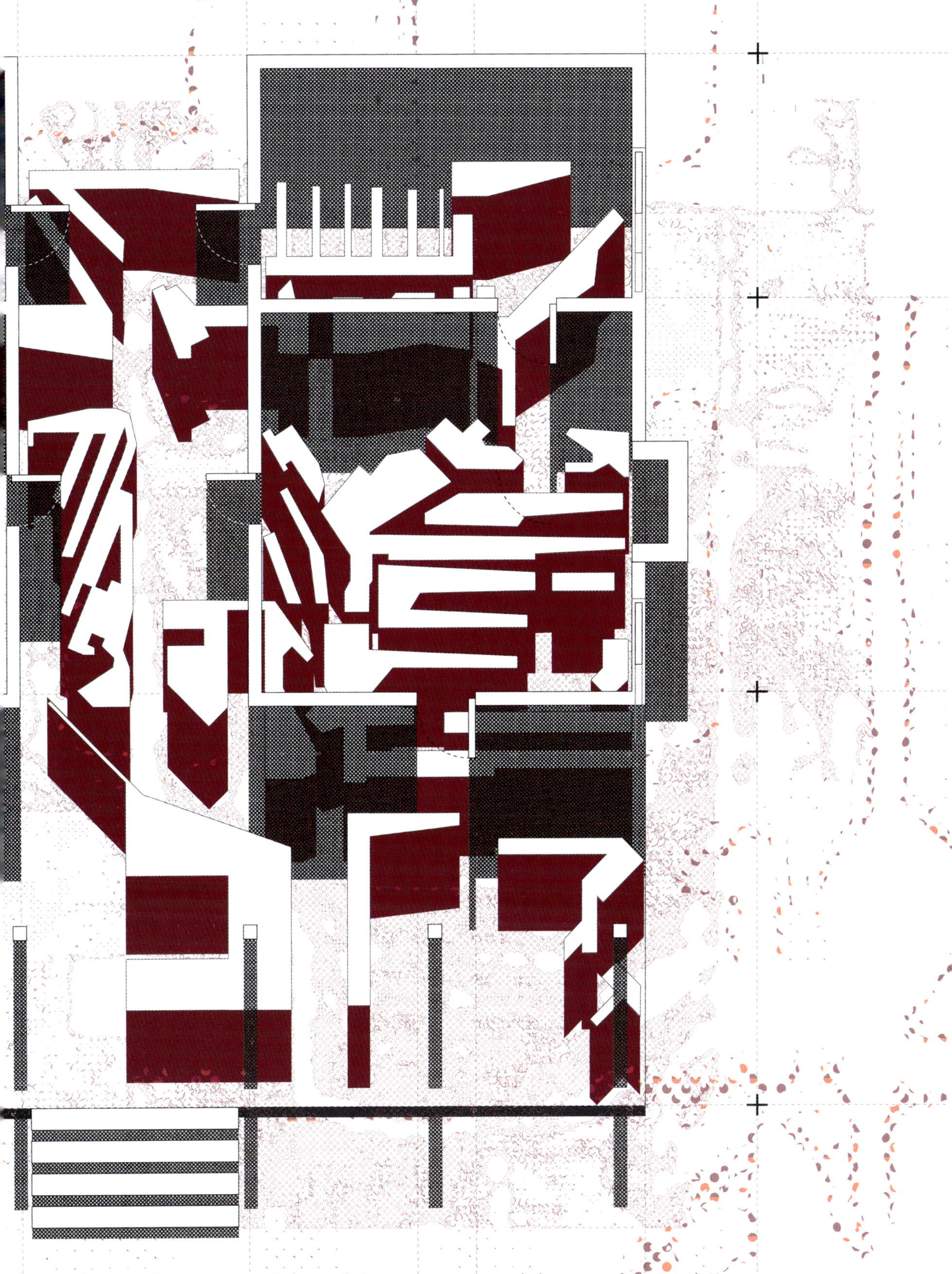

ANTI-SLAVERY
MEETINGS!
To be Addressed by
Turn Out!

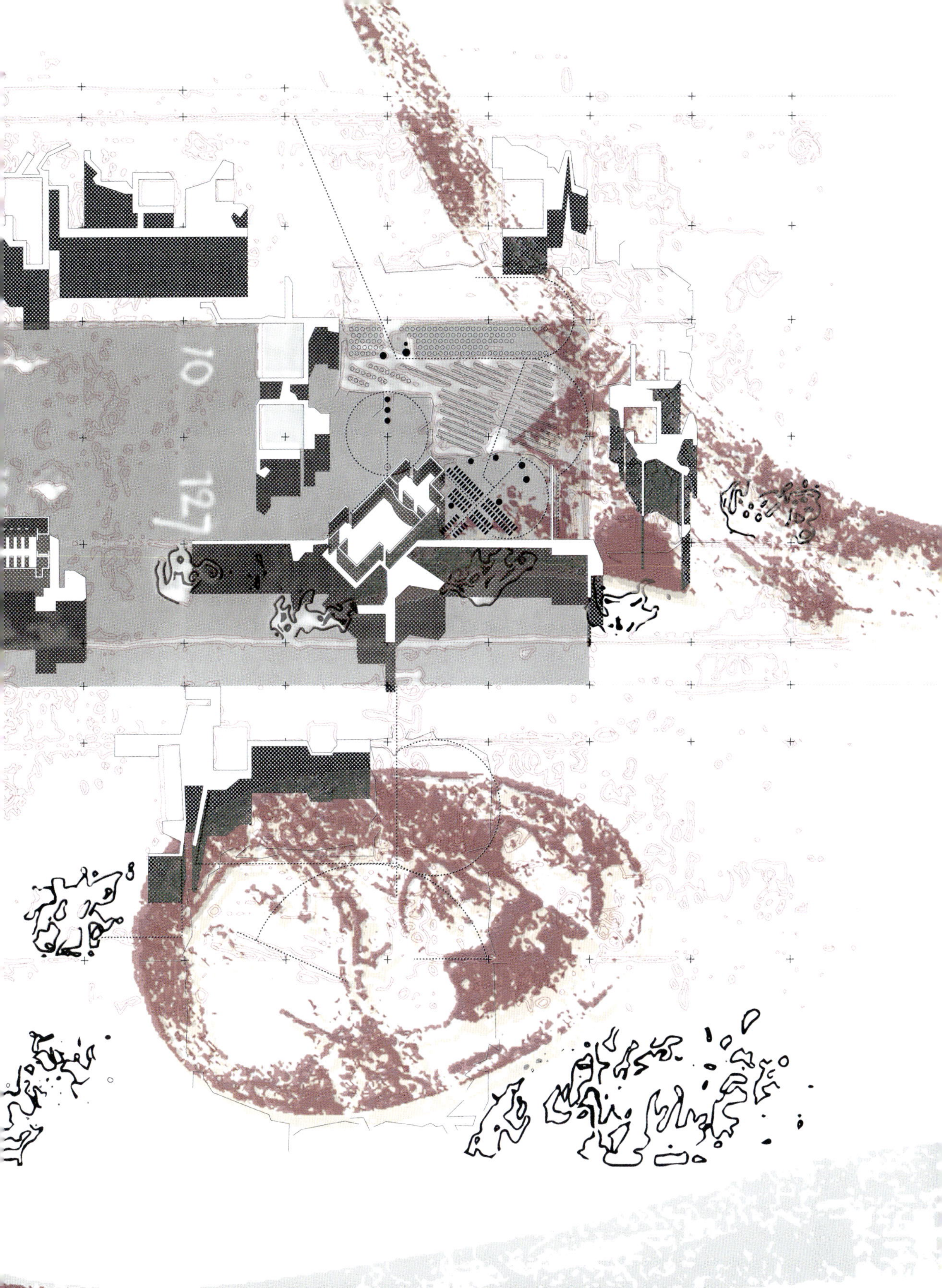

5.4 Diffracted Archipelagos and the Fantasy of Erasure

In *MT3*, Tschumi explores two seemingly unrelated architectural programs: first, an 'archetypal sequence of spaces' and their transformation; and second, a 'zooming operation' to configure a 'continuous and vertical sequence of spaces.' [373] The programs are extruded with axonometric projections derived from spatial conditions, first explained in plan, and 'through the introduction (transgression) of movement patterns. ... MT3 thus sees event and movement coincide in formal terms, even if the event's cultural implications inevitably differ from the significance of the movement pattern (which in this case it taken to be neutral).' [374] The extrusion is fundamental for activating spatial (and temporal) conditions, but in the second sequence the vertical axonometry is revealed through the stacking up of spaces at different levels. The falling body is the event that shapes the excavated space, a top-down excavation of the extrusion followed by the sedimentation of the resulting architecture along a vertical axis.

Tschumi's axonometries in the *Transcripts* mostly show one frontal face and the top, which works as an undistorted floor plan of the architecture. At first, they seem to correspond to what Stan Allen describes as *axonometric degree zero*, or 90-degree axonometry, a type of drawing in which 'both plan and front elevation are undistorted and the sides have collapsed to nothing.' [375] Out of the different possible axonometric angles with which to construct a drawing, the 90-degree is where the ambiguity between extrusion and flatness becomes more evident. The non-rotated 90-degree axonometry, which complicates descriptive qualities normally present in other types of axonometries, is 'slightly awkward, even naïve ... something almost childlike, or coming from somewhere other than the Western canon of visual representation.' [376]

Drawing mostly from John Hejduk's 1960s *Diamond Series* – an investigation the architect started while still teaching in Texas and which eventually led to his seminal pedagogy involved in the nine-square grid problem [377] – Allen argues that one of the strengths of this type of drawing comes from its being less of a projection and more of a folding or hinging that brings about the capacity for measuring. The collapse of all sides but the frontal, which Allen associates with Hejduk's interests in Cubist painting, generates a 'layered space activated by a moving spectator and unfolding in time. Time is compressed more than dilated.' [378] Tschumi's drawings share some similarities with Hejduk's approach, namely in that they draw attention to the drawing as artifice by 'depict[ing] abstract objects floating in space,' that is, objects without a correspondence to their external context. In Hedjuk's *Diamond House*, as much as in his nine-square problem, the context is offered by the grid, which also works as a frame to develop the architecture. In the *Transcripts*, Tschumi also reinforces the isolation of the *architecture of the event*. It is known and explicit that the movement of a falling body in *MT3* activates the sequence, but nothing else. The collision between space, event and movement is totalizing in the image, to the point where nothing else seems to matter. One doesn't know whose body is falling, where is it falling from or when or why, for that extra context is not the generator. In that sense, Tschumi's extrusions are isolated from any other contextual adjacencies. However, the drawings seem to be less of a folding or hinging as Allen suggests, and more of an excavation of extrusions notated in parallel projection. It is as if Tschumi sculpts the movement of his protagonists along the extrusion resulting from the 90-degree axonometry.

Allen makes a clear distinction between Hejduk's axonometries and more recent resurgences of this technique in architectural discourse, which invest in the contextualization of the architecture in its (mundane) context, 'the whole thing rendered as a scene … in a carefully poised interplay with the abstract, measurable character historically associated with the axonometric.' [379] Even though Hejduk's aforementioned project and pedagogy did reinforce an idea of architecture happening in the abstract, it might be worth noting that he was also interested in site and vernacular conditions, and that those interests were not uncommon within the New York Five. [380] His approach to architecture combined pure geometrical abstraction with site-specific conditions. To some architects of this métier – Eisenman, for example, or Libeskind, who studied at the Cooper Union – Berlin seemed to have played a pivotal interest in site during the late 1970s and 1980s, namely with a potent and charged ground that would eventually become a laboratory for architectural ideas with the reunification of Germany after 1989. When some of their architectural approaches were used to study cities, the projects become indexical to the stories of how things existed and why eventually some of them disappeared. Eisenman's *Cities of Artificial Excavation* (1978–1988) is an important case in point, where architecture doesn't happen in pure abstraction or on a neutral ground. On the contrary, the project de-sediments Berlin with the selective extrusion of historical elements, which emerge from a set of embedded conditions in a thickened and apparently solid, even if broken, ground. Ground is extruded and excavated almost as a series of three-dimensional sequential montages. Derrida's influence is not accidental here: the 1986 *Project for a Garden* in Parc de la Villette, for example, started out as an intended collaboration between Eisenman and the philosopher.

Some notations in the *Transcripts* result from transgressions, like *MT2– 'The Street,'* where Tschumi describes an unusual journey on 42nd Street: borders between private and public are crossed; architectural programs are overlapped. In the long drawing, the sequence is narrated with a mixture of notations and collages unfolding, both in space and time (indeed, one gets the impression that the drawing could also work as a timeline). The drawing also 'introduces the notion of transference, by which a space reappears as a kind of ghost-image, an afterimage of an earlier organization.'[381] With transgression and transference Tschumi recreates a non-linear cross-section of the street with which to question space.[382]

Questions of space, in fact, an active questioning *of* space, were in Tschumi's mind before the *Transcripts*. In conjunction with critic and curator RoseLee Goldberg while still in London, Tschumi invested in the study of a relation between architecture and performative art, with an emphasis on space as an eventual link, as well as a point of tension, between the two.[383] Questioning space was at the center of Tschumi's reticence in defining conceptual architecture, the paradox lying in the 'relationships between architecture as a product of the mind – a conceptual and dematerialized discipline – and architecture as the sensual experience of space and as spatial praxis.'[384] For him, it was, therefore, impossible to question the nature of space and, simultaneously, to make or experience real space.[385]

When Tschumi moved to New York, his interest in performative art continued. Transgression, transference and performance became recurrent themes in Tschumi's practice to define questions of space. In 1982, Tschumi organized an exhibition in New York called *Architecture: Sequences* for which he selected five emerging architects – Philippe Guerrier, Jenny Lowe, Lorna McNeur, Deborah Oliver and Peter Wilson (some of whom had been Tschumi's students at the AA) – to explore the nature of sequential architecture in establishing routes and rituals, 'movement as well as method, program as well as narrative.'[386]

One of McNeur's projects showcased at the exhibition, simply called *Central Park*, is an exploration of the landscape as a reactive plan of Manhattan against the grid. The project reconceptualized the park as a lost city in ruins, where built forms and infrastructure are extruded, while lawns, meadows and water drop down. As a result, the park is 'exposed … as an island, with the edge and the towers which stand outside it suggesting the walls of a medieval city. The labyrinthine paths also have a medieval quality,

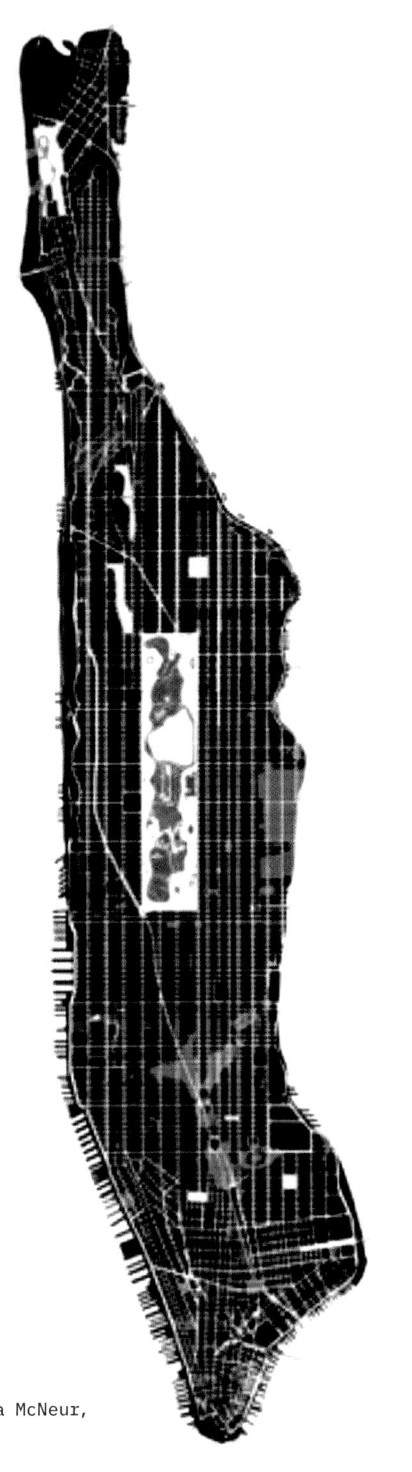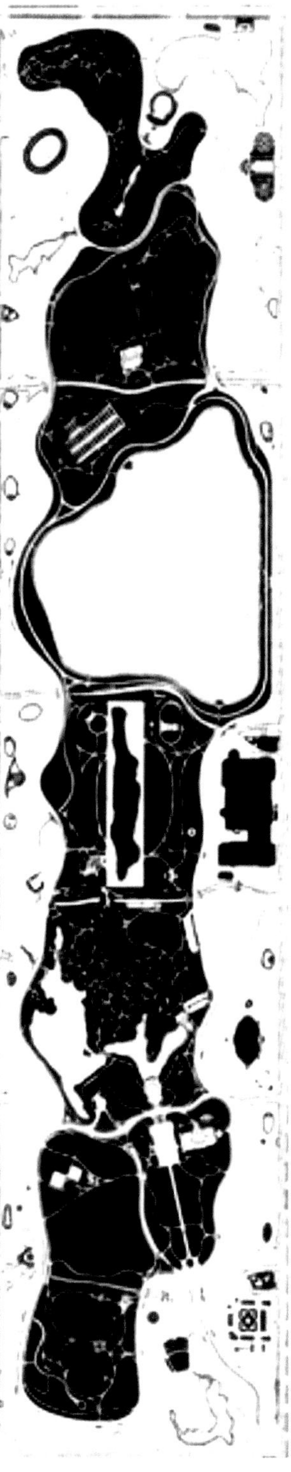

41 *Central Park City*, Lorna McNeur,
1979–1983.

while the overlaid axis of the Grand Promenade recalls ancient Rome, or its revival in the Renaissance.' [387] The project informed the longer speculative research *Central Park City*, developed by McNeur between 1979 and 1983 with support from faculty and students at the Cooper Union, including Hejduk. It raised questions about Central Park as a cultural construct, provoking the imagination as a colossal miniature of the city, and eventually pushing the limits of what a map can do. [388] Critically reflecting on her own research project, McNeur questions how useful the 'discovery' of New York's plan 'embedded within Central Park [to] inform the design of the city in a real and tangible way ...' might have been. She proposes that 'a more realistic approach might be to reinstate Broadway as the Grand Promenade of New York City.' [389] She developed a series of related projects – some of which with students in adjacent studios – to explore Broadway as a ritualistic sequence of architectural events in the city. The new spaces along the main artery became the architectural resolution of the city among thickened conditions of ground, which extrudes, sometimes in uncertain ways. Ground seems unsettled, de-sedimented through an attitude not too dissimilar from Eisenman's *Cities of Artificial Excavation.*

Tschumi's axonometries in the *Transcripts* reveal the architectural space as an excavation of the extrusion. In turn, McNeur's project begins to reveal a carving out of a thickened and unsure ground that is the city itself. Excavation no longer responds only to internal logics involved in a SEM relationship, for context is expanded and more closely aligned with geo-references.

Architectural notation rendered as a contextualized scene becomes important in the Anthropocene, especially since ground here is proposed as a condition that dissolves boundaries between natural and synthetic, or between geology and archeology. If architecture is engaged in an ethics of ground to excavate it, it then demands a contextualization of what is excavated, or scoped for, or eventually found. Excavation is less of an act of hollowing out to create space and more of a de-layering or a peeling-off to reveal space.

In *Archaeologics of Domesticity* the generative context for extruding emerges from an integration between space, movement patterns, programmatic occupation and geo-archaeological practices with their own logics. The political context of this work – one in which the spatial conditions of Central Park are both a point of departure and a generator – dissolves into several ambiguities: past and future merge in the *now*; domestic and public juxtapose; map projections and analytical cuts of the ground collapse in axonometric section and confound what is found and what is imagined, what once existed, what exists now and what is eventually yet to come.

Archipelago of Dependencies

The development of the virtual exhibition created the possibility of animating sequential drawings in a way different from the methods Tschumi used. Living between the static drawing and video – both widely used in architecture – the animated drawings that inform the design exploration demand an active participation from the user, even if unconscientious at first. The drawings are animated by a relation between the eye and the hand of the beholder in a continuous scrolling down that determines the tempo in which the sequence unfolds. Similar to Tschumi's interest in dragging events and movement laterally to the frame, several entangled conditions are also dragged to the screen frame – including models pertaining to the analogue, material world – continuously, like a long, uninterrupted shot scene. The technique allows for a different form of storytelling that potentiates both linear and non-linear unfoldings and complicates cause and effect.

The scrolling down – similar in many ways to the long smooth zoom effect that has become somewhat ubiquitous in digital software – enacts a mental (de)-sedimentation of the drawings, distinct from the sort of sedimentation usually facilitated by turning the pages of a book. In a way, it promotes a more diffracted understanding of the work produced.

The third and last notational event explores tensions between adjacent territories in and beyond Manhattan. The idea is to read the nuances of the insular conditions that emerge within social, political, cultural and racial, as well as geological and hydrological isolation.

The model produced to study some of the identified insular conditions defines three interrelated stages. First, a vertical backstage rescues the notation of Central Park in *Under the Rug* as a broken territory made of several pieces of dry land, connected or separated by ramified conditions of wetness. Second, a horizontal central stage explores Manhattan's archipelagic conditions with other adjacent islands along the East River and Hudson Bay. And third, two side stages positioned vertically receive shadow projections of these islands and construct new spatial and transcalar relations, both in space and time.

The physical artifact replicates some of the techniques involved in the construction of a shadow puppet theatre – a piece called *Shadow Island Theatre*. It was assembled inside and within the constraints of an existing leather suitcase.

The model makes use of paper constructions which flatten the excavated extrusions onto the two dimensions of the paper space. This quasi-three-dimensionality, something that Hejduk and many after him explored extensively, becomes interesting in the context of a three-dimensional model, in that they force the beholder into a specific position with a perfect viewpoint that activates the three-dimensional reading of the paper elements. The 'forceful' positioning is perhaps more akin to the perspective technique – where the position is made explicit through the establishment of a horizon line and vanishing point to which all drawn lines converge – and less to the axonometric technique. In that sense, the model problematizes Lissitzky's idea that the axonometric is a view detached from the ground.

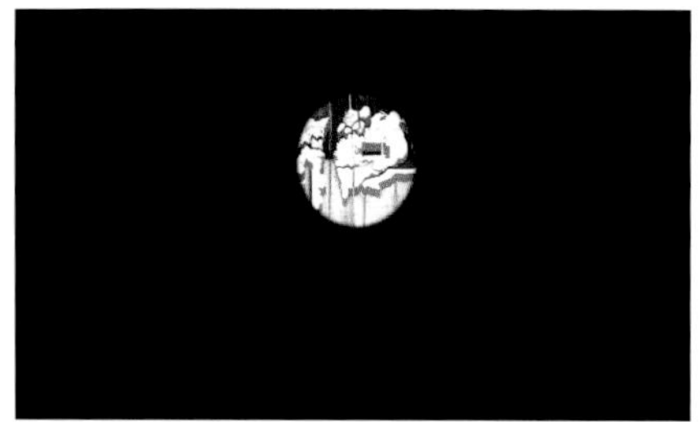

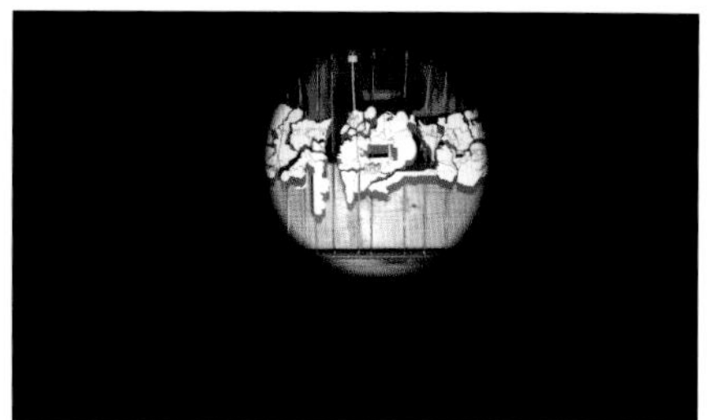

Sneak peek through the stage peephole.
A blurry shiny spot.
Come closer.
A scene under the spotlight.
Come closer.
A stage of sorts.
Even closer.
Three stages, in fact.
A broken park occupies the frontal,
vertical stage.
Interconnected islands,
an archipelago maybe,
occupy the bottom, horizontal one.
On each side,
paper veils receive shadow projections
of island pieces
floating across the stage.
Everything is
neither two nor three dimensional,
but a sort of transition in between.
A thick-two,
or maybe a thin-three?
Axonometries
that depend on the position.
They become
a matter of perspective.

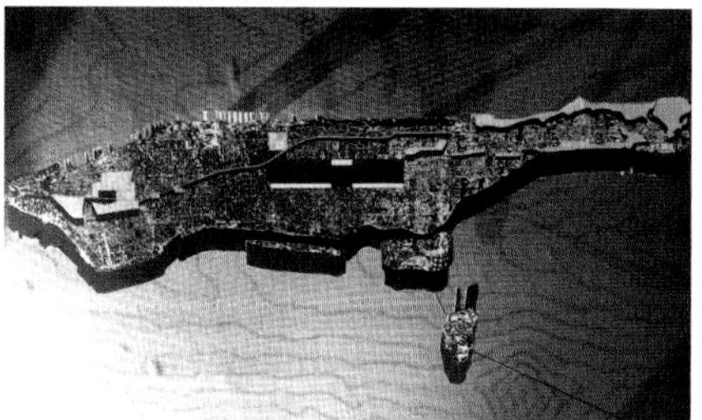

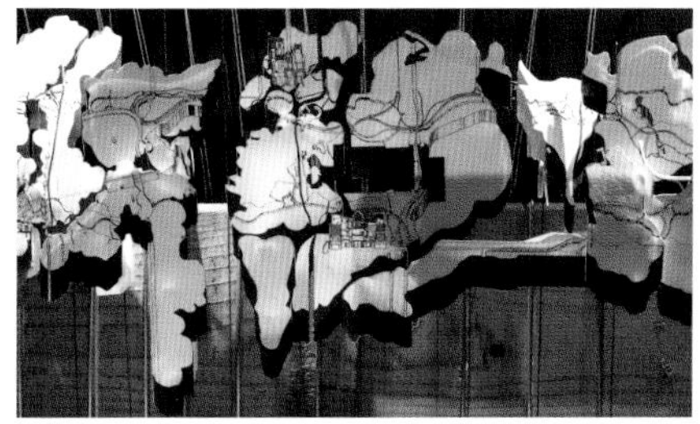

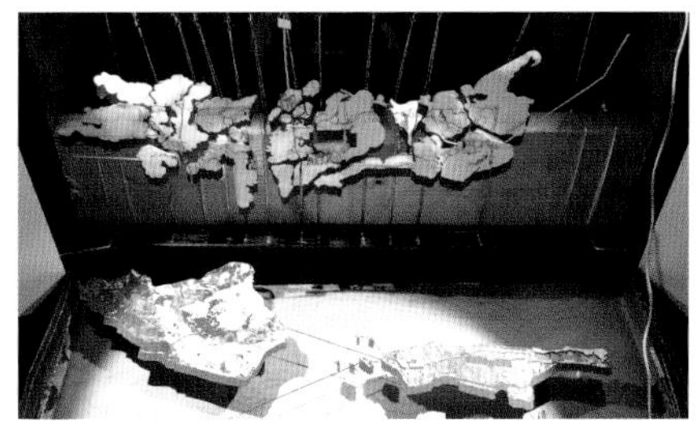

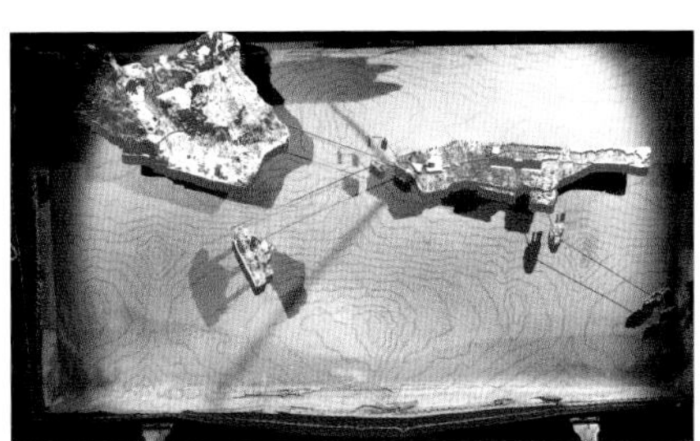

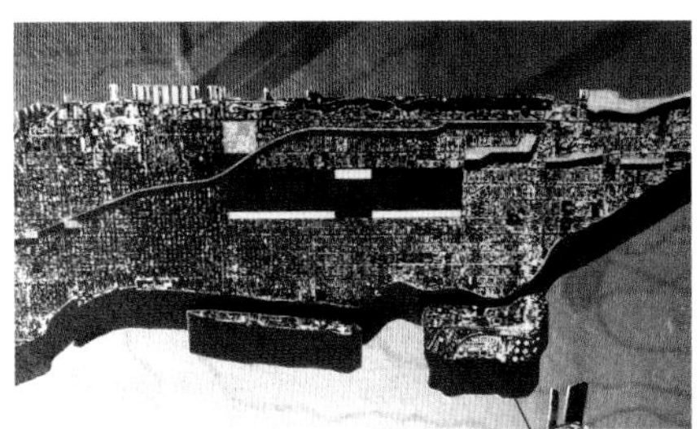

(this and next pages) *Shadow Island Theatre*, Views of the model and studies for *Archipelago of Dependencies*.

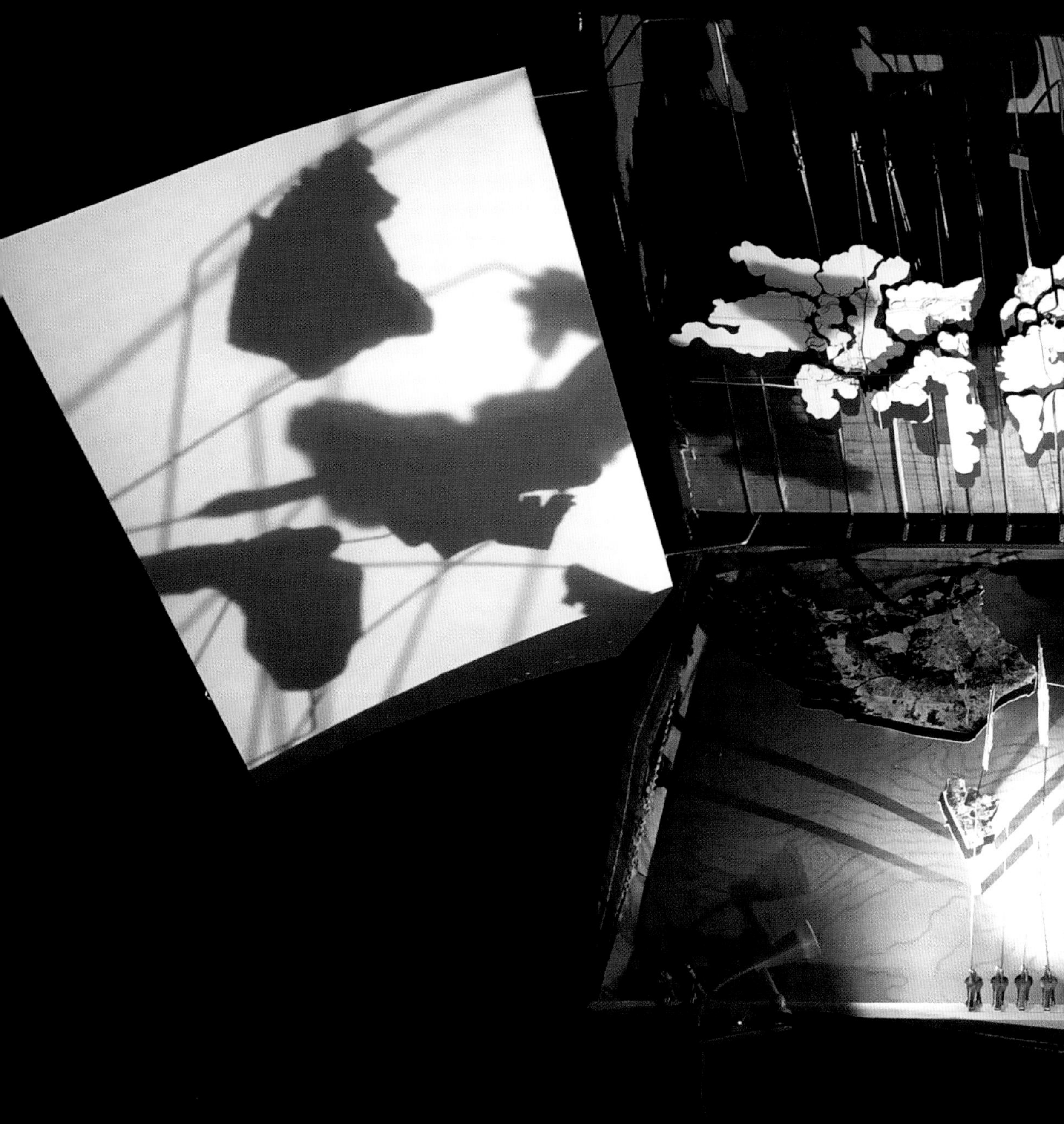

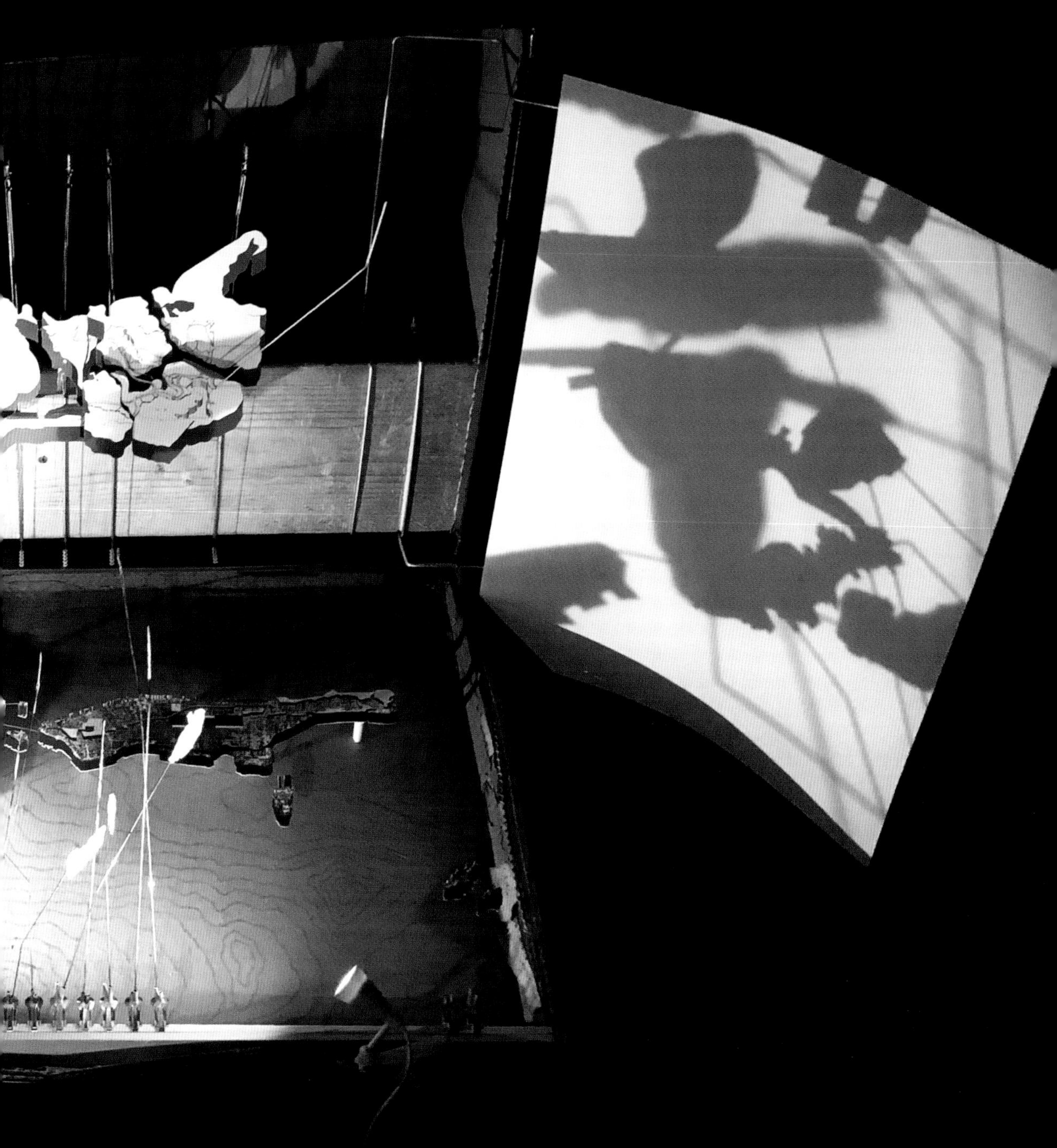

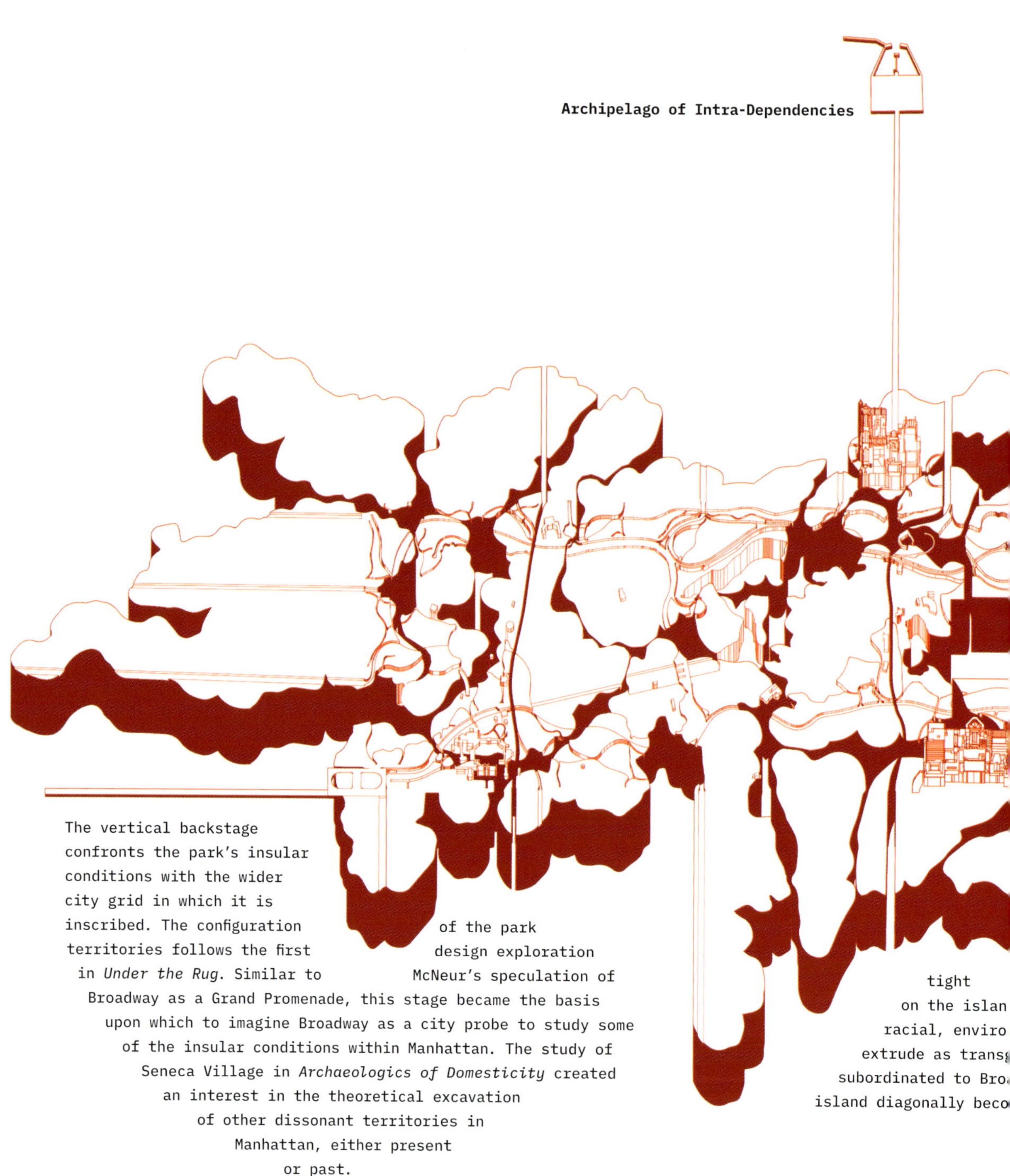

The vertical backstage
confronts the park's insular
conditions with the wider
city grid in which it is
inscribed. The configuration
territories follows the first   of the park
                                                design exploration
in *Under the Rug*. Similar to   McNeur's speculation of
Broadway as a Grand Promenade, this stage became the basis
    upon which to imagine Broadway as a city probe to study some
        of the insular conditions within Manhattan. The study of
        Seneca Village in *Archaeologics of Domesticity* created
            an interest in the theoretical excavation
                of other dissonant territories in
                    Manhattan, either present
                        or past.

                                                            tight
                                                        on the islan
                                                        racial, enviro
                                                        extrude as transg
                                                        subordinated to Bro
                                                        island diagonally beco

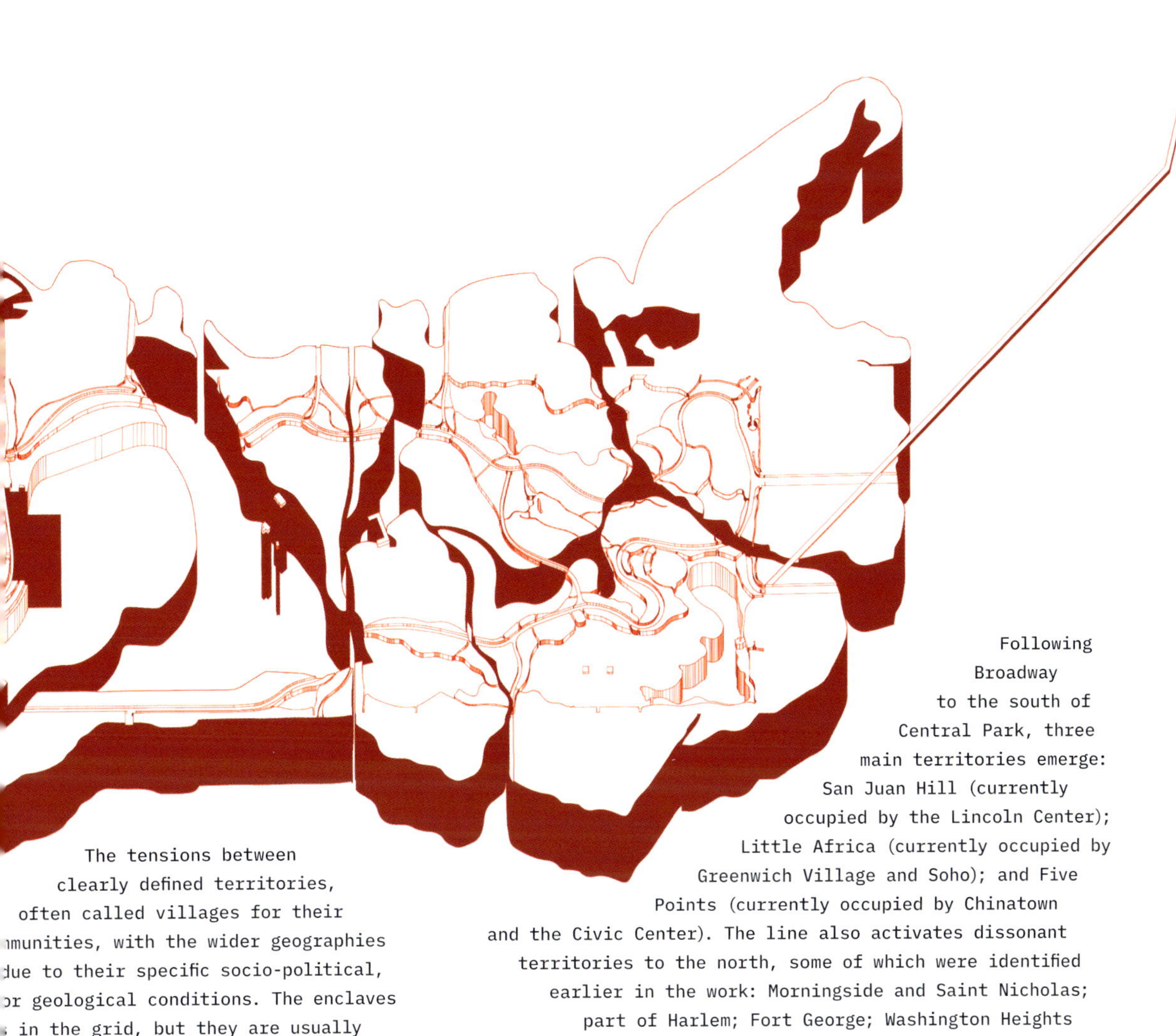

Following
Broadway
to the south of
Central Park, three
main territories emerge:
San Juan Hill (currently
occupied by the Lincoln Center);
Little Africa (currently occupied by
Greenwich Village and Soho); and Five
Points (currently occupied by Chinatown
and the Civic Center). The line also activates dissonant
territories to the north, some of which were identified
earlier in the work: Morningside and Saint Nicholas;
part of Harlem; Fort George; Washington Heights
and Inwood Hill. Through this study, Manhattan
emerges as an *Archipelago of
Intra-Dependencies*.

The tensions between
clearly defined territories,
often called villages for their
munities, with the wider geographies
due to their specific socio-political,
or geological conditions. The enclaves
in the grid, but they are usually
inuous path. The axis crossing the
facto line of investigation.

The horizontal central stage positions Manhattan within the wider geographical conditions where the island
the bay and the Atlantic Ocean.
From an exploration of the insular conditions of villages that once existed in Manhattan, the island is th
Manhattan as an emblematic insular cultural construct is questioned against the notion of its existence al
not limited to: Staten, Coney, Ellis, Liberty and Governors islands to the southwest in the bay; Roosevelt,
Brothers, City and Hart islands further up along the East River. Some of the islands operate (or operated)

of matter coming from the city, such as Staten or Coney Islands. Some operate as extensions of the cit
Hart Island in the Bronx. Through this second, interrelated study, Manhattan is then conceived as an A

t the end of the Hudson River and its confluence with the East River, at the point when they both drain into

nted with its own relationalities with some of the other islands orbiting around it.
 an archipelago of islands with complementary functions that support the city. These include, but are
 Mill Rock and Randal's islands wrapping around Manhattan along the East River; Rikers, North and South
strative centers, as for example Governors or Ellis Islands, while others work as territories of reception

oosevelt, Randal's, Rikers or City, while others work as reformatories, prisons, or burial sites, as for example
o of Inter-Dependencies.

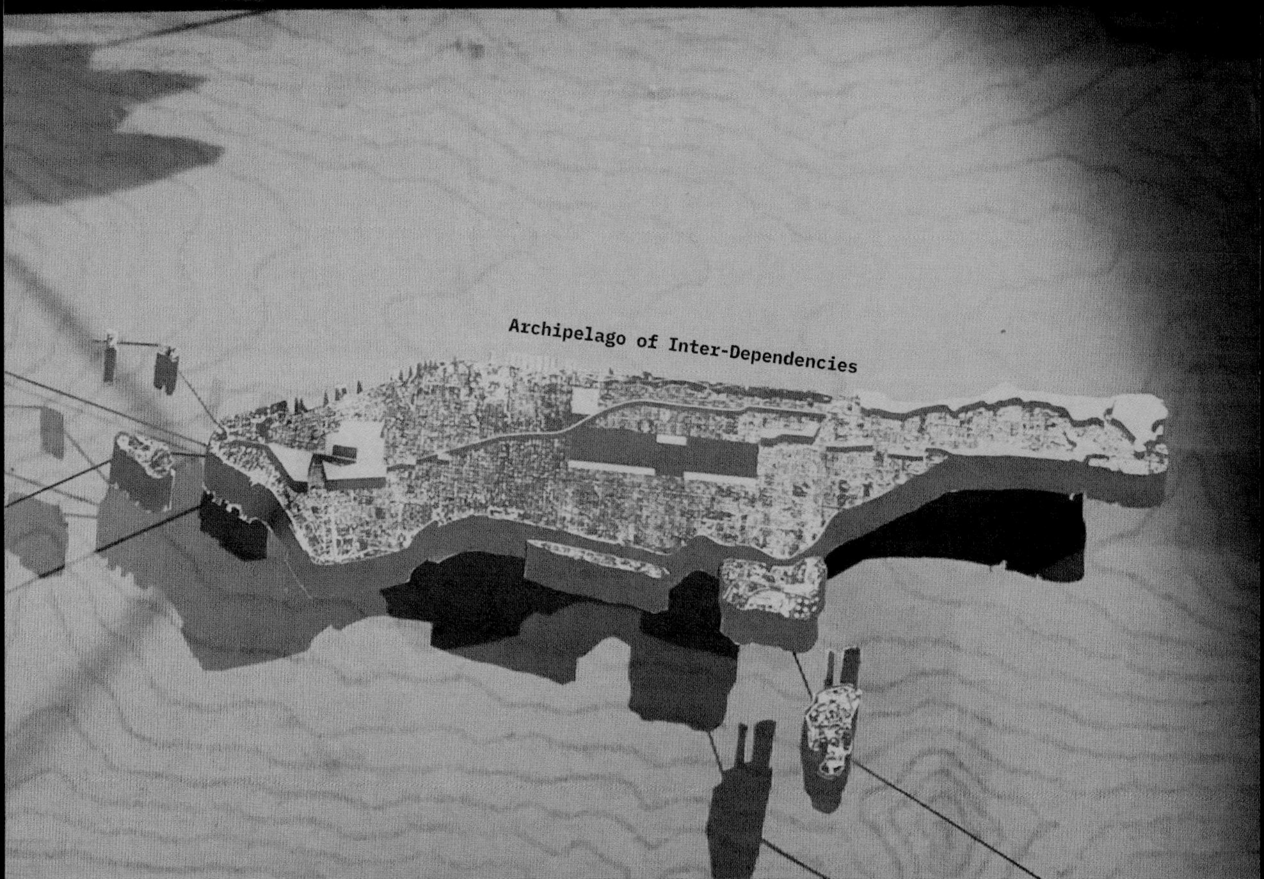

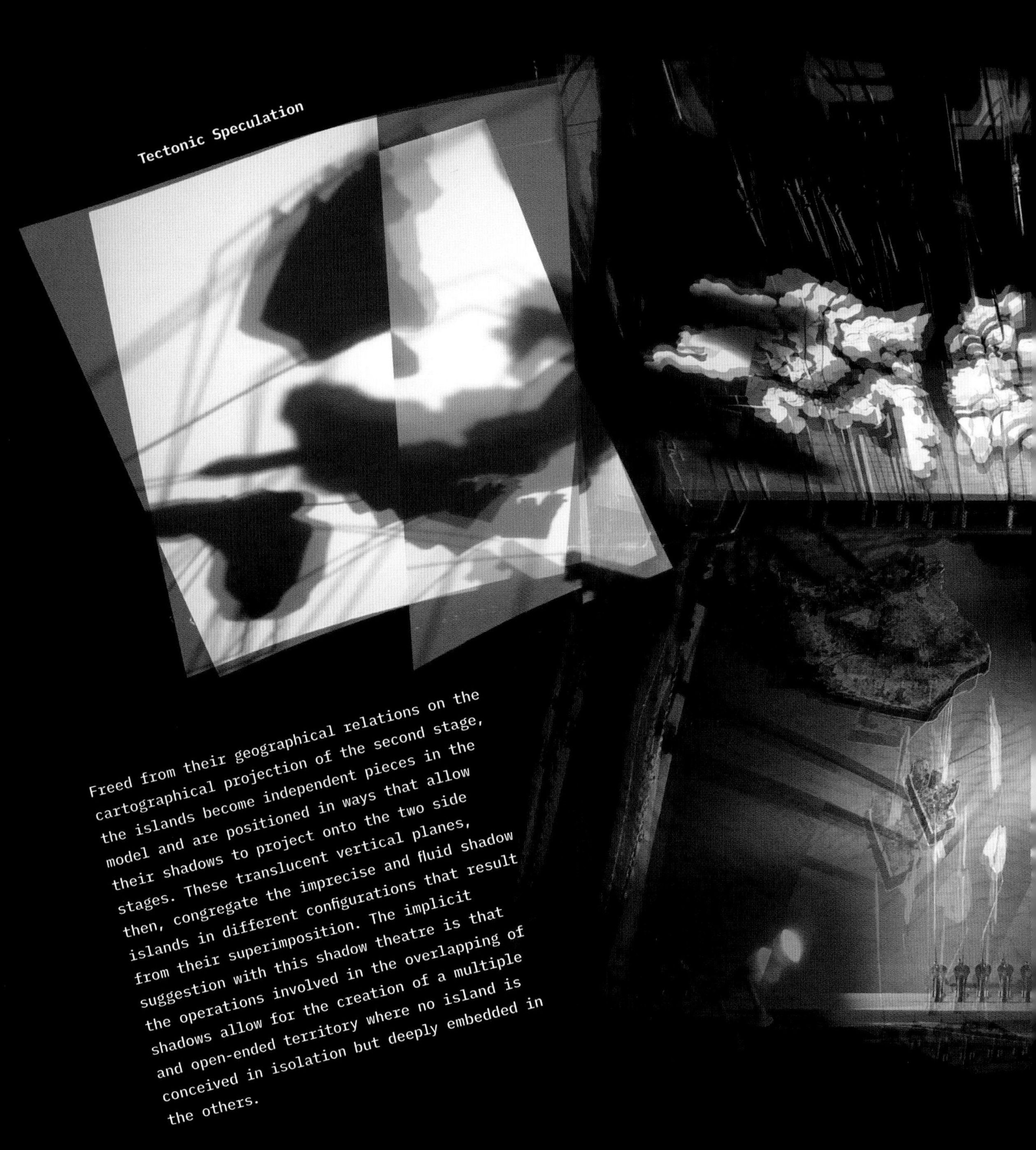

Freed from their geographical relations on the cartographical projection of the second stage, the islands become independent pieces in the model and are positioned in ways that allow their shadows to project onto the two side stages. These translucent vertical planes, then, congregate the imprecise and fluid shadow islands in different configurations that result from their superimposition. The implicit suggestion with this shadow theatre is that the operations involved in the overlapping of shadows allow for the creation of a multiple and open-ended territory where no island is conceived in isolation but deeply embedded in the others.

Earlier, Manhattan was conceived as a rocky draft adrift in a semi-liquid mantle. The idea was that the island was not a definitive territory but rather a transitional condition that ought to engage with the Earth's plate tectonics. Here the territories in and around Manhattan, previously extruded in their own context, become destabilized or de-sedimented. Like tectonic plates moving slowly along the Earth's crust, these shadow projections invite the beholder to imagine them also as constantly reconfigured territories.

Ways of thinking geologically about Manhattan, together with the archipelago of which it is just but a subcomponent, as fluid and open-ended territories might be attuned to the Anthropocene if the process of thinking *with* and *through* them activates conceptual and operative possibilities. The island is conceived less as an emblematic cultural construct and more as a constant geo-social and cultural becoming; a territory of reinvention and renovation, of material movement within and beyond its own boundaries; a set of mutable conditions that defy their own boundaries precisely because they are constantly renegotiating them.

Previously in the book, the idea of *constant becoming* was positioned in relation to Donna Haraway's *naturecultures* – fluid organizations that dissolve the human with the non-human – as well as to Karen Barad's idea of *agential cuts* – ethical, responsible, and accountable cuts of the world. It was argued that both bring important ethico-epistemological considerations into the field of architecture. Such considerations are valid also for a retrospective appraisal of Tschumi's practice, but in this case, it might be important to introduce yet another idea from Barad about *diffraction* and the making of temporality. [390]

For Barad *diffraction* – a reading diffractively for patterns of differences that make a difference – is a practice. If one practices with it, it becomes slightly easier to accept that the past is not inevitable and the future does not unfold in a cause-followed-by-effect relation. [391] Instead, they are 'iteratively reconfigured and enfolded through the world's ongoing *intra-activity*. There is no inherently determinate relationship between past, present, and future.' [392] Haraway suggests that 'diffraction patterns record the history of interaction, interference, reinforcement, difference. Diffraction is about heterogeneous history, not about originals.' [393] It moves away from the notion of undoing past discrete moments, given that 'the fantasy of erasure is not possible,' and instead proposes opportunities for reparation, the idea being that the past accepts change in a sort of productive reconfiguration in an 'iterative unfolding of *spacetimemapter.*' [394] With this idea, Barad defends a sedimentation of events that is inscribed in the world and cannot be erased, 'so changing the past is never without costs, or responsibility.' This is a type of sedimentation that emerges from the Derridean notion of *justice-to-come*, that is, the opposite of a 'justice which we presume we know what it is in advance, and which is forever fixed.' [395] *Diffraction*, then, practices a sort of de-sedimentation not only for the purpose of analysis, but also for the prospect of regeneration.

Throughout this chapter, the reading of Central Park within a thickened context is concerned with two main aspects: first, how the park is cut off from the city and inscribed in a rectilinear boundary that makes it immediately recognizable, and second, how an ethico-environmental approach concerned with pre-park landscape features helps to reconfigure some of the park's political and urban conditions. The provocative unleashing of the park to the city then becomes a notated event.

The construction of Central Park was executed with a selective predetermined sense of justice, which the city as a collective presumed was known in advance and was forever fixed. The park itself resulted from the erasure of everything that did not fit. Eminent domain was used as a sweeping out of *personae non gratae*, and the park was inscribed in a causal historical process. Questions of what the park 'tried' to erase – for erasure is a fantasy – and has been 'hiding' ever since occupied a core part of the design investigation. It was within the context of a diffracted reading of the park for patterns of difference that make a difference that the focus on Seneca Village emerged. At this point, notational sequence was used to carve out or extrude other notations in maps and plans from around the time when the park was being constructed. A notated Seneca Village emerged, and with it, a sense of domesticity that scarred the landscape before it became formalized as a public park.

A diffracted reading of Manhattan can be one that de-sediments the idea of the grid as totalizing and instead accepts it as a series of cuts that enact the 'experience of permeability.' [396] Manhattan becomes less of an insular totality and more of a coalescence of dissonant conditions, which were often erased for not conforming to the grid's capitalist-driven logics. Manhattan's internal dependencies are iteratively reconfigured and enfolded through its productive *intra-activity*. Permeability is also useful in the notation of the island's inter-activity, or the set of reciprocal relations with the archipelago it belongs to.

It was mentioned earlier that an Anthropocenic *architecture of the event* is a seismic scoping that de-structures the city from within. To that, one might now add that it is also a geo-archaeological excavation that continuously regenerates the ground into productive configurations. Thus configured, it is as if Tschumi's *architecture of the event*, an architecture in the *now* (maintenant), somehow never ceases to continuously reconfigure space. If the architectural space is generated in the event, there may never be something left behind after the excavation of an extrusion, for that excavation is always already in the making. A diffracted reading of the events that occupy Tschumi and Derrida, in action and thought, is one that distributes them 'across multiple times and spaces.' [397] Architecture gains the responsibility of facilitating a fluid and open-ended (de-)sedimentation in contexts where 'questions of social [but also political and environmental] justice have to be thought about in terms of a different kind of causality.' [398] This is, in a way, an architecture concerned with an ethics of matter that is not added to 'questions of matter but rather is the very nature of what it means to matter.' [399]

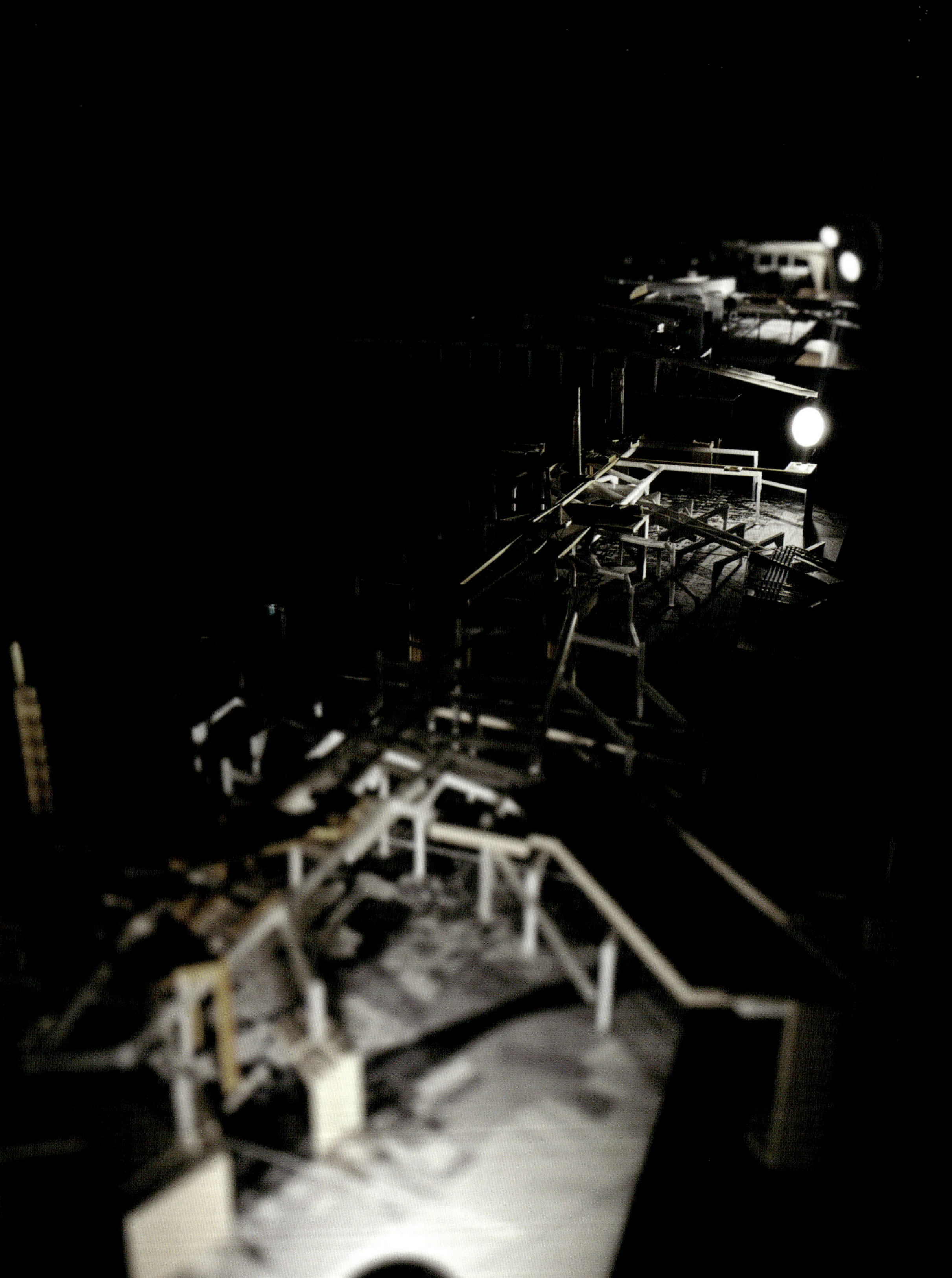

6 Intra-Act
Architecture as a Geologic Condition

6.1 Contact Zones: Architecture as a Condition for the Fault

Works such as the ones presented throughout this book may never be final; the results of each exploration always lead to new lines of enquiry. The last critical reflection here showcased happened as an installation that was exhibited in Lisbon in 2022. In sympahy with the work feeding this book, it synthetized the work done before while opening new questions, some of which will continue to be examined for some time.

The experiment departed from the initial argument that Manhattan is a territorial condition which negotiates its existence between an orthogonal grid that has determined its growth and a fractured geomorphological condition that affects the way it exists and evolves. The idea of what a fault is, or what it represents and how it can be represented, occupied a central position in the design exploration. However, over the years the meaning of what the faults crossing the island are, either structurally or conceptually, and what they might mean for the work, requires a more complete articulation of what their impact in representation might be and could possibly mean.

A fault can be made of many and multiple things: it is made of accumulation, sedimentation and erosion; it is made of grinding, overlapping and cutting; it is made of pressure, tension, coexistence, sometimes even contradiction; it is made of geological matter with a physical presence as much as it is of ideas and concepts about what it is and what it represents. It is transcalar, meaning that it cuts across the many scales it affects, from the planetary scales of tectonic plates down to the subatomic scales of chemical exchange. It is also transdisciplinary, meaning that it is defined by many different disciplines tangentially and interconnectedly: a fault for seismology is different than a fault for structural engineering, but they certainly inform each other. It is also certainly different from what it may mean as a philosophical provocation or as an architectural possibility.

With this in mind, and from a conceptual standpoint emerging from

In *Architecture as a Condition for the Fault,* Manhattan is explored as a territory that negotiates its existence between an orthogonal grid and an old and fractured geomorphological condition. The study plays out through a series of extrusions of contact zones that conceptually resulted from modelling conditions in and around the passive fault lines crossing the island. (next pages) Drawings and images of exhibition.

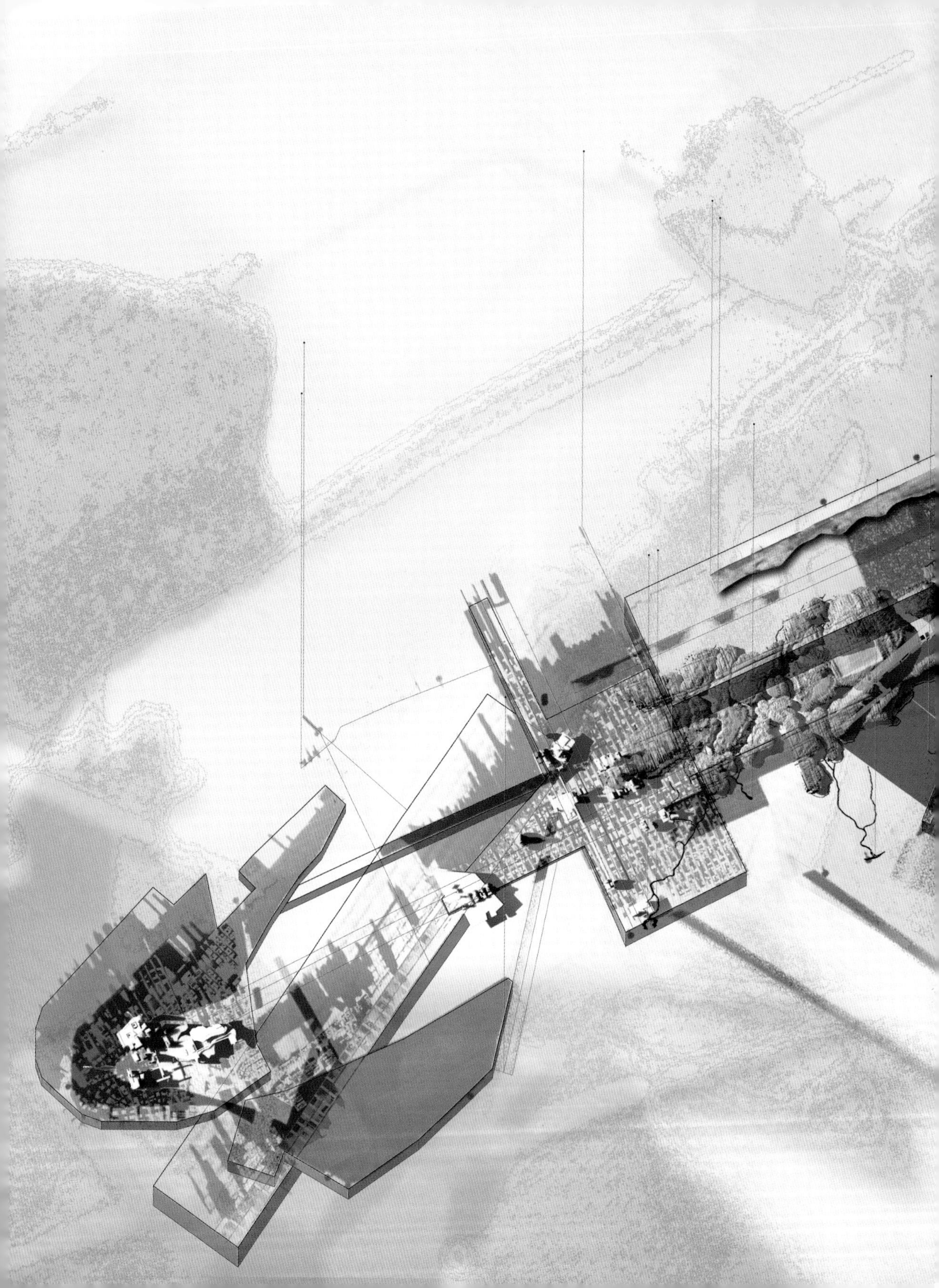

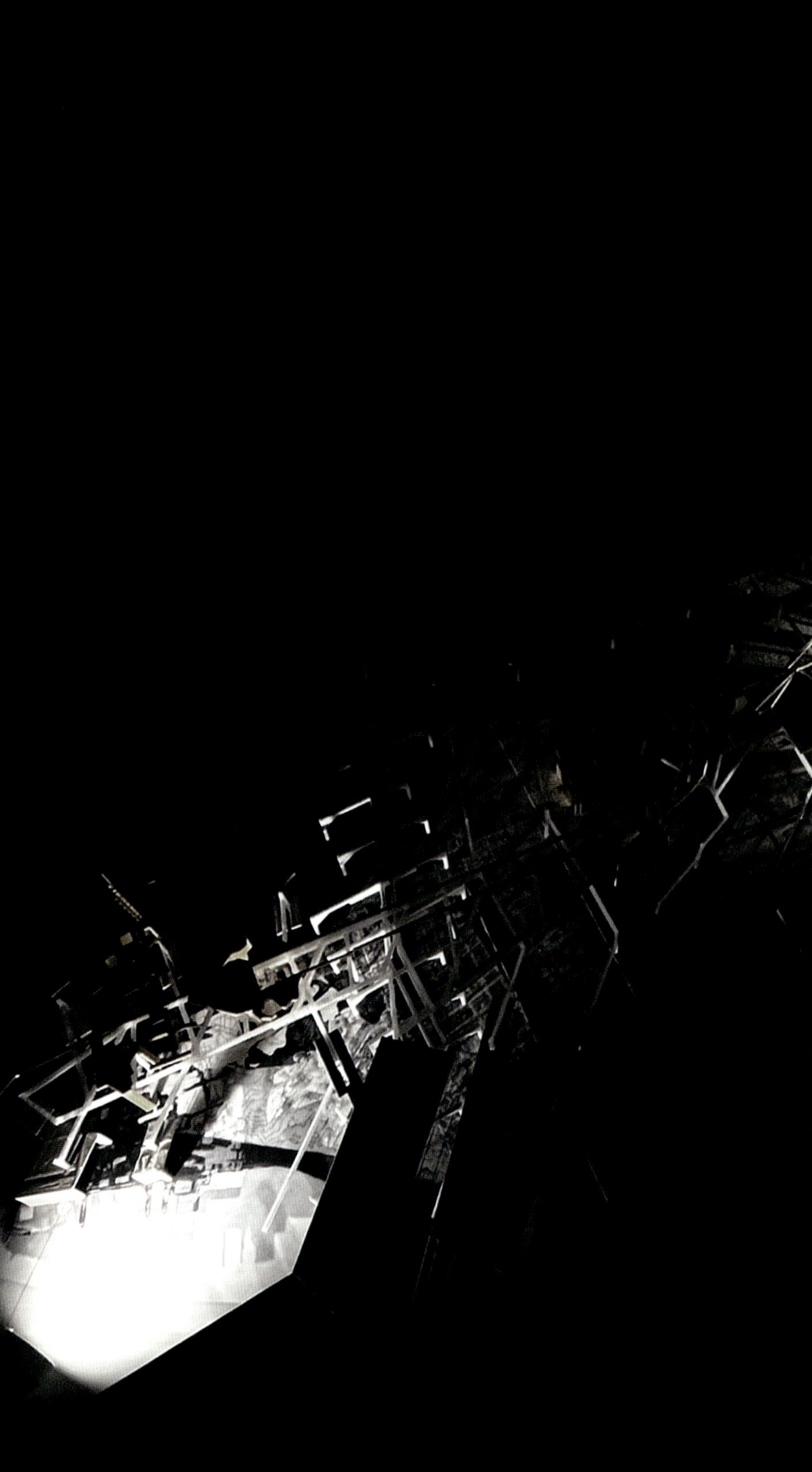

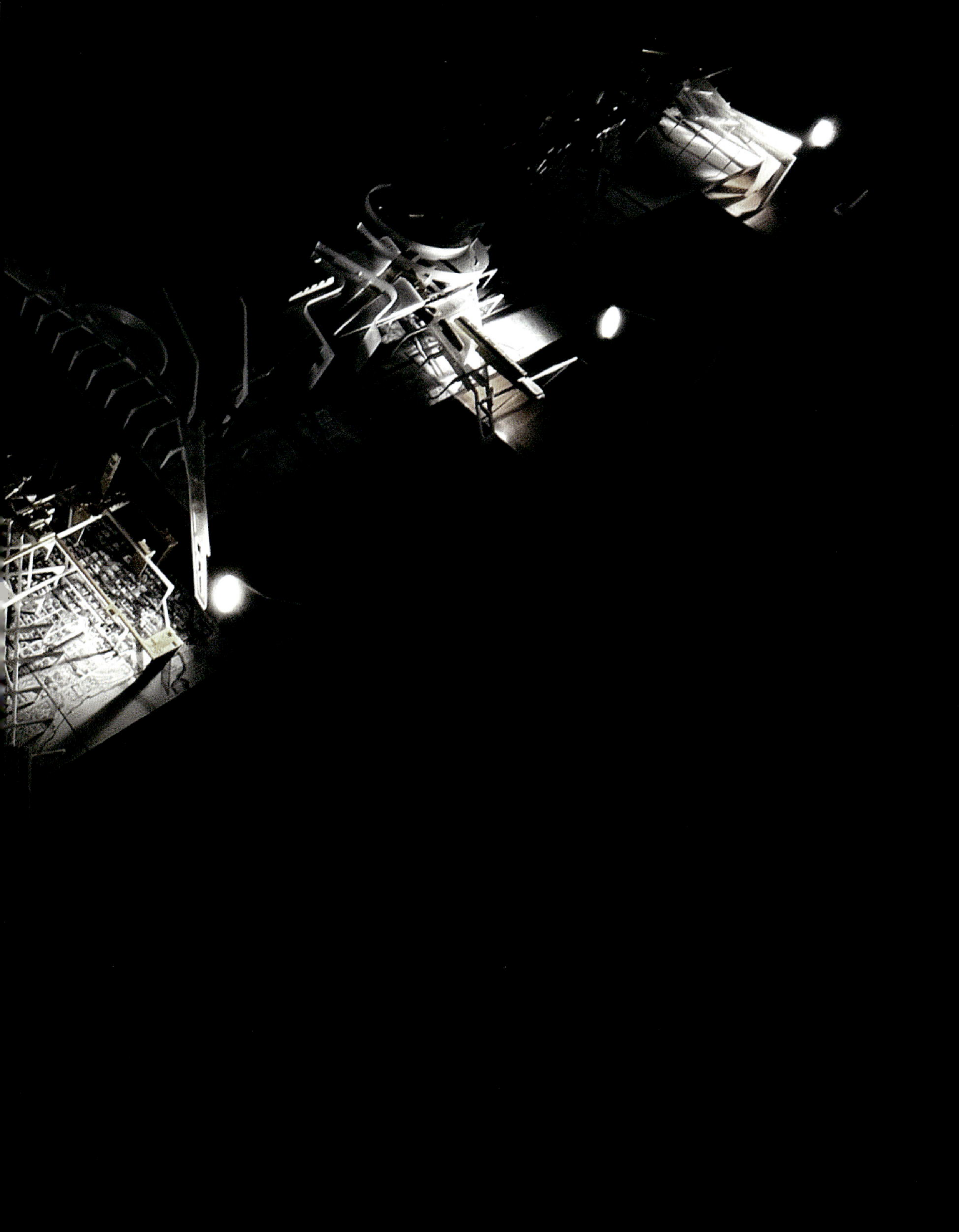

within the work, a fault may be essentially a condition that affects the territories that exist in its adjacency. The perimeter of those adjacencies as something qualitatively different than the area that lies beyond them is here called the *contact zone*. Contact zone is a concept carrying specific meaning for disciplines such as geography or geology to denote areas of adjacency in direct or indirect contact with each other, but which nevertheless carry with them properties that result from a negotiation emerging from that overlap. In ecology, for example, these areas of contact are usually referred to as ecotones, and they are described as ecological zones not only carrying properties of the areas that are in contact with one another, but also, eventually, developing other, unique qualities of their own; an ecotone is usually ecologically richer that any of the areas whose overlaps initially originated it. A similar, albeit more speculative, theory exists in anthropological studies, where areas adjacent to fault lines, that is, planetary regions where different tectonic plates grind on each other, are considered to be the birthplaces of many civilizations, precisely because they are bio-ecological hotspots.

In the experimental work, perhaps more humbly, contact zone helps describe most of the territories and conditions in and around some of the passive geological faults crossing the island. In Manhattan these contact zones might be interesting because they foreground, sometimes perhaps even stage, the constant negotiation between the city and the geology that supports it. They put into evidence logics other than capitalism, and, in that sense, they can be considered condensers of the wider thesis being made for the island. The city, or better put, those who regard the city as a synthetic, thin and flat carpet on which to grow the city and extrude architecture, may define these contact zones as anomalies. And using the logics postulated by neoliberal capitalism, they are, indeed, anomalies. But more importantly to the work, they correspond to spatial adjacencies that can not only be explained in relation to a fault but also help explain why the city operates the way it does, that is, according to the geologics this book argues for.

The work developed for this installation began with a layered drawing that laid out the many distinct moments of the body of design work. It became a useful exercise to spatialize the many different moments in relation to each other, not only to examine the tensions between them, but also to understand how they forcefully coexist.

Initially composed as a synthesis of the different experiments which inform the work, the drawing then began to generate certain architectural conditions that resulted from selectively extruding parts of it. The extrusions were selected mostly to foreground the faults and their contact zones. They were sustained by constructions that, in turn, tried to negotiate space with the faults, in similar ways to, for example, how structural engineering and hydrology construct infrastructure in the city with inventions such as the trestle bridge. In other words, in a rather conceptual way, the extrusions are supported by an infrastructural network that extrudes and lifts the contact zones.

The installation was conceived with three main moments, called tables not just for the

Architecture as a Condition for the fault. From concept, to drawing and finally to modelling. (next pages) Views of the installation.

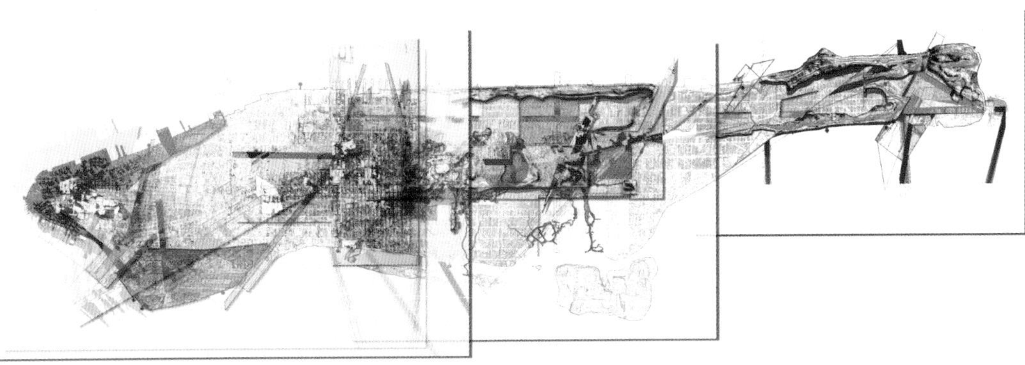

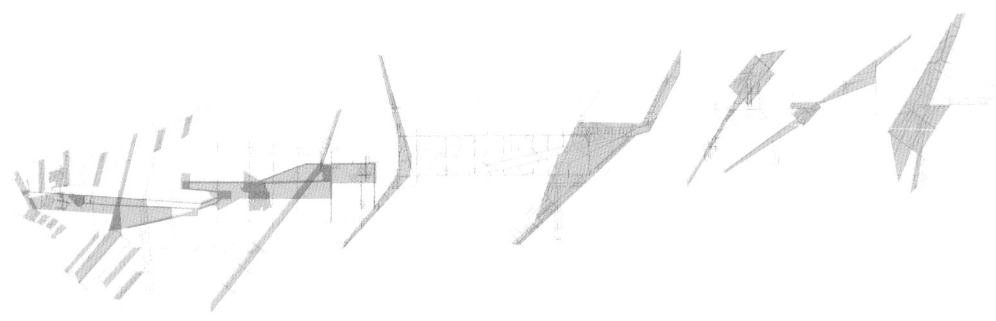

obvious reason that they were constructed as tables, but also because of their quality as tables of operations. The three pieces synthesized different moments of design production and different zones in Manhattan that received particular attention.

Table 1 examines the island's northern territories, including Inwood Hill Park and other pronounced geologies at the edges of the island – Fort Tyron, Fort George, Washington Heights. This is an area in Manhattan with pronounced faults which determine conditions of accumulation in the contact zones. These contact zones are, therefore, full of material conditions that exist adjacent to the faults. This northern part of the island was a fertile territory to explore early ideas that emerged in relation to Woods' *Lower Manhattan*, even though the depiction itself focuses on the southern tip of the island. The argument in this book derives from Woods' rhetoric of ground and claims that the architect uses it, even if never fully articulated, to frame architecture as a creative practice for dealing with indeterminacy. Indeterminacy becomes a meaningful concept to explore in New York, because it both explains and consistently undermines capitalism. It corrodes the needed ideas of stability of the markets for real estate investment, and it forces the city to come to terms not only with the idea of publicness, but also more recently with climate change, sea level rise or super storms.

Table 2 focuses on the island's central territories, between Harlem and Midtown's northern end. The faults in this area determine certain logics of superimposition and negotiation through overlapping. These territories also include Central Park, which extends between and connects the two faults here defined. As mentioned before, the park is regarded less as a Koolhaasian synthetic carpet and more as a complicated archipelagic construction of dry islets bounded by thresholds of humidity in what is otherwise a very complex drainage basin moving the water diagonally from the park's western edge. In this new approach, Central Park becomes a contact zone itself, precisely because it connects across the faults and becomes a territory of adjacencies.

This central part of the island is where most of the ideas in relation to Tschumi's

Transcripts emerged. The *Transcripts* include a series of notational drawings that activate Tschumi's SEM sequence through which, he claims, the spaces of and for architectural sequence may be anticipated from montaged programs of extreme nature that explore conflicts and tensions between pleasure and violence, their two driving theoretical forces. Architecture in this sense may result from sequential movement, often in articulation with some form of transgression, other times with a more gestural touch that carves out space for it. It was useful to relate the idea of notation – as well as of point-like grid – to Derrida's ideas around de-sedimentation, which naturally influenced Tschumi. Derrida conceives of such grids as the experience of permeability which may anticipate an architecture of multiplicity and heterogeneity – what both Tschumi and Derrida call an *architecture of the event*.

The research on Central Park eventually focused on Seneca Village, which in the book, and despite its own very important socio-political history, became an interesting condition with which to counterbalance Central Park as a curated construction of publicness. The argument here is that the village may come closer to an idea of commons and, more importantly, a condition that transpires intimacy and domesticity forged in the city by marginalized communities. The exploration encouraged a shifting from questions of space – which may have been Tschumi's main focus – to questions of ground, and how the latter may be investigated with a diffracted approach.

Table 3 examines the most southern,

and arguably most well-known, part of Manhattan occupied by Downtown and Midtown, as well
the valley in between, informally called the Villages. The area in this table was defined by two
far less pronounced faults (even though the one that stretches along what is today Canal Street
has some physical presence in the city's current configuration), both because they were probably
less pronounced on a geological scale, and also because they are crossed and affected by the
field conditions where the city invested the most in applying the orthogonal logics. These field
conditions are defined and described, even if diffusively, by Koolhaas in *Delirious New York*. In
affirming himself as Manhattanism's ghost-writer Koolhaas describes a literary city where a
haunting past, a congested present and a fantastical future provide alternative images to the
 New York that actually exists. The research examined Koolhaas' use of the PCM to then generate
paranoid critical approaches to the creative extrusion, mining and quarrying of some of the city's
architecture and urban fragments.

The complexity of the logics in these contact zones could be explained as both a dislocation
of material conditions from oblique directions into north-south orthogonal ones, as well as
from a quarrying of resources and dispersion of architectures that define what most people
conceive as Manhattan, and even New York. One could go as far as to argue that there are
some metonymic qualities to this third table, in that it stands for the whole of Manhattan and,
therefore, for the city in the whole installation. Yet, the argument here also forcefully refutes
such metonymic qualities, precisely because an architecture as a condition for the fault is
hyper-contextual.

Material configurations in white correspond to areas in the city that are directly on top of the
fault. The darker extrusions correspond to important geological features usually contained in
parks in the city's current configuration. The pieces in the midtone are areas of either landfill or
excavation, that is, infrastructural work which changed the topography more drastically to validate
certain urban configurations.

The serial pieces expand radially around the main spine, which correspond to parts of the
southern crown around the island that have been landfilled to create the port-like edge we know
today, that is, the edge that made New York what is has become. Since the second half of the
twentieth century, these perimeters have been identified as areas threatened by sea level rise
and bigger and more frequent storm surges, which are therefore, more prone to flooding.

6.2 Towards an Ethics of Ground

It could be argued in more ways than one that Manhattan is not a
representative city of the twenty-first century, a moment when urban
territories have diffused far beyond any possibility of clearly defining their
boundaries. Yet, the island remains in collective imaginaries as an idea of
what a city is or represents. While recognizing humans as the dominant
geomorphic force altering the planet, the Anthropocene also registers the
human condition, both individually and collectively, as a subcomponent
of more-than-human assemblages. Human action impacting the planet
ought to be read within timeframes that are more closely articulated with
temporalities of the earth. If Manhattan is regarded beyond its totalizing
aspect as a socio-cultural construct which has pre-empted Modernism and is
conceived within its wider and more fluid archipelagic conditions – something
the book argues for – its representational cosmos becomes inevitably tangled
with shifting planetary conditions in ways that help problematize the ways in
which the city reconciles its existence with its indeterminant context.

The focus of this work relies on the analysis of Manhattan's historical,
socio-cultural and environmental contexts to thicken city depictions. In
response to the Anthropocene, these thickened architectural representations
should also be enmeshed within wider conditions of connectivity across
scale. And while the study of how these conditions manifest requires a
type of thinking that is necessarily multiscalar, it is also important to
acknowledge that some of those conditions are observed differently at specific
scales or sets of scales. In other words, the representation of entanglements
includes not only a thinking across different scales but also, at times, a
sharpening on specific scales. Thinking spatially both across and at scale
has always arguably been a task of architecture. However, the expansion
of scales proposed by the Anthropocene, which in turn brings about the
constant negotiation needed to represent important scalar shifts, also
demands new ways of framing architecture, both in theory and practice.

The use of the *geologic* as a lens for reframing knowledge-making
practices activates a positioning of the city within an expanded context which
includes the geological layers beneath as well as the atmospheric conditions
around and above it, and how they project the city across wider temporal and
material frames. Even when it acknowledges New York's old and relatively
stable geomorphology, this research rhetorically argues for an understanding
of ground as something essentially dynamic and indeterminant. Less a

palimpsest where events are kept as traces over time, ground here is conceptualized more as a set of active actions of (de-)sedimentation, where layers with information are in constant transformation and mediation. Architecture cannot be simply inscribed on the ground because it must negotiate its existence with it. The argument laid out in this book, which began with an invitation to imagine Manhattan cut across a deep section, in fact, suggests that this approach demands a type of architectural practice that accepts the city as an entanglement with ground – essentially an architecture of ground.

When Bruno Latour worries that critique might be running out of steam, he refers to how inherent uncertainties – scientific or otherwise – with which facts are constructed are being efficiently used to undermine the values embedded in collective ways of being and knowing. The necessarily unsure ground on which realities are contested and constructed is muddying creations of different realities, rather than advancing or eventually validating them. If 'there is no sure ground even for criticism,' the only way forward, he claims, is to actively reimagine our more-than-human *lifeworlds* through *matters of concern*. [400] The current planetary sense of groundlessness – where socio-environmental struggles are real, as well as inequality, racism and classism – impacts us all, but very differently. To 'stay [and deal] with the trouble,' the matters of concern ought to be envisioned through an ethics of care that is interdependent. [401] A practice of reading diffractively the recordings of histories and stories of interaction, interference and differentiation involved in power relations should also be concerned with opportunities for reparation that are only possible if existence is seen less as self-contained and independent and more as a series of constantly evolving and forcefully heterogenous intra-relating entanglements. After a rather long line of philosophical and scientific thought, Barad defends that, from this perspective, the measuring of the world is never neutral, objective or external, but rather profoundly enmeshed in the productive reconfiguration of material intra-actions that dilute oppositions between 'creation and renewal, beginning and returning, continuity and discontinuity.' [402] The extension of responsibility in the responses to a world that is not defined by pre-existing interationsinteractions, but it is rather constantly becoming within the intra-actions of its entanglements, requires a refined and nuanced ethics with which to 'disrupt patterns of thinking that see the past as finished and the future as not ours or only ours.' [403]

Ground as an idea of earth media where events and actions across scale can never be fully erased offers a contextual positioning that cares not just about why things exist or have existed, but also how they exist. It demands of architecture ethical approaches to ground and matter which de-sediment social, political and environmental situations. De-sedimentation in the context of the work here presented aims to de-structure and destabilize some of the existing orders, ideas and power relations about the city to then be able to construct other types of meaning and *response-ability* to material entanglements.

The use of a type of geologic imagination that aims to unsettle conventional architectural representations often means pushing the limits of representability beyond what is usually depicted. In other words, it means trying to represent the unrepresented, which also often means attempting to represent the unfathomable, or even the unknown. The exercise raises several questions in terms of how to bring conditions usually lying outside of representation into its realm. It involves creative and critical approaches to thinking about the city which dilute binary oppositions between nature and culture, human and inhuman, figure and ground. The same ethical approach that reads matter diffractively should also relate to a discussion of aesthetics that necessarily comes with the problematization of representation as a type of synthesis and knowledge construction that reads the city as an entanglement, for both ethics and aesthetics can and, in this case, do unsettle conventional epistemologies.

The book delved into the speculative worlds of Woods, Koolhaas and Tschumi with the recognition of the historical folds to which their practices are inevitably bound. But the experimental recontextualization of their work from perspectives offered by the Anthropocene facilitates alternative understandings related to concerns perhaps extraneous to the architects' initial preoccupations, or at the very least complementary to them.

The active search for context that allows for a deeper understanding of architectural meaning led the research to initially tangential lines of enquiry which cut across the nebula of the influences, interactions and interests of the three practitioners. Some of these lines of flight were more stabilized in the argument, when they facilitated what is perceived here as a more solid integration of how their approaches came to exist. Even if the discourses foregrounded in their pieces may suggest individual attitudes to architectural practice that distinguish them from their peers – which were successful to a certain extent, especially for Koolhaas and Tschumi – the significance of several influences to each of them could not go unnoticed, especially when the research came to a point of not being able to disentangle the influences from the architects themselves. Thus, it could be argued that their architectural practices also result from their intra-actions with some of their colleagues, with important female practitioners necessarily coming to the fore.

The same attitude of scoping laterally or diagonally brought into the frame, sometimes quite literally, collectivities and forms of existence which had been almost pushed to oblivion in the shaping of Manhattan, even though their contribution helps explain some of the stories explored in the work. This expansion of the Modernist and Post-Modernist canons of architecture and landscape architecture is important if one is to believe that Manhattan can be used to explain how other cities, forms of collectivity and urban existences may be regarded less as individualized occurrences in the world and more as shifting territories that are inevitably connected with planetary forces.

The design explorations showcased in the book have benefited from the noticing and making sense of these entanglements to suggest alternative possibilities for thinking about the city through representation. It is perhaps in this sense that the work can begin to expand beyond its focus on New York and be eventually accepted as a methodology to represent the world and some of its many contemporary territories, where the ethical and aesthetic concerns of what is represented are less about what there is and more about what there could be. In other words, if representation is a synthesis of a knowledge that is in constant expansion, it becomes less about the depiction of conditions of certainty or totality, and more about indeterminacy and critical partiality. This is not an invitation to ignore altogether existing city representations and cartographic conventions that give voice to a privileged few, but rather to examine how they perpetuate unjust and unbalanced power relations, to then de-sediment them as they are folded into more complex representational mechanisms concerned with the suggestion of alternative *lifeworlds*. Even with all the limitations that exist in architectural production concerned with representation – for the claim here is not that representation alone, or even design practice more widely, can singlehandedly improve the world – could iterations of this methodology still be useful in dismantling legacies of structural racism, colonialism and imperialism, extractive exploitation, resource dilapidation or climate change? Could they facilitate an understanding of how existing power relations, value systems and ethical approaches determine space across scale and point to alternatives that encourage coexistence, cohabitation or collectivity? Could they empower those who have been historically excluded from elitist forms of representation that obfuscate those relations? Could they help propel spatial practice into the complex challenges of the present, especially in the diffuse, metropolitan, networked, even continental urban territories of the present?

While the explorative nature of these design processes determines their rather fluid existence, the moments when they were curated and installed in the form of brief installations worked both as invitations to slow down for critical reflection and catalysts for propelling the work forward with new enquiries. The installations hinge on being both a sedimentation through design exploration, with recognized moments of crystallization of the work, and their de-sedimentation, meaning the forging of new, sometimes unexpected relations amongst their different constituents, which transcend an obvious relation between observer and observed. They are thick, dense spaces that encourage immersion in their constructed temporalities and sense of materiality. These characteristics frustrate attempts at describing the work as a linear progression of knowledge-making and encourage a more fragmentary and fleeting understanding of it through glimpses that may be impossible to fully document, but which are, nevertheless, productive.

Exhibitions have been described as 'a philosophical problem that travels along with the thematic or conceptual research [they] do.'[404] The problem raises the question of 'what, when, and how to exhibit a given set of concerns or ways of working, of various epistemological trajectories or commitments, of intersecting or interfering versions of a given narrative,' which eventually enables 'a persistent rhythm that drives and animates research.'[405] While this description might be concerned with the exhibitions' recurrent problems of (re)presentation and communication, it can still offer some useful considerations regarding the type of installations informing the book, which were perhaps less concerned with any potential to communicate ideas about Manhattan than they were in conceiving of architecture in their own right, even forging imagined new city conditions. For this reason, they often lacked obvious clues as to how to read the work and obvious relations between visitors and the work being experienced. The fragments exhibited through physical models and devices, drawings and video projections, and virtual pieces encouraged more porous and blurry streams of unconscious consciousness, which are perhaps not unusual in creative activities supported by methods akin to the PCM.

In its dense immersion, the architectural space created by the installation can also be conceived as a philosophical problem that slows us down and attunes us to their flow, transitionality and sense of materiality. The installation becomes an architecture that allows for the event it constructs not to exist completely or solidly but to be briefly manifested, with a type of vibrancy that demands stillness. It is in this space of the installation that the representation of Manhattan can be fully questioned and perhaps proposed differently.

Architecture, then, may become that which has a possibility to happen, even if briefly and not fully formed, through a series of fragments which animate and affect the event with their shimmery quality. And just like Woolf noticing dust forming on the windowsill, design experimentation can happen through ways of noticing and de-sedimenting this vibrancy. If we engage with this way of thinking about architecture as a possibility, or as a potential or ability for new things to happen, we are also, perhaps in a fundamental way, accepting the possibility of thinking about architecture geologically.

Terminological Positions

The positional terms presented throughout the book emerged alongside the development of the design work. They argue for understandings that are often specific and sometimes partisan. Rather than providing an exhaustive list of important ideas, the selected definitions aim to support theoretical claims and design explorations and activate a series of divergent entry points into the work.

Even if has not been yet accepted as the technical term in geology and stratigraphy to describe the contemporary geological age of the earth, the use of the Anthropocene as a theoretical framework is sustained by the revision and expansion of other important terms, such as time, frame or ground, and their repositioning among more complex, rhizomatic and, therefore, also unpredictable constituencies – natureculture, geosocial formation or hyperobject. The knowledge emerging from the debate also grows thanks to intersections with certain influential currents in late-twentieth-century French thought and Feminist positionings, and more recently with Object-Oriented Ontology, Intersectional Studies and New Materialism.

The described terms do not all hold the same value for the arguments in the book. A first group is composed of important ontological divergencies or expansions. A second set becomes valuable as methodological tools for steering theoretical discourse, design experiments and representational techniques. A third group includes important lenses which inform practices for reading, noticing and bearing witness to spatial, temporal and scalar conditions. Finally, the focus of the book on the island-territory of Manhattan demanded the inclusion of some terms that help the reader understand its insular, territorial, landscape and field conditions.

Anthropocene

See also Geologic; Geosocial Formation; Hyperobject; Natureculture

Initially formulated as a hypothesis within the earth sciences in the early 2000s, the Anthropocene refers to a proposed new geological epoch in which humans have become the dominant geomorphic force altering the earth. [406] The Anthropocene poses at least three important problems, primarily the need to define *Anthropos*, the subject of the Anthropocene. It raises concerns both about how it impacts all humans but in different ways, [407] and about the fact that humans are always already entangled in more-than-human assemblages. [408] The second problem is the tendency for the Anthropocene to become a grand narrative that some claim to be new. While the current geological epoch is witnessing human-induced change accelerating exponentially and becoming potentially irreversible (the mathematical asymptote as a new aesthetic paradigm), the idea that the earth was ever in equilibrium is incorrect, even though evidence suggests the speeding up of some conditions at a global level, i.e., the rise in temperature or sea level. [409] The final problem is the idea of progressive and inevitable collapse, which frequently opposes nihilists, for whom the world is not worth preserving, to technofixers, who believe that all problems can be fixed. A third group advocating for resilience and adaptation to change includes, among others, ecofeminists, who defend an active searching for possibilities of living and 'staying with the trouble.' [410] Borrowing from earlier debates in Feminism, the Anthropocene theory questions binary thinking that opposes nature to culture, subject to object, human to non-human, even figure to ground. Instead, it accepts more fluid notions such as *natureculture, geosocial formation*, or *hyperobject*. The Anthropocene sustains an ongoing trans-disciplinary debate in the humanities that intersects with climate change, deep ecological thinking, critical race theory, post-colonialism and intersectionality.

Assemblage

See also Field; Hyperobject

Imprecise translation of the French concept of *agencement*, first proposed by Gilles Deleuze and Félix Guattari in 1980, to describe the arrangement or fitting together of different components. [411] Deleuze defines the term as a multiplicity of heterogenous elements and the unstable relations between them. It was further theorized by Manuel De Landa as an ontological framework for analyzing social complexity. [412] The theory states that assemblages are 'characterized by "relations of exteriority" that are not predetermined or strictly defined, but rather in constant reconfiguration.' [413]

Assemblage is a useful concept for thinking about heterogenous conditions which make up cities and complex territories. [414] Under this optic, cities are not considered stable totalities, because their properties and manifestations depend on fluctuating internal and external part-to-part relations, and their rhizomatic *modus operandi* is not exhausted by those relations. [415]

In the Anthropocene, assemblage helps describe complex more-than-human conditions and relations that manifest across scale, from the local to the planetary. It has influenced New Materialists such as Jane Bennett, for whom assemblage is used to explain matter's vibrancy, or Anna Tsing, for whom the idea helps explain open-ended and unpredictable becoming-together in a place. Assemblage has also been quite influential to philosophers such as Graham Harman or Timothy Morton.

Cut
See also Deep Section; Fault

Action performed to divide or separate something into segments to single out or isolate a particular set of conditions. In the architectural disciplines, the cut is an important tool for analyzing and revealing spatial conditions in planimetric or sectional views. Architectural sections involve speculative creative and critical thinking about assumed points of view which escape common perception and encourage representation across and at scale.

The idea of cut has undergone an expansion as it became nested more closely within the Anthropocene debate. When defining an ethics of matter, Karen Barad introduces the notion of *agential cut*, whose intention is not to separate the whole into parts or separate one thing from (an)other, but rather to cut with an ethics of 'responsibility and accountability for the lively relationalities of becoming, of which we are a part.' [416] The agential cut is performed as a subjectification, and it exists between the conditions observed with the cut and the possibilities inherent in the very process of becoming a subject. Similarly, Joanna Zylinska's *minimal ethics* propose the idea of *ethical injunction* as a series of incisions that are made in the world and allow for more accountability. [417]

Cyborg
See also Natureculture

A cybernetic organism with both organic (even if fully synthetically produced) and robotic (biomechanic) body parts. Cyborgian configurations appear as important characters and tricksters in different early cultures, even if they are not referred to as cyborgs. In the mid-nineteenth century the idea of a man-machine system was used more regularly in science-fiction, for example in stories by Edgar Allen Poe. [418] The term itself was coined in 1960 by scientists Manfred E. Clynes and Nathan S. Kline to describe an enhanced human being who could survive in extra-terrestrial environments. The concept became influential under the speculative thinking of cyberneticist Gregory Bateson in the context of the space race and the Cold War. The idea also has had important resonance in the conception of cities and architecture.

More recently, the term was expanded as a feminist figure of thought and speech, specifically by Donna Haraway in her influential 'A Cyborg Manifesto' (1985). Haraway's notion of the cyborg still accepts the ammalgamation of the organic with the machinic, but it is used to describe possibilities for thinking teleologically about things that aren't 'born.' She utilizes the cyborg to question binary thinking and as a trope for 'living within and honoring the skills and practices of contemporary technoculture.' [419]

Deep Section

See also Cut; Fault; Frame; Representation; Thickness

A type of section concerned with the representation of a wide range of thick site-specific conditions – architectural, geological, biochemical, hydrological, ecological or infrastructural. It usually makes use of an expanded representational framing of the cut being performed to include the deeper layers of ground and atmosphere. The deep section has been used in the natural sciences to convey the complexity of the landscapes and territories analyzed, with the famous example of Alexander von Humboldt's annotated mountain and volcano *tableaux physiques*. More recently, it has become associated with urban and landscape design practices to represent the articulation of thick and unstable ground conditions. [420]

Deep Time

See also Anthropocene; Frame; Geologic

An incommensurably large temporal frame when compared to human life, which includes the age of the earth and its processes, sometimes also called *geological time*. [421] Deep time corresponds to a scientific paradigm shift introduced by James Hutton to the conventions about the geological processes of the earth's crust. It revolutionized the ways in which to read and represent a planet that was much older than what had been accepted by religious dogma. [422] The term was adopted in mainstream knowledge much later, namely with John McPhee's reference in a 1981 *The New Yorker* article. [423]

Ideas of time were significantly expanded in the twentieth century, both in science, with theories such a relativity or quantum field theory, and in philosophical thought. [424] Some Anthropocene theorists accept time as entangled and scalarly diffracted conditions of 'material configurings of spacetimemattering.' [426]

The Anthropocene theory generally accepts a convergence between earth and human temporalities, [426] encouraging the contemplation of how human-induced worlds are distributed across spacetime and affect more-than-human formations. It also complexifies it by including several kinds of time, 'from longue durée evolutionary rapprochements to the quick boom and bust of investment capital,' and giving meaning to their inevitable encounters, superpositions and entanglements. [427]

In the book, deep time becomes both an embedded condition of the geologic – geo-time – as well as a practice for noticing things that have been consigned to the margins of modernity's dominant logics. [428]

Design Practice

See also Cut; Representation; Thickness

Here understood as a particular kind of situated generative practice for knowledge-making that is first creative and critical. It results from iterative ways of thinking and making, and ways of noticing and bearing witness, which place emphasis on material explorations, translations and mediations. In this optic, design demands both a *thick* (contextual) attention to site-specificity and a *foreign* (necessarily external) drive to invention and transformation that gestures beyond repetition and mimicry. [429] Landscape and architectural design practices are entangled in spacetime conditions that operate along an infinitely connected continuum both at specific (and irreducible) scales and across scale. This is a type of transcalar analysis and imagination that is required when design practice is situated within an Anthropocenic framework and which, therefore, is reappraised within processes of constant becoming. Thus configured, design carries with it an ethics of *response-ability*. [430]

Event

`See also Assemblage; Glimpse`

Broadly defined as 'something that happens,' event has received considerable attention in theoretical debates since the turn of the twentieth century. Setting aside other contemporary uses of the word, namely for something that is planned, as well as the many philosophical reflections on the notion, the focus of the argument in the book lies in event as defined, albeit differently, by philosophers such as Gilles Deleuze, Jacques Derrida, Alain Badiou, or Michel Foucault.

Events for Deleuze are part of rhizomatic, ever changing and ongoing processes of becoming and differentiation. [431] They are connected through these processes, yet they do not comprise a unified whole but rather an emerging multiplicity because they are differentiated.

For Derrida, event is what happens in the now, 'something singular and non-repeatable' associated with the singularity of organic life. [432] Both Deleuze and Derrida accept event as an emergence of disparate multiplicities, which may have an eventual spatial character open to invention and possibility. [433] Bernard Tschumi draws from these definitions to propose the event as a 'sudden intensity generated by the juxtaposition and superimposition of differences,' a '"disjunctive synthesis,"' that operates on real, continuous and uninterrupted disjunctions. [434] Tschumi also draws influence from Michel Foucault to accept event less as a 'logical sequence of words or actions,' and more as an expansion that problematizes '"the very assumptions of the setting within which a drama may take place – occasioning the chance or possibility of another, different setting."' [435]

Extrusion

`See also Cut; Deep Section; Ground; Thickness`

Force applied to material that pushes it out and gives it shape. In geology, extrusion refers to 'the breaking-out of igneous rock from below the Earth's surface ... whether it is ejected through a volcano's cone or through pipe-like channels or fissures in its crust,' and its section constantly varies in relation to situational forces and encounters. In some artisanal and industrial practices, extrusion corresponds to 'the forcing of metals, clays or plastics at optimum temperature through a die to make rods, tubes and various hollow or solid sections,' which maintain their regularity throughout. [436]

In the book, extrusion becomes a design operation to examine architectural and city fragments together with their contextual conditions. It is mostly revealed stratigraphically through deep sections cutting across the city. Thus utilized, extrusion expands the usual limits of representability of the city to reveal its perhaps lesser-known entanglements while, at the same time, attempting to rescue them into the realm of architectural practice.

Fault

See also Cut; Deep Section; Geologic

Fracture along a planet's crust caused by pressure and accompanied by fast or slow rock-mass displacement of one side of the fracture in relation to the other and usually parallel to the fault line or trace. Faults can be explained by geometric rules and receive different names depending on both the angle the plane makes with the earth's surface and the direction of the slip along the plane. Larger faults in the earth's crust commonly result from movements and forces of tectonic plates. [437]

In the book, fault is first a figure of thought for reading territorial conditions, sometimes taken literally – along Manhattan's passive faults – other times metaphorically – cuts along the city which demonstrate fault-like qualities. It also becomes a condition for design experimentation that allows for the testing and enactment of possibilities for architectural, landscape and urban change of the current island-city configuration.

Field Condition

See also Assemblage; Hyperobject

Referring to *field* as an expandable spatial condition containing speed vectors, Stan Allen defines field condition as 'any formal or spatial matrix capable of unifying diverse elements while respecting the identity of each.' [438] Field conditions are relational and fluid assemblages more dependent on the internal relationships of their parts, scale and repetition, than on their overall shape, and they escape conventions of 'axiality, symmetry, or hierarchy.' [439] They correspond to a mode of thinking that accepts differentiation as incremental and repetitive, instead of being made through disjunctive breaks imposed from the outside. [440] Allen uses grid, moiré, flock, school, swarm or crowd as manifestations of field conditions, which encompass complex dynamics related to desire, operating at the edge of control and interacting in 'less predictable patterns.' [441]

In landscape and architectural discourses, field condition seems to operate at the intersection between three understandings: first, a land-related spatiality – field as an old term with imprecise origins used to describe a clearly recognizable portion of land, either open or enclosed, used for agricultural, military, or industrial operations.; [442] second, a mathematical spatiality – field as a set of elements that are affected and effected by forces (functions) with vectors and speeds – with important ramifications in twentieth-century physics (relativity) and quantum field theory; and third, a disciplinary spatiality that defines knowledge hierarchically, systematically and intra- and inter-disciplinarily. Thus defined, field conditions can sometimes operate in both the background and foreground of architectural production, namely in representation, where field becomes the graphic system – a surface, a paper or a table of operations – with which the extracts will later be organized.' [443]

Frame

`See also Glimpse; Ground; Representation; Scale`

Both a noun used to describe 'something composed of parts fitted together and united,' which define an enclosing border, and a verb to describe the actions of enclosing, giving expression or adjusting to 'something on for an end.' [446] In art and design disciplines concerned with space, *frame* is an important tool of representation and perception, and it is used to describe, reveal or conceal context and experience. In landscapes, cities or buildings *framing* can be experimented with to manipulate the perception of spatial conditions, from the establishment of visual connections to the revelation of thicker conditions. Influenced by film techniques, serial framing also became influential in architecture and urban practices, namely to describe spatial and temporal transitions. [445]

More recent techno-scientific advances across expanded scales – from sub-atomic scales to outer space – have had a profound impact on questions related to frame. [446] The challenges posited by the Anthropocene determine an active questioning of the frames utilized to define any given problem and to reverse some of the assumed spatial and temporal orders of modernity in questions of subjectivity (who or what is centrally or marginally represented), narrative (whose story is told), totality (never being able to grasp the whole) and scale (a scalefulness that verges on scalelessness). [447] The Anthropocene demands further expansion of onto-epistemological frames of knowledge and reference, as well as of the spatial, temporal and material frames of representation and experience of profoundly enmeshed and connected planetary conditions.

Future Perfect

`See also Design Practice; Glimpses`

Verb construction that results from the combination of the future and perfect tenses; used to describe events in relation either to the moment when they occurred or to a retrospective temporal marker. [448] It establishes a temporal relation between the future moment when the event happens and either a present (will have done) or past (would have done) reference point. In the latter case, it constructs a 'past of the future of the past,' that is, a construction where the event happens before a time that occurs after the past time of reference or perspective. This more complex construction is often referred to as the 'conditional perfect.' [449]

The grammatical construction supports the constitution of a rhetorical tool in the book with which to offer a retrospective contextualization of the three architectural manifestos and their authors' practices from the contemporary perspectives offered by the Anthropocene theory and its many debates.

Geologic

`See also Anthropocene; Assemblage; Geosocial Formation; Glimpse; Ground; Hyperobject`

Distinct from geological – an adjective used to described material configurations in geology – geologic corresponds to an expansion in 'cultural meaning and aesthetic sensation.' [450] The Anthropocene demonstrates that '[g]eology does not refer exclusively to the ground under our feet,' but to expanded understandings of the *geo* in relation to political, socio-cultural, technological and eco-environmental conditions. [451] In this context, geology is regarded as a medium that reveal 'sites of transformation where the earth becomes an object of systematized knowledge' about resources extracted for technological production, geopolitics and 'increasingly a global survey of the minerals of the earth.' [452]

The actions involved in thinking geologically about landscape and architectural conditions include a 'thinking with' as well as a 'feeling through' the idea of geologic, [453] through which human existence is read as being entangled in more-than-human materialities which unfold across deep time and at multiple scales. Ways of thinking attuned to the geologic can only partially reveal the complexity of infinitely connected conditions. Rather than gesturing towards the whole, these thoughts – or lines of flight, as Deleuze would call them – focus on fluid part-to-part relations.

In the book, geologic is used to describe logics in thought and experimentation that encourage the imagination of alternative ways of reading, understanding and representing city and landscape conditions.

Geosocial Formation

See also Anthropocene; Cyborg; Natureculture

Specific or concrete manifestation of dynamic and ever-changing spatio-temporal processes. [454] The term was first coined by Nigel Clark and Kathryn Yusoff in 2017 to describe the confluence of earth and social conditions. Following a period of two centuries, when the idea of the earth, having been formed through periods of geological instability, was divorced from the more recent period of Holocenic stability (and outside of philosophical significance, according to Hegel), the Anthropocene theory supports more recent scientific inquiries which suggest that the planet has never been in equilibrium, even if sometimes it seems to exist suspended in momentary periods of stability. 'Formation' denotes the dual meaning as process and outcome, and its use aims to integrate the examination of 'the current global environmental predicaments' with the necessary understandings of how 'social futures [might] engage with the geologic in ways other than at present.' [455] Geosocial formations encourage a more active thinking about the together-becomings of earth and society, and help probing 'the richly layered formations we have inherited for the overlooked, marginalized or as yet unactualized geosocial possibilities murmuring within them.' [456]

Glimpse

See also Design Practice; Event; Frame; Geologic

Process of thinking through the image that is deeply intertwined with a process and style of writing, where images can only be seen in fleeting impressions – or glimpses. [457] Developed by Georges Didi-Huberman as both a theory of and a method for image critique, glimpse translates from the French *aperçue*, and offers poetic descriptions of images which re-veal 'affinities and insights which appear when images are juxtaposed by means of montage.' [458] The meaning of the image is in flux with the instances of that image flaring up and fading away. [459] Didi-Huberman considers glimpses always in the plural as he refers to multiple singularities invoked and coming together only during the brief moment of the impression. Albeit with some differences, the concept shares some theoretical affinity with Deleuze's *lines of flight*, as well as with Zylinska's more recent definition of *shards of thought*. [460]

In the book, glimpses are used as a practice of writing diffractively about a multitude of marginal events and conditions that inform each other and the design experimentation. [461]

Ground

See also Anthropocene; Extrusion; Geologic; Landscape; Representation; Stratigraphy; Thickness

Set of diffuse geo-bio-chemical conditions in which natural materials such as rocks, minerals, fossils and soil exist in entangled formations with synthesized materials such as concrete, asphalt, synthetic debris, plastic or radionuclides. [462] The Anthropocene theory recognizes the impossibility of disentangling the natural from the synthetic as well as the geological from the geopolitical. [463] Ground is contemplated geo-archaeologically, as natural and synthetic matter organized stratigraphically and containing a collection of vestigial traces of violence, erasure and constant reworking. It is considered geopolitically, as unsettled, disturbed and (re)claimed thicknesses which reveal habits of coexistence and tension. It is read geometrically and geographically, as constantly renegotiated gradients and vectors which dissolve differences between figure and ground and question dominant logics – Cartesian, Imperialist, Colonialist. It is accepted critically and creatively, as a figure of thought for practice; the action verb grounding. Ground exists across massively distributed scales; it conceals and reveals violent traces of systemic racism, military-industrial explorations, exploitations and extractions, eco-erasures and bio-mass-destructions; it is deterritorialized and terraformed in new *spacetimematterings*. [464] Grounding becomes a probing for non-hierarchical ways of thinking about spacetime thickness, sedimentation, archive and media. [465]

In the book, ground informs analytical lenses to read context, critical lenses to construct rhetoric, and creative lenses to practice and imagine newly positioned landscapes as ground registrations that acknowledge the 'differences that make a difference' and enable ways of connecting differently with the world. [466]

Hyperobject

See also Anthropocene; Assemblage; Deep Time

Object 'massively distributed in time and space relative to humans,' first defined by Timothy Morton. [467] A hyperobject can be a black hole, a planet, or the entire solar system. It can be all the nuclear materials on earth or just plutonium. It can be global warming, the internet, oil or capitalism. Hyperobjects 'are "hyper" in relation to some other identity,' whether synthesized or not. Distinct as they might be, hyperobjects share properties in common: viscosity, non-locality, temporal undulation, phasing and inter-objectivity. [468] The term can be useful for thinking of more-than-human entanglements across transcalar conditions of connectivity.

Island

See also Assemblage; Geologics; Ground

A specific geological and geographical condition – simply defined as a tract of land detached from larger landmasses or surrounded by water – as much as an idea with profound trans-cultural onto-epistemological implications. Deleuze considers the island's speculative importance as a place of reinvention containing the possibility to begin anew, whereas Foucault highlights its discursive and spatial qualities as a heterotopia. [469] Sloterdijk builds on these ideas to conceptualize islands as prototypical 'world models in the world' and refers to the notion of *connected isolation* to denote that no island is absolutely isolated. [470] Morton aligns with this position when describing an island's edges as ambiguous – or *molten* – depending on the scale of observation. [471] Island is a seminal manifestation in important philosophical probes and literary *topoi*. [472]

Islandness defines a set of physical and conceptual conditions that establish a means of unsettling differentiation within an operative field and through which it becomes possible to productively 'connect and disconnect parts and wholes.' [473] These conditions are explored in the book specifically in relation to Manhattan, a quintessential island-territory of the nineteenth and twentieth-century city, whose sense of isolation seems to be discursive and reinforced by its status as an emblematic cultural construct. [474]

Landscape

See also Assemblage; Cyborg; Deep Time; Field Condition; Geologic; Ground; Natureculture

Sets of material conditions media and ways of being and knowing fluidly configured across and at scale in space and time, which support the *lifeworlds* of more-than-human communities.

Benefitting from meaningful transformations in theory and practice from the 1970s onwards, the idea of landscape expanded with Feminist critical theorists such as Elizabeth Meyer, who defend the questioning of binary thinking as it is applied to assumed divisions between nature and culture, architecture and landscape, or figure and ground. Meyer's thinking positions landscape as a hybrid (or cyborg) at the intersection of these concepts. [475] The Anthropocene theory corroborates Meyer's proposition, further expanding on ideas of time, space, or ground. It also questions previous notions of landscape as a palimpsest on which traces can be constantly erased and rewritten, to instead claim that Anthropogenic landscapes result from a confluence of multiple past occupations and imagined futures in the *now*. [476] More specifically, New Materialists suggest that landscapes haunted by these synchronic and diachronic confluences become 'strange topologies: "[e]very bit of spacetimemattering is ... entangled with all others."' If landscapes enact 'more-than-human rhythms,' they also demand new trans-disciplinary approaches with which to offer newly hybrid histories and stories 'crossing the sciences and humanities,' that may question narratives of progress, capitalism and techno-optimization. [477]

Natureculture

See also Anthropocene; Assemblage; Cyborg; Geosocial Formation; Landscape

Synthesis of nature and culture that accepts their inseparable entanglement in ecological relationships, first coined by Donna Haraway. [478] The term emerged from eco-feminist scholarly inquiry questioning the dualisms dominant in western forms of binary thinking, which frequently oppose nature to culture and accept human exceptionalism. Questioning the supposed division between nature and culture, *natureculture* repositions the human as a subcomponent of much wider and non-binary formations that are 'both biophysically and socially formed.' [479] The term has been appropriated in landscape and architectural critical theory and has further supported a critique on the assumed rifts between human and nature, architecture and landscape, object and context or figure and ground. [480]

Representation

See also Frame; Design Practice; Scale; Thickness

Representation can be defined etymologically as the act of 'making present' something which is absent, often through the function of 'a sign or symbol "standing for" that to which it refers.' [481] Setting aside the myriad applications of the term in different onto-epistemological systems, in design contexts representation refers to the critical and creative processes of thought and production, including the apparatuses of tools and methods, to analyze, construct, and synthetize knowledge. [482]

Representation can be accepted as a set of practices that 'co-produce' and contemplate together with the material world – less of a representation of the world and more of a representation with the worlds-in-the-making. The Anthropocene considers representation also as a geoaesthetic contemplation, demanding not only an expansion of the scales and frames to represent a more active *geo*, but also a critical reflection on what such expansion might mean to different kinds of representation – materially, metaphorically, and methodologically. [483]

The representational production manifested through the work in the book pays particular attention to the contextual conditions in which such representations might occur as well as to the context being represented. The former – the context of a representation – is here called *thick representation*, whereas the latter – an expanded context being represented – is called *representation of thickness*. [484]

Scale

See also Representation; Deep Time; Frame; Geologic; Hyperobject

Relationship between objects, spatial conditions, or temporal frames through measurement, which constructs a referential, or system of reference. It can also denote a studied relationship between a space or territory and their representational abstraction. In design disciplines, scale is a core notion in practicing along and across the spacetime continuum. Landscape, urban and architectural practices are activated by and often enacted through multiscalar thinking, manifested both at and across scale. [485]

The Anthropocene requires multiscalar thinking to reflect on how 'human agency [acts] over multiple and incommensurable scales at once.' [486] Scale is implicated in the multiple relations and positionings of more-than-human formations both at the planetary and local scales. Increasing techno-scientific, industrial and design precision in scaling – 'the quality called *scalability'* – means the ability to expand incommensurably. [487] Yet, the apparent possibilities of smoothly transitioning from one set of scales to another with the support of complex techno-material and representational apparatuses – sometimes also called *long zoom effect* – must be challenged by the acknowledgment that human activities affecting the scale of geology are 'marked at certain points, and that these points are to scale.' [488]

Spherography

See also Frame; Geologic; Ground; Representation; Stratigraphy

Practice of reading and understanding the positioning of something within the earth's crust. This approach – both spherographical and spherological – accepts that the spherical volume of the planet affects the planar Cartesian conventions often used in architectural and landscape representation: the horizontal becomes an arc of the earth, the vertical a radius and the oblique a tangent. The ambition of the book to position and conceive of Manhattan within much wider planetary conditions benefits from such an approach, which is not necessarily new, [489] but which nevertheless was considerably reappraised more recently by Peter Sloterdijk in his trilogy of philosophical books *Spheres*. [490]

Stratigraphy

See also Assemblage; Deep Section; Geosocial Formation; Ground; Geologic

Branch of geology focused on the study of rock layering and stratification which includes both lithologic (rock and mineral) and biologic (fossil) formations. [491] The Anthropocene activates a more conceptual use of stratigraphy in the arts and humanities also as a practice of cutting across infinite conditions of connectivity to understand, even if only partially, specific conditions of wide geosocial formations or assemblages. [492]

In the book, stratigraphy also becomes a practice of reading spatial conditions entangled in their context. It supports the conceptual cuts and sections enacted in Manhattan as ways of reading and understanding entanglements between the city and the geologic conditions that support it.

Thickness

See also Deep Section; Field Condition; Ground

Approach to spatial analysis and design that navigates and attempts to reconcile the apparent tension between local site-specificity and global universalism in an increasingly more interconnected planet. The notion gained prominence through Clifford Geertz's anthropological and ethnographic descriptions – often called *thick descriptions* – and is compelling in landscape and architectural practice, especially as related to both context and the methods of analysis and production involved in dealing with it. James Corner utilizes *thickness* as a condition to describe landscapes planimetrically, sectionally, geographically, materially, ecologically and culturally. [493] This understanding borrows from Stan Allen's idea of the *thick-2D* – moments of intensity in urban fields defined by thickened surfaces – and Sébastien Marot's notion of *sub-urbanism* – the site-specific ground that steers a particular place. [494]

Endnotes

1. Interact
Indeterminant New York

1 F. Scott Fitzgerald, *The Great Gatsby* (1925).

2 H. G. Wells, *The War in the Air* (1908); and F. Scott Fitzgerald, *My Lost City* (1933).

3 It is accepted that the term gained traction at the hand of atmospheric chemist Paul Crutzen, who coined the term at a conference on stratigraphy and climate change and then further refined it in a series of related articles and papers.

Suggestions about its eventual starting point in time diverge, ranging from earlier beginnings twelve thousand years ago and coinciding with the invention of agriculture and the first sedentary civilizations, to the Industrial Revolution and the introduction of petrochemicals at a global scale, or to the more recent period of the Great Acceleration and the rise of the nuclear in the second half of the twentieth century and after WWII. See also Timothy Morton, *The Ecological Thought* (Cambridge: Harvard University Press, 2010).

4 The popularization of the term was first due to the publication of several articles in mainstream media. One such article was written in 2011 by Elizabeth Kolbert. The term eventually permeated media, politics, socio-cultural events and publications, art manifestations and literary pieces. See Elizabeth Kolbert, 'Enter the Anthropocene—Age of Man.'

5 As of 2024, the International Commission on Stratigraphy has 'voted down a proposal to declare the start of the Anthropocene,' claiming that it is still too early to accept the current geological time as something radically different than the Holocene. Even when acknowledging human's undeniable influence in contemporary planetary changes, the group of scientists led by Jan A. Zalasiewicz has stated a preference to 'describe the Anthropocene as an "event," not an "epoch."' (Raymond Zhong, 'Are We in the "Anthropocene," the Human Age? Nope, Scientists Say,' *The New York Times* March 25, 2024). The research and discussion spanning almost two decades includes the identification of a geological marker for the Anthropocene to eventually accept it as the name of the current geological epoch (Meera Subramanian, 'Anthropocene now: influential panel votes to recognize Earth's new epoch,' *Nature* (2019). The work has been controversial, with some supporting the unprecedented attempt to identify a period on the deep geological time scale that is still ongoing and probably in its early stages, while others state that 'the stratigraphic evidence overwhelmingly indicates a time-transgressive Anthropocene with multiple beginnings rather than a single moment of origin,' that is, looking for a single geological marker – for example, radionuclide signals – may be useless and 'imped[e] rather than facilitat[e] scientific understanding of human involvement in Earth system change.'(Matt Edgeworth quoted in Subramanian, 'Anthropocene now.') For a more complete discussion on the *Anthropocene* see Terminological Positions (end of book).

6 See Haraway, *Staying with the Trouble.*

7 The idea of de(sedimentation) is explored later in the book.

8 A conceptualization of geology as media has been proposed by several scholars and more recently reformulated within the Anthropocene theory by Jussi Parikka. See Jussi Parikka, *A Geology of Media* (Minneapolis: University of Minnesota Press, 2015). For a more articulated explanation of these ideas, see the definition of *Ground* in Terminological Positions (end of book).

2. Imagine
The Deep Section as a Tool for Thinking About Context

9 Robert Smithson, 'Frederick Law Olmsted and the Dialectal Landscape,' in Jack Flam (Ed.), *Robert Smithson: The Collected Writings* (1973, Berkeley, CA: University of California Press, 1996).

10 Sectional depictions have a long tradition in architecture and landscape architecture as determinant modes of representation. In their article 'The Performative Ground: Rediscovering the Deep Section', Stephanie Carlisle and Nicholas Pevzner discuss the importance of deep sections not only as a means for grasping the complexity inherent in the landscape's thickness and performance but also as 'a critical tool for interdisciplinary collaboration and design exploration' (Stephanie Carlisle and Nicholas Pevzner, 'The Performative Ground: Rediscovering the Deep Section,' in *Scenario Journal 02*, 2009).

11 Karen Barad, 'Matter feels, converses, suffers, desires, yearns and remembers,' interviewed by Rick Dolphijn and Iris van der Tuin, in Rick Dolphijn and Iris van der Tuin (Eds.), *New Materialism: Interviews and Cartographies* (London: Open Humanities Press, 2012), 69.

12 See Joanna Zylinska, *Minimal Ethics for the Anthropocene* (London: Open Humanities Press, 2014). Zylinska's interest in ethics stems from Emmanuel Levinas's 'turning towards something' and from Jacques Derrida's 'horizon of infinite justice.' See also Joanna Zylinska, in conversation with Benek Çinçik and Tiago Torres-Campos, 'A Local Museum of the Anthropocene,' in *Postcards from the Anthropocene: Unsettling the Geopolitics of Representation* (Barcelona: DPR-barcelona, 2022).

13 Timothy Morton compares the restricted human perception of a *hyperobject* to an architectural section. He writes that '[s]ince hyperobjects occupy a higher-dimensional phase space than we can experience directly, we can only experience somewhat constrained slices of them at any one time.' In architectural practice, this comparison may imply that the slice – one could also call it section – is a truncated representation of a set of conditions that occupy higher-dimensions in space and time (Timothy Morton, *Hyperobjects: Philosophy and Ecology after the End of the World* [Minneapolis: University of Minnesota Press, 2013], 1.) For a more complete definition of *hyperobject* see Terminological Positions (end of book).

14 Lebbeus Woods, 'Lower Manhattan Revisited,' in *Lebbeus Woods Blog* (2012).

15 Mark Dorrian, 'Adventure on the Vertical. Powers of Ten and the mastery of space by vision', in *Cabinet* 44 (2011).

16 Ibid.

17 Ibid.

18 Ibid.

19 For more information on a *spherographic approach*

see Terminological Positions (end of book).

20 Derek Woods, 'Scale Critique for the Anthropocene,' in Minnesota Review 83 (2014) (New Series) For a more complete elaboration on the notion of *scale* see Terminological Positions (end of book).

21 Ibid.

22 Some ideas explored in the next paragraphs were originally published in an essay by the author. See Tiago Torres-Campos, 'Manhattan's Geologic Delineations', in *Ground-Up Journal of Landscape Architecture* 05 Delineations (Berkeley: University of California, 2016), 58–63.

23 The idea of the city as a geologic force was postulated by artists and writers Elizabeth Ellsworth and Jamie Kruse. See Elizabeth Ellsworth and Jamie Kruse, *Geologic City: A Field Guide to the Geoarchitecture of New York* (New York: Friends of the Pleistocene, 2011).

24 Woods, 'Lower Manhattan Revisited.'

25 The application of the idea of a surveyor's chain, also called *Gunther's chain*, as an operation to describe Manhattan's geological behavior was developed in tandem with student-led ideas in response to the syllabus of a joint MArch/MLA design studio co-taught by Adrian Hawker, Victoria Claire Bernie and the author. See Adrian Hawker, Victoria Claire Bernie and Tiago Torres-Campos, 'Island Territories VI: Manhattan Scapeland Estrangement / Displacement,' MArch and MLA (The University of Edinburgh, School of Architecture and Landscape Architecture, 2018–2020).

26 Charles Merguerian and John E. Sanders, *Geology of Manhattan and the Bronx: Guidebook for On-The-Rocks* (New York: New York Academy of Sciences, 1991).

27 The idea of Manhattan's park systems operating geologically as a constellation was first presented as part of an essay by the author. See Tiago Torres-Campos, 'Inwood's Geofollies and Other Witnesses of Dissonance,' in Ed Wall (Ed.), *AD The Landscapists: Refining Landscape Design as a Critical Medium* (New York: Wiley, 2020), 38–45.

3. Stratify
Towards a Rhetoric of Ground

28 Examples of such projects are the proposals coming out of the international design competition Rebuild by Design – the most mediatic of them being Bjarke Ingels Group's *Big U* – or the perhaps more impactful infrastructural proposal for the New York Harbor Storm Surge Barrier.

29 *Lower Manhattan* was first published in the Italian magazine *Abitare*, May 1999. See Lebbeus Woods, 'Lower Manhattan,' *Abitare* 384 (1999).

30 Lebbeus Woods in conversation with Geoff Manaugh, 'Without Walls: An Interview with Lebbeus Woods,' in *BLDG BLOG* (2007).

31 Lewis Wallace, 'Lebbeus Woods: The Architect Who Dared to Ask 'What If?,' *Wired* (2013).

32 Woods, 'Lower Manhattan.'

33 The writings by and about Lebbeus Woods, both about himself – the person and the architect – and his work, exist in many formats: from academic books and short publications to articles and essays in specialized magazines, to interviews and talks. Some of the studied sources are explicitly (auto)biographical – Woods often reflected on his personal experiences and their influence in his understanding of the world. Whenever relevant, the experiences are mentioned in the text or in a footnote. Towards the end of his life, as Woods progressively expanded his focus from objects to fields, he also expanded his forms of practicing. A particular reference should be given to his prolific reflective and creative writings in the form of a blog. See *Lebbeus Woods Blog.*

Shannon Mattern describes 'Lebbeus' blogging voice' as being 'much less prone to manifesto-like proclamation than in his earlier writing,' a form of writing that she describes as being 'generous and elegantly conversational and marked by sage humility.' This '"free-zone" web architecture' is utilized in the first section of this chapter as an attempt to capture Woods' reflections on several relevant matters of concern (Shannon Mattern, 'Lebbeus Woods: The Politics of Small Things,' in *Words in Space: Shannon Mattern* (2014).

34 The architect states that '[i]f you're doing work on a certain level, it's always autobiographical.' The son of a military officer, Woods grew up around the military-industrial complex – watching with interest the construction of military bases and aircrafts – an experience he links directly with his later period at the School of Engineering at Purdue University, before studying Architecture at the University of Illinois. When reflecting on his trip to Sarajevo in 1993, soon after the massive destruction of the city by the Yugoslav People's Army, the architect considered his 'involvement with the concept of war and architecture' to have been more influenced by his interest in the engineering poetic pragmatism in constructing things and 'dealing with complex and difficult practical problems.' Woods adds that 'when I was drawn into this Sarajevo situation … I brought that knowledge or that memory into that situation but on a new level, certainly nothing that I had ever thought of as a child.' The Sarajevo projects, included in the publication 'War and Architecture,' were aimed at deriving guiding principles with which Woods believed his conceptual work could make a meaningful contribution to the reconstruction of the city, as well as other places devastated by war. See Lebbeus Woods, *Lebbeus Woods: the Vico Morcote Interview*, (SCI-Arc Archives, 1998).

35 In a 2008 interview for the *New York Times*, Woods adds: '[a]ll my work is still meant to evoke real architectural spaces. But what interests me is what the world would be like if we were free of conventional limits. Maybe I can show what could happen if we lived by a different set of rules. See William Yardley, 'Lebbeus Woods, Architect Who Bucked Convention, dies at 72,' in *The New York Times* (2012).

36 Ibid.

37 Lebbeus Woods, 'Why I Became An Architect,' in *Lebbeus Woods Blog* (2012).

38 Lebbeus Woods, 'RIEA: the Back Story,' in *Lebbeus Woods Blog* (2011). Woods describes the two-day founding event in upstate New York, later called RIEA's First Conference, as an occasion which gathered practicing architects from different parts of the world around a common focus on experimental architecture. He points out that one thing that united them at the time – apart from himself, the group included Gordon Gilbert, Michael Webb, Hani Rashid, Michael Sorkin, Ken Kaplan, Ted Krueger, Peter Cook and Neil Denari – was the fact that none of them 'had built much if anything but [they] had made ground-breaking conceptual projects.'

39 Ibid.

40 Lebbeus Woods in conversation with John Szot, 'Terrible Beauty,' *MAS Context* Issue Aberration (2011).

41 The linking underground city unfolded beneath Fredrick Strasse and next to Checkpoint Charlie. Taking advantage of two existing crossing U-Bahn lines, the project evolved into an inverted city of civic spaces for living and working carved out of the earth's planetary mass. The new underground city is developed through a series of individual site-specific interventions that are, nevertheless, intricately connected 'like the vertebrae in a spine. It is an imagined urban condition that resolves a geopolitical truncation by means of expanding the underground' (Lebbeus Woods, *Centricity: The Unified Urban Field*, Excerpt from Public Lecture at SCI-Arc (SCI-Arc Archives, 1988)). The expansion of the reference datum of the city is crucial to the reflections about *Lower Manhattan* in relation to the Anthropocene theory which is further developed later in the book.

42 Woods' idea for this reconstruction focused on the exploration of the 'consequences of freedom and choice,' and it was perhaps unique in its advocacy for 'spontaneous architecture without predetermined purpose and meaning evolving through the unpredictable exchanges by electronic means of people living there' (Lebbeus Woods, 'Terrible Beauty').

When asked about his defense of Berlin's public space, Woods discusses his interest in boundaries instead of property lines. To this discussion about urban delineations, he adds that '[t]he idea of "owning" a part of the earth does not appeal to me personally, though I understand that it has been, and remains, a great influence on how we live and are able to live.' See Lebbeus Woods in conversation with Leo Gullbring, in *Azure* (2008), 34.

43 Ibid. In an earlier interview Woods distinguishes, once again, between boundaries and property lines. He explains that 'the least present aspect is the idea of property lines. There are certainly boundaries – spatial boundaries – because, without them, you can't create space. But the idea of fencing off, or of compartmentalizing

– or the capitalist ideal of private property – has been absent from my work over the last few years.' (Woods, 'Without Walls').

44 Woods refers to an 'architecture constructed, transformed, or completed by their effects – an architecture that uses earthquakes, converting to a human purpose the energies they release, or the topographical transformations they bring about – an architecture that causes earthquakes, triggering microquakes in order that "the big one" is defused—an architecture that inhabits earthquakes, existing in their space and time.' See Lebbeus Woods, *Radical Reconstruction* (New York: Princeton Architectural Press, 1997), 21–22.

45 Lebbeus Woods in conversation with Corrado Curti, 'Architecture: The Solid State of Thought,' in *Lebbeus Woods Blog* (2010).

46 Ibid. Woods adds that '[a]rchitects have largely ignored earthquakes and other natural, if violent, transformations, political walls, and wars, feeling that they were outside of architecture's proper domain, which is to design the known building typologies for the known and stable social conditions.'

47 Ibid.

48 It seems relevant to note here that Woods' conception of architecture as field may have benefitted from Stan Allen's notion of *field conditions*. For a deeper discussion of *field conditions* see Chapter 4 and Terminological Positions (end of book).

It could also be argued that Woods' interest in constructing relationships between architecture and context came earlier on in his life, for example, when he describes his acts of drawing out the conditions of *Underground Berlin*:

> … 'with the idea of a landscape in mind. In other words, that architecture is really part of the world. And the use of perspective drawing places architecture within a total landscape, something which is not architectural. So, our usual means of representing architecture – plan, section, elevation, and so on – tend to isolate architecture out, and what I'm trying to do in these drawings it to put architecture back

into the idea of a landscape, even though this is a totally self-referential landscape' (Woods, *Centricity*).

49 Haraway defines cyborgs as figures for living within contradictions, attentive to the naturecultures of mundane practices, opposed to the dire myths of self-birthing, embracing mortality as the condition for life, and alert to the emergent historical hybridities actually populating the world at all its contingent scales. See Donna Haraway, *The Companion Species Manifesto: Dogs, People, and Significant Otherness* (Chicago: Prickly Paradigm Press, 2003). See also Nicholas Malone and Kathryn Ovenden, 'Natureculture', Agustín Fuents (Ed.), *The International Encyclopaedia of Primatology* (New Jersey: John Wiley & Sons, 2017). See Terminological positions at the end of the book for a more complete definition of *cyborg* as a figure of thought and *natureculture* in relation to the Anthropocene studies.

50 A line of theoretical enquiry that brings together Woods and Haraway can be supported by the influence cybernetics played in their modes of thinking and their respective bodies of work. In his young adulthood, Woods was profoundly influenced by Austrian-American scientist Heinz von Foerster, who is considered to be one of the originators of second-order cybernetics, or the 'cybernetics of cybernetics,' devoted to the epistemological and ethical study of 'observing systems.' See Ranulph Glanville, 'The Purpose of second-order cybernetics,' *Kybernetes* 33 (9/10) (2004),1379–1386.

Woods' architecture is made of complex self-referential, self-organizing systems, where 'circularity is taken seriously'. In turn, in 'A Cyborg Manifesto' Haraway states that cyborgs are defined '"cybernetic organisms," named in 1960 in the context of the space race, the cold war, and imperialist fantasies of technohumanism built into policy and research projects.' Haraway refers to American cyberneticist Gregory Bateson as a key figure in her development of speculative thinking about cyborgs. See Donna Haraway, *SF: Science Fiction, Speculative Fabulation, String Figures, So Far*, Acceptance Speech for Pilgrim Award, 2011 July 7 (California and Dublin: SFRA Meetings, 2011), 7.

51 Tiago Torres-Campos, 'Duck and Cover:

Experiencing the Anthropocene in 21ˢᵗ Century Manhattan', in *Pidgin Magazine* 27 (Princeton: Princeton University School of Architecture, 2020), 132–147.

52 Lebbeus Woods, 'Architecture: The Solid State of Thought'.

53 Woods used this description of Manhattan in a 2010 summer studio he instructed at Cornell, titled 'Vertical Manhattan: between the earth and the stars.' Lebbeus Woods, 'AS401: Vertical Manhattan I,' *Lebbeus Woods Blog* (2010).

54 Ibid.

55 Lebbeus Woods, 'Without Walls'.

56 Bobbette's interest in the series does not lie in any particular geologic or photographic quality of the images but rather on the limits they expose: the spatial and temporal vastness of geology; the technical and technological limits of emerging photographic activities; and the limits of precision challenged by the link that Harrison creates between the two. See Adam Bobbette, 'Episodes from a History of Scalelessness,' in Etienne Turpin (Ed.), *Architecture in the Anthropocene: Encounters Among Design, Deep Time, Science and Philosophy* (Open Humanities University Press, 2013), 47–58.

57 Ibid. These complex relationships between figure and ground are notorious in Harrison's photographs, even though fossil and rock are clearly distinguished from a geological standpoint in his written work.

58 Ibid.

59 For a more complete definition of *geosocial formation* see Terminological Positions (end of book).

60 A similar argument is made in a study of Gaetano Pesce's *The Church of Solitude*, a project for an underground church beneath a parking lot in Manhattan. See Tiago Torres-Campos, 'Silence in the Middle Ground. Aesthetic Immersion in the Geologic,' in Mark Dorrian & Christos Kakalis (Eds.), *Place of Silence. Architecture / Media / Philosophy* (London: Bloomsbury, 2020), 149–162.

61 Ibid.

62 Morton, *Hyperobjects*.

63 In this expanded understanding of the entanglement between city and bedrock, it may be interesting to mention *Lower Manhattan*'s aesthetic quality as a hyperobject. The

relation is interesting mostly in its potential to activate different meanings around the idea of fossilization and, in the specific case of *Lower Manhattan*, also of fossilized impressions of city, rock and planet as pertaining to an entangled formation which is difficult, if not impossible, to disentangle (see Morton, *Hyperobjects*).

64 Morton compares the restricted human perception of a hyperobject to an architectural section. He writes that '[s]ince hyperobjects occupy a higher-dimensional phase space than we can experience directly, we can only experience somewhat constrained slices of them at any one time.' In architectural practice, this comparison may imply that the slice – one could also call it section – is a truncated representation of a set of conditions that occupy higher-dimensions in space and time (Morton, *Hyperobjects*).

65 Barad, 'Matter feels.' See also Barad, *Meeting the Universe*. For a contextualization of agential cut within a more complete definition of *cut* see Terminological Positions (end of book).

66 For a more complete definition of *deep section* see Terminological Positions (end of book).

67 Jean-François Lyotard, 'The Sublime and the Avant-Garde,' in *The Bloomsbury Anthology of Aesthetics* (New York: Continuum, 2012), 537.

68 In her delineation of the *sublime*, Emily Brady defends that 'paradigm cases of the sublime involve qualities related to overwhelming vastness [mathematical sublime] or power [dynamic sublime] coupled with a strong emotional reaction of excitement and delight tinged with anxiety.' In her opinion, these are qualities that most artworks lack, even if some art can still be sublime. The same thing applies to classical examples of architecture – pyramids, temples, artificial lakes, canals, etc. – or contemporary, such as skyscrapers, both individually, when looking from the ground up into the sky, and collectively, when looking at the 'huge horizontal skyline, like a mountain range, looming from a distance.' See Emily Brady, *The Sublime in Modern Philosophy: Aesthetics, Ethics, and Nature* (Cambridge: Cambridge University Press, 2013), 119.

69 Brady draws on Edmund Burke's philosophy to the

notion of *mathematical sublime* (Ibid).

70 Chandos Michael Brown, 'The First American Sublime,' in Timothy M. Costelloe (Ed.) *The Sublime: From Antiquity to the Present* (2012, Cambridge: Cambridge University Press, online version 2015), 147–170. Hutton's paradigmatic notion of deep time reformulated conventions about earth and its geology. For a more detailed account of his influence see the definition of *deep time* in Terminological Positions (end of book).

71 Interested in Burke's more physiological theorization of the sublime and how it may be explained through the Avant-Garde, Lyotard also draws from Kant's notion of the *mathematical sublime* to state that art related to this movement 'expresses the sublime insofar as it is able to present the "unpresentable."' Lyotard's reference to an inability to comprehend derived from an inability to represent, which also lies at the heart of the Romantic notion of the sublime, is interesting in its deliberate gesture towards the limits of representability (Lyotard, 'The Sublime,' 537). See also Lyotard quoted in Brady, *The Sublime*, 137–38.

72 Supported by a powerful relationship between geology, nature, wilderness and remoteness, these ideas were foundational in the construction of a new national history for the then-young United States. This enmeshed relationship was perhaps no longer available in Europe, which had destroyed most of its sublime landscapes, but in the United States it became a tool with which to 'negotiate the essential tension of the American sublime.' See Brown, 'The First American Sublime.'

73 Contemporary scholars have outlined meaningful ways in which to bring additional relevance to the sublime in relation to the existential planetary threats lying ahead of us. Brady regards the sublime as being able to inform alternative modes of thinking in environmental ethics and aesthetics and to contribute to 'our moral attitudes toward natural environments' (Brady, *The Sublime*, 184–96).

74 Idem, 203.

75 Claire Colebrook establishes a relatively similar, if slightly more critical, line of thought about the sublime in contemporary attitudes to nature, namely the Kantian idea of sublime as being conducive of constructing nature architectonically. Instead, her proposed notion of *geological sublime* is generated though the perception of what is presented and the critical thinking 'about it not being that which it signifies, such that it is the distance and distinction of the word that renders it sublime' See Claire Colebrook, 'The Geological Sublime,' in Tom Cohen, Claire Colebrook and J. Hillis Miller (Eds.), *Twilight of the Anthropocene Idols* (London: Open Humanities Press, 2016), 117–125.

76 Claire Colebrook, 'The Geological Sublime,' 122.

77 Idem, 124–125.

78 Joanna Zylinska theorizes about post-apocalypticism in the context of the environmental threats posed by climate change and mass extinction. See Joanna Zylinska, *The End of Man: A Feminist Counterapocalypse* (Minneapolis: Minnesota University Press, 2018).

79 Brady, *The Sublime*, 117.

80 See David Nye, *American Technological Sublime* (Cambridge, Mass: MIT Press, 1994).

81 Starting with the completion of the Croton Aqueduct's first version in 1842, the water infrastructures ended up including a myriad of complex upgrades, which progressively extended the hydrological network upstate until it captured all the water over a gigantic territorial watershed. These works profoundly transformed the landscape of this entire region, which Gandy describes as an easily overlooked 'life-sustaining circulatory system through the interaction of the flow of water and the flow of money.' See Mathew Gandy, *Concrete and Clay: Reworking Nature in New York City* (Cambridge: MIT Press, 2002), 18 and 32–34.

82 The *Viele Map* might have benefitted from information traced from other seminal maps of Manhattan, namely a copy of *The British Headquarters Map* (circa 1782/1783), or equally the collection of John Randel Jr.'s ninety-two *Farm Maps* detailing the fiduciary land division of pre-grid Manhattan.

83 Tiago Torres-Campos, 'The Grid and the Bedrock. Manhattan through a Cartographic Geo-Tale,' in Bernd Upmeyer (Ed.), *MONU—Magazine on Urbanism* 29 Narrative Urbanism (Rotterdam: MONU, 2018), 49–50.

84 This idea is further explored in Chapter 5.

85 Torres-Campos, 'The Grid and the Bedrock,' 50. One could argue that maps such as the *Viele Map* should be explained not just in terms of their representational qualities but also within the wider mapping agencies for and contexts in which they were created. As *thick representations*, they require a contextual explanation of the ways they affect readings of the city. On the other hand, as operative devices, which compress disparate spatio-temporal moments onto their horizontal surfaces, these maps can be understood also as *representations of thickness*. This thickness is less of a palimpsest and more of a process similar to sedimentation, where layers of information are overlapped, fractured, merged, eroded or weathered. For a more detailed explanation of *thickness* in relation to representation see Terminological Positions (end of book).

86 Nye posits that this new aesthetic sensibility can be considered as a definite step in the consolidation of the American sublime, distinct from the Romantic attitudes from the previous century, namely by Hudson River School (Nye quoted in Gandy, *Concrete and Clay*, 34).

87 For a more complete definition of *technosphere* see Peter Haff, 'Humans and technology in the Anthropocene: Six rules,' in *The Anthropocene Review* 1(2) (2014), 126–136.

88 See Bruno Latour's definition of *actant* (translated from the original French term *actant*) within *Actor-Network Theory* (ATN). In very simple terms, *actant* refers to both human and non-human (a vast category that includes animals, plants, viruses, as well as technology, etc.) actors, who are entangled in networks shaped by the nature and virtue of their relations with one another. Rejecting an external influence on these networks of relations, ATN accepts no difference between the ability of humans and non-humans to act and, in acting (as in engaging) on a network, they become a subcomponent of the network itself.

89 Woods, 'Architecture: The Solid State of Thought.'

90 Woods, 'Without Walls'.

91 Wallace, 'Lebbeus Woods'.

92 Ibid.

93 Woods, *Centricity.*

94 Some ideas explored in this section were originally published in an essay by the author. See Tiago Torres-Campos, 'Foregrounding the Geologic: A Device for Working in Manhattan's Faults,' in Diana Periton (Ed.), *Journal of Architecture and Culture* 4(4) (London: Taylor & Francis, 2016), 163–166.

95 Steven Kurutz, 'When There Was Water, Water Everywhere,' *The New York Times* (2012).

96 Charles A. Baskerville, 'The foundation geology of New York City,' in Robert F. Legget (Ed.), *Geology under Cities* (Boulder, Colorado: The Geological Society of America, 1982), 95-117.

97 Eric W. Sanderson, *Mannahatta: A Natural History of New York City* (New York: Abrams, 2009). When describing the conditions of the old *Mannahatta* (the name that the Lenni Lenape used to designate the island and meaning 'the land of many hills') before the establishment of the first colonies, Sanderson refers to a luxuriant and very diverse landscape, crossed by many streams that nourished fertile valleys, wetlands and dense forests.

98 Similar lines of exploration underpin the investigation led by scientists such as the geologist Charles Merguerian, the geophysicist Alan Kafka or the climatologist and seismologist Klaus Jacob in the city of New York. Their separate studies investigate processes and constantly scan for signs in the city's geology, biosphere and atmosphere that can be measured and somehow related to our human-scale while also accounting for scales of space and time which are very difficult to grasp: the study of the nature and geometry of the faults existing in the tunnels that perforate Manhattan in order to assess the geological behavior of the island; or the movement and temperature of different types of rock and water beds to infer the small, yet constant movements of massive plates; or the analysis of ecologies of plants, animals and fungi to understand behavioral patterns and relationships across this shared territory. Despite their impressive body of work, which certainly puts into evidence relations of size and scale between the city and everything that supports or is supported by it, the aforementioned scientists – among many other illustrious names – have also expressed on many occasions the alarming lack of awareness in the collective mind of New Yorkers not only of the natural dynamics of the territory they live in, but inclusively of potential hazards or the absence of robust emergency plans in case of sudden rise of water levels, earthquakes or superstorms. See Lilah Raptopoulos, '"Are we safe? Of course not": climate scientist's NYC warning after Sandy,' *The Guardian* (November 2014); Charles Merguerian, 'NYC Earthquakes: Fact or Fiction,' Talk at the *The Asian American / Asian Research Institute (AAARI)* (CUNY, 2007); Charles Merguerian, *Stratigraphy, Structural Geology and Ductile – and Brittle Faults of New York City* (Hempstead: Hofstra University, 1996); and Fred Graver and Charlie Rubin, 'Waiting for the big one,' in *New York Magazine* Special Issue Earthquake (1995).

99 A more complete definition of *heterotopia* can be seen in Michel Foucault's 1967 seminal lecture 'Des Espaces Autres' – in English 'Of Other Spaces.' In the text, the philosopher explains his concept to an audience mainly composed of architects. See Michel Foucault, 'Of Other Spaces,' *Diacritics* 16(1), Jan Miskowiec (Trans.) (Spring, 1986), 22–27.

100 Foucault, 'Of Other Spaces,' 21.

101 Some ideas explored in this section were originally published in an essay by the author. See Torres-Campos, 'Inwood's Geofollies,' 38–45.

102 Charles Merguerian and J. Mickey Merguerian, *Field Trip Guidebook: Isham and Inwood Parks, NYC* (Lamont-Doherty Earth Observatory, Manhattan Prong Workshop) (Durham, NC: Hofstra University Geology Department and Duke Geological Laboratory, 2014). Offering views across the Hudson to the Palisades in New Jersey and to other hills in the vicinity, the park was once an important settlement of the indigenous Lenni Lenape people. It was also the place where Peter Minuit, Director General of the Dutch North American colony of New Netherland, allegedly purchased the island in 1626 from the local tribes. These communities called the island *Mannahatta*, often translated as 'the land of many hills,' 'place for gathering wood to make bows', 'the island where we all became intoxicated' or, simply, 'island.' See Robert Juet, *Journal of Hudson's 1609 Voyage*, entry 2 October (Albany, NY: New Netherland Museum / Half Moon, 2008).

103 Kathryn Yusoff, *A Billion Black Anthropocenes or None* (Minneapolis: University of Minnesota Press, 2019), Preface.

104 See Jane Bennett, *Vibrant Matter: A Political Ecology of Things* (Durham, NC: Duke University Press, 2010). The concept of *material witness* was first developed by Susan Schuppli. See Susan Schuppli, *Material Witness: Media, Forensics, Evidence* (Cambridge: MIT Press, 2020).

105 From a deforested landscape during the eighteenth-century wars between the British Empire and the rebellious colonies to a place of many asylums and weekend retreats for the rich merchants coming from New York's downtown in the nineteenth and early twentieth centuries, Inwood Hill has experienced significant landscape change. See Judith M. Fitzgerald and Robert E. Loeb, 'Historical Ecology of Inwood Hill Park, Manhattan, New York,' *Journal of the Torrey Botanical Society* 135(2), (2008), 281–93. Following the archaeological works which uncovered several caves that had once served as dwellings for the Lenni Lenape, the city first considered the possibility of creating a park here in the 1930s. Robert Moses used his position as Park Commissioner to initiate a process of demolishing the mansions and asylums that occupied the ridges. See Arthur H. Graves, 'Inwood Park, Manhattan,' *Torreya* 30 (5) (1930), 117–129. The old, fractured geology bears witness to the many uses and occupancies related with sheltering and leisure, as well as forced treatment and incarceration.

With the surrounding rivers revealing meaningful tidal variations at this point around the hill, salt gradients used to define most of the boundaries between land and water. Inwood, with the last salt marsh in Manhattan, evokes what once were valuable tidal habitats feeding the island, such as reed, kelp or oysters. But, in fact, the existing retaining wall that protects the park from the marshland's cyclic flooding equally registers the process of city growth which progressively replaced all soft waterscapes on the island with clear-cut port-like edges.

Most woodlands in Manhattan were harvested, either to give place to urbanization in times of peace, or for timber production for guns and fortifications in times of war. Some were also replanted. Moses's decision to erase the cultural landscape and replant the woodland that currently exists in the park is perhaps one of the most recent actions in a long succession of sowing and harvesting on this hill. While they decisively contributed to the park's value as an ecological haven, these actions may also be described as an act of white cleansing based on an abusive power relation in the city against human as well as vulnerable nonhuman minorities who once inhabited the hill.

Moses's resolution in the 1930s was closely aligned with the new planning policy to create public outdoor spaces throughout the city. As the grid carved its way across Manhattan's topography, several parks of different sizes were defined in areas where the rock was either too big or too hard to cut. A closer critical cartographic analysis of the several plans for the northern boroughs developed along the early decades of the twentieth century reveals that many options for bringing the city grid up Inwood Hill were considered.

The creation of a park in Inwood reflects some of the wider geopolitical dynamics behind the creation of Manhattan's park systems, especially north of Central Park. The majority of these landscapes are limited by significant streets or avenues, which do not conform to the orthogonal grid but distort it instead. Some of these significant boundaries lie directly on top of geological faults spreading across the island, and they also divide the city into its different administrative areas (Merguerian and Sanders, *Geology of Manhattan*). Inwood's geology, for example, is part of a complex system defined by the Dyckman fault, which runs beneath the street carrying the same name. The fault separates Inwood Hill and Isham Park, to the north, from the two long systems running south, one in the west composed by the parks of Fort Tryon and Fort Washington, and the other in the east composed by the parks of Harlem River, Highbridge and Jackie Robinson.

106 The machine supports the exploration of some of Inwood's highly site-specific dynamics: atmosphere and tides exchanging salt; drainage of run-off and underground water along the steep geology; and finally, compression, permeability and erosion caused by gravity. The machine equally brings into the project its own operating materials, by moving atomized and liquefied paint mixed with salt across the model to test principles of fluidity usually related with landscapes of salt – saturation, crystallization, erosion and sedimentation. As the salty ink slowly dries up due to gravity and evaporation, it creates a new undulating topography.

107 Arata Isozaki, 'Osaka's Green Crossroads,' in Pamela Johnston and Dennis Crompton (Eds.), *Osaka Follies* (London: Architectural Association, 1991), 5.

108 Ibid.

109 Mark Dorrian, 'Art/Architecture/Concept,' in W. Davidts, S Holden and A Paine (Eds.), *Trading Between Architecture and Art: Strategies and Practices of Exchange* (Amsterdam: Valiz, 2019), 16–25.

110 Idem, 23.

111 Idem, 24.

112 Cedric Price, 'The Folly,' in Johnston and Crompton, *Osaka Follies*, 7.

113 For a thorough account of dark humor in relationship to ecological thought, see Timothy Morton, *Dark Ecology: For a Logic of Future Coexistence* (New York: Columbia University Press, 2018). For a more complete explanation of the importance of serious playfulness in challenging its direct, corporativist opposite, playful seriousness, see Timothy Morton in conversation with Sean Lally, in *Night White Skies* episode 002 (2016).

114 For a thought-provoking exploration of the museum as a space of historical alienation, see Peter Sloterdijk, 'Museum – School of Alienation,' in *Art in Translation* 6 (4) (2007, London: Bloomsbury, 2014), 437–448.

115 Woods, *Centricity*.

116 Ibid.

117 Ibid.

118 Wallace, 'Lebbeus Woods.'

119 Lebbeus Woods, *Vico Morcote Interview*. Woods describes *Deconstructivism* as 'a fake avant-garde movement in the late [19]80s, manufactured by Phillip Johnson and Peter Eisenmann, with the help of a few others in New York,' as a consequence of the recognition of certain visual affinities between the works of certain architects, while disregarding what he considers to be significant conceptual differences. *Deconstruction* is discussed in more detail in Chapter 5 and in specific relation to Bernard Tschumi's *architecture of the event* and *The Manhattan Transcripts*.

120 Woods refers to this definition of his practice as something other than building several times (see, for example, Lebbeus Woods, *Centricity*). Later in life, he also made public statements detaching himself from other architects of his generation who had focused their careers on transforming their architectural ideas into actual buildings.

121 Yardley, 'Lebbeus Woods.'

122 Lebbeus Woods had at least three direct contacts with Hollywood's film industry: first in 1990 as a 'conceptual architect' consultant for Vincent Ward's *Alien II*I, whose production was then abandoned; second as a co-writer of a screenplay where his *Underground Berlin* project would project architecture as a vital instrument of social change; and third in 1995 when his 1987 project *Neomechanical Tower (Upper) Chamber* was copied for one of the sets in architect-director Terry Gilliam's production of *12 Monkey*s, which Woods sued and won. See Wallace, 'Lebbeus Woods;' and Jimmy Stamp, 'Lebbeus Woods and 12 Monkeys,' in *Life Without Buildings* (2006).

123 Haraway, *SF*, 9–10.

124 Idem, 10.

125 Idem, 6.

126 Idem, 9.

127 Idem, 12.

128 Clark and Yusoff, 'Geosocial formations,' 3–4.

129 Ibid.

130 See Benjamin H. Bratton, *The Terraforming* (Moscow: Strelka Press, 2019). The concept of *terraforming* has been presented as both a scientific approach and a science-fictional possibility. Carl Sagan, for example, admitted an eventual terraforming of planets such as Venus in the 1960s. And examples of terraforming alien planets make them amenable to human and earth-life existences. Some authors claim that the term was coined in 1942 by Jack Williamson in his short story *Astounding Science Fiction*, while others recognize previous uses of the word in popular culture.

131 Geoff Manaugh, 'Lebbeus Woods, 1940–2012,' in *BLDG BLOG* (2012).

132 Ibid.

133 See Haraway, *Staying with the Trouble*.

134 Haraway quotes what she considers to be an important lesson from social anthropologist Marilyn Strathern. The original quote is from Marilyn Strathern, *The Gender of the Gift* (Berkeley: University of California Press, 1988), quoted in Haraway, *SF*, 4. A similar argument is made by the author in relation to the experience of Manhattan's environmental phenomena in Torres-Campos, 'Duck and Cover.'

135 Torres-Campos, 'Duck and Cover,' 145.

136 Ibid.

137 Manaugh, 'Lebbeus Woods'.

4. Extrude
Delirious Fields and Paranoid Critical Fragments

138 Rem Koolhaas, *Delirious New York. A Retroactive Manifesto for Manhattan* (New York: The Monacelli Press, 1994).

139 Rem Koolhaas, Bernard Tschumi, Ana Miljacki, Amanda Reeser Lawrence and Ashley Schafer, '2 Architects 10 Questions on Program,' in *PRAXIS: Journal of Writing + Building* 8 RE:PROGRAMMING (2006), 6–15.

140 Rem Koolhaas, 'Why I Wrote Delirious New York and Other Textual Strategies,' in *ANY: Architecture New York* May/June 1993, Writing in Architecture (1993), 42–43.

141 Idem, 43.

142 Koolhaas, *Delirious New York*, 10.

143 Teresa Stoppani, *Paradigm Islands: Manhattan and Venice. Discourses on Architecture and the City* (London: Routledge, 2011), 16–20. Stoppani reads delirium as 'an intentional erasure and censorship' to argue that Koolhaas' method becomes '"operative"'.

144 Ibid.

145 Koolhaas, *Delirious New York*, 20.

146 Idem, 42.

147 Idem, 43. Through an aphoristic literary construction, *Delirious New York* encourages different reading exercises. One possible way of reading the book is not linear but rather as blocks of text. In fact, Koolhaas describes the book as blocks of text in the first few pages in a paragraph titled 'Blocks' (Koolhaas, *Delirious New York*, 11).

148 Idem, 294–295.

149 MoMA's archives, Madelon Vriesendorp's website and OMA's website all present slightly different versions of the image.

150 The problematization of geology as having the capacity for architectural inhabitation has been argued within the socio-urban and geological context of Manhattan in Torres-Campos, 'Silence in the Middle Ground.'

151 The image reveals OMA's homage to physically built projects, such as the Trylon and Perisphere from the 1939's New York International Fair, the RCA Building or the Berlin Wall. The homage extends, however, to important architectural ideologies, such as Le Corbusier's *Plan Voisin*, or Malevich's Suprematist Arkhitektons. Finally, the visual exploration reaches out to fields outside of architecture such as cinema with a reference to *The Cabinet of Doctor Caligari* (Robert Wiene, 1920), or painting with a reference to *Millet's Architectonic Angelus* (Salvador Dalí, 1933).

152 Koolhaas, *Delirious New York*, 7.

153 When reflecting on a direct relationship between *Delirious New York* and his subsequent endeavors – namely his finalist entry to the Parc de la Villette in 1982 – Koolhaas admits the influence his understanding of Central Park as a horizontal skyscraper had. (Koolhaas et al., '2 Architects,' 12).

154 Ibid.

155 The legendary purchase of the island by Peter Minuit in 1626 for twenty-four dollars is surrounded by misinterpretation, mistranslation and falsehood. Koolhaas exposes this troublesome transaction – which he calls a 'phantom sale' – when he states that it 'is a falsehood; the sellers do not own property. They do not even live there. They are just visiting' (Koolhaas, *Delirious New York*, 16–18). One could argue that Koolhaas' understanding is also troublesome, in that it does not rid itself completely of both a Westernized and colonial bias. Similar to other Native American communities, the Lenni Lenape had a totally different concept of property from the Eurocentric capitalist one; a notion that did not necessarily involve actually owning something as land or territory. Yet, they used this territory for their subsistence. Literary and archaeological reports reveal and demonstrate their daily camping grounds in some parts of the island, as well as their daily and seasonal movements on the island to get food and water. One example is the daily commute the Lenni Lenape made between their camping grounds around Collect Pond and the southern tip of the island. This commute along the ridge, which eventually became Broadway, was related to the harvesting of shellfish, especially oyster (information found on multiple sources, including Native-American literature on the Lenni Lenape).

156 Stoppani, *Paradigm Islands*, 18.

157 Koolhaas, *Delirious New York*, 9.

158 Koolhaas, *Delirious New York*, 18–19.

159 Stan Allen, 'Field Conditions Revisited,' in Benjamin Wilke (Series Ed.), *Four Projects, Source Books in Architecture* 10 (Novato: Applied Research + Design Publishing, 2017), 21. For a more complete definition of *field conditions* see Terminological Positions (end of book).

160 When referring to the rectilinear grid as 'one of architecture's oldest and most persistent organizing devices,' Allen also explains two of the most persistent difficulties often associated with it in city making or territorial division: either too much meaning deriving from its potential metaphysical or cosmological associations, or not enough meaning from its association with technical and technocratic efficiencies. However, he adds, these two extremes require a nuanced reading. The Public Land Survey System, for example, was used to divide and sell land in regular plots as a means to control the territory whilst raising money for the new country in debt. Unfolding like a continental carpet, the rectilinear system had to receive several distortions or correction lines to 'impose measure on the immeasurable expanse of the American landscape.' In urban contexts, Manhattan's grid is arguably the most iconic. Initially built to be a 'convenient starting point' and 'not as an overarching ideal,' the grid facilitated the construction of cheap and convenient houses, also allowing for much denser occupations on the island, and its many iterations also show an adaptation to the territories' real conditions. (Allen, 'From Object to Field').

161 Koolhaas' focus is not accidental – these areas are the most congested of the island – and there are roughly two arguments as to why that is. The geological argument contends that the city's skyline mirrors the depth of the bedrock, with the datum of the rock close to the surface beneath Downtown and Midtown and an abrupt depth between the two areas. The financial argument supports the idea that investments in skyscrapers are so large that they could justify any rentable location in the city. The latter explains the absence of high-rise buildings between the two areas with the former existence of big slums and problematic neighborhoods, such as Five Points, which investors wanted to avoid.

162 Allen, 'From Object to Field,' 21.

163 Koolhaas, *Delirious New York*, 82.

164 Ibid.

165 In his description of the Woolworth, Koolhaas oscillates between pragmatism and spirituality, mass, disembodiment and antigravitation to finally define the building as an early example of automonumentality in the city. Discussing the building's scale beyond its sheer size, Koolhaas mentions that it becomes a city in itself. The automonument can be read as a field condition inside the city itself (Koolhaas, *Delirious New York*, 100). Allen analyzes how buildings can become field conditions in his description of the Mosque of Córdoba, where a sense of directionality provided by columns and arches built over the centuries makes the building inherently expandable (Allen, 'From Object to Field,' 220–26).

166 Such an exercise of the imagination could, for example, be supported by the principle of property law, which dates from medieval times and is encapsulated in the Latin phrase 'Cuius est solum, eius est usque ad coelum et ad inferos' (loosely translated as 'whoever's is the soil, it is theirs all the way to Heaven and all the way to Hell'). Even though the principles known in their abbreviated forms as *ad coelum* and *ad infernum* – the former as the right to own the air above ground and the latter as the right to own the subsurface below ground – are no longer fully applied in modern property law, the owner of a piece of land still benefits from certain rights both above and below ground. See John G. Sprankling, 'Owning the Center of the Earth,' *UCLA Law Review* 979 (2008).

167 Koolhaas, *Delirious New York*, 26–27.

168 In 1853 the international fair standing on what would become Bryant Park prominently featured two colossal structures. Manhattan's Crystal Palace was a cruciform glass building, 'whose intersection is topped by an enormous dome,' as means to inscribe the half sphere in the grid expanding northwards (Koolhaas, *Delirious New York*, 23). Standing right next to the globe, the Latting Observatory – a long needle-like panoramic tower and perhaps the '"World's first Skyscraper"' – offered the city the first ever opportunity to look back at itself and inspect its insular domain (Idem, 25). In 1939 needle and globe reappear as central features and separated yet interconnected 'formal poles' of the international fair and 'the theme exhibit – Trylon and Perisphere' (Idem, 275). While the needle of the Trylon remains empty, the almost perfect globe of the Perisphere – 'the largest ever built in the history of mankind' and with a diameter measuring two hundred feet, or the exact 'width of a Manhattan block' – represents 'the pure archetype of Manhattan's Skyscraper: a Globe tall enough to be a Tower' (Idem, 277). Its pristine white exterior surface conceals a hollow interior, where 'an elaborate model of the elusive City of the Machine Age: "Democracity,"' marks the triumph of Modernism and its eventual arrival in New York as a 'garden city of tomorrow,' where high, monolithic Corbusian towers exist on an Arcadian green carpet.

169 Koolhaas, *Delirious New York*, 26.

170 Idem, 61.

171 Idem, 71.

172 Ibid.

173 Idem, 75.

174 Idem, 91–94.

175 Stoppani, *Paradigm Islands*, 26

176 Koolhaas, *Delirious New York*, 95.

177 The Rockefeller Center, including RCMH, was designed by architect Raymond Hood together with Wallace K. Hamson and Andrew Reinhard.

178 Koolhaas, *Delirious New York*, 210.

179 The discussion of the globe as an architectural problem often focuses on the qualities of the interior it generates. David Gissen, for example, reflects on Manhattan's vast interior atmospheres of corporate mega-buildings and qualifies them as a significant type of anthropogenic biome. See David Gissen, *Manhattan Atmospheres: Architecture, the Interior Environment, and Urban Crisis* (Minneapolis: University of Minnesota Press, 2014).

Mark Dorrian studies the idea of globe more widely, and in its many architectural configurations, in relation to weather control and manipulation. See Mark Dorrian, 'Utopia on Ice: The Climate as Commodity Form,' in Etienne Turpin (Ed.), *Architecture in the Anthropocene: Encounters Among Design, Deep Time, Science and Philosophy* (London: Open Humanities Press, 2013), 143–152.

180 Idem, 168–169.

181 Idem, 117.

182 Ibid.

183 Idem, 169.

184 Idem, 9.

185 Stoppani, *Paradigm Islands*, 65.

When describing the park as a leap of faith at the time of its creation – for it existed before the city around it – Koolhaas considers the park as a record of the city's progress: 'a taxidermic presentation of nature that exhibits forever the drama of culture outdistancing nature' (Koolhaas, *Delirious New York*, 21).

186 Ibid, 23.

187 The artpiece's original name was *Grösse Kugelkaryatide*, or *Great Spherical Caryatid*.

188 When it was initially built, One World Trade Center was the tallest building in New York. The early, unfounded rumors of its height, which allegedly allowed for the contemplation of the earth's curvature at the top of its panoramic terrace, reinforce the idea of a needle that has become galactic. In other words, the building becomes an axis that projects itself radially from the earth's surface into outer space.

189 The political decisions here mentioned are the subject of a more in-depth analysis in Chapter 5.

190 Koolhaas, *Delirious New York*, 235–245.

191 Ibid.

192 Ibid.

193 Ibid.

194 Koolhaas explains that the PCM was used, for example, by explorer Christopher Columbus in his never proven theory that 'he would reach India by sailing westward.' Equally meaningful is Koolhaas' linkage of the PCM to processes of colonization and the power relations they triggered in the attempt to subjugate all non-White humans. Another interesting example of the use of the PCM activity prior to Dalí is Jollain's 1672 bird's-eye view depiction of New Amsterdam, which Koolhaas describes as 'the only true representation of New York as project.' Through the use of the PCM, the representation of Manhattan accommodates a series of influential European urban precedents and exposes the island as an invention of 'projections, misrepresentations, transplantations and grafts.' When analyzed retrospectively, Jollain's map becomes an increasingly accurate 'portrait of a paranoiac Venice, archipelago of colossal souvenirs, avatars and simulacrums that testify to all the accumulated "tourisms" – both literal and

mental – of Western culture.' (Koolhaas, *Delirious New York*, 238, 243 and 245). Curiously, the map does not represent either New Amsterdam or Venice, but pre-earthquake Lisbon instead (see also Library of Congress, *Nowel Amsterdam en Lamerique*).

195 Koolhaas, *Delirious New York*, 237.

196 Hsu, 'Delirious New York,' 169.

197 Ibid.

198 Hubert Damisch, 'The Manhattan Transfer,' in J. Lucan (Ed.) *OMA/Rem Koolhaas: Architecture 1970–1990* (New York: Princeton Architectural Press, 1991), 21–32,

Endnotes

quoted in Hsu, 'Delirious New York', 170.

199 Koolhaas, *Delirious New York*, 261. Koolhaas mentions that, upon his arrival, Dalí found out 'that in Manhattan Surrealism is invisible.'

200 The framing of the version utilized for the book, dated from 1978, excludes both the Rockefeller Building catching the other two, post-coitus, as it opens the bedroom door, and an armless Statue of Liberty, resembling the famous Greek statue Venus de Milo, amongst the crowd of other Manhattan buildings – anthropomorphized and judging the scene – outside the window. The lamp on the bedside table is a fragment of the same statue.

201 Fosco Lucarelli, 'Madelon Vriesendorp's Manhattan Project,' in *Socks* (February 2, 2015).

202 See Nicholas Jarr, *The Fabrication of Evidence in Rem Koolhaas' Delirious New York* (Extended essay, dissertation, University of Brighton, 2014), 26. Jarr agrees with theorist Neil Leach when discussing the drawing to 'observe the influence of Dalí on Vriesendorp.' See also the studies on Vriesendorp work by theorists Charles Jenks, Shumon Basar, Stephen Truby or Briony Fer.

203 Shumon Basar and Stephen Truby (Eds.), *The World of Madelon Vriesendorp* (London: AA Publications, 2008), 263–264. Vriesendorp's statement is included in her interview with Beatriz Colomina and is featured in the book.

204 Ibid.

205 Vriesendorp with Colomina, quoted in Basar and Truby, *The World of Madelon Vriesendorp*.

206 For a more complete explanation of how extrusion expands the limits of representability, see Terminological Positions (end of book).

207 Koolhaas, *Delirious New York*, 236–237. It is perhaps interesting to discuss this tension also in relation to 'Woman,' a text block where Koolhaas makes the only mention to a female individual (Vriesendorp herself is never mentioned). Arguing that Manhattan's pursuit of the sky is a masculine endeavor without any female accompaniment, the architect mentions that 'among the 44 men on the stage, there is a single woman, Miss Edna Cowan, the "Basin Girl"' (Koolhaas, *Delirious New York*, 130). The passage could be read as a tension between the ambition of vertical growth through architectural extrusion and the realistic limits of structural integrity in the geological substrate. When describing the process of architectural cannibalism involved in the development of the Empire State, Koolhaas explains that the new Empire's heavy weight can only be supported due to the existence of a solid bedrock beneath it, that '"has been dug away … [so that] a useful load in the form of a building … [could be] placed there by man"' (Koolhaas, *Delirious New York*, 126–127 and 139).

208 Idem, 125.

209 Idem, 174–177.

210 An earlier building from Hood, the McGraw-Hill skyscraper, deserves an even more metaphorical description:

Once again Hood has combined two incompatibles in a single whole: its golden shades pulled down to reflect the sun, the McGraw-Hill Building looks like a fire raging inside an iceberg: the fire of Manhattanism inside the iceberg of Modernism. (Koolhaas, *Delirious New York*, 171).

211 Torres-Campos, 'Silence in Middle Ground,' 156.

212 Interested in radical architectural syntheses that offered sustained critique to existing societal forms and ideologies of urbanism, Superstudio developed their 'discorso per immagini' – or discourse by images – utilizing sophisticated narratives with photocollages and lithographs See Felicity Scott, 'Superstudio,' in *Artforum International* 42 (7) (New York, 2004), 177–178 and 202. See also Giacomo Pala, 'Architecture as a Margin within the Negotiation between Reality and Utopia,' *sITA – studii de Istoria și Teoria Arhitecturii* 4 (2016), 216–224.

Continuous Monument was initially prepared for the Tri-National Biennial of Graz in 1969 and consisted of three pieces: a series of photomontages, a physical installation and a storyboard.

213 See Barbara Pierpaoli, 'Cincuenta años de Superstudio. Una lectura contemporánea,' in *rita* 7 (2017), 110-119.

214 Working almost in tandem with the participation in the biennial, Superstudio developed *Grazerzimmer*, a parallelepiped volume from floor to ceiling capped by a white plastic laminated with a tiled texture, resembling the abstract tiled materiality of the monument in the photomontages. Unlike the scaleless architectures in the collages, the extrusion of the installation was carefully scaled to the height of the room while its holes worked as arched passages. *Grazerzimmmer* could be yet another fragment of *Continuous Monument* – an interior of an interior, or its almost opposite, an exterior without an interior – as much as an alternative vision for the city of Graz, or even the possibility of architectural freedom operating under the structure and constraints of the discipline (Peter Cook, 'Natalini Superstudio', in *The Architectural Review* 171 (1982), 49; and Pierpaoli, 'Cincuenta años de Superstudio,' 117).

215 Rather than a stratified vision of the monument offered by the photomontages, the sequences in the complementary storyboard offer fragments structured around the power of a precise yet open-ended and constantly reinvented narrative (Pierpaoli, 'Cincuenta años de Superstudio,' 117).

Starting with a fast-paced historical approach to aesthetic references in architecture, the story quickly moves towards the study of the abstractedness of a cube and the multiple possibilities that occur with its progressive multiplication. It then embarks on the development of *Continuous Monument* traversing a myriad of different contexts to which it often barely reacts. The visual narrative finishes with speculations on the emission of the structure, potentially to envelop the whole planet. Through the carefully assembled sequence – and its 'being put into circulation' as a path to totality – the storyboard may then help further analyze the geoaesthetic value of the monument.

216 Cook, 'Natalini Superstudio,' 49.

Felicity Scott refers to the models organized in a grid on the floor of the gallery space in relation to their enactment of scale, 'generating objects ranging in scale from furniture to environments.' She also mentions that the apparently homogeneous and isotropic matrix of plastic laminate is, in fact, far from neutral (Scott, 'Superstudio').

217 Pierpaoli, 'Cincuenta años de Superstudio,' 11.

218 Pala, 'Architecture as a Margin,' 218.

219 The project was produced for the *Pamphlet Architecture* series.

220 Lebbeus Woods, 'The Vagrant Light of Stars,' in *Lebbeus Woods* (September 27, 2009). See also Lebbeus Woods, 'Einstein Tomb,' in *Pamphlet Architecture* 6 (New York: Princeton Architectural Press, 1980). By incorporating Einstein's Theory of Relativity into his own architectural proposal, Woods makes use of the 'gravity-warped structure of space' to justify the architecture's 'return to Earth in sidereal time, an infinite number of times, or at least until the end of time and space at the death of the universe.' See Fernando Díaz–Pinés Mateo, 'Delirio y Anomia em la Obra de Lebbeus Woods,' *Arquitecturas al margen* 18 (Seville: Universidad de Sevilla, 2018; my translation), 108.

221 Operating as an empty vessel 'following an immense and subtle arc through the stars,' Woods' cenotaph consists of four extruded slabs touching one another perpendicularly in a three-dimensional cross, a shape that contains a meaningful symbolic role in both religion and philosophy. The extremes of two of the slabs receive sculptural extensions figuring what could be considered winged mythological figures on top of extruded plinths (Woods, *Einstein Tomb*).

222 Mateo, 'Delirio y Anomia,' 108. Mateo positions *Einstein Tomb* along a much longer line of architectural discourse through practice through which Woods eloquently travels along the edges of the discipline and gets progressively closer to delirium, 'persisting in fantasist experimentation and in his refusal to build' (Mateo, 'Delirio y Anomia'). The *Light Pavilion*, concluded one week before Woods' death, is described in this argument as the condenser of the architect's delirious ideology. Considering Koolhaas' work and method, the light installation can also be described as the result of Woods' professional lifetime PCM.

Thirty years after producing *Einstein Tomb*, Woods described it as a 'film strip' depicting a 'microcosmic scene ... at a moment of the alignment of the Moon, the Earth, and the Sun – a moment of mythic or perhaps especially portentous energy.' Woods describes the architecture as being more of a memorial than a tomb –

for it is empty and not carrying Einstein's ashes – and also as a 'foreign object [that] intrudes and reveals itself to be rectangular solid, akin to the Monolith described by Arthur C. Clarke and Stanley Kubrick in "2001."' Equally, Woods importantly wonders, even if indirectly, whether the scalelessness of the cruciform architecture could mean that the expansions on its two opposing ends were, perhaps, skyscrapers. It then becomes possible to read the architecture proposal as an emitted extruded city that can transcend the speed of light, and thus, explore the edges – if not rise above – the Einsteinian limits of space-time travel in the universe. See Lebbeus Woods, 'Einstein Tomb @ 30,' in *Lebbeus Woods* (June 09, 2010.

223 Frances Hsu, 'Delirious New York: A Retroactive Manifesto for Manhattan,' in *Journal of Architectural Education* 64(2) (2011), 169–170.

224 Rem Koolhaas, 'Why I Wrote Delirious New York,' 43.

225 The design inquiry can be regarded also as a retrospective reading of a text written in 1978, which is meaningful to the temporality of the texts themselves. This chapter is roughly at the same temporal distance from *Delirious New York* than the latter is from the post-Great Depression era of the construction of the high-rise buildings that are the lightning conductors of Koolhaas' attention – and pivotal in the formulation of *Manhattanism*.

226 Koolhaas, *Delirious New York*, 10.

227 Idem, 210.

229 Ibid.

229 Besides the description of RCMH, the other two explicit references to gold in *Delirious New York* are both related to Raymond Hood. The first is the reference to Hood's early bankruptcy when his office was left half-gilded. The second is description of the creation of the American Radiator Building, also by Hood, in a text block titled 'Gold.' In the latter, Koolhaas describes Hood's pragmatism as the cause for severing 'all connections between gold and any possible associations with Ecstasy' (Koolhaas, *Delirious New York*, 162 and 165).

230 The reserve bank allows only for short and highly controlled visits to the underground chambers, eighty feet below street level. Once inside the vaults, visitors can finally grasp the enormity of the reserves, organized in shiny brick-like walls of gold bars and ingots.

231 Ellsworth and Kruse, *Geologic City*, 1.

232 Current scientific research no longer accepts Supernovas of the type II as the birthplace of gold. Some astrophysicists point to the outer rims forming around collisions between neutron stars, while others situate gold's origin at the event horizon of black holes. See Joshua Sokol, 'A New Blast May Have Forged Cosmic Gold,' in *Quanta Magazine* (2017).

233 Ellsworth and Kruse, *Geologic City*, Site #5.

234 Ibid.

235 Susan Schuppli, 'Slick Images: The Photogenic Politics of Oil,' in Mihnea Mirca and Vincent W. J. van Gerven Oei (Eds.), *Allegory of the Cave Painting* (Antwerp: Extra City, 2015), 426–427. Quote from Gilles Deleuze in *Cinema 2: The Time Image*, Hugh Tomlinson and Barbara Habberjam (Trans.) (London: Continuum, 1989), 112–113.

236 Schuppli, 'Slick Images,' 429–430.

237 Ibid.

238 Writing about gold's beauty, power and allure in 1959, English numanist C. H. V. Sutherland describes a generalized yet complex human attraction to the precious metal. Gold holds value for the geologist and the chemist for its almost total reactive inertia. It holds value for the metallurgic and the goldsmith for its malleability and plasticity. It holds value for the economist and the businessman for its resolute capacity to annex and stabilize finances. It holds value also for the anthropologist for its civilizational influence in power relations. Sutherland also refers to gold's extremely high gravity, explaining that the fifty thousand tons of extracted gold existing at that time in the world could be compressed into a cube of less than fourteen meters in each direction. See Carol Humphrey Vivian Sutherland, *Gold: its beauty, power and allure* (London: Thames & Hudson, 1959), 8–10. More recently, revised estimates of extraction size the theoretical golden cube between twenty and twenty-two meters on its side (see World Gold Council; see also Donald A. Singer, 'World class base and precious metal deposits; a quantitative analysis,' in *Economic Geology* 90(1) (1995), 88–104).

239 In *Delirious New York*, Koolhaas quotes surrealist painter Salvador Dalí to describe the artist's PCM. The method will be further explained ahead. See Salvador Dalí, *La Femme Visible* (Paris: Éditions Surréalistes, 1930); Salvador Dalí, 'The Conquest of the Irrational,' appendix to *Conversations with Dalí* (New York: Dutton, 1969), 115, quoted in Koolhaas, *Delirious New York*, 235–237.

240 Through the voice and thought of an unnamed narrator, the tale tells the story of a destitute friend, William Legrand, who, after finding and being allegedly bitten by a golden beetle on Sullivan's Island, near Charleston, South Carolina, deciphers a cryptogram inscribed in an old parchment and eventually drags his African-American servant, Jupiter, and the narrator himself out for an adventure that will lead them to a buried treasure of incalculable value, believed to have once belonged to the legendary Scottish pirate Captain Kidd.

241 Despite being a very early example of adventurous tales for the youth, the short tale was not the first of its kind. Some of the nuanced literary constructions it portrays bear structural resemblance to Daniel Defoe's 1719 *Robinson Crusoe*, a relation identified by English professor Shawn James Rosenheim, namely regarding the use of cryptography (see Shawn James Rosenheim, *The Cryptographic Imagination: Secret Writing from Edgar Poe to the Internet* (Baltimore: Johns Hopkins University Press, 1997), 42–64).

Perhaps more striking is the long lineage that can be traced after Poe's tale, from Robert Louis Stevenson to Jules Verne or Jorge Luis Borges. Directly influencing Robert Louis Stevenson's 1883 *Treasure Island*, 'The Gold Bug''s second translation to French, in 1856 by Charles Baudelaire, contributed to the expansion of Poe's impact across Europe, eventually influencing early science-fiction authors such as Jules Verne. Later, Poe's influence dispersed into many genres and to authors from many disparate origins, such as T. S. Eliot, Jorge Luis Borges, Stephen King, or Richard Powers. See Thomas C. Carlson, 'Review of Poe and His Times: The Artist and His Milieu,' in *The Mississipi Quarterly* 46 (1) (Winter 1992), 140–142.

242 Poe moved together with his wife Virginia and her mother to a farmhouse in upper Manhattan belonging to the Brennan family (Tom Miller, 'The Lost Brennan House – 84th Street and Broadway,' in *Daytonian in Manhattan* (2017)).

243 In 1848, only five years after the publication of the short tale, the United States would witness the Californian Gold Rush, one of the largest and most intense migrations of people across the country to the West Coast in search of gold. Once again, however, it is important to note the existing tension between the geographically located pursuit of gold, even if across a continent, and the open-ended expansion of the grid, both at the urban and the continental scales.

244 J. Woodrow Hassell Jr., 'The Problem of Realism in "The Gold Bug,"' *American Literature* 25 (2) (1953), 179–180.

245 It is important to note that Poe's avid intellectual appetite for natural history perhaps meant that he was knowledgeable of the local fauna and flora of Sullivan's Island, especially having spent time in his youth in the nearby Fort Moultrie during his military service (Carroll Laverty, 'The Death's-Head on the Gold-Bug,' in *American Literature* 12 (1) (1940), 88–91). Entomologist Ellison A. Smyth Jr. describes Poe's bug as '"the blending of several beetles into the one composite insect deemed necessary for the purposes of the tale"' (see Ellison A. Smyth Jr., 'Poe's *Gold Bug* from the Standpoint of an Entomologist,' in *Sewanee Review* XVIII (1910), 67–72, quoted in Laverty, 'Death's-Head').

While partially agreeing with this observation, literary scholar Carroll Laverty questions the entomologist's perhaps too simplistic observation of '"the writer's fertile imagination"' and adds that the blend of the beetle for the sake of verisimilitude in the narrative was intentional, given Poe's knowledge of beetles. A more recent entomological study of Poe's beetle emphasizes again the intentional hybridization of the insect, since the described anatomy points to certain possible scarab genotypes, whereas the golden color alludes to other genera. See Laverty, 'Death's-Head.' See also Donald B. Thomas, Ainsley Seago and David C. Robacker, 'Reflections on Golden Scarabs,' *American Entomologist* 53 (4) (2007), 224–230.

246 Salvador Dalí, *La Femme Visible*, and 'The Conquest of the Irrational,' appendix to *Conversations with Dalí* (New York: Dutton, 1969), 115, quoted in Koolhaas, *Delirious New York*, 235–237.

247 The *Golden Record* was part of the Voyager space discovery missions. It reinforces a planetary valuation of gold as a material becoming a special envoy or ambassador of Earth to outer space.

248 The scarab, also known as the dung beetle, was accorded a significant status in ancient Egypt, as an animal with a rich mythology linked to *Khepri*, the god of the rising sun. Historians such as Plutarch refer to the translation of the hieroglyphic image of the scarab as a *come into being* or a *becoming*, in relation to transformation, denoting the insect's potential meaning in existential, ontological and fictional terms. Ancient Egyptian culture connected the scarab to cycles of cosmological renewal – such as the sunrise and the sunset, and the subordinated planetary orbits, through which planets were considered to rise to the sun and set to the ground – and to cycles of biological renewal through life and death. See Plutarch, 'Isis and Osiris,' in *Moralia* V (public domain, edition of 1936). See also Carol Andrews, *Amulets of Ancient Egypt* (Texas: University of Texas Press, 1994).

249 Georges Bataille, *The Solar Anus* (1927, Paris: Éditions de la Galerie Simon, 1931). Bataille interweaves disparate themes and conceptual preoccupations, from life, death and decay, to nature, copulation, love and excrement. He uses a 'parodic-travestying mimicry' to question the apparent cosmological order of planetary rotation, which he pairs up with sexual movement as 'two primary motions ... whose combination is expressed by the locomotive's wheels and pistons' (ibid). Equally provocative is the essayist's description of the tide as '[t]he simplest image of organic life united with rotation.' For Bataille, '[f]rom the movement of the sea, uniform coitus of the earth with the moon, comes the polymorphous and organic coitus of the earth with the sun' (ibid). Bataille frames the sun as the origin of life on earth, but also of its inevitable death from its unrestricted expelled energies, which he compares to an 'integral erection' when he screams 'I AM THE SUN.' As the essay approaches its open end, Bataille deploys the full conceptual strength of his cosmogony linked to a theoretical urge for thinking through and feeling with the endless becomings of a cosmological balance between expansion and destruction.

250 The dung beetle refers, in fact, to a group of beetles that feed, partially or completely, on feces of other animals. Some insects in this group navigate, orientate themselves, and transport the dung balls using the Milky Way. In ancient Egypt, the scarab's feeding regime with feces commonly stored underground was also believed to be connected to the underworld and, therefore, to the dead. The insect was often utilized as an amulet depicted in religious representations as well as in pieces of jewelry built in precious metals, including gold. It was often poised on mummified corpses and it was believed that it offered protection in life and death. In popular science there are frequent references to the orientation of the scarab along the line of diurnal solar movement. However, the only scientific proof to date refers to the African dung beetle *Scarabeus satyrus*, a nocturnal insect which navigates geographically utilizing the Milky Way. See Marie Dacke, Emily Baird, Marcus Byrne, Clarke J. Scholtz and Eric J. Warrant, 'Dung Beetles Use the Milky Way for Orientation,' *Current Biology* 23 (4) (2013), 298–300.

251 Thomas F. Thornton and Yadvinder Malhi, 'The Trickster in the Anthropocene,' in *The Anthropocene Review* (2016), 1–4.

252 Idem, 4.

253 Gold's massively distributed presence across the earth and its heavy accumulation in Manhattan can be explained as part of a wider study of its vast networks of formation, sedimentation, ungrounding and structural recrystallization, with the idea of exploring gold as a horizon of human entropy. The use of *ungrounding* here follows closely John Rajchman's exploration of the Deleuzian concept of *éffondement*. See John Rajchman, 'Grounds', in *Constructions* (Cambridge: MIT Press, 1998), 77–89.

Through the methodological narrative, these networks that weave gold and city are conceptualized as horizons working stratigraphically in similar ways to their conceptualization in geology. Yet, the concept of *horizon* here also acquires a more symbolic role linked to the delineation of human entropy. Gold's almost total lack of reactivity with any other materials on Earth makes it extremely durable and stable across deep time. That condition, coupled with its apparent rarity and delirious appeal to human senses, makes it, it could be argued, an impeccable delineator of human existence.

This generative intensity also motivates a conceptual and creative reading of Manhattan as a hyper-dense mineralogic accumulation. This conception does not necessarily register a strict resemblance with geological and geometric rules of mineral or crystal growth, such as proximity, interface, supersaturation or existence of impurities. Instead, it creatively accepts that the island-territory may be changed through processes that can be loosely described by creatively borrowing from them.

254 The mechanisms involved in the search and digging for gold share meaningful connections with other human senses of adventure, even related to delirium. Gold may be conceived as a material trigger for the notion of progress, a fundamental pillar sustaining the project of modernity. Gold's distributed networks of extraction, distribution and accumulation certainly come to mind at this point. Following Jussi Parikka, a critical understanding of geology in the Anthropocene contemplates not only its geophysical aspects but its geopolitical dimensions too. See Parikka, 'Materiality,' in *Geology of Media*. In that sense, gold must be also problematized politically, within the complex and often highly unbalanced power relations it generates. Gold has been at the foundation of civilizations, empires and some of the largest fortunes in the world. The cost of these accumulations is tremendously high, from the intense, dangerous and poorly paid conditions offered to miners for its extraction to the risky and threatening conditions of high security involved in its unbalanced distribution and accumulation and finally to its volatile transferring and codification into digits that create or destroy globalized virtual markets. As a mechanism of power and wealth, gold leaves behind a trail of destruction and destabilization.

Max Page utilizes a similar antagonistic notion to explain the mechanisms involved in the construction of Manhattan from 1900 until 1940. Page borrows the term 'creative destruction' from economist Joseph Schumpeter to describe New York as a 'provisional city' witnessing unprecedented capitalist urban development 'not defined by simple expansion and growth but rather by a vibrant and often chaotic process of destruction and rebuilding.' Page comes close to Koolhaas' provocative description of Manhattan's urbanism as 'a form of architectural cannibalism.' See Max Page, *The Creative Destruction of Manhattan 1900-1940* (Chicago: The Chicago University Press, 1999); see also Koolhaas, *Delirious New York*, 132–139, 204.

The design exploration creatively conceives of Manhattan as an imagined city where its fragments agglomerate without ever completely disappearing. The *Geotaxonomies* benefit from this temporal and spatial compression and are organized in a pseudo-taxonomical classification according to relations of proximity, affinity, kinship and differentiation in the grid and the ground that sustains it. As congested agglomerations of cultural, architectural and landscape ideas and existences, the nine proposed theoretical taxa result from both physical and imagined realities, which question precisely hierarchical orders by accepting many confluent and dissident systems of tension, acceptance, contradiction, fluidity and queer performativity.

255 The first collection explores, albeit not literally, a meaning of emission as 'a putting into circulation,' similar to how *Continuous Monument* was analyzed earlier in the book, that is, as a megastructure extending and extruding beyond the island to embrace the curvature of the Earth. Like *Continuous Monument*, which traps and envelops certain monumental complexes, so do does the *Geotaxonomies*' megastructure capture, reorganize and enable the recrystallization of the many gathered city fragments. The second collection of framed drawings explores a meaning of emission as something 'sent forth by emitting,' such as radiation or an object from a celestial body, similar to how *Einstein Tomb* was studied earlier. Here, the *Geotaxonomies*' megastructure is emitted to space to become a planetary ambassador into the universe.

Endnotes

256 Some ideas explored in this section were originally published in an essay by the author. See Tiago Torres-Campos, 'Architecture Passes: Noticing Entropy, Anxiety and Indeterminacy,' in *On Site Review* 43 – Architecture and Time (2023), 38–41.

257 Morton relates the Freudian formulation of two states of mind – the conscious and the unconscious – to the boundary between the *real* (actuality) and *reality* (the feeling of real or how things are accessed), thus critiquing a Hegelian-Lacanian mode of thinking about boundary as something rigid or thin (Morton and Lally, *Night White Skies*).

258 *To the Lighthouse* narrates the stories of the Ramsay family in their holiday house in the Hebrides, in Scotland. See Virginia Woolf, *To the Lighthouse* (1927, London: Penguin Books, 1992). In 'Time Passes' the reader witnesses a world of crumbling matter and witnesses it through the 'eyes' of the house. The reader may assume the house is the narrator which slows down time to the point where matter in space becomes weird. During this slowing down, important accounts about characters are provided in short sentences inside parentheses. It is almost as if time passing by slowly distances oneself from the minds of the different characters through streams of consciousness. The lighthouse, a beacon of light which maintains a certain distance yet is present throughout the whole novel, replaces the human eye and brain with a blind eye which pulsates rhythm into the inside of the house. Through the witnessing blind eyes of the house, people disappear, walls crumble, furniture dissolves and so does space itself. And as day and night go by, as seasons go by, as years go by, the house is suspended in a viscous state. Things inside and outside this space are not completely solid anymore, but not also completely liquid. The revelation of an otherwise invisible world of these insentient characters can be understood as not necessarily being the opposite of consciousness. The insentient blind eyes are dehumanized, in that they are not human or human-like, even though they do not necessarily escape a certain anthropomorphism. Assuming a thick, porous and blurry border between the real and reality, the blind eyes register moments when the *stream of consciousness* also becomes a *stream of unconscious consciousness*, or in other words, something very close to a delirium.

259 In *To the Lighthouse* architectural space is revealed through light and dust, engaging even if in a free, literary sense, to the wave-particle quantum model, which Woolf was aware of through her interests in the scientific discoveries of her time. See Paul Tolliver Brown, 'Relativity, Quantum Physics, and Consciousness in Virginia Woolf's "To the Lighthouse,"' *Journal of Modern Literature* 32 (3) (2009), 39–62; and Mark Hussey, 'To the Lighthouse and Physics: The Cosmology of David Bohm and Virginia Woolf,' in Helen Wussow (Ed.), *New Essays on Virginia Woolf* (Dallas: Contemporary Research Press, 1995), 79–97.

260 In conversation with architect Tom Wiscombe, Morton refers specifically to 'Time Passes' to discuss architecture. He says that in Woolf's narrative of the house 'there's [sic] no people in it. It is just dust falling in the sunlight in the window frame and that kind of stuff. And it is so beautiful. … And it is how you have to think if you are in architectural space' (Morton with Wiscombe, *Sci-Arc*).

261 The noun *sediment* was first registered in the English language in 1547, while the transient verb to *sediment* was first registered only in 1859.

262 David Cunningham conceptualizes the *abstract* as the challenging modern problem of thinking about totality. Distancing the epic novel from its common formulation as a new kind of *concreteness*, he explores it instead as a form of abstract art, which reflects the qualities and limits involved in the capacity to think abstractly about the totality of the capitalist system. See David Cunningham, 'Capitalist epics. Abstraction, totality and the theory of the novel,' *Radical Philosophy* 163 (2010), 11–23.

263 Borrowing from the *Hegelian idea* as well as Karl Marx's *Das Capital*, Cunningham states that the '"subject of history" … is neither, strictly, the bourgeoisie nor the proletariat, but, more obviously, self-valorizing capital itself' and that 'the "*shape of money*"' is what 'constitutes the "real" social being of modernity here' (Cunningham, 'Capitalist epics,' 19–20).

264 Woolf's work relates to and influences other

important discoveries of her time. In a brief essay about cinema, then still an emerging art, Woolf focuses on the qualities of the real that the moving picture eventually adds to still photographs, mainly through the manipulation of time (Virginia Woolf, 'The Cinema,' *The Nation and A nthenaeum* 39 (13) (1926), 381–383). 'The Cinema' was published in 1926, at the same time as Woolf was writing *To the Lighthouse*. The influence cinema was exerting on her work at this time is perhaps easy to grasp in 'Time Passes,' which has been described as 'a form of experimental cineplay.' The ten years between the first and third chapters of the novel also have an important resemblance in the gap of ten years that Woolf alludes to in 'The Cinema.' In the essay, these ten years pass between 'the present in which the early films are being viewed and the past of the realities they record.' See Laura Marcus, *The Tenth Muse: Writing about Cinema in the Modernist Period* (Oxford: Oxford University Press, 2007), 120, quoted in Caleb Sivyer, *The Politics of Gender and the Visual in Virginia Woolf and Angela Carter* (PhD Thesis, School of English, Communication & Philosophy, Cardiff University, 2015), 22; see also Laura Marcus, 'Cinema and Modernism', in *Discovering Literature: 20th Century* (2016). In 'The Cinema', Woolf seems to load the marginal with endless possibility when she describes shadows flickering across the screen in a movie theatre that pull her out from the story into a suspended state of fear or anxiety (Woolf, 'Cinema,' 382).

265 Walter Benjamin, *Illuminations* (Hannah Arendt, ed., Harry Zohn, trans.) (London: Fontana, 1973), 229–230, quoted in Avishek Parui, 'All is hubble-bubble,' 11.

266 Didi-Hüberman, *Glimpses*. For a more complete definition of *glimpse* as a practice of reading and writing diffractively about space see Terminological Positions (end of book).

267 See sub-chapter 3.3.

5. De-Sediment
Seismic Forces
Through the Slightest Tremor

268 Bernard Tschumi, *The Manhattan Transcripts* (London: Academy Editions, 1994). The statement was informal, made at the beginning of a round table with other architects, where Tschumi was also present. It was anecdotal – Tschumi waved amused from across the stage, and Koolhaas' coetaneous book, *Delirious New York*, was the one claiming to be a 'retroactive manifesto' – and its provocation may extend beyond its obvious ego-related implications.

269 Bernard Tschumi, Rem Koolhaas and Stephan Trüby, 'A Conversation,' in *GTA Events* (ETH, 2011).

270 Ibid.

271 Bernard Tschumi, *Red is not a Color* (New York: Rizzoli, 2012), 6–7. The first part of the book, called 'Space Event Movement' (SEM), begins with an extended photo-essay (to which Tschumi returns at the beginning of each of the subsequent parts) which aphoristically lays the ground for the constructed scene that is to come. Here, the *Transcripts* are described as an event in which many disparate plot lines converge. The *Transcripts* are also a preamble to the climactic event of Tschumi's first public project of international reputation, Parc de La Villette (competition 1982–1983; completion in 1998), explored later in the chapter. See also Bernard Tschumi in conversation with Enrique Walker, 'The Manhattan Transcripts: Bernard Tschumi conversa con Enrique Walker,' in *Traspasos* (Universidad de Chile, 2020).

272 Tschumi, *Transcripts*, 7.

273 Idem, 8.

274 As a philosophical or critical method, *deconstruction* 'asserts that meanings, metaphysical constructs, and hierarchical oppositions (as between key terms in a philosophical or literary work) are always rendered unstable by their dependence on ultimately arbitrary signifiers' (Merriam Webster Dictionary, s.v. 'Deconstruction'). See also Lawlor, 'Jacques Derrida.'

275 Larousse Dictionary, s.v. 'Déconstruction.' Translated to English from the original in French: 'En philosophie, [déconstruction] analyse critique d'une structure. Opération critique consistant à montrer que les discours signifient autre chose que ce qu'ils énoncent.'

276 Royle notes that 'Derrida himself has no great fondness for the work,' in reference to its use in the late

Endnotes

1970s and 1980s, especially in American academia, namely by what came to be known as the 'Yale School' of deconstruction. See Nicholas Royle, *Jacques Derrida* (London: Routledge, 2003).

Unlike perhaps more conventional understandings of the word, *deconstruction* is not an actual synonym of demolition; 'instead it means "breaking down" or analyzing something (especially the words in a work of fiction or nonfiction) to discover its true significance, which is supposedly almost never exactly what the author intended' (Merriam Webster, s.v. 'Deconstruction').

277 Idem, 23–25.

278 Jacques Derrida in conversation with Maurizio Ferraris and Giorgio Varrimo, 'I Have a Taste for the Secret,' in *A Taste for the Secret*, Jacques Derrida and Maurizio Ferraris (Cambridge: Polity, 2001), 3–92. See also Royle, *Jacques Derrida*, 23–25.

279 Kirby Dick and Amy Ziering Kofman, *Derrida* (Los Angeles: Jane Doe Films, 2002).

280 Lawlor, 'Jacques Derrida.'

281 Ibid.

282 Royle, Jacques Derrida, 25–28. See also Jacques Derrida, 'Force and Signification,' in *Writing and Difference*, Alan Bass (Trans.) (1967, London: Routledge, 1978), 3–30; Jacques Derrida, *Of Grammatology*, Gayatri Chakravorty Spivak (Trans.) (Baltimore: John Hopkins University Press, 1976).

283 Derrida, 'Point de Folie,' 70.

284 Ibid.

285 Idem, 65.

286 Ibid.

287 Idem, 75.

288 Tschumi, *Architecture*, 256.

289 Tschumi, *Red*, 176. For the complete essay 'Six Concepts' see Tschumi, *Architecture and Disjunction.*

290 Ibid.

291 Ibid.

292 Christian Beck and François-Xavier Gleyzon, 'Deleuze and the event(s),' in *Journal for Cultural Research* 20 (4) (2016), 329, note 433.

Even though Tschumi didn't write or practice an *architecture of the event* explicitly embedded in this epistemological framework, his thinking was interestingly aligned with a Deleuzoguattarian formulation of assemblage, which accepts heterogeneity, divergence and contradiction as conditions of coexistence.

293 See, for example, Bennett, *Vibrant Matter.*

294 Richard Dagenhart, 'Urban Architectural theory and the contemporary city: Tschumi and Koolhaas at the Parc de la Villette,' *Eikistics* 56 (334/335) Space Sintax: Social Implications of Urban Layouts (1989), 84–92.

295 Tschumi, *Architecture*, 177.

296 Ghosh, *Great Derangement.*

297 Tschumi, *Red*, 108–109.

298 Ibid.

299 Stengers, *Catastrophic Times*, 9.

300 It is worth mentioning, for example, the vibrant exchange of ideas, and even design collaborations, between Derrida and Peter Eisenmann.

Besides the need to pay attention to Derrida's cautious note against its direct or literal applications in architectural practice, *deconstruction* should not be confounded with *deconstructivism*, the architectural movement of postmodern architecture in the 1980s and early 1990s, defined by a fragmentary tectonic approach, sometimes to fragmentation also as an ornament or desired architectural form. The movement was, however, strongly influenced by Jacques Derrida and pushed forward by Mark Wigley together with Philip Johnson, at the time both working at MoMA. In 1988, Wigley and Johnson organized a seminal exhibition titled *Deconstructivist Architecture*, which included Tschumi, Rem Koolhaas, Zaha Hadid, Peter Eisenman, Frank Gehry, Daniel Libeskind and Coop Himmelb(l)au. However, *deconstructivism* is not directly derived from the Derridean deconstruction; instead, it finds its foundations in contrast to the Russian Constructivism movement.

301 The international design competition to design Parc de La Villette was organized by the French Government in 1982 on a 125-acre expanse of land on the outskirts of Paris (19th arrondissement). The desire to build a park for the 21st century integrated President Mitterrand's socialist agenda, used to reassert France's cultural prominence and, more specifically, Paris' urban relevance, both informed by a socio-political strategy known as *Grand Projets*. The competition attracted over 472 contestants and happened over two time periods. The first, in 1982, identified a series of finalists – including Rem Koolhaas, Zaha Hadid, Jean Nouvel and Tschumi – while the second, in 1983, awarded the first prize to Tschumi's proposal. Controversial ever since its initial competition phases, Tschumi's project juxtaposed those who consider it the 'single most significant project in terms of forging a new architecture of the landscape' with those who consider it an oversimplification of, or perhaps even a total disregard to site specificity, a '"non-landscape park" that fails to engage the most important system – the landscape itself.' See Elizabeth Meyer, 'The Public Park as Avant-Garde (Landscape) Architecture: A Comparative Interpretation of Two Parisian Parks, Parc de la Villette (1983–1990) and Parc des Buttes-Chaumont (1864–1867),' in *Landscape Journal* 10 (1) Special Issue: The Avant-Garde and the Landscape: Can They be Reconciled (1991), 16–26; and Julia Czerniak, 'Parc de la Villette. Bernard Tschumi,' in David Leatherbarrow and Alexander Eisenschmidt (Eds.), T*he Companions to the History of Architecture IV Twentieth-Century Architecture* (New York: John Wiley & Sons, 2017), 2–13.

302 Derrida, 'Point de Folie,' 70.

303 At the beginning of the essay, Derrida explains that La Villette's follies should be regarded in relation to the plural 'madnesses' (les follies) and not the singular 'madness' (la follie).

304 See Dorrian, 'Art/Architecture/Concept,' 16–25. More widely, follies have been used for a long time in landscape architecture, and they acquired maximum artistic and symbolic expression in the West with the English garden of the Romantic period, when they were conceived as artificial ruins capable of distorting time and space. Associated with delight and fantasy, follies established a field of possible paths in the landscape – mostly visual but sometimes also structural – on top of the park's other features.

305 Derrida, 'Point de Folie,' 73.

306 Bernard Tschumi, 'La Case Vide,' in Derrida, 'Point de Folie,' 66. Woven in several directions, like a fabric, the point grid is a construction the architect had tested a few years earlier with his city screenplays, and it was something always implicit in the *Transcripts*, almost flowing under the sequential drawings. But only in La Villette does the grid, and each of the points (follies), get the opportunity to be fully explored.

307 Koolhaas's proposal for La Villette included a series of architectures dispersed throughout the park which he called confetti. They constituted a network on top of the main ribbon-like structure with which Koolhaas resolved disparate programs.

308 This idea is further explored later in the chapter.

309 Tschumi, 'La Case Vide,' in Derrida, 'Point de Folie,' 66.

310 Roy Rosenzweig and Elizabeth Blackmar, *The Park and The People: A History of Central Park* (Ithaca: Cornell University Press, 1992), 1–15.

311 Idem, 3.

312 Idem, 7.

313 Idem, 5–6.

314 Idem, 18.

315 Ibid.

316 Frederick Law Olmsted, *The Papers of Frederick Law Olmsted. Vol. III: Creating Central Park, 1857 1861*, Charles Capen McLaughlin (Ed.) (Baltimore, Maryland, 1983), 212–13, quoted in Lorna McNeur, 'Central Park City,' *AA Files 23* (Summer 1992), 65.

317 The idea of Central Park as an anti-Manhattan was also explored, albeit in a different context, by Umberto Eco, who compared the experience of walking in Central Park at night with a medieval venture into the woods surrounding a medieval town. See Umberto Eco, *Travels in Hyper-Reality* (1973, London, Harcourt Brace Jovanovich, 1986), quoted in McNeur, 'Central Park City,' 68.

318 McNeur, 'Central Park City,' 65.

319 Egbert L. Viele, 'The Central Park. Report of Egbert L. Viele Esq., Engineer-in-Chief, 'Interesting Notes Concerning the Topography and Drainage of the Central Park. Proposed Plan of Improvement,' *The New York Times* (January 20, 1857).

320 The competition brief required some common elements for the new landscape, including 'a parade ground, a drive, three ballfields, an area for a winter skating ground, a grand fountain, an observatory, a flower garden, a music hall, four roads traversing the park, and a budget of no more than $1.5 million' (see Marissa Castrigno, 'The Competition: 33 Plans for Central Park in 1858,' in *Central Park Conservancy Magazine* (2019).

321 Rosenzweig and Blackmar, *Park and People*, 9–11.

322 Tschumi, *Transcripts*, 6. Tschumi's murdering chase in *MT1–'The Park,'* for example, is not that different from Umberto Eco's *city inferno* (see note 317). The sheltering park to the inclement during the day is the same landscape that protects the nocturnal beasts, human and otherwise. The suspension of the idea of public park in the city's socio-cultural imaginaries entails the foundational myths about the conflict between nature and culture, with which humans narrate their own stories since the beginning of their existence. In the *Transcripts*, Tschumi used architectural notation as yet another way of telling some of those stories.

323 Idem, 6.

324 Ibid.

325 Ibid. In the *Transcripts*, Tschumi refers to two seminal essays he published while developing the book – 'The Pleasure of Architecture' and 'Violence of Architecture' – in which he explores such thematic preoccupations. It is worth noting at this point the influence that ideas from Georges Bataille, Roland Barthes and Jacques Lacan played in Tschumi's definition of the concepts.

326 Bernard Tschumi, 'The Pleasure of Architecture,' in *Architecture and Disjunction* (Cambridge: MIT Press, 1996). The essay 'originally appeared in a different format in *AD (Architectural Design)*, March 1977.'

327 Tschumi, 'Pleasure,' 91–93. In the *Transcripts* Tschumi explains that 'the architecture of pleasure lies where conceptual and spatial paradoxes merge in the middle of delight, where architectural language breaks into a thousand pieces, where the elements of architecture are dismantled and its rules transgressed.' See also Tschumi, *Transcripts*, Postscript (1994 edition), xxviii.

328 Bernard Tschumi, 'Violence of Architecture,' in *Architecture and Disjunction* (Cambridge: MIT Press, 1996).

329 Tschumi, *Transcripts*, Postscript (1994 edition), xxviii. Tschumi states that 'programmatic violence … favor[s] those activities generally considered negative and unproductive: "luxury, mourning, wars, cults; the construction of sumptuous monuments, games, spectacles, arts; perverse sexual activity."'

330 Bernard Tschumi, 'Violence,' 121–122. There is an inevitable conceptual relation between Tschumi's understanding of violence and Michel Foucault's philosophy and, to a certain extent, also to Jacques Lacan's psychoanalytical theory. More specifically in relation to Foucault, Tschumi writes a final note on madness as a third sensation (the first two being pleasure and violence), with a quote from 'Historie de la Folie': '"In madness equilibrium is established, but it masks that equilibrium beneath the cloud of illusion, beneath feigned discorded; the rigor of the architecture is concealed beneath the cunning arrangement of these disordered violences."' See also the first part of Bernard Tschumi, 'Madness and the Combinative,' in *Architecture and Disjunction* (Cambridge: MIT Press, 1996). The essay 'originally appeared in *Precis* (New York: Columbia University Press, 1984).'

331 Ibid.

332 Idem, 7. Some of these themes were adapted from philosophical ideas. One such adaptation comes from Georges Bataille's idea of *expenditure* (explored earlier in the book), which Tschumi replaces with *architecture* to further contextualize his practice.

333 Tschumi elaborates on his tension:
The architectural origin of each episode is found within a specific reality and not in an abstract geometrical figure. Manhattan is a *real* place; the actions described in it are *real* actions. … Yet the role of the *Transcripts* is never to represent; they are not mimetic. So, at the same time, the buildings or events depicted are not real buildings or events, for distancing and subjectivity are also themes of the transcription. Thus the reality of its sequences does not lie in the accurate transposition of the outside world, but in the internal logic these sequences display (Tschumi, *Transcripts*, 7–8).

334 Notation is a seminal form of architectural

representation in Tschumi's practice and something he kept using in several projects after the *Transcripts*, such as Parc de la Villette, Tokyo's Opera House or Le Fresnoy.

335 Tschumi, *Red*, 80.

336 Bernard Tschumi, 'Sequences,' in *Architecture and Disjunction* (Cambridge: MIT Press, 1996). The essay 'originally appeared in *The Princeton Journal: Thematic Studies in Architecture*, vol.1 (1983).

337 For a detailed comparison between Sergei Ejzenštejn's compositional montage or Moretti's theoretical writings on spatial sequences and their influence on Tschumi's practice see Carla Molinari, 'Sequences in architecture: Sergei Ejzenštejn and Luigi Moretti, from images to spaces,' *The Journal of Architecture* (2021).

338 Tschumi, *Transcripts*, 10.

339 Idem, 11.

340 Idem, 12.

341 Ibid.

342 This convergence between geological and archaeological practices explored by the Anthropocene theory is discussed later in this chapter.

343 Tschumi, *Red*, 94.

344 Tschumi, *Transcripts*, 7.

345 Idem, 7–10.

346 Lázló Moholy-Nagy, *Painting, Photography, Film* (London: Lund Humphries, 1967), 38–40 and 122–137. Moholy-Nagy describes *typophoto* as 'the visually most exact rendering of communication' combining typography and photography. Writing in a moment when film was in its early stages, Moholy-Nagy anticipated the influence it would have in shaping socio-cultural and media events. *Typophoto* is defined as a potentially different type of communication from conventional typography or photography, in that it could benefit from techniques of image and text repetition and reproduction, and 'the new tempo of the new visual literature' (Idem, 40). Moholy-Nagy developed innovative works in architecture and interior and stage design, and his tradition in Modernism and Constructivism deserved attention by architects such as Tschumi, who saw in the artist a source of inspiration. The sketches for film scripts, as well as his equally influential stage directions, could be regarded – and

were probably seen by Tschumi – as notations with a powerful architectural appeal.

347 Tschumi, *Transcripts*, 10.

348 Idem, 11.

349 The complexity of the concept from epigenetics, originally proposed by biologist Conrad Waddington, extends beyond this quick observation, but it is perhaps important to mention that, when reframed by critical Feminist approaches, it encourages an active questioning of modes of representation that favor determinism and reductionism to instead promote epistemological entanglements that accept ambiguity and multidisciplinarity. When applied to art practices and, more specifically, to spatial disciplines, the concept may help inform design attitudes that welcome indeterminacy, open-endedness and conflicting positionings. See Susan Merrill Squier, *Epigenetic Landscapes: Drawing as Metaphor* (Durham: Duke University Press, 2017). The book studies several landscapes and their designers in relation to the concept of *epigenetic landscape*, including Ian McHarg, Dilip da Cunha and Anuradha Mathur.

350 Some of the properties of light and how they may affect architectural practice are explained in Chapter 4.

351 The idea of material movement and the reciprocities it entails was proposed by Jane Hutton, who traces the materials that make New York City back to their original production landscapes. In doing so, she demonstrates dialectics that are otherwise almost invisible to the city. See Jane Hutton, *Reciprocal Landscapes: Stories of Material Movements* (New York: Routledge, 2020).

352 Diana diZerega Wall, Nan A. Rothschild and Cynthia Copeland, 'Seneca Village and Little Africa: Two African American Communities in Antebellum New York City,' *Historical Archaeology* 42 (1), Living in Cities Revisited: Trends in Nineteenth- and Twentieth-Century Urban Archaeology (2008), 97–107.

353 Diana diZerega Wall, Nan A. Rothschild, Meredith B. Linn and Cynthia Copeland, *Seneca Village, a Forgotten Community: Report on the 2011 Excavations* (New York: Institute for the Exploration of Seneca Village History, Inc., 2018).

354 Rosenzweig and Blackmar, *Park and People.*

355 Idem, 65–73.

356 Their work, supported by larger teams – namely the New York Historical Society – culminated in a *de facto* groundbreaking archaeological dig in Central Park in 2011, to collect and study religious, domestic, fashion and agricultural artifacts. The extensive excavations report goes well beyond the description and interpretation of Seneca's material cultures and ventures into the conditions of the landscape pre-Central Park, including considerations of an eventual 'original ground' (pre-park), local architectures, and pre-existing native ecologies alien to the current park configuration. In the decade building up to the excavations, Copeland recalls the reports of passers-by walking along the park paths where the village once existed and stumbling upon clay pipes, glass shards and bits of ceramic. These were not dug from the ground, she adds, they were 'kind of pushed up in the earth after rain in these spaces.' They were moving upwards in what is an unsettled, disturbed ground. Once historically documented, the artifacts provided additional justification for the 2011 campaign. See Cynthia Copeland in conversation with Liz H. Strong, *Saving Preservation Stories: Diversity and the Outer Boroughs. The Reminiscences of Cynthia Copeland* (New York: New York Presentation Archive Project, 2017).

357 The notion of *lifeworld* is used in the way Anna Tsing conceptualized it. See Anna Tsing, *The Mushroom at the End of the World. On the Possibility of Life in Capitalist Ruins* (Princeton: Princeton University Press, 2015).

358 See, for example, Kenneth Jackson and David Dunbar (Eds.), 'Selected Writings on Central Park, Frederick Law Olmsted (1858–1870),' in *Empire City: New York through the Centuries* (New York: Columbia University Press, 2002).

359 Koolhaas' idea of Central Park as *Arcadian synthetic carpet* was explored in Chapter 4. See also Koolhaas, *Delirious New York.*

360 Matt Edgeworth, 'The Relationship between Archaeological Stratigraphy and Artificial Ground and Its Significance in the Anthropocene,' in *Geological Society, London*, Special Publications (2014), 91–108.

361 Idem, 91–95.

362 Yusoff, *Black Anthropocenes*, xiii–xiv. This idea is explored in Chapter 3.

363 Ibid.

364 Marilyn Nelson, *My Seneca Village* (South Hampton, NH: Namelos, 2015).

365 In literary terms, the poems vary in form, from more common quatrains (four-line rhyming stanzas), usually organized in classic (Shakespearean) sonnets, to the less common styke of Petrarchan sonnets. Most poems in the book employ exact rhyme and slant rhyme, with some revealing what Nelson calls 'conceptual rhyme,' which '"echoes" related intellectual concepts. Iambic pentameter is also used in most poems. The meter is common in the English language, both in poetry, drama, and even pop songs, as it comes close to the rhythm of speaking informally or a heartbeat (Nelson, *Seneca Village*, 85–87).

366 Tschumi, *Transcripts*, 8.

367 Ibid.

368 Ibid.

369 The plan is included in the 2011 excavations report (Wall et al., *Seneca Village Report*).

370 Ibid. They also relied on two important maps that supported the 2011 excavations: Egbert Viele's 1856 *Map of the Lands Included in The Central Park from a Topographical Survey* (published in 1857), and Gardner Sage's *Central Park Condemnation Map*, from the same year. The *Condemnation Map* was particularly useful when it came to underline 'the middle-class nature of the community. Most of the denizens of Seneca Village lived in substantial houses.' It was cross-referenced with the listing in the 1850 and 1855 Federal census to help draw a profile of the African Americans who lived in Seneca Village.

371 Peter Sloterdijk considers pampering the *conditio humana*, that is, the topological difference that, unlike genetics, may explain how humans became humans from being great apes. See Peter Sloterdijk in conversation with Thomas Macho, 'Raising Our Heads: Pampering Spaces and Time Drifts,' in Peter Sloterdijk, *Selected Exaggerations: Conversations and Interviews*

1993–2012 (Chicester: Polity Press, 2016), 82–105.

372 The dogtrot was a common house type throughout the southeastern United States during the nineteenth and early twentieth centuries, possibly even earlier in the South Carolina Low Country. The design included two one-story cabins connected by a breezeway (or dogtrot), all under a common roof. One cabin was usually used for cooking and dining, and the other was a private living space, usually a bedroom. Here it is speculated that the design may have been used as a starting point for some of the houses of the free African American families in Seneca Village.

373 Tschumi, *Transcripts*, 11.

374 Ibid.

375 Stan Allen, 'John Hejduk's Axonometric Degree Zero,' *Drawing Matter* (September 2019).

In his study of the oblique drawing, architect Massimo Scolari states that different types of parallel projection have been utilized as representational devices for more than two thousand years. In the West, they have been widely used in techno-mechanical and military applications for the 'rapid measurability' that other techniques (namely perspective) could not offer. See Massimo Scolari, *Oblique Drawing: A History of Anti-Perspective* (Cambridge: MIT Press, 2012).

376 Allen, 'John Hejduk's.'

377 See Timothy Love, 'Kit-of-Parts Conceptualism: Abstracting Architecture in the American Academy,' in *Harvard Design Magazine* 19 Architecture as Conceptual Art? Blurring Disciplinary Boundaries (2003). See also Hedjuk in MoMA and Cooper Union, *Education of an architect: a point of view* (New York: MoMA, 1971).

378 Allen, 'John Hejduk's.'

379 Ibid. Advocating for the need of disciplinary concerns in a world where technology is increasingly dissolving them, Allen defends that, unlike Hejduk's personal approach to engage the discipline, contemporary practices 'look outward, to architecture as a body of collective knowledge, and to the world beyond. They are a reminder that technical expertise and a deep knowledge of history are not in conflict with architecture's political mandate.'

380 The *New York Five* was a group composed of five American architects – Peter Eisenman, Michael Graves, Charles Gwathmey, John Hejduk and Richard Meier – whose work was featured in the 1972 book *Five Architects*.

381 Tschumi, *Transcripts*, 11.

382 See Bernard Tschumi, 'Questions of Space' (1976), *Architecture and Disjunction* (Cambridge: MIT Press, 1994), 53–64. For more information on Tschumi's interest in conceptual art and performance as a means of creating space see Sandra Kaji-O'Grady, 'The London Conceptualists: Architecture and Performance in the 1970s,' in *Journal of Architectural Education* 61 (4) (2008), 43–51.

383 Kaji-O'Grady, 'London Conceptualists,' 46. Both residing and working in London at the time – Tschumi worked at the AA, while Goldberg directed the Royal College of Art – architect and critic organized a series of exhibitions, perhaps epitomized by their 1976 *A Space: A Thousand Words*, 'the culmination and turning point of the three-year program of cross-fertilization between their respective institutions.'

384 Bernard Tschumi, 'Architecture and Transgression,' in *Oppositions* 7 (1976), 57, quoted in Kaji-O'Grady, 'London Conceptualists, 44. For Tschumi's complete essay, see Tschumi, *Architecture and Disjunction*.

385 Kaji-O'Grady, 'London Conceptualists,' 44.

386 Bernard Tschumi, 'Architecture: Sequences,' Excerpt from exhibition catalogue (1982), in *The Renaissance Society*.

387 McNeur, 'Central Park City,' 67.

388 The project's narrative follows a rather long lineage in literature exploring the role of cartographies detailed beyond their representational limits, that includes Lewis Carroll, Jorge Luis Borges, Jean Baudrillard and Umberto Eco.

389 McNeur, 'Central Park City,' 68–69.

390 Barad, 'Matter feels,' 54.

391 Idem, 51. The understanding of time as non-causality is related to Deleuze's formulation of time.

392 Idem, 66 (my emphasis).

393 Donna Haraway quoted in Barad, 'Matter feels,' 51.

Endnotes

394 Barad, 'Matter feels,' 66–67 (my emphasis).

395 Jacques Derrida, *Specters of Marx: The State of the Debt, the Work of Mourning and the New International*, P. Kamuf (Trans.) (1993, New York: Routledge, 2006), quoted in Barad, 'Matter feels,' 67–68.

396 Derrida, 'Point de Folie,' 73.

397 Barad, 'Matter feels,' 68–70.

398 Ibid.

399 Ibid.

6. Intra-Act
Architecture as
a Geologic Condition

400 See Bruno Latour, 'Why Has Critique Run out of Steam? From Matters of Fact to Matters of Concern,' in *Critical Inquiry* 30 (Chicago: The University of Chicago, 2004). Part of the argument on Latour's statement has been examined in an essay by the author. See Tiago Torres-Campos, 'Common Ground: Approaches to Space and Matter,' in Jamie Vanucchi, Ozayr Saloojee & Sarah Dooling (Eds.), *Design Research for Uncertain Futures* (Barcelona and San Francisco: Actar and ORO Publishers, 2024).

401 See Barad, 'Matter feels.' See also María Puig de la Bellacasa, *Matters of Care: Speculative Ethics in More Than Human Worlds* (Minneapolis: University of Minnesota Press, 2017); and Isabelle Stengers, 'We Are Divided,' in *e-flux Journal* #114 (December 2020).

402 Barad, *Meeting the Universe*, ix.

403 Idem, x–xi.

404 Anne-Sophie Springer and Etienne Turpin, 'Exhibition as a Philosophical Problem,' in *GAM—Graz Architecture Magazine* 14 Exhibiting Matters (Graz, 2018), 117–118.

405 Ibid.

Terminological Positions

406 The term gained traction at the hand of atmospheric chemist Paul Crutzen, who proposed it at a conference on stratigraphy and climate change and then further refined it. As mentioned before, the term has not yet been accepted to describe the current geological epoch, with scientists preferring to refer to it as an undeniable event (see note 5). Suggestions about its eventual starting point in time diverge, ranging from earlier beginnings twelve thousand years ago and coinciding with the invention of agriculture and the first sedentary civilizations, to the Industrial Revolution and the introduction of petrochemicals at a global scale, or to the more recent period of the Great Acceleration and the rise of the nuclear in the second half of the twentieth century and after WWII. See Timothy Morton, *The Ecological Thought* (Cambridge: Harvard University Press, 2010).

407 The problem of the constitution of an adequate subject has sparked controversy in the naming of the current situation: Capitalocene, Chthulucene, Anthrobscene, Plantationocene, Misanthropocene, among others. See Haraway, 'Tentacular Thinking,' in *e-flux journal* #75 (2016).

408 The notion of entanglement is here used in the specific sense given by Karen Barad. See Karen Barad, *Meeting the Universe Halfway: Quantum Physics and the Entanglement of Matter* (Durham: Duke University Press, 2007).

409 The idea of the earth in equilibrium finds its roots in the analysis of the twelve-thousand-year period of moderate stability called Holocene, by some also described as the period of agro-logistics.

410 See Donna Haraway, *Staying with the Trouble: Making Kin in the Chthulucene* (Durham: Duke University Press, 2016).

411 See Deleuze and Guattari, *Thousand Plateaus*, 12.

412 See Manuel DeLanda, *A New Philosophy of Society: Assemblage Theory and Social Complexity* (London: Continuum Books, 2006).

413 Brent Milligan, 'Landscape Migration. Environmental design in the Anthropocene,' *Places Journal* (2015).

414 See Gilles Deleuze and Clairy Parnet, *Dialogues* (New York: Columbia University Press, 2007). See also Colin McFarlane, 'The City as Assemblage: Dwelling and Urban Space,' in *Environment and Planning D: Society and*

Space 29 (4) (2011), 649–671.

415 See McFarlane, 'City as Assemblage.' See also Manuel DeLanda, *Assemblage Theory* (Edinburgh: Edinburgh University Press, 2016). Part-to-part relations have also been explored from the perspectives offered by Actor-Network Theory (ANT), first developed at the Centre de Sociologie de l'Innovation, by French sociologists BrunoLatour, Michel Callon and Madeleine Akrich. See Ignacio Farías, 'Introduction: Decentring the Object of Urban Studies,' in Ignacio Farías and Thomas Bender (Eds.), *Urban Assemblages: How Actor-Network Theory Changes Urban Studies* (New York: Routledge, 2010), 1–24.

The use of the rhizome here refers to an image of thought proposed by Deleuze and Guattari for conveying non-hierarchical, unpredictable and ad-hoc relations, unlike the more hierarchical metaphor of the tree and its root. Defined as infinitely connected, 'the rhizome connects any point to any other point. ... It has neither beginning nor end, but always a middle (milieu) from which it grows and overspills in linear mulitiplicities.' (Deleuze and Guattari, *Thousand Plateaus*, 6).

416 Barad, 'Matter feels.' 69.

417 See Zylinska, *Minimal Ethics*. Zylinska's interest in ethics stems from Emmanuel Levinas's 'turning towards something' and from Jacques Derrida's 'horizon of infinite justice.' See also Joanna Zylinska, in conversation with Benek Çinçik and Tiago Torres-Campos, 'A Local Museum of the Anthropocene,' in *Postcards from the Anthropocene: Unsettling the Geopolitics of Representation* (Barcelona: DPR-barcelona, 2022).

418 In 1843 Edgar Allen Poe wrote the short story 'The Man That Was Used Up' in which a man with extensive prostheses was described.

419 Donna Haraway, 'A Cyborg Manifesto: Science, technology and socialist-feminism in the late twentieth century,' in David Bell and Barbara M. Kennedy (Eds.), *The Cybercultures Reader* (New York: Routledge, 2000). Haraway describes cyborgs as 'figures for living within contradictions, attentive to the naturecultures of mundane practices ... alert to the emergent historical hybridities actually populating the world at all its contingent scales.' She returns to the idea of the cyborg in her book *Companion Species Manifesto.*

420 See endnote 10.

421 James Hutton famously wrote that with deep time '...we find no vestige of a beginning, – no prospect of an end.' See Hutton, *Theory of the Earth* (Edinburgh: Royal Society of Edinburgh, 1788).

422 Competing with Neptunism – a dominant explanation of the earth's history at the University of Edinburgh – James Hutton's new theory of the planet's formation as the result of volcanic activity – known as Plutonism – formulated the earth as a 'beautiful machine'. This new way of thinking eventually reverberated across the discipline of geology and slowly spread to other disciplines, including biology, chemistry and physics.

423 See John McPhee, 'Basin and Range,' *The New Yorker* (1981).

424 Notions of time were further complicated in scientific thought with theories such as Relativity, which propose spacetime as an inseparable and non-linear continuum. These ideas percolated across the humanities and influenced contemporary philosophy, especially in late-twentieth-century French thought. Deleuze, for example, proposes formulations of time that move away from its understanding as an external linear progression – in which effect follows cause – and instead embrace it as a constant reworking and enfolding of past and future in the moment of *now.*

425 Barad, 'Matter feels.' See also Barad, *Meeting the Universe.* The idea of *spacetimemattering* in used here in the context given by Donna Haraway and Karen Barad.

426 See Dipesh Chakrabarty, 'Postcolonial Studies in the Era of Climate Change,' *New Literary History* 43 (2012). See also Dipesh Chakrabarty, 'The Climate of History: Four Theses,' *Critical Inquiry* 35 (2009).

427 Anna Tsing, Elaine Gan, Heather Swanson and Nils Burbandt, 'Haunted Landscapes of the Anthropocene,' in Anna Tsing et al. (Eds.), *Arts of Living on a Damaged Planet: Ghosts and Monsters of the Anthropocene* (Minneapolis: Minnesota University Press, 2017), 5.

428 Amitav Ghosh, *The Great Derangement: Climate Change and the Unthinkable* (Chicago: University of Chicago Press, 2016), 62–63. In the context of the Anthropocene

Endnotes

debate, Ghosh states that 'the Anthropocene has reversed the temporal order of modernity: those at the margins are now the first to experience the future that awaits all of us.'

429 James Corner, 'The Thick and the Thin of It,' in Christophe Girot and Dora Imhof (Eds.), *Thinking the Contemporary Landscape* (New York: Princeton Architectural Press, 2016), 117–135.

430 Donna Haraway describes *response-ability* as a 'praxis of care and response … in ongoing multispecies worlding on a wounded terra.' See Donna Haraway, 'Awash in Urine: DES and Premarin® in Multispecies Response-ability,' *WSQ: Women's Studies Quarterly* 40: 1 & 2 (2012).

431 Christian Beck and Gleyzon, 'Deleuze and the event(s),' 329. For a more complete line of thought on *event* according to Deleuze, see Gilles Deleuze, *Difference and Repetition*, Paul Patton (Trans.) (New York: Columbia University Press, 1994) and Gilles Deleuze, *The Logic of Sense* (New York: Columbia University Press, 1993).

432 Leonard Lawlor, 'Jacques Derrida,' in Edward N. Zalta (Ed.), *The Stanford Encyclopedia of Philosophy* (Fall 2021 Edition). See also Jacques Derrida, 'Typewriter Ribbon: Limited Ink (2) ("within such limits"),' in Barbara Cohen et al. (Eds.), *Material Events: Paul de Man and the Afterlife of Theory* (Minneapolis: University of Minnesota Press, 2001).

433 Derrida, 'Point de Folie,' 65–75.

434 Bernard Tschumi, *Architecture and Disjunction* (Cambridge: MIT Press, 1994), 227–259. *Disjunctive synthesis* is a term Tschumi borrows from Kant. The event's real, continuous, and uninterrupted operations relate to Deleuze's definition.

435 Idem, 256. Tschumi's idea of the event as expansion was borrowed from Michel Foucault and his notion of the *event of thought*.

436 Oxford Encyclopedia, s.v. 'Extrusion' (Oxford: Oxford University Press, 2018).

437 See Frederick Lutgens, Edward Tarbuck and Dennis Tasa, *The Essentials of Geology* (13th Edition) (London: Pearson, 2015).

438 Stan Allen, 'From Object to Field: Field Conditions in Architecture + Urbanism', in *Practice: Architecture,*

Technique and Representation (New York: Routledge, 2009), 218.

439 Ibid. Field conditions are concerned with part-to-part relations, and they question any attempts at grasping the whole. They advance 'from the whole down to the part … but from part to part … moving outwards from the smallest part to the whole' (Idem, 226).

440 Idem, 229. Allen's field conditions are perhaps less concerned with form than with process. By describing the American city grids 'as prototypical field conditions,' he clearly refers not only to spatial but equally to temporal scales. Over time, repetitions in the grid based on studied intervals and measure start registering accumulations of small variations which counter-act its universal orthogonal geometry. And instead of being disrupted, the grid accommodates the topographical, hydrological and cultural accidents fluidly, thus creating local variation through pragmatism. 'The order adjusts to local contingency without compromising its overall sense of coherence. Variation and consistency; difference and order – the very American ideals of individual freedom and collective responsibility – are held in delicate balance.'

441 Idem, 237. See also Stan Allen, 'Field Conditions,' in *Points + Lines: Diagrams and Projects for the City* (New York: Princeton Architectural Press, 1999), 100.

442 In this sense, the French term *milieu* seems to be meaningful. Meaning '"surroundings," "medium," and "middle,"' milieu 'has neither beginning nor end, but is surrounded by other middles, in a field of connections, relationships, extensions, and potentials.' See James Corner, 'The Agency of Mapping: Speculation, Critique, and Invention,' in James Corner and Alison Bick Hirsch (Eds.), *Landscape Imagination: Collected Essays of James Corner 1990–2010* (New York: Princeton Architectural Press, 2014), 208.

443 Corner, 'Agency of Mapping,' 213. The field as a graphic system becomes an agential milieu of representational production where an 'extensive and rhizomatic set of field operations precipitates, unfolds, and supports hidden conditions, desires, and possibilities nested within a milieu. Here, the concern becomes less about the design of form and space *per se*, and more about engaging, accelerating, and networking interactions amongst forces in time' (Idem, 233).

444 Merriam Webster Dictionary, s.v. 'Frame.'

445 While serial framing was a technique used before, at the turn of the twentieth century, film significantly expanded the notion of the representational frame. Moving image had a profound impact on everyday life, as well as in the sciences, arts, and humanities. It informed new aesthetic approaches in literature, fine arts, and architecture which underpinned several movements, such as Impressionism, Cubism and Modernism, among others. When discussing artwork, Derrida considers frame as a construction that creates an inside and an outside, both physically (the frame of a painting) and conceptually (art separate from art critique. See Jonathan R. Fardy, 'Double Vision: Reviewing Man Ray and Marcel Duchamp's 1920 Photo-text,' MA Thesis (Graduate College of Bowling Green University, 2008). See also Jacques Derrida, *The Truth in Painting*, Geoff Bennington and Ian McLeod (Trans.) (Chicago: University of Chicago Press, 1987).

446 The framing of less stable and phase-spaced sub-atomic particles differs significantly from the more stable atomic and super-atomic framing. Equally, the framing of the whole earth with images such as the *Blue Marble*, or the capacity to capture and represent much larger formations in the universe challenges the discursive capacities of conventional framing methods and techniques. These scalar expansions require distinct onto-epistemological frameworks of analysis and operation. See Mark Dorrian, 'Adventure on the Vertical. Powers of Ten and the mastery of space by vision', in *Cabinet 44* (2011) and Mark Dorrian, 'On Google Earth,' in Mark Dorrian and Frédéric Pousin (Eds.), *Seeing from Above: The Aerial View in Visual Culture* (London: I. B. Tauris & Company, 2013).

447 See Ghosh, *Great Derangement*. See also Tom Cohen and Claire Colebrook, 'Preface,' in Tom Cohen, Claire Colebrook and J. Hillis Miller (Eds.), *Twilight of the Anthropocene Idols* (Open Humanities Press, 2016), 7–19.

448 See Bernard Comrie, *Tense* (Cambridge: Cambridge University Press, 1985).

449 Ibid.

450 Elizabeth Ellsworth and Jamie Kruse, 'Evidence: Making a Geologic Turn in Cultural Awareness', in Elizabeth Ellsworth and Jamie Kruse (Eds.), *Making the Geologic Now. Responses to Material Conditions of Contemporary Life* (New York: Punctum Books, 2013), 6.

451 Jussi Parikka, *The Anthrobscene* (Minneapolis: University of Minnesota Press, 2014), 36–37.

452 Idem, 4.

453 Heather Davis and Etienne Turpin, 'Art & Death: Lives Between the Fifth Assessment & the Sixth Extinction,' in Heather Davis and Etienne Turpin (Eds.), *Art in the Anthropocene: Encounters Among Aesthetics, Politics, Environments and Epistemologies* (London: Open Humanities Press, 2015), 3.

454 Nigel Clark and Kathryn Yusoff, 'Geosocial formations and the Anthropocene', in *Theory, Culture & Society 34* (2017), 3–23.

455 Idem, 6.

456 Ibid.

457 Georges Didi-Huberman, 'Glimpses,' Keynote lecture at the European Graduate School (2015). See also Georges Didi-Huberman, 'Glimpses. Between Appearance and Disappearance,' in Lorenz Engell and Bernhard Siegert (Eds.), *Zeitschrift für Medien und Kulturforschung* (Hamburg: Meiner Verlag, 2016), 109–110.

458 Stijn De Cauwer and Laura Katherine Smith, 'Critical Image Configurations,' *Angelaki* 23 (4) (2018), 1-2.

459 Didi-Huberman, 'Glimpses.'

460 For an explanation of *shards of thought* see Zylinska, *Minimal Ethics*.

461 Didi-Huberman, 'Glimpses.'

462 The notion of *ground* received renewed attention in the nineteenth century, mostly with artists from the Romantic period, and it was expanded and complicated throughout the twentieth century with scientific theories such as *continental drift* (1950s–60s), which eventually evolved into the more contemporary *plate tectonics*. The idea of a planet in constant regeneration – also supported by the *Gaïa* hypothesis – changed the conception of ground to an unsure, fluid, unsettled and fractured thickness. Ground is key to landscape and architectural practices, especially when understood less as a passive, palimpsestic recipient and more as an active, non-neutral agent with memory. See Elizabeth Meyer, 'The Expanded Field of Landscape Architecture,' in George F. Thompson and Frederick R. Steiner (Eds.), *Ecological Design and Planning* (New York: John Wiley & Sons, 1997). See also Robin Dripps, 'Groundwork,' in Carol J. Burns and Andrea Kahn (Eds.), *Site Matters: Design Concepts, Histories, and Strategies* (New York: Routledge, 2005).

463 Deleuze and Guattari's *rhizome* as a thinking from the milieu without reference to any specific ground strata may help resolve the tensions of ground-specificity between the local and the global, but it also demands attention to the current planetary sense of *groundlessness*.

464 Barad, 'Matter Feels.'

465 See Parikka, *Geology of Media* and Parikka, *Anthrobscene*.

466 Barad, 'Matter Feels,' 49. See also Haraway, *SF,* 7.

467 The term was coined by Timothy Morton in 2010 and borrows conceptually from OOO, which critiques the reduction of philosophical enquiry to a correlation between thought and being, also known as the *human-world gap*. In this view, objects are not simply products of human cognition (so they are no longer ontologically defined only by their relations with humans), but exist independently and forge relations with one another, even between non-human entities. The idea emerges from Morton's alignment with deep ecological thought which promotes a dissolution human and earth temporalities and expands spatial and materials frames. It borrows some important influences also from Deleuze's reformulation of time as well the Deleuzoguattarian definition of assemblage, and it comes close to New Materialism's notion of *vibrant matter* (see Morton, *Hyperobjects*). For a discussion on vibrant matter see Bennett, *Vibrant Matter.*

468 For a more detailed description of the properties of hyperobjects see Morton, *Hyperobjects.*

469 See Gilles Deleuze, 'Desert Islands,' in *Desert Islands and Other Texts 1953–1974* (Cambridge, MA: The MIT Press, 2004).

Michel Foucault refers to and outlines the notion of *heterotopia* at least on three occasions between 1966 and 1967, the most well-known of them being a talk titled 'Of Other Spaces' ('Des Espaces Autres') delivered in 1967 to an audience of architects and published in the French journal *Architecture/Movement/Continuité* in 1984. Foucault defines heterotopias as worlds within the world which both mirror and upset what is outside. He also refers to heterotopia as a condition of *otherness* in his preface to *The Order of Things*, in this case discussing texts rather than socio-cultural spatial conditions. See Michel Foucault, *The Order of Things: An Archaeology of the Human Sciences* (New York: Vintage Books, 1971).

Even if perhaps less relevant to this discussion, Lyotard's idea of *scapeland* may still deserve some attention, for its inversion underscores a sense of displacement that is fundamental to both the understanding and definition of the term. 'Estrangement [dépaysement – or sense of estrangement caused by dislocation] would seem to be a precondition for landscape [paysage].' Scapeland can be read in a relatively close alignment with both Deleuze's sense of radical dislocation to begin anew, and Foucault's heterotopia as that which dislocates the outside into an inside of otherness. See Jean-François Lyotard, 'Scapeland,' in *The Inhuman: Reflections on Time* (1988, Cambridge, UK: Polity Press, 1991).

470 In *Spheres* (*Sphären*) Peter Sloterdijk explores multiple *spaces of coexistence* through a reinterpretation of Western metaphysics. Even though in *Foams*, the third volume in the trilogy, Sloterdijk develops what can be called a theory of insulation, and proposes a tripartite categorization of islands as absolute, climatic and anthropogenic – the first being a capsule like a space station, for example – he also suggests a conceptual position that he calls connected isolation, that is, a link between a human right of isolation and the need for interconnection. See Peter Sloterdijk, *Foams, Spheres Volume III: Plural Spherology* (Cambridge, MA: The MIT Press, 2016), 294 and 307.

471 The scales Morton refers to can range, for example, from an apparently rigid and thin separation between land and water from the air to a complex ridged topography that is extensionally distinct from the perspective of a small crawling beach creature. See

Timothy Morton, 'Molten Entities,' in Daniel Daou and Pablo Pérez-Ramos (Eds.), *New Geographies 08: Island* (Cambridge, MA: Harvard University Press, 2016), 72–75).

472 To mention a few: a sense of rebirth, from Plato's Atlantean myth in *Timaeus* (360 BCE) to Francis Bacon's 1623 *New Atlantis*; a disengagement from humanity and development of a new humanness in isolation, from Ibn Tufayl's seminal 12th-century book *Hayy ibn Yaqzán* to Daniel Defoe's 1719 *Robinson Crusoe*; a utopian place, from Thomas More's 1516 *Utopia* to Jonathan Swift's 1726 *Gulliver's Travels*; as well as a dystopian reality, from H. G. Wells 1896 *Island of Doctor Moreau* to William Golding's 1954 *Lord of the Flies* or Aldous Huxley's 1962 *Island*; and finally a space of subversive reinvention, from Michel Tournier's 1972 *Friday, or the Limbo of the Pacific* to J. G. Ballard's 1973 *Concrete Island*. See Robin MacKay, 'Philosopher's Islands,' *New Geographies* 08, 56–83.

473 Marc Shell, 'Islandology,' in *New Geographies* 08, 44–54.

474 As explored in chapter 3, Manhattan at the same time also seems less isolated than other islands due to its characteristics as a radically interconnected territory. The argument in this book is that the depiction of Manhattan as a totalizing territory where island and grid overlap irreducibly is supported and reinforced by dominant logics of neo-liberal capitalism, and explores alternatives rooted in *geologics* that acknowledge its condition as a coalesced territory of heterotopic, divergent, heterogeneous yet somehow reconciled space-time configurations.

Sloterdijk posits that Modernity has created a nesopoietic project regarding the idea of island: from found to made. While Manhattan corresponds to a geographical definition of island, it is also a made cultural construct of island. In this category, one might also include other islands, such as Venice (Sloterdijk, *Foams*, 292–293).

475 This operative definition benefits from ideas developed over time in the fields of landscape architectural theory and associated fields. See, for example John Brinckerhoff Jackson, 'The Word Itself,' in *Discovering the Vernacular Landscape* (New Haven: Yale Univ. Press, 1984), 3–8.; John R. Stilgoe, 'Preface,' in *What is Landscape?* (Cambridge: MIT Press, 2015), ix–xiv; Stanislaus Fung, 'Mutuality and Cultures of Landscape Architecture,' in James Corner (Ed.), *Recovering Landscape: Essays in Contemporary Landscape Architecture* (New York: Princeton Architectural Press, 1999), 141–152; and Meyer, 'Expanded Field'. The definition moves away from an understanding of landscape as 'a portion of the earth's surface that can be comprehended at a glance,' suggested by J. B. Jackson, and tries to reconcile the origins of the concept as a pictorial or scenic notion in some western cultures both with its Anglo-Saxon roots as a working milieu and its Latin roots as an administrative territorial circumscription. (Ideas of landscape in non-western cultures are left purposefully outside of this brief train of thought, even though they were considered in the formulation of the operative definition. Landscape benefits from multicultural understandings that gesture beyond any disciplinary cannons and decolonized approaches.) The definition has at least three important implications. First, it aims to rescue the artistic and eidetic imaginaries of landscape as a socio-cultural construction and clarify its distinction from and interrelation with concepts such as nature, environment or wilderness. Second, it alludes to 'a deep and intimate mode of relationship not only among buildings and field but also among patters of occupation, activity, and space.' Third, it reveals an ambition for the concept to become both a foregrounded field of operations and a backgrounded infrastructural support in complex contemporary territories. See James Corner, 'Eidetic Operations and New Landscapes,' in Corner, *Recovering Landscape*, 153–170.

476 Tsing et al., 'Haunted Landscapes,' 6. According to the authors:

As humans reshape the landscape, we forget what was there before. Ecologists call this forgetting the "shifting baseline syndrome." Our newly shaped and ruined landscapes become the new reality. Admiring one landscape and its biological entanglements often entails forgetting many others. Forgetting, in itself, remakes landscapes, as we privilege some assemblages over others. Yet ghosts remind us. Ghosts point to our forgetting, showing us how living landscapes are imbued with earlier tracks and traces (Ibid).

477 Idem, 12.

478 See Haraway, *Companion Species Manifesto*.

479 Nicholas Malone and Kathryn Ovenden, 'Natureculture', in Agustín Fuents (Ed.), *The International Encyclopaedia of Primatology* (New Jersey: John Wiley & Sons, 2017).

480 See for example Meyer, 'Expanded Field;' and James Corner, 'Terra Fluxus,' in Charles Waldheim (Ed.), *The Landscape Urbanism Reader* (New York: Princeton Architectural Press, 2006), 21–33.

481 Oxford Reference, 'Representation,' in *Oxford Reference, Media Studies* (Oxford: Oxford University Press).

482 Representation gestures beyond the domain of the visual – a depiction – to the eidetic – an image. It invokes reality; it both expresses perceptual factors and reveals what cannot be expressed; it is critical, non-neutral, and agential; it becomes a constant negotiation between histories of production, construction and deconstruction of ideas embedded in specific value systems and power relations; it synthesizes past and present histories and stories and allows the imagination of future possibilities and alternatives. See Çinçik and Torres-Campos, 'Postcard Notes on the Anthropocene,' in *Postcards*.

483 Elizabeth Grosz defends representation less as a defining human cultural achievement and more as a reorganized materialization of 'imperceptible cosmic, biological, and geologic forces of the universe ... on the body; sensations that allow our becoming-otherwise.' See Elizabeth Grosz, Kathryn Yusoff, Arun Saldanha, Catherine Nash and Nigel Clark, 'Geopower: a panel on Elizabeth Grosz's Chaos, Territory, Art: Deleuze and the Framing of the Earth,' *Environment and Planning D: Society and Space* 30 (2012), 971.

484 Both *thick representation* and *representation of thickness* draw influence from Clifford Geertz's anthropological and ethnographic notion of *thick description*, a type of description of human socio-cultural action that positions behavior in close relation to both context and actors, as a way of making it more accessible and better understood to an outsider. The term has been utilized outside of its original disciplinary circumscription, namely in literary criticism. See Clifford Geertz, *The Interpretation of Cultures* (New York: Basic Books, 1973).

485 First, multiscalar thinking manifested at scale encourages an understanding of how a set of spacetime conditions operates at a specific scale, as well as the capacity for translating and mediating how those conditions may be represented at a different scale. Scaling, an operation for this translation, 'involves the displacement, reduction/enlargement, and multiplication of prominent ... figures ...' (Corner, 'Agency of Mapping,' 222–223).

Second, multiscalar thinking across scale operates with different sets of conditions at distinct scales, which are read and eventually understood in relation to each other. The expansion of the human onto progressively larger and radically different scalar domains 'can be read in terms of the domination and control of the realms that it pictures,' while the corresponding projection of human-derived subjectivity onto them raises questions about the meaning and kind of representations required to ground and situate ourselves, gesturing towards eventual limits in representability where scalefulness begins to verge on scalelessness (see Dorrian, 'Adventure on the Vertical').

486 Chakrabarty, 'Postcolonial Studies,' quoted in Derek Woods, 'Scale Critique for the Anthropocene,' in *Minnesota Review* 83 (2014) (New Series), 133.

487 Anna Tsing, 'On Nonscalability: The Living World Is Not Amenable to Precision-Nested Scales,' in *Common Knowledge* 18 (3) (2012), 505-506 (italics in the original).

488 See Tom Cohen et al., (Eds.), *Twilight of the Anthropocene Idols*, 8–9 (italics in the original). See also Isabelle Stengers, *In Catastrophic Times. Resisting the Coming Barbarism* (Open Humanities Press, 2015), 9.

This is a recognition of, on one hand, the 'existence of real discontinuities that subject objects, bodies, and systems to different constraints at different scales,' and on the other hand, that scaling up raises profound implications on the subject of representation (who or what is being represented) (see Woods, 'Scale Critique'). See also Bruno Latour, 'Anti-zoom,' in Laurence Bossé, Hans Ulrich Obrist, Claire Staebler (Eds. and Curators), *Olafur Eliasson: Contact, Suzanne Pagé* (Paris: Flammarion, 2014), 122–125; and Clark and Yusoff, 'Geosocial formations,' 9.

It is also a theoretical critique of onto-epistemologies where material and spacetime conditions are conceptually organized in 'precision-nested scales,' towards what Anna Tsing calls a theory of *nonscalability* to register and acknowledge the importance of 'wild diversity of life on earth' (Tsing, 'On Nonscalability,' 506). See also Zylinska, *Minimal Ethics*, 25–36.

489 Several approaches to understanding global positionings using logics related to the sphere can be identified across different civilizations. More specifically, at the turn of the twentieth century some European geographers led by Élisée Reclus advocated for the development of *spherography* to 'counter the popularity of map making.' See Joyce Hsiang and Bimal Mendis, 'The City of Seven Billion,' *New Geographies* 08, 204–211.

490 For a contextualization of Sloterdijk's *Spheres* see note 470.

491 The practice of reading the earth's age and aging through information contained in geological layers emerged in Europe in the seventeenth and eighteenth centuries and expanded in scope and precision with the disciplinary reformulation of geology in the nineteenth century.

Stratigraphy contributes to the determination of the earth's periods – epochs, eras, eons, etc. – by providing evidence of significant change in the geo-bio-chemical layers of the earth as well as the identification of geological markers, technically called Global Boundary Stratotype Section and Points (GSSP) but often named 'golden spikes.' These are reference points in a stratigraphic section which define the lower boundary of a period on the geologic time scale. See Felix M. Gradstein, James G. Ogg, Mark B. Schmitz, Gabi M. Ogg (Eds.), *Geologic Time Scale 2020* (Amsterdam: Elsevier, 2020).

492 Zylinska, among others, recognizes the importance of stratigraphic readings in the construction of an ethics for the Anthropocene, when she mentions that through 'our human ability to tell stories and to philosophize, we can not only grasp the deep historical stratification of values through an involvement in what Deleuze and Guattari call "a geology of morals" (1987) but also work out possibilities for making better differences across various scales' (Zylinska, *Minimal Ethics*, 21).

493 See James Corner, 'The Thick and the Thin.'

494 For a more complete description of *thick-2D* see Stan Alen, 'Field Conditions.' For a more complete description of *sub-urbanism* see Sébastien Marot, *Sub-Urbanism and the Art of Memory* (London: Architectural Association Publications, 2003). See also Corner, 'The Thick and the Thin.'

List of Figures

1 *Hutton's unconformity at Jedburgh*, John Clerck of Eldin, 1787.

2 *Géographie des plantes équinoxiales. Tableau physique des Andes et Pays voisins*, Alexander von Humboldt, 1803. © Société des Lettres, sciences et arts 'La Haute-Auvergne.'

3 Studies of exponential variation in Manhattan's geology, series, 2016 [image by the author].

4 Earth's tectonic plates (series), in 'Lower Manhattan Revisited,' Lebbeus Woods, blog, March 8, 2012, https://lebbeuswoods.wordpress.com/2012/03/08/lower-manhattan-revisited/. © The Estate of Lebbeus Woods.

5 *Geologic map and sections of Manhattan Island*, State of New York, 1898.

6 *Lower Manhattan*, Lebbeus Woods, 1999. © The Estate of Lebbeus Woods.

7–9 *Underground Berlin 19*, Elevation View, Lebbeus Woods, 1988. Graphite and pastel on paper; 12 1/2 x 20 1/4 in. (31.8 x 51.4 cm). San Francisco Museum of Modern Art, Purchase through a gift of the FOG Forum © The Estate of Lebbeus Woods.

10 *Pinnacle of Chalk*, William Jerome Harrison, W. of Sheringhamm, 1886, in Adam Bobbette, 'Scalelessness' © British Geological Survey.

11 *Sanitary & Topographical Map of the City and Island of New York*, Egbert L. Viele, 1865.

12 *Delirious New York*, Original book cover, Rem Koolhaas, 1978. © OMA.

13 *The City of the Captive Globe*, Rem Koolhaas and Madelon Vriesendorp, 1972. © OMA. Madelon Vriesendorp.

14 *Commissioners' Plan*, 1811. The definition of Manhattan as a field condition. © Library of Congress.

15 *Dreamland at Night*, Coney Island, New York, Unknown, Museum of City of New York, ca. 1905.

16 'From Fair to Fair', in Delirious New York, Rem Koolhaas, 1978. © OMA.

17–19 Interior of Radio City Music Hall. © Library of Congress.

20 Lobby with Globe inside the Daily News Building, Raymond Hood [photograph by the author].

21 Postcard 'Madison Square East, New York', 1909, in Delirious New York, 1978.

22–24 *Exodus, or the Voluntary Prisoners of Architecture*, Rem Koolhaas, Madelon Vreisendorp, Elia Zenghelis, and Zoe Zenghelis, 1972. © OMA. MoMA Archives.

25–29 Fragments of *Delirious New York*, Original book cover, Rem Koolhaas, 1978. Image adapted from *Flagrant Délit*, Madelon Vriesendorp, 1975.

30 *Continuous monument*, Superstudio, New York, 1969. © Superstudio. Courtesy of Drawing Matter

31 *Modella della Zimmer in Graz, Sketchbook 12*, Superstudio, 1969. © Superstudio. Courtesy of Drawing Matter

32 *Einstein Tomb*, Lebbeus Woods, 1980. (top left) *Drawing for Einstein Tomb*, Lebbeus Woods, 1980. Graphite and ink on board; 21 3/8 in. x 14 1/2 in. (54.29 cm x 36.83 cm). San Francisco Museum of Modern Art, Purchase, by exchange, through a gift of PeggyGuggenheim © The Estate of Lebbeus Woods. (top right and bottom two) *Pamphlet Architecture 6: Einstein Tomb*

[Color study] [pages 3, 5 and 6] Lebbeus Woods, 1980. Colored pencil on pigment print; 8 1/2 x 7 in. (21.6 x 17.8 cm) San Francisco Museum of Modern Art, Gift of the Estate of Lebbeus Woods © The Estate of Lebbeus Woods.

33 *The Manhattan Transcripts*, Original book cover, Bernard Tschumi, 1981. © Bernard Tschumi.

34 *The Manhattan Transcripts*, Introductory Triptych and excerpt of MT1–'The Park', Bernard Tschumi, 1981. © Bernard Tschumi.

35 *The Manhattan Transcripts*, MT3–'The Tower' (The Fall), excerpt, Bernard Tschumi, 1981. © Bernard Tschumi.

36 *Proposal for Parc de la Villette*, General Plan, Bernard Tschumi Architects, 1982. © Bernard Tschumi Architects.

37 *Map of Central Park*, Calvert Vaux and Frederick Law Olmsted, 1870. © Central Park Arsenal.

38 *Greensward Plan, Proposal for Central Park*, Calvert Vaux and Frederick Law Olmsted, 1858. ©NY Historical Society and Central Park Arsenal.

39 *Map of the Lands Included in The Central Park from a Topographical Survey*, Egbert Viele, June 17, 1856. ©NY Public Library.

40 *Plan for the Improvement of The Central Park*, Adopted by the Commissioners, Egbert Viele, June 03, 1856. ©NY Public Library.

41 *Central Park City*, Central Park drawing, Lorna McNeur, 1979–1983. ©Lorna McNeur.

Bibliography

Aggarwala, Rohit T., 'Review of Manhattan Atmospheres: Architecture, the Interior Environment, and Urban Crisis', in *Buildings and Landscapes* 22 (2) (2015).

Allen, Stan, 'Field Conditions Revisited', in *Four Projects, Source Books in Architecture 10* (series ed. Benjamin Wilke) (Novato: Applied Research + Design Publishing, 2017)

Allen, Stan, 'From Object to Field: Field Conditions in Architecture + Urbanism', in *Practice: Architecture, Technique and Representation* (New York: Routledge, 2009), 217–242.

Allen, Stan, 'John Hejduk's Axonometric Degree Zero,' in *Drawing Matter* (September 2019), online: https://drawingmatter.org/john-hejduks-axonometric-degree-zero/].

Allmer, Acalya, 'Scissors versus T-square: on El Lissitzky's Representations of Space,' in *Online Journal of Art and Design* 3 (3) (2015), 19–32.

Andrews, Carol, *Amulets of Ancient Egypt* (Texas: University of Texas Press, 1994).

Badiou, Alain, 'The Event in Deleuze,' in *Parrhesia* 2 (2007), 37–44.

Barad, Karen, 'Matter feels, converses, suffers, desires, yearns and remembers,' interviewed by Rick Dolphijn and Iris van der Tuin, in Rick Dolphijn and Iris van der Tuin (Eds.), in *New Materialism: Interviews and Cartographies* (London: Open Humanities Press, 2012), 48–70.

Barad, Karen, *Meeting the Universe Halfway: Quantum Physics and the Entanglement of Matter* (Durham: Duke University Press, 2007).

Basar, Shumon, and Stephen Truby (Eds.), *The World of Madelon Vriesendorp* (London: AA Publications, 2008).

Baskerville, Charles A. 'The foundation geology of New York City', in Robert F. Legget (Ed.), *Geology under Cities* (Boulder, Colorado: The Geological Society of America, 1982), 95–117.

Bataille, Georges, *The Solar Anus* (1927, Paris: Éditions de la Galerie Simon, 1931).

Beck, Christian, and François-Xavier Gleyzon, 'Deleuze and the event(s),' in *Journal for Cultural Research* 20 (4) (2016), 329–333.

Benjamin, Walter, *Illuminations* (Hannah Arendt, Ed., Harry Zohn, Trans.) (London: Fontana, 1973).

Bennett, Jane, *Vibrant Matter: A Political Ecology of Things* (Durham, NC: Duke University Press, 2010).

Bobbette, Adam, 'Episodes from a History of Scalelessness', in Etienne Turpin (Ed.), *Architecture in the Anthropocene: Encounters Among Design, Deep Time, Science and Philosophy* (Open Humanities University Press, 2013), 47–58.

Boldt-Irons, Leslie Anne, 'Bataille's "The Solar Anus" or the Parody of Parodies,' in *Studies in 20th Century Literature* 25 (2), Article 3 (2001), 354–375.

Botar, Oliver, 'Review: [Untitled], Films by Lázló Moholy-Nagy,' in *Journal of the Society of Architectural Historians* 67 (3) (University of California Press on behalf of the Society of Architectural Historians, September 2008), 460–462).

Brady, Emily, *The Sublime in Modern Philosophy: Aesthetics, Ethics, and Nature* (Cambridge: Cambridge University Press, 2013).

Bratton, Benjamin H., *The Terraforming* (Moscow: Strelka Press, 2019).

Brown, Chandos Michael, 'The First American Sublime', in Timothy M. Costelloe (Ed.), *The Sublime: From Antiquity to the Present* (2012, Cambridge: Cambridge University Press, online version 2015), 147–170.

Brown, Paul Tolliver, 'Relativity, Quantum Physics, and Consciousness in Virginia Woolf's "To the Lighthouse,"' *Journal of Modern Literature* 32 (3) (2009), 39–62.

Carlisle, Stephanie, and Nicholas Pevzner, 'The Performative Ground: Rediscovering the Deep Section', *Scenario Journal* 02 (2009), online: https://scenariojournal.com/article/the-performative-ground/

Carlson, Thomas C., 'Review of Poe and His Times: The Artist and His Milieu,' in *The Mississipi Quarterly* 46 (1) (Winter 1992), 140–142.

Chakrabarty, Dipesh, 'The Climate of History: Four Theses,' *Critical Inquiry* 35 (2009).

Chakrabarty, Dipesh, 'Postcolonial Studies in the Era of Climate Change,' in *New Literary History* 43 (2012).

Chilvers, Ian, and John Glaves-Smith (Eds.), 'Abstract Sublime', in *Dictionary of Modern and Contemporary Art* (2nd ed.) (Oxford: Oxford University Press, 2009).

Clark, Nigel, and Kathryn Yusoff, 'Geosocial formations and the Anthropocene', in *Theory, Culture & Society* 34 (2017), 3–23.

Cohen, Tom, and Claire Colebrook, 'Preface,' in Tom Cohen, Claire Colebrook and J. Hillis Miller (Eds.), *Twilight of the Anthropocene Idols* (Open Humanities Press, 2016), 7–19.

Colebrook, Claire, 'The Geological Sublime', in Tom Cohen, Claire Colebrook and J. Hillis Miller (Eds.), *Twilight of the Anthropocene Idols* (London: Open Humanities Press, 2016), 117–125.

Comrie, Bernard, *Tense* (Cambridge: Cambridge University Press, 1985).

Corner, James, 'Eidetic Operations and New Landscapes,' in James Corner (Ed.), *Recovering Landscape: Essays in Contemporary Landscape Architecture* (New York: Princeton Architectural Press, 1999), 141–152.

Corner, James, 'Terra Fluxus,' in Charles Waldheim (Ed.), *The Landscape Urbanism Reader* (New York: Princeton Architectural Press, 2006), 21–33.

Cook, Peter, 'Natalini Superstudio,' in *The Architectural Review* 171 (1982), 48–51.

Copeland, Cynthia, in conversation with Liz H. Strong, *Saving Preservation Stories: Diversity and the Outer Boroughs. The Reminiscences of Cynthia Copeland* (New York: New York Presentation Archive Project, 2017).

Corner, James, 'The Agency of Mapping: Speculation, Critique, and Invention,' in James Corner and Alison Bick Hirsch (Eds.), *Landscape Imagination: Collected Essays of James Corner 1990–2010* (1990, New York: Princeton Architectural Press, 2014), 197–239.

Corner, James, 'The Thick and the Thin of It,' in Christophe Girot and Dora Imhof (Eds.), *Thinking the Contemporary Landscape* (New York: Princeton Architectural Press, 2016), 117–135.

Cunningham, David, 'Capitalist epics. Abstraction, totality and the theory of the novel,' in *Radical Philosophy* 163 (2010), 11–23.

Czerniak, Julia, 'Parc de la Villette. Bernard Tschumi,' in David Leatherbarrow and Alexander Eisenschmidt (Eds.), *The Companions to the History of Architecture IV Twentieth-Century Architecture* (New York: John Wiley & Sons, 2017), 2–13.

Dagenhart, Richard, 'Urban Architectural theory and the contemporary city: Tschumi and Koolhaas at the Parc de la Villette,' in *Eikistics* 56(334/335) Space Sintax: Social Implications of Urban Layouts (1989), 84–92.

Dalí, Salvador, *La Femme Visible* (Paris: Éditions Surrealistes, 1930).

Dacke, Marie, Emily Baird, Marcus Byrne, Clarke J. Scholtz, Eric J. Warrant, 'Dung Beetles Use the Milky Way for Orientation,' in *Current Biology* 23(4) (2013), 298–300.

Dalí, Salvador, 'The Conquest of the Irrational,' appendix to *Conversations with Dalí* (New York: Dutton, 1969).

Damisch, Hubert, 'The Manhattan Transfer,' in J. Lucan (Ed.), *OMA/Rem Koolhaas: Architecture 1970–1990* (New York: Princeton Architectural Press, 1991), 21–32.

Davis, Heather and Etienne Turpin, 'Art & Death: Lives Between the Fifth Assessment & the Sixth Extinction,' in Heather Davis and Etienne Turpin (Eds.), *Art in the Anthropocene: Encounters Among Aesthetics, Politics, Environments and Epistemologies* (London: Open Humanities Press, 2015), 3–30.

De Cauwer, Stijn and Laura Katherine Smith, 'Critical Image Configurations,' in *Angelaki* 23(4) (2018), 1-2.

DeLanda, Manuel, *A New Philosophy of Society: Assemblage Theory and Social Complexity* (London: Continuum Books, 2006).

DeLanda, Manuel, *Assemblage Theory* (Edinburgh: Edinburgh University Press, 2016).

Deleuze, Gilles, *Cinema 2: The Time Image* (Hugh Tomlinson and Barbara Habberjam, trans.) (London: Continuum, 1989).

Deleuze, Gilles, 'Desert Islands,' in *Desert Islands and Other Texts 1953–1974* (Cambridge, MA: The MIT Press, 2004).

Deleuze, Gilles, *Difference and Repetition*, Paul Patton (Trans.) (1968, New York: Columbia University Press, 1994).

Deleuze, Gilles, *The Logic of Sense* (1969, New York: Columbia University Press, 1993).

Deleuze, Gilles and Clairy Parnet, *Dialogues* (1977, New York: Columbia University Press, 2007).

Deleuze, Gilles and Félix Guattari, *A Thousand Plateaus. Capitalism and Schizofrenia*, Brian Massumi (Trans.), (1980, Minneapolis: University of Minnesota Press, 1987).

Derrida, Jacques, 'Force and Signification,' in *Writing and Difference*, Alan Bass (Trans.) (1967, London: Routledge, 1978), 3–30.

Derrida, Jacques, *Of Grammatology* (Gayatri Chakravorty Spivak, trans.) (1967, Baltimore: John Hopkins University Press, 1976).

Derrida, Jacques, 'Point de Folie – Maintenant l'Architecture. Bernard Tschumi: La Case Vide – La Villette, 1985,' in *AA Files* 12 (Summer 1986), 65–75.

Derrida, Jacques, *Specters of Marx: The State of the Debt, the Work of Mourning and the New International,*

P. Kamuf (Trans.) (New York and London: Routledge, 2006),

Derrida, Jacques, *The Truth in Painting*, Geoff Bennington and Ian McLeod (Trans.) (Chicago: University of Chicago Press, 1987).

Derrida, Jacques, in conversation with Maurizio Ferraris and Giorgio Varrimo, 'I Have a Taste for the Secret,' in Jacques Derrida and Maurizio Ferraris, *A Taste for the Secret* (Cambridge: Polity, 2001), 3–92.

Derrida, Jacques, 'Typewriter Ribbon: Limited Ink (2) ("within such limits"),' in Barbara Cohen et al. (Eds.), *Material Events: Paul de Man and the Afterlife of Theory* (Minneapolis: University of Minnesota Press, 2001).

Didi-Huberman, Georges, 'Glimpses. Between Appearance and Disappearance,' in Lorenz Engell and Bernhard Siegert (Eds.), *Zeitschrift für Medien und Kulturforschung* (Hamburg: Meiner Verlag, 2016), 109–110.

Dorrian, Mark, 'Adventure on the Vertical. Powers of Ten and the mastery of space by vision', in *Cabinet* 44 (2011)

Dorrian, Mark, 'On Google Earth,' in Mark Dorrian and Frédéric Pousin (Eds.), *Seeing from Above: The Aerial View in Visual Culture* (London: I. B. Tauris & Company, 2013).

Dorrian, Mark, 'Utopia on Ice: The Climate as Commodity Form', in Etienne Turpin (Ed.), *Architecture in the Anthropocene: Encounters Among Design, Deep Time, Science and Philosophy* (London: Open Humanities Press, 2013), 143–152.

Dorrian, Mark, 'Art/Architecture/Concept,' in W. Davidts, S. Holden and A. Paine (Eds.), *Trading Between Architecture and Art: Strategies and Practices of Exchange* (Amsterdam: Valiz, 2019), 16–25.

Dripps, Robin, 'Groundwork,' in Carol J. Burns and Andrea Kahn (Eds.), *Site Matters: Design Concepts, Histories, and Strategies* (New York: Routledge, 2005).

Eco, Umberto, *Travels in Hyper-Reality* (1973, London, Harcourt Brace Jovanovich, 1986).

Edgeworth, Matt, 'The Relationship between Archaeological Stratigraphy and Artificial Ground and Its Significance in the Anthropocene,' in *Geological Society* (London: Special Publications, 2014), 91–108.

Ellsworth, Elizabeth, and Jamie Kruse, *Geologic City: A Field Guide to the Geoarchitecture of New York* (New York: Friends of the Pleistocene, 2011).

Ellsworth, Elizabeth, and Jamie Kruse, 'Evidence: Making a Geologic Turn in Cultural Awareness', in Elizabeth Ellsworth and Jamie Kruse (Eds.), *Making the Geologic Now. Responses to Material Conditions of Contemporary Life* (New York: Punctum Books, 2013), 6–26.

Farías, Ignacio, 'Introduction: Decentring the Object of Urban Studies,' in Ignacio Farías and Thomas Bender (Eds.), *Urban Assemblages: How Actor-Network Theory Changes Urban Studies* (London; New York: Routledge, 2010), 1–24.

Fardy, Jonathan R., 'Double Vision: Reviewing Man Ray and Marcel Duchamp's 1920 Photo-text,' MA Thesis (Graduate College of Bowling Green University, 2008)

Fitzgerald, Judith M., and Robert E. Loeb, 'Historical Ecology of Inwood Hill Park, Manhattan, New York', *Journal of the Torrey Botanical Society* 135(2), (2008), online: http://www.jstor.org/stable/40207578, 281–93.

Foucault, Michel, *The Order of Things: An Archaeology of the Human Sciences* (1966, New York: Vintage Books, 1971).

Foucault, Michel, 'Of Other Spaces', *Diacritics* 16 (1) (Jan Miskowiec, trans.) (Spring, 1986), 22–27.

Freud, Sigmund, Civilization and Its Discontents (New York: W. W. Norton & Company, 2010).

Fung, Stanislaus, 'Mutuality and Cultures of Landscape Architecture,' in James Corner (Ed.), *Recovering Landscape: Essays in Contemporary Landscape Architecture* (New York: Princeton Architectural Press, 1999), 141–152.

Gandy, Mathew, *Concrete and Clay: Reworking Nature in New York City* (Cambridge: MIT Press, 2002).

Geertz, Clifford, *The Interpretation of Cultures* (New York: Basic Books, 1973).

Ghosh, Amitav, T*he Great Derangement: Climate Change and the Unthinkable* (Chicago: University of Chicago Press, 2016), 62–63.

Gissen, David, *Manhattan Atmospheres: Architecture, the Interior Environment, and Urban Crisis* (Minneapolis: University of Minnesota Press, 2014).

Glanville, Ranulph, 'The Purpose of second-order cybernetics', *Kybernetes* 33 (9/10) (2004),1379–1386.

Gould, Stephen Jay, *Time's Arrow, Time's Cycle. Myth and Metaphor in the Discovery of Geological Time* (Cambridge: Harvard University Press, 1987).

Gorki, Maxim, 'The Kingdom of Shadows,' in Gilbert Adair (Ed.), *Movies* (Harmondsworth: Penguin, 1999), 10-11.

Gradstein, Felix M., James G. Ogg, Mark B. Schmitz and Gabi M. Ogg (Eds.), *Geologic Time Scale 2020* (Amsterdam: Elsevier, 2020).

Graves, Arthur H., 'Inwood Park, Manhattan', *Torreya* 30 (5) (1930), available online: http://www.jstor.org/stable/40596696, 117–129.

Graver, Fred, and Charlie Rubin, 'Waiting for the big one', in *New York Magazine* Special Issue Earthquake (1995).

Grosz, Elizabeth, Kathryn Yusoff, Arun Saldanha, Catherine Nash and Nigel Clark, 'Geopower: a panel on Elizabeth Grosz's Chaos, Territory, Art: Deleuze and the Framing of the Earth,' *Environment and Planning D: Society and Space* 30 (2012), 971–988.

Haff, Peter, 'Humans and technology in the Anthropocene: Six rules', in *The Anthropocene Review* 1(2) (2014), 126–136.

Haraway, Donna J., 'A Cyborg Manifesto: Science, technology and socialist-feminism in the late twentieth century,' in David Bell and Barbara M. Kennedy (Eds.), *The Cybercultures Reader* (New York: Routledge, 2000).

Haraway, Donna J., *The Companion Species Manifesto: Dogs, People, and Significant Otherness* (Chicago: Prickly Paradigm Press, 2003).

Haraway, Donna J., *SF: Science Fiction, Speculative Fabulation, String Figures, So Far*, Acceptance Speech for Pilgrim Award, 2011 July 7 (California and Lublin: SFRA Meetings, 2011).

Haraway, Donna J., 'Awash in Urine: DES and Premarin® in Multispecies Response-ability,' in *WSQ: Women's Studies Quarterly* 40 (1 & 2) (2012).

Haraway, Donna J., *Staying with the Trouble: Making Kin in the Chthulucene* (Durham: Duke University Press, 2016).

Haraway, Donna J., 'Tentacular Thinking: Anthropocene, Capitalocene, Chthulucene', in *e-flux journal* #75 (2016), online: https://www.e-flux.com/journal/75/67125/tentacular-thinking-anthropocene-capitalocene-chthulucene/.

Harman, Graham, 'The Road to Objects,' *Continent* 3 (1) (2011), 171–179.

Hawker, Adrian, Victoria Claire Bernie and Tiago Torres-Campos, 'Island Territories VI : Manhattan Scapeland Estrangement / Displacement,' MArch and MLA (The University of Edinburgh, School of Architecture and Landscape Architecture, 2018–2020).

Hassell Jr., J. Woodrow, 'The Problem of Realism in "The Gold Bug,"' in *American Literature* 25 (2) (1953), 179–192.

Hsiang, Joyce, and Bimal Mendis, 'The City of Seven Billion,' in Daniel Daou and Pablo Pérez-Ramos (Eds.), *New Geographies* 08: Island, (Cambridge, MA: Harvard University Press, 2016), 204–211.

Hsu, Frances, 'Delirious New York: A Retroactive Manifesto for Manhattan,' in *Journal of Architectural Education* 64 (2) (2011), 169–170.

Hussey, Mark, 'To the Lighthouse and Physics: The Cosmology of David Bohm and Virginia Woolf,' in Helen Wussow (Ed.), *New Essays on Virginia Woolf* (Dallas: Contemporary Research Press, 1995), 79–97.

Hutton, James, *Theory of the Earth* (Edinburgh: Royal Society of Edinburgh, 1788).

Hutton, Jane, *Reciprocal Landscapes: Stories of Material Movements* (New York: Routledge, 2020).

Isozaki, Arata, 'Osaka's Green Crossroads,' in Pamela Johnston and Dennis Crompton (Eds.), *Osaka Follies* (London: Architectural Association, 1991), 5–6.

Jackson, John Brinckerhoff, 'The Word Itself,' in *Discovering the Vernacular Landscape* (New Haven: Yale Univiversity Press, 1984), 3–8.

Jackson, Kenneth, and David Dunbar (Eds.), 'Selected Writings on Central Park, Frederick Law Olmsted (1858–1870),' in *Empire City: New York through the Centuries* (New York: Columbia University Press, 2002).

Jarr, Nicholas, 'The Fabrication of Evidence in Rem Koolhaas' Delirious New York,' Extended essay, dissertation (University of Brighton, 2014).

Juet, Robert, *Journal of Hudson's 1609 Voyage*, entry 2 October (Albany, NY: New Netherland Museum / Half Moon, 2008), online: http://newnetherlandmuseum.org/Juets-modified.pdf.

Kaji-O'Grady, Sandra, 'The London Conceptualists: Architecture and Performance in the 1970s,' in *Journal of Architectural Education* 61 (4) (2008), 43–51.

Koolhaas, Rem, 'Why I Wrote Delirious New York and Other Textual Strategies', in *ANY: Architecture New York* May/June 1993, Writing in Architecture (1993), 42–43.

Koolhaas, Rem, *Delirious New York. A Retroactive Manifesto for Manhattan* (New York: The Monacelli Press, 1994).

Koolhaas, Rem, Bernard Tschumi, Ana Miljacki, Amanda Reeser Lawrence and Ashley Schafer, '2 Architects 10 Questions on Program', *PRAXIS: Journal of Writing + Building* 8 RE:PROGRAMMING (2006), 6–15.

Latour, Bruno, 'Why Has Critique Run out of Steam? From Matters of Fact to Matters of Concern,' in *Critical Inquiry* 30 (Chicago: The University of Chicago, 2004), 225–248.

Latour, Bruno, 'Anti-zoom,' in Laurence Bossé, Hans Ulrich Obrist, Claire Staebler, Suzanne Pagé (Eds. and Curators), *Olafur Eliasson: Contact* (Paris: Flammarion, 2014), 122–125.

Laverty, Carroll, 'The Death's-Head on the Gold-Bug,' in *American Literature* 12 (1) (1940), 88–91.

Lawlor, Leonard, 'Jacques Derrida,' in Edward N. Zalta (Ed.), *The Stanford Encyclopaedia of Philosophy* (Fall 2021 Edition), online: https://plato.stanford.edu/entries/derrida/.

Lissitzky, El, 'A. und Pangeometrie,' in C. Einstein and P. Westheim (Eds.), *Europa Almanac* (S. Lissitzky-Kuppers, trans.) (Potsdam: Kiepenheuer, 1925).

Love, Timothy, 'Kit-of-Parts Conceptualism: Abstracting Architecture in the American Academy,' *Harvard Design Magazine* 19 Architecture as Conceptual Art? Blurring Disciplinary Boundaries (2003), online: http://www.harvarddesignmagazine.org/issues/19/kit-of-parts-conceptualism-abstracting-architecture-in-the-american-academy.

Lucarelli, Fosco, 'Madelon Vriesendorp's Manhattan Project,' in *Socks* (February 2,2015), online: http://socks-studio.com/2015/02/02/madelon-vriesendorps-manhattan-project/.

Lutgens, Frederick, Edward Tarbuck and Dennis Tasa, *The Essentials of Geology* (13th Edition) (London: Pearson, 2015).

Lyotard, Jean-François, 'Scapeland,' in *The Inhuman: Reflections on Time* (1988, Cambridge, UK: Polity Press, 1991).

Lyotard, Jean-François, 'The Sublime and the Avant-Garde', in *The Bloomsbury Anthology of Aesthetics* (New York: Continuum, 2012), 531–542.

MacKay, Robin, 'Philosopher's Islands,' in Daniel Daou and Pablo Pérez-Ramos (Eds.), *New Geographies 08: Island* (Cambridge: Harvard University Press, 2016), 56–83.

Malone, Nicholas, and Kathryn Ovenden, 'Natureculture', in Agustín Fuents (Ed.), *The International Encyclopaedia of Primatology* (New Jersey: John Wiley & Sons, 2017).

Marcus, Laura, *The Tenth Muse: Writing about Cinema in the Modernist Period* (Oxford: Oxford University Press, 2007).

Marot, Sébastien, *Sub-Urbanism and the Art of Memory* (1999, London: Architectural Association Publications, 2003).

Mattern, Shannon, 'Lebbeus Woods: The Politics of Small Things', in *Words in Space: Shannon Mattern* (2014), available online: http://wordsinspace.net/shannon/2014/04/19/lebbeus-woods-the-politics-of-small-things/.

Mateo, Fernando Díaz–Pinés, 'Delirio y Anomia en la Obra de Lebbeus Woods', in *Arquitecturas al margen* 18 (Seville: Universidad de Sevilla, 2018), 102–122.

McFarlane, Colin, 'The City as Assemblage: Dwelling and Urban Space,' in *Environment and Planning D: Society and Space* 29 (4) (2011), 649–671.

McNeur, Lorna, 'Central Park City,' in *AA Files* 23 (Summer 1992), 65–74.

Merguerian, Charles, *Stratigraphy, Structural Geology and Ductile – and Brittle Faults of New York City* (Hempstead: Hofstra University, 1996).

Merguerian, Charles, 'NYC Earthquakes: Fact or Fiction', Talk at the The *Asian American / Asian Research Institute (AAARI)* (CUNY, 2007), available online: https://aaari.info/07-03-02merguerian/.

Merguerian, Charles, and J. Mickey Merguerian, *Field Trip Guidebook: Isham and Inwood Parks, NYC* (Lamont-Doherty Earth Observatory, Manhattan Prong Workshop) (Durham, NC: Hofstra University Geology Department and Duke Geological Laboratory, 2014).

Merguerian, Charles, and John E. Sanders, *Geology of Manhattan and the Bronx: Guidebook for On-The-Rocks* (New York: New York Academy of Sciences, 1991).

Meyer, Elizabeth, 'The Public Park as Avant-Garde (Landscape) Architecture: A Comparative Interpretation of Two Parisian Parks, Parc de le Villette (1983–1990) and Parc des Buttes-Chaumont (1864–1867), *Landscape Journal* 10 (1) Special Issue: The Avant-Garde and the

Landscape: Can They be Reconciled (1991), 16–26.

Meyer, Elizabeth, 'The Expanded Field of Landscape Architecture,' in George F. Thompson and Frederick R. Steiner (Eds.), *Ecological Design and Planning* (New York: John Wiley & Sons, 1997).

Milligan, Brent, 'Landscape Migration. Environmental design in the Anthropocene,' in *Places Journal* (2015), online: https://placesjournal.org/article/landscape-migration/.

Moholy-Nagy, Lázló. *Painting, Photography, Film* (London: Lund Humphries, 1967).

Molinari, Carla, 'Sequences in architecture: Sergei Ejzenštejn and Luigi Moretti, from images to spaces,' *The Journal of Architecture* (2021).

MoMA and Cooper Union, *Education of an architect: a point of view* (New York: MoMA, 1971).

Morton, Timothy, *The Ecological Thought* (Cambridge: Harvard University Press, 2010).

Morton, Timothy, *Hyperobjects: Philosophy and Ecology after the End of the World* (Minneapolis: University of Minnesota Press, 2013).

Morton, Timothy, 'Molten Entities,' in Daniel Daou and Pablo Pérez-Ramos (Eds.), *New Geographies 08: Island* (Cambridge: Harvard University Press, 2016), 72–75.

Morton, Timothy, *Dark Ecology: For a Logic of Future Coexistence* (New York: Columbia University Press, 2018).

Nelson, Marilyn, *My Seneca Village* (South Hampton, NH: Namelos, 2015).

Nye, David, *American Technological Sublime* (Cambridge: MIT Press, 1994).

Olmsted, Frederick Law, *The Papers of Frederick Law Olmsted. Vol. III: Creating Central Park, 1857–1861*, Charles Capen McLaughlin (Ed.) (Baltimore, Maryland, 1983)

Oxford Encyclopedia, s.v. 'Extrusion' (Oxford: Oxford University Press, 2018).

Oxford Reference, 'Representation,' in Oxford Reference, Media Studies (Oxford: Oxford University Press).

Page, Max, *The Creative Destruction of Manhattan 1900–1940* (Chicago: The Chicago University Press, 1999).

Pala, Giacomo, 'Architecture as a Margin within the Negotiation between Reality and Utopia', in *sITA – studii de Istoria și Teoria Arhitecturii* 4 (2016), 216–224.

Parikka, Jussi, *The Anthrobscene* (Minneapolis: University of Minnesota Press, 2014).

Parikka, Jussi, *A Geology of Media* (Minneapolis: University of Minnesota Press, 2015).

Parui, Avishek, '"All is hubble-bubble, swarm and chaos": The cognitive contingencies and possibilities in Virginia Woolf's "The Cinema," in *Postgraduate English* 23 (2011), 1–23.

Pierpaoli, Barbara, 'Cincuenta años de Superstudio. Una lectura contemporánea,' in *rita* 7 (2017), 110-119.

Plutarch, 'Isis and Osiris,' in *Moralia* V (public domain, edition of 1936), online: http://penelope.uchicago.edu/Thayer/E/Roman/Texts/Plutarch/Moralia/Isis_and_Osiris*/home.html.

Puig de la Bellacasa, María, *Matters of Care: Speculative Ethics in More Than Human Worlds* (Minneapolis: University of Minnesota Press, 2017).

Rajchman, John, 'Grounds,' in *Constructions* (Cambridge: MIT Press, 1998), 77–89.

Rosenheim, Shawn James, *The Cryptographic Imagination: Secret Writing from Edgar Poe to the Internet* (Baltimore: Johns Hopkins University Press, 1997), 42–64.

Rosenzweig, Roy, and Elizabeth Blackmar, *The Park and The People: A History of Central Park* (Ithaca: Cornell University Press, 1992).

Royle, Nicholas, *Jacques Derrida* (London: Routledge, 2003).

Sanderson, Eric W., *Mannahatta: A Natural History of New York City* (New York: Abrams, 2009).

Schuppli, Susan, 'Slick Images: The Photogenic Politics of Oil,' in Mihnea Mirca and Vincent W. J. van Gerven Oei (Eds.), *Allegory of the Cave Painting* (Antwerp: Extra City, 2015), 425–447.

Schuppli, Susan, *Material Witness: Media, Forensics, Evidence* (Cambridge: MIT Press, 2020).

Scott, Felicity, 'Superstudio', in *Artforum International* 42 (7) (New York, 2004), 177–178 and 202.

Shell, Marc, 'Islandology,' in Daniel Daou and Pablo Pérez-Ramos (Eds.), *New Geographies* 08: Island, (Cambridge: Harvard University Press, 2016), 44–54.

Singer, Donald A., 'World class base and precious metal deposits; a quantitative analysis', in *Economic Geology* 90 (1) (1995), 88–104.

Sivyer, Caleb, 'The Politics of Gender and the Visual in Virginia Woolf and Angela Carter, PhD Thesis (School of English, Communication & Philosophy, Cardiff University, 2015).

Sloterdijk, Peter, 'Museum – School of Alienation,' *Art in Translation* 6 (4) (2007, London: Bloomsbury, 2014), 437–448.

Sloterdijk, Peter, *Foams, Spheres Volume III: Plural Spherology* (Cambridge: The MIT Press, 2016).

Sloterdijk, Peter, in conversation with Thomas Macho, 'Raising Our Heads: Pampering Spaces and Time Drifts,' in Peter Sloterdijk, *Selected Exaggerations: Conversations and Interviews 1993–2012* (Chicester: Polity Press, 2016), 82–105.

Smyth Jr., Ellison A., 'Poe's Gold Bug from the Standpoint of an Entomologist,' *Sewanee Review* XVIII (1910), 67–72.

Sokol, Joshua, 'A New Blast May Have Forged Cosmic Gold', *Quanta Magazine* (2017), online: https://www.quantamagazine.org/did-neutron-stars-or-supernovas-forge-the-universes-supply-of-gold-20170323/.

Sprankling, John G., 'Owning the Center of the Earth', *UCLA Law Review* 979 (2008).

Springer Anne-Sophie, and Etienne Turpin, 'Exhibition as a Philosophical Problem,' in *GAM—Graz Architecture Magazine* 14 Exhibiting Matters (Graz, 2018).

Squier, Susan Merrill, *Epigenetic Landscapes: Drawing as Metaphor* (Durham: Duke University Press, 2017).

Stafford, Norman, 'Edgar Allan Poe's "The Gold-Bug," the Trickster, and the "Long-Tail'd Blue,"' in *Thalia* 18 (1) (1998), 72–83.

Stengers, Isabelle, *In Catastrophic Times. Resisting the Coming Barbarism* (Open Humanities Press, 2015).

Stengers, Isabelle, 'We Are Divided,' *e-flux Journal* #114 (December 2020), online: https://www.e-flux.com/journal/114/366189/we-are-divided/.

Stewart, Jack F., 'Light in To the Lighthouse,' *Twentieth Century Literature* 23 (3) (1977), 377–389.

Stilgoe, John R., 'Preface,' in *What is Landscape?* (Cambridge: MIT Press, 2015), ix–xiv.

Stoppani, Teresa, *Paradigm Islands: Manhattan and Venice. Discourses on Architecture and the City* (London: Routledge, 2011).

Sutherland, Carol Humphrey Vivian, *Gold: its beauty, power and allure* (London: Thames & Hudson, 1959).

Thomas, Donald B., Ainsley Seago and David C. Robacker, 'Reflections on Golden Scarabs,' in *American Entomologist* 53 (4) (2007), 224–230.

Thornton, Thomas F. and Yadvinder Malhi, 'The Trickster in the Anthropocene', in *The Anthropocene*

Review (2016), 1–4.

Torres-Campos, Tiago, 'Foregrounding the Geologic: A Device for Working in Manhattan's Faults',
Diana Periton (Ed.), *Journal of Architecture and Culture* 4 (4) (London: Taylor & Francis, 2016),
163–166.

Torres-Campos, Tiago, 'Manhattan's Geologic Delineations', *Ground-Up Journal of Landscape
Architecture* 05 Delineations (Berkeley: University of California, 2016), 58–63.

Torres-Campos, Tiago, 'The Grid and the Bedrock. Manhattan through a Cartographic Geo-Tale',
Bernd Upmeyer (Ed.), *MONU—Magazine on Urbanism* 29 Narrative Urbanism (Rotterdam: MONU,
2018), 48–53.

Torres-Campos, Tiago, 'Duck and Cover: Experiencing the Anthropocene in 21st Century Manhattan',
Pidgin Magazine 27 (Princeton: Princeton University School of Architecture, 2020), 132–147.

Torres-Campos, Tiago, 'Inwood's Geofollies and Other Witnesses of Dissonance', in Ed Wall (Ed.),
AD The Landscapists: Refining Landscape Design as a Critical Medium (New York: Wiley, 2020), 38–45.

Torres-Campos, Tiago, 'Silence in the Middle Ground. Aesthetic Immersion in the Geologic', in Mark
Dorrian & Christos Kakalis (Eds.), *Place of Silence. Architecture / Media / Philosophy* (London:
Bloomsbury, 2020), 149–162.

Tschumi, Bernard, 'Architecture and Transgression," in *Oppositions* 7 (1976).

Tschumi, Bernard, 'Questions of Space' (1976), in *Architecture and Disjunction* (Cambridge: MIT Press,
1994), 53–64.

Tschumi, Bernard, 'Architecture: Sequences,' Excerpt from exhibition catalogue (1982), in *The
Renaissance Society*, online: https://renaissancesociety.org/exhibitions/315/architecture-
sequences/.

Tschumi, Bernard, *Architecture and Disjunction* (Cambridge: MIT Press, 1994), 227–259.

Tschumi, Bernard, *The Manhattan Transcripts* (London: Academy Editions, 1994).

Tschumi, Bernard, 'Madness and the Combinative,' in *Architecture and Disjunction* (Cambridge: MIT
Press, 1996).

Tschumi, Bernard, 'Sequences,' in *Architecture and Disjunction* (Cambridge: MIT Press, 1996).

Tschumi, Bernard, 'The Pleasure of Architecture,' in *Architecture and Disjunction* (Cambridge: MIT
Press, 1996).

Tschumi, Bernard, 'Violence of Architecture,' in *Architecture and Disjunction* (Cambridge: MIT
Press, 1996).

Tschumi, Bernard, *Red is not a Color* (New York: Rizzoli, 2012).

Tschumi, Bernard, Rem Koolhaas and Stephan Trüby, 'A Conversation,' in *GTA Events* (ETH, 2011),
online: https://video.ethz.ch/events/2011/d-arch_gta/75db5f75-5ff9-41af-a221-c48ab14f8aa5.
html.

Tsing, Anna, 'On Nonscalability: The Living World Is Not Amenable to Precision-Nested Scales,' in
Common Knowledge 18 (3) (2012), 505–524.

Tsing, Anna, *The Mushroom at the End of the World. On the Possibility of Life in Capitalist Ruins* (Princeton:
Princeton University Press, 2015).

Tsing, Anna, Elaine Gan, Heather Swanson and Nils Burbandt, 'Haunted Landscapes of the
Anthropocene,' in Anna Tsing et al. (Eds.), *Arts of Living on a Damaged Planet: Ghosts and Monsters
of the Anthropocene* (Minneapolis: Minnesota University Press, 2017), 1–14.

Bibliography

Viele, Egbert L., 'The Central Park. Report of Egbert L. Viele Esq., Engineer-in-Chief, 'Interesting Notes Concerning the Topography and Drainage of the Central Park. Proposed Plan of Improvement,' *The New York Times* (January 20, 1857).

Wall, Diana diZerega, Nan A. Rothschild and Cynthia Copeland, 'Seneca Village and Little Africa: Two African American Communities in Antebellum New York City,' in *Historical Archaeology* 42 (1), Living in Cities Revisited: Trends in Nineteenth- and Twentieth-Century Urban Archaeology (2008), 97–107.

Wall, Diana diZerega, Nan A. Rothschild, Meredith B. Linn and Cynthia Copeland, *Seneca Village, a Forgotten Community: Report on the 2011 Excavations* (New York: Institute for the Exploration of Seneca Village History, Inc., 2018).

Woods, Derek, 'Scale Critique for the Anthropocene,' *Minnesota Review* 83 (2014) (New Series), 133–142.

Woods, Lebbeus, 'Einstein Tomb', *Pamphlet Architecture* 6 (New York: Princeton Architectural Press, 1980).

Woods, Lebbeus, *Radical Reconstruction* (New York: Princeton Architectural Press, 1997).

Woods, Lebbeus, 'Lower Manhattan', *Abitare* 384 (1999).

Woods, Lebbeus, 'After Forms', *Perspecta* 38 Architecture after All (Boston: MIT Press, 2006).

Woods, Lebbeus, in conversation with Leo Gullbring, *Azure* (2008).

Woolf, Virginia, 'The Cinema,' *The Nation and Anthenaeum* 39 (13) (1926), 381–383, online: https://www.bl.uk/collection-items/the-cinema-by-virginia-woolf-from-the-nation-and-athenaeum.

Woolf, Virginia, *To the Lighthouse* (London: Penguin Books, 1992).

Yusoff, Kathryn, *A Billion Black Anthropocenes or None* (Minneapolis: University of Minnesota Press, 2019), Preface.

Zylinska, Joanna, *Minimal Ethics for the Anthropocene* (London: Open Humanities Press, 2014).

Zylinska, Joanna in conversation with Benek Çinçik and Tiago Torres-Campos, 'A Local Museum of the Anthropocene,' in *Postcards from the Anthropocene: Unsettling the Geopolitics of Representation* (Barcelona: DPR-barcelona, 2022).

Zylinska, Joanna, *The End of Man: A Feminist Counterapocalypse* (Minneapolis: Minnesota University Press, 2018).

Web Sources

Castrigno, Marissa, 'The Competition: 33 Plans for Central Park in 1858,' in *Central Park Conservancy Magazine* (2019), online: https://www.centralparknyc.org/articles/plans-for-central-park.

Didi-Huberman, Georges, 'Glimpses,' Keynote lecture at the European Graduate School (2015), online: https://www.youtube.com/watch?v=60GdzcKKdwE.

Eakin, Emily, 'THINK TANK; What Did Poe Know About Cosmology? Nothing. But He Was Right.,' *The New York Times* (November 2, 2002), online: https://www.nytimes.com/2002/11/02/books/think-tank-what-did-poe-know-about-cosmology-nothing-but-he-was-right.html.

Kolbert, Elizabeth, 'Enter the Anthropocene—Age of Man,' *National Geographic* (2011), online https://www.nationalgeographic.com/magazine/article/age-of-man.

Kurutz, Steven, 'When There Was Water, Water Everywhere', *The New York Times* (2012), online:

http://www.nytimes.com/2006/06/11/nyregion/thecity/11viel.html?_r=2&oref=slogin&.

Larousse Dictionary, s.v. 'Déconstruction,' online: https://www.larousse.fr/dictionnaires/francais/déconstruction/22357.

Library of Congress, *Nowel Amsterdam en Lamerique*, 1672, online: https://www.loc.gov/maps/.

Manaugh, Geoff, 'Corporate Gardens of the Anthropocene', *BLDG Blog* (2017), online: http://www.bldgblog.com/tag/david-gissen/.

Manaugh, Geoff, 'Lebbeus Woods, 1940–2012', *BLDG BLOG* (2012), online: http://www.bldgblog.com/2012/10/lebbeus-woods-1940-2012/.

McPhee, John, 'Basin and Range,' *The New Yorker* (1981).

Merriam Webster Dictionary, s.v. 'Deconstruction,' online: https://www.merriam-webster.com/dictionary/deconstruction.

Merriam Webster Dictionary, online (Merriam Webster Inc.), s.v. 'Frame,' online: https://www.merriam-webster.com/dictionary/frame.

Miller, Tom, 'The Lost Brennan House – 84th Street and Broadway,' in *Daytonian in Manhattan* (2017), online: http://daytoninmanhattan.blogspot.com/2017/06/the-lost-brennan-house-84th-street-and.html.

Morton, Timothy in conversation with Sean Lally, in *Night White Skies* episode 002 (2016), online: https://soundcloud.com/user-561947272/ep-002_timothy-morton.

Morton, Timothy in conversation with Tom Wiscombe, *Sci-Arc* (2016), online: https://www.youtube.com/watch?v=x2lbtwd3KZU.

Raptopoulos, Lilah, '"Are we safe? Of course not": climate scientist's NYC warning after Sandy, *The Guardian* (November 2014), online: https://www.theguardian.com/us-news/2014/nov/05/climate-scientist-klaus-jacob-warning-new-york-city-hurricane-sandy.

Stamp, Jimmy, 'Lebbeus Woods and 12 Monkeys', in *Life Without Buildings* (2006), online: http://lifewithoutbuildings.net/2006/09/lebbeus-woods-12-monkeys.html.

Subramanian, Meera, 'Anthropocene now: influential panel votes to recognize Earth's new epoch,' *Nature* (2019), online: https://www.nature.com/articles/d41586-019-01641-5.

Tschumi, Bernard in conversation with Enrique Walker, 'The Manhattan Transcripts: Bernard Tschumi conversa con Enrique Walker', in *Traspasos* (Universidad de Chile, 2020), online: https://ma.uchilefau.cl/traspasos/ and https://www.youtube.com/watch?v=R82ZZIjeP5Q.

Wallace, Lewis, 'Lebbeus Woods: The Architect Who Dared to Ask 'What If?', *Wired* (2013), online: https://www.wired.com/2013/02/lebbeus-woods-conceptual-architect/.

Woods, Lebbeus, 'AS401: Vertical Manhattan I', *Lebbeus Woods Blog* (2010), online: https://lebbeuswoods.wordpress.com/2010/08/15/as401-vertical-manhattan-1/.

Woods, Lebbeus, *Centricity: The Unified Urban Field*, Excerpt from Public Lecture at SCI-Arc (SCI-Arc Archives, 1988), online: https://www.youtube.com/watch?v=j1JMNIFYZnc (part 1) and https://www.youtube.com/watch?v=hwoFnBxzSGQ (part 2).

Woods, Lebbeus, 'Einstein Tomb @ 30', *Lebbeus Woods Blog* (June 09, 2010), online: https://lebbeuswoods.wordpress.com/2010/06/09/einstein-tomb-30/.

Woods, Lebbeus, *Lebbeus Woods: the Vico Morcote Interview*, (SCI-Arc Archives, 1998), online: https://www.youtube.com/watch?v=KO7-sGk6O8g.

Woods, Lebbeus, 'Lower Manhattan Revisited,' *Lebbeus Woods Blog* (2012), online: https://

lebbeuswoods.wordpress.com/2012/03/08/lower-manhattan-revisited/.

Woods, Lebbeus, 'RIEA: the Back Story', *Lebbeus Woods Blog* (2011), online: https://lebbeuswoods.
wordpress.com/2011/06/25/riea-the-back-story/.

Woods, Lebbeus, 'The Vagrant Light of Stars', *Lebbeus Woods Blog* (September 27, 2009), online:
https://lebbeuswoods.wordpress.com/2009/09/27/the-vagrant-light-of-stars/.

Woods, Lebbeus, 'Why I Became An Architect', *Lebbeus Woods Blog* (2012), online: https://
lebbeuswoods.wordpress.com/2012/02/06/why-i-became-an-architect-part-1/ (part 1) and
https://lebbeuswoods.wordpress.com/2012/02/08/why-i-became-an-architect-part-2/ (part 2).

Woods, Lebbeus in conversation with Corrado Curti, 'Architecture: The Solid State of Thought,'
Lebbeus Woods Blog (2010), online: https://lebbeuswoods.wordpress.com/2010/12/10/
architecture-the-solid-state-of-thought-complete/, and in *Cluster* (2010), online: http://www.
cluster.eu/2010/11/18/architecture-as-the-solid-state-of-thoughts-a-dialogue-with-lebbeus-
woods-part-1/.

Woods, Lebbeus in conversation with Geoff Manaugh, 'Without Walls: An Interview with Lebbeus
Woods,' *BLDG BLOG* (2007), online: http://www.bldgblog.com/2007/10/without-walls-an-
interview-with-lebbeus-woods/.

Woods, Lebbeus in conversation with John Szot, 'Terrible Beauty,' *MAS Context Issue Aberration*
(2011), online: https://www.mascontext.com/issues/12-aberration-winter-11/terrible-beauty/.

World Gold Council, online: https://www.gold.org/about-gold/gold-supply/gold-mining/how-much-
gold.

Yardley, William, 'Lebbeus Woods, Architect Who Bucked Convention, dies at 72', *The New York Times*
(2012), online: https://www.nytimes.com/2012/11/01/arts/lebbeus-woods-unconventional-
architect-dies-at-72.html.

Films

Dick, Kirby and Amy Ziering Kofman, *Derrida* (Los Angeles: Jane Doe Films, 2002).

Acknowledgements

As most books unfold, so does life. Neither of them could have happened in the same way without the incredible support I got.

This book is the result of a ten-year long period of research, discovery and experimentation. I thank the support of Gordon Goff, who believed in this project strongly than others, and Kirby Anderson, who helped me made it possible. Thank you also to Rhode Island School of Design for its generous institutional support.

The book began with a PhD in Architecture by Design that I completed while still teaching at the University of Edinburgh. I am grateful to Mark Dorrian, my supervisor, for a type of mentorship that goes beyond the scope of a thesis. His guidance and support through the different stages in the research (and my life) were significant and impactful, especially in moments of doubt. I'm equally thankful to Emily Brady, my second supervisor, for the valuable insights she provided to my work.

My work is profoundly shaped by the people I interact with, both in my personal and professional spheres. I am indebted to the fruitful exchanges of ideas I had with faculty, students and staff both at the University of Edinburgh and, more recently, at the Rhode Island School of Design. The names are too many to mention here, but I thank in particular my colleagues and friends Benek, Francisca, Lisa, Elinor, Ella, Vicky, Adrian (Edinburgh), Ed and Tim (Greenwich) and Emily, Suzanne, Johanna and Amy (RISD). I owe them the improvement of ideas and hypotheses in my investigation through our conversations, reviews, joint studios and other experimentations.

Since my life and work deeply intertwine, a final thanks to my family. Ben, for his love and a renewed sense of what truly matters in life. Luis, for his loving friendship and strong support in every step of the way. My mom, for her unconditional love and deep care. My dad, for his strong values and sense of purpose. My sister and brother, nephews and nieces, for always bringing me back home.

Obrigado.